LEONBATTISTA ALBERTI   NICCOLÒ LEONICENO   JOHANN GEORG GRAEVIUS

LONARDO DA VINCI   JOHANNES TRITHEMIUS   GIOVANNI PICO DELLA MIRANDOLA

ETA   NICOLAUS COPERNICUS   ARO CONTARINI

GRICOLA   FRANÇOIS RABELAIS   PH   STOPHER WREN

POSTEL   MIGUEL SERVET   WOL   MAGLIABECHI

NITO ARIAS MONTANO   JOHN DEE   JEAN BODIN   JOHANN JOACHIM BECHER

EPH SCALIGER   JOHANN THOMAS FREIGIUS   TYCHO BRAHE   ROBERT HOOKE

TER RALEIGH   ISAAC CASAUBON   LORENZO MAGALOTTI   WILLIAM PLAYFAIR

TOMMASO CAMPANELLA   BARTHOLOMÄUS KECKERMANN   NICHOLAS STENO

LAUDE PEIRESC   HUGO GROTIUS   JOHN SELDEN   DANIEL GEORG MORHOF

CLAUDE SAUMAISE   FRANCISCUS JUNIUS   OLOF RUDBECK THE YOUNGER

US MARCI   JUAN EUSEBIO NIEREMBERG   RENÉ DESCARTES   NICOLAES WITSEN

AMUEL HARTLIB   BATHSUA MAKIN   CONRAD SAMUEL SCHURZFLEISCH

NS   JOHN JONSTON   JOHANN HEINRICH BISTERFELD   THOMAS BROWNE

HURMAN   JOHN WILKINS   VINCENT PLACCIUS   GILBERT BURNET

ELISABETH, PRINCESS PALATINE   ISAAC VOSSIUS   HENRY OLDENBURG

RCUS MEIBOM   BLAISE PASCAL   WILLIAM PETTY   OTTO MENCKE

GEL   QUEEN CHRISTINA OF SWEDEN   FRANCESCO REDI   EUSEBIO KINO

ISAAC BARROW   OLOF RUDBECK THE ELDER   CARLOS SIGÜENZA Y GÓNGORA

TER JUANA INÉS DE LA CRUZ   HENRI BASNAGE   BERNARD DE FONTENELLE

PEDRO DE PERALTA Y BARNUEVO   JOHN WOODWARD   HERMAN BOERHAAVE

BURKHARD GOTTHELF STRUVE   JOHANN JACOB SCHEUCHZER   SCIPIONE MAFFEI

DANIEL GOTTLIEB MESSERSCHMIDT   NICHOLAS FRÉRET   EMANUEL SWEDENBORG

SAMUEL REIMARUS   JOHANN ANDREAS FABRICIUS   HENRY HOME, LORD KAMES

BUFFON   LEONHARD EULER   CARL LINNAEUS   ALBRECHT VON HALLER

MIKHAIL LOMONOSOV   DENIS DIDEROT   JAMES BURNETT, LORD MONBODDO

RGUSON   ADAM SMITH   ANNE ROBERT TURGOT   CHRISTIAN GOTTLOB HEYNE

ST VON SCHLÖZER   JOSÉ ANTONIO DE ALZATE   NICOLAS MASSON DE MORVILLIERS

MAS JEFFERSON   ANTOINE LAVOISIER   NICHOLAS, MARQUIS DE CONDORCET

WOLFGANG VON GOETHE   JOHANN GOTTFRIED EICHHORN   STANISŁAW STASZIC

WILHELM VON HUMBOLDT   GEORGES CUVIER   ALEXANDER VON HUMBOLDT

S YOUNG   HENRY PETER BROUGHAM   MARY SOMERVILLE   ANDRÉS BELLO

LES BABBAGE   JOHN HERSCHEL   WILLIAM WHEWELL   THOMAS CARLYLE

O CATTANEO   ANTOINE COURNOT   GUSTAV FECHNER   GEORGE P. MARSH

THE POLYMATH

THE POLYMATH

A CULTURAL HISTORY FROM LEONARDO DA VINCI TO SUSAN SONTAG

PETER BURKE

YALE UNIVERSITY PRESS
NEW HAVEN AND LONDON

For information about this and other Yale University Press publications, please contact:
U.S. Office: sales.press@yale.edu   yalebooks.com
Europe Office: sales@yaleup.co.uk   yalebooks.co.uk

Set in Adobe Garamond Pro by IDSUK (DataConnection) Ltd
Printed in Great Britain by Gomer Press Ltd, Llandysul, Ceredigion, Wales

Library of Congress Control Number: 2019952805

ISBN 978-0-300-25002-2

A catalogue record for this book is available from the British Library.

10 9 8 7 6 5 4 3 2 1

Nothing is more beautiful than to know everything

(Plato)

Ah, but a man's reach should exceed his grasp,
Or what's a heaven for?

(Robert Browning, *Andrea del Sarto*)

Specialization is for insects

(Robert Heinlein)

In memory of Asa Briggs, David Daiches, Martin Wight and the Sussex project to 'redraw the map of learning'
And for Maria Lúcia, who is able to do three things at the same time

CONTENTS

PLATES

13. Portrait of Thomas Young (1773–1829), by Henry Briggs (1822).
14. John Herschel (1792–1871), photo by Julia Margaret Cameron (1867).
15. Portrait of Alexander von Humboldt (1769–1859), self-portrait (1814).
16. Portrait of Mary Somerville (1780–1872), by Thomas Phillips (1834).
17. *Philosophers (S. N. Bulgakov and P. A. Florensky)*, by Mikhail Nesterov (1917).
18. Portrait of Herbert Simon (1916–2001), by Richard Rappaport (1987). Richard Rappaport / CC BY 3.0.
19. Paul Otlet (1868–1944) at his desk (1937).
20. Susan Sontag (1933–2004), photo by Jean-Regis Rouston (1972). Roger Viollet via Getty Images.
21. Fuld Hall, Institute for Advanced Study, Princeton, photographer unknown (early 1950s). From the Shelby White and Leon Levy Archives Center, Institute for Advanced Study, Princeton, NJ, USA.
22. The University of Sussex, prospectus photo by Henk Snoek (1964). Henk Snoek / RIBA Collections.

PREFACE AND ACKNOWLEDGEMENTS

For the last twenty years or so I have been working, on and off, on the history of knowledge, publishing a general survey, *A Social History of Knowledge* (2 vols., 2000–2012), an introduction to the subject, *What is the History of Knowledge?* (2016), and most recently *Exiles and Expatriates in the History of Knowledge* (2017). Like the book on exiles, the present study developed out of the general survey to become a book on its own. I have been drawn to this topic for a long time. Although my mathematical and scientific illiteracy makes polymathy out of the question, I have long shared the view famously expressed by the French historians Lucien Febvre and Fernand Braudel that one writes better history by escaping from the confines of that discipline, at least from time to time.

As a student at Oxford, taking a three-year course in history, I went to lectures in other disciplines – to Gilbert Ryle on philosophy, for instance, to Roy Harrod on economics, to J. R. R. Tolkien on medieval literature, to Michael Argyle on psychology and – most important for my future – to Edgar Wind on art history. As a postgraduate student, I began reading in sociology and anthropology, and attended seminars in the history of science as well as one organized by Norman Birnbaum and Iris Murdoch on the concept of alienation.

When I heard that the new University of Sussex was going to be organized in an interdisciplinary manner, I immediately applied for a position there and taught in the School of European Studies from 1962 to 1979, collaborating in teaching with colleagues in art history, sociology, and English and French literature. Thanks to these experiences, at Sussex in particular, I felt that this was a book that I really had to write, about individuals and small groups concerned with the big picture as well as with detail and often engaged in the transfer or 'translation' of ideas and practices from one discipline to another.

It has been a pleasure to keep company, however indirectly, with this gifted group of men and women, the polymaths discussed in this book, some of whom were old acquaintances, and in a few instances personal friends, while the achievements of others were discovered only in the course of the research.

I should like to thank Tarif Khalidi and Geoffrey Lloyd for their comments on chapter 1; Waqas Ahmed for sending me a questionnaire on polymaths in 2013 as well as an early draft of his book; Christoph Lundgreen, Fabian Krämer and the 'Zwei Kulturen' Research Group at the Berlin Brandenburgische Akademie der Wissenschaften for a fruitful discussion of my ideas; and Ann Blair, Steven Boldy, Arndt Brendecke, Chris Clark, Ruth Finnegan, Mirus Fitzner, José Maria García González, Michael Hunter, Gabriel Josipovici, Neil Kenny, Christel Lane, David Lane, Hansong Li, Robin Milner-Gulland, William O'Reilly, Ulinka Rublack, Nigel Spivey, Marek Tamm and Marianne Thormählen for information, suggestions and references.

Some of my thoughts about polymaths have been presented in print as well as in lectures.[1] I hope that this fuller version is an improvement on its more sketchy predecessors. Presenting the same ideas in different places or contexts has often suggested modifications. Hence I am extremely grateful to the audiences of my lectures on this topic in Belo Horizonte, Berlin, Brighton, Cambridge, Copenhagen, Engelsberg, Frankfurt and Gotha for their various questions and comments. My warm thanks also go to Robert Baldock and Heather McCallum at Yale University Press for welcoming the manuscript, and to their two anonymous readers and my copy-editor Richard Mason for their constructive suggestions. As usual, Maria Lúcia read the whole manuscript and offered wise advice.

INTRODUCTION
WHAT IS A POLYMATH?

'History,' it has been said, 'is unkind to polymaths.' Some are forgotten, while many are 'squashed into a category we can recognize'.[1] They are remembered, as we shall see again and again in what follows, for only one form or a few forms of their varied achievements. It is time to redress the balance. In fact, an increasing number of studies of individual polymaths have been published in recent years, perhaps in reaction against our culture of specialization. I have made grateful use of many of these monographs, which include not only studies of intellectual giants such as Leonardo and Leibniz but also some near-forgotten figures such as Dumont Durville and William Rees.[2] General surveys are more difficult to find, although their number is increasing, especially in the form of short contributions to journals or radio programmes.[3]

In attempting such a survey, this book offers an approach to the cultural and social history of knowledge. All forms of knowledge, practical as well as theoretical, deserve to have their histories written. Hunter-gatherers needed a wide range of knowledges to survive, while farmers were celebrated as 'many-sided' by the geographer Friedrich Ratzel, who was a polymath himself.[4] Artisans, midwives, merchants, rulers, musicians, footballers and many other groups require and possess a segment of knowledge in which some individuals excel. In the last few years, the term 'polymath', once confined to scholars, has been extended to individuals whose achievements range from athletics to politics.

DEFINITIONS

The 'polymath discussion group', for instance, has defined the polymath as 'someone who is interested in and learning about many subjects'.[5] This book, on the other hand, will concentrate on academic knowledge, formerly known as 'learning'. It focuses on scholars with interests that were 'encyclopaedic' in the original sense of running around the whole intellectual 'course' or 'curriculum', or at any rate around a major segment of that circle.

For this reason I have excluded two entrepreneurs: Elon Musk, who took degrees in economics and physics before founding Tesla and other companies, and Sergei Brin, who studied mathematics and computer science before founding Google together with another computer scientist, Larry Page. I also hesitated before including that many-sided man John Maynard Keynes, since most of his sides were not academic. Keynes was described by his friend Leonard Woolf as 'a don, a civil servant, a speculator, a businessman, a journalist, a writer, a farmer, a picture-dealer, a statesman, a theatrical manager, a book collector, and half a dozen other things'. On the other hand, Keynes himself remarked that 'the master economist must possess a rare combination of gifts. He must reach a high standard in several different directions and must combine talents not often found together. He must be mathematician, historian, statesman, philosopher – in some degree.' On that criterion, not to mention his interest in the many interests of Isaac Newton, Keynes certainly qualifies.[6]

A few famous writers of fiction will be discussed in the chapters that follow, notably Johann Wolfgang von Goethe, George Eliot, Aldous Huxley and Jorge Luis Borges, but this is essentially because they also produced non-fiction, usually essays. In similar fashion, Vladimir Nabokov is included, not as the author of *Lolita* but as a literary critic, an entomologist and a writer on chess, while August Strindberg appears as a cultural historian rather than as a dramatist. Conversely, Umberto Eco will appear in these pages as a scholar who also wrote novels.

DISCIPLINES

Defining a polymath as an individual who has mastered several disciplines raises the question: what is a discipline? The history of academic disciplines is a double one, both intellectual and institutional. The term 'disciplines' in the plural comes from 'discipline' in the singular, itself derived from the Latin word *discere*, 'to learn', while *disciplina* translated the ancient Greek word *askesis*, meaning 'training' or 'exercises'. In classical antiquity, the idea of discipline moved back and forth between at least four domains: athletics, religion, war and philosophy. Discipline was learned by following the rule of a master (thus becoming his 'disciple') and internalizing it, practising a kind of asceticism of self-control, both of the mind and the body.

In the course of time, the term 'discipline' came to refer to a particular branch of knowledge. In ancient Rome, the study of thunder and lightning was known as *disciplina etrusca*, because specialists in this practice were Etruscans. In the fifth century, Martianus Capella wrote about seven 'disciplines', otherwise known as the seven liberal arts: grammar, logic, rhetoric, arithmetic, geometry, music and astronomy. The idea of 'disciplines' in the plural implied organization, institutionalization and indeed the beginning of a long process of specialization.[7] In order to avoid projecting later attitudes onto the past, I include magic as a discipline when writing about the sixteenth and seventeenth centuries, and try to avoid referring to 'biology', 'anthropology' and so on when discussing the time before these names came into use.

Making life more difficult for the historian, the criteria for calling a scholar a 'polymath' have changed over the last six hundred years. As traditional disciplines have fragmented, the idea of 'many' disciplines has been diluted and the bar set lower. A recent article describes living individuals who have made original contributions to two disciplines, such as law and economics, as 'polymaths'. However odd it may seem to call two 'many', it has become a significant achievement to keep two intellectual balls in the air at one time.[8]

AIMS AND METHODS

This study is based for the most part on a prosopography, a collective biography of a group of five hundred individuals active in the West between the fifteenth century and the twenty-first, listed in the Appendix.

Appropriately enough, what he called 'the prosopography of scholars' was one of the 'passions' of Pierre Bayle, a leading polymath of the seventeenth century.[9] Despite its concern with collective biography, the book does not make much use of statistics. Although it will note the numbers of males and females, clerics and laity in the group, many other questions cannot be answered in this precise manner.

Even deciding which polymaths were Catholic or Protestant presents its difficulties. Converts from Catholicism to Protestantism include Sebastian Münster and Philip Melanchthon. Converts from Protestantism to Catholicism include Lucas Holstenius, Christina of Sweden, Peter Lambeck and Nicholas Steno, while Justus Lipsius moved backwards and forwards between the two faiths. Benito Arias Montano was officially a Catholic, but apparently a member of a secret sect, the Family of Love. Jean Bodin may have converted to Judaism. Giordano Bruno seems to have invented his own religion. Isaac Newton was officially an Anglican, but did not believe in the Trinity.

Besides generalizations, the book offers case studies. It focuses on the giants, the 'monsters of erudition', a phrase that goes back to the Dutchman Herman Boerhaave, who was active at the turn of the eighteenth century and himself made contributions to medicine, physiology, chemistry and botany. It also offers thumbnail sketches of polymaths of the second rank, discussing individual itineraries and peculiarities.

This book aspires to be more than a gallery of individual portraits, however fascinating their sitters may have been. The portraits need framing, sometimes by comparison and more often by contextualization. One of the principal aims of this study is to describe some intellectual and social trends and so to answer general questions about forms of social organization and climates of opinion that are favourable or unfavourable to polymathic endeavours. It will be necessary to distinguish places and times where curiosity is encouraged or discouraged, the latter often for religious reasons, as in the famous case of St Augustine, who included 'the investigation of nature' among the 'things that it does no good to know and that men only want to know for the sake of knowing'. But Augustine also felt the pleasure of knowledge (*rerum cognitione laetitia*).[10]

The thread through the history that follows is composed of the opposite but entwined stories of specialization and synthesis. It is usually if not always a mistake to reduce any kind of history to a simple linear story. Many major trends have been accompanied by a movement in the opposite direction. The rise of organized specialization has coexisted for a considerable time as the counter-movement of organized interdisciplinarity. As the division of intellectual labour has increased, even polymaths have become a kind of specialist. They are often known as 'generalists' because general knowledge, or at least the knowledge of many disciplines, is their speciality. Their distinctive contribution to the history of knowledge is to see connections between fields that have been separated and to notice what specialists in a given discipline, the insiders, have failed to see. In this respect their role resembles that of scholars who leave their native country, whether as exiles or expatriates, for a place with a different culture of knowledge.[11]

A major concern in this study is the survival of polymaths in a culture of increasing specialization. One might have expected the species to have become extinct in the eighteenth, nineteenth or at the latest the twentieth century, but it has shown an astonishing resilience. To explain this resilience involves studying the habitat of the species, its cultural niche, often but not always the university. Universities have been by turns favourable and unfavourable to polymaths. Some polymaths have preferred a career outside the university because it offered more freedom. Others have moved from one faculty or department to another, as if rebelling against restriction to a particular discipline. A few universities have been flexible enough to accommodate these moves, as we shall see.

At a more personal level, questions about polymaths include: what drove these individuals? Was it a simple yet omnivorous curiosity, what Augustine called knowing 'for the sake of knowing', or does something else underlie what a memoir of the political scientist Harold Lasswell calls his 'passion for omniscience'?[12] What prompts shifts from one discipline to another? Is it a low threshold of boredom or an unusual degree of open-mindedness? How have polymaths found the time and the energy for their many-sided studies? How have they made a living?

5

TYPES OF POLYMATH

Distinctions between types of polymath will recur in these pages. It seems useful to describe some of them as passive (as opposed to active); limited (as opposed to general); or serial (as opposed to simultaneous). By 'passive' polymaths I mean individuals who seem to know everything but produce nothing (or, at any rate, nothing new). On the frontier between passive and active are the systematizers or synthesizers such as Francis Bacon or Auguste Comte. 'Limited' polymaths is an obvious oxymoron, but a term is needed for scholars who master a few related disciplines, whether in the humanities, the natural or the social sciences. In what follows, this type will be described as 'clustered'.

Scholars who juggle several subjects more or less simultaneously may be contrasted with what might be called 'serial' polymaths – on the model of serial polygamists – who move from field to field in the course of their intellectual lives. One of them, Joseph Needham, began an auto-biographical essay with the question 'How did it happen that a biochemist turned into a historian and sinologist?'[13] Following the trail and attempting to understand trajectories of this kind has been one of the great pleasures of writing this book.

Another possible typology distinguishes just two varieties of poly-math, the centrifugal type, accumulating knowledge without worrying about connections, and the centripetal scholar, who has a vision of the unity of knowledge and tries to fit its different parts together in a grand system. The first group rejoices in or suffers from omnivorous curiosity. The second group is fascinated – some would say obsessed – with what one of them, Johann Heinrich Alsted, called 'the beauty of order'.[14]

This distinction between centrifugal and centripetal echoes the contrast offered by Isaiah Berlin in a famous lecture on Tolstoy, between what he (following the ancient Greek poet Archilochus) called 'foxes', who know 'many things', and 'hedgehogs', who know 'one important thing'.[15] The contrast should not be made too sharp, as Berlin himself recognized when he described Tolstoy as a fox who believed that he ought to be a hedgehog. Most if not all polymaths can be located on a continuum between the two extremes, and a number of them were (and are) pulled in both directions, a creative tension between centripetal and centrifugal forces.

Take the case of the seventeenth-century German Johann Joachim Becher, a physician turned mathematician, alchemist and adviser to the emperor Leopold I on what we call 'economic policy'. In the language of his time, Becher was a 'projector', an individual with ambitious and often unrealistic schemes, which in his case included turning sand or lead into gold. 'He published works on chemistry, politics, commerce, universal language, didactic method, medicine, moral philosophy and religion.' Becher's interests appear to be centrifugal, but what held them together, so it has been suggested, was the idea of circulation, both in nature and society.[16]

THE MYTHOLOGY OF THE POLYMATH

The knowledge of individual polymaths has often been exaggerated, so much so that we might speak of the 'mythology' of the species. They are sometimes described as knowing everything, rather than as mastering the academic knowledge of their particular culture. This kind of description goes back a long way. The medieval poet John Gower described Ulysses as 'a clerk knowende of everything'. The seventeenth-century Jesuit Athanasius Kircher has been described as 'the last man who knew everything'.[17] Later candidates for the title include the Cambridge don Thomas Young, the American professor Joseph Leidy and, most recently, the Italian physicist Enrico Fermi, who was described more than once in this way in his own time, although, as a recent biographer points out, 'His knowledge of science beyond physics was superficial, and his knowledge of history, art, music and much else besides was limited, to say the least'.[18] The facile use of the adjective 'last' underlines the need for a study concerned, like this one, with the long term.

Somewhat more modestly, a book of essays about Umberto Eco was subtitled, appropriately enough for an admirer of Alfred Hitchcock, 'the man who knew too much', a phrase that has also been applied to the computer scientist and cryptanalyst Alan Turing and to the natural philosopher Robert Hooke.[19] In similar fashion, more than one polymath has been described as 'the last Renaissance man' – the philosopher Benedetto Croce, for instance, and the behavioural scientist Herbert Simon. The biochemist–sinologist Joseph Needham has been called a 'twentieth-century Renaissance man' and the critic George Steiner 'a late, late, late Renaissance man'. Hooke has been described as 'London's Leonardo', Pavel Florensky as 'Russia's unknown Da Vinci', and Harold Lasswell 'A kind of Leonardo da Vinci of the behavioural sciences', 'as close to the discipline's Renaissance person as any political scientist who has ever lived'.[20] The term 'Renaissance Woman' has also been applied widely, from musicology to 'sexology'.[21]

The language used in the previous paragraphs reinforces the myth of the solitary genius who achieves everything by him- or herself, as in the famous story of Blaise Pascal's childhood, rediscovering geometry without the benefit of books or tutors. Some polymaths are indeed relatively solitary, Leonardo more than most, but the young Leonardo was a renowned performer at the court of Milan. Again, Giambattista Vico, often described as solitary, led a sociable life in Naples, at least in his youth. Small groups often stimulate the creativity of their members and some polymaths have become famous for ideas that probably originated in group discussions of the kind discussed in chapter 8.[22] All the same, if I did not believe that certain polymaths made a difference in the world of learning, I would not have written this book.

Many achievements will be discussed or at least mentioned here, but this study does not offer a simple success story. Polymathy comes at a price. In some cases, those of the so-called 'charlatans' discussed below, the price includes superficiality. The idea that polymaths are frauds goes back a long way, at least as far as ancient Greece, when Pythagoras was denounced as an impostor. The seventeenth-century bishop Gilbert Burnet, a man of broad enough interests to experience the problem himself, wrote that 'Very often those who deal in many things are slight and Superficiall in them all'.[23] In other cases, we find what might be called the 'Leonardo syndrome', in other words a dispersal of energy that shows itself in fascinating or brilliant projects that are abandoned or simply left unfinished.

The book concentrates on Europe and the Americas, North and South, from the fifteenth century to the twenty-first. It begins with the *uomo universale* of the Renaissance but focuses on the long-term consequences of what might be called two crises of knowledge, the first in the middle of the seventeenth century and the second in the middle of the nineteenth, both of them responses to the proliferation of books (it is still too early to predict the long-term consequences of a third crisis, following the digital revolution). All three crises produced what might be called 'explosions' of knowledge, in the sense of both rapid expansion and fragmentation. Responses to fragmentation will be discussed in due course.

In order to remind readers that the modern West is not the only region in which polymaths have flourished, the following chapter offers brief sketches of some wide-ranging scholars from the ancient Greeks to the end of the Middle Ages, together with still briefer remarks about China and the Islamic world. Writing that chapter required the author to move out of his own intellectual comfort zone, but in order to write about polymaths one has to be prepared to swim out of one's depth.

~ 1 ~

EAST AND WEST

In a pre-disciplinary epoch, or in a period such as the Middle Ages in which only a few academic disciplines existed, there might seem to be little need for a concept such as 'polymath'. Wide-ranging curiosity was normal at this time and might even be described as the default setting. So was the practice of writing books about a wide range of topics. Since there was less to know than would become the case from the Renaissance onwards, it was possible – with a mighty effort – to master at least the dominant forms of knowledge (leaving aside the knowledges required by many everyday practices). All the same, in classical antiquity (both Greek and Roman), traditional China, the Islamic world and the Western Middle Ages, a number of individuals were already admired for their unusual breadth of knowledge – and a few were already criticized for lacking depth.

THE GREEKS

Like many debates, a discussion of the value of knowledge is first recorded in ancient Greece. The philosopher Heraclitus (c.535–c.475 BC), discussing a variety of many-sided individuals, claimed that 'much learning (*polymathiē*) does not teach understanding (*noos*)' (Fragment 40).[1] On the other side of the debate, the philosopher Empedocles (c.495–435 BC) asserted that 'learning (*mathē*) increases wisdom' (Fragment 17), while it is surely significant that some Greeks revered the goddess Polymatheia.

In various forms this debate would recur over the centuries, always the same in essence yet always different in emphases and circumstances. The essential conflict is between breadth and depth, between Isaiah Berlin's 'fox', who 'knows many things', and his 'hedgehog', who 'knows one great thing'. However, this contrast becomes entangled in different places and periods with conflicts between amateurs and experts, theory and practice, pure and applied knowledge, detail and the big picture, rigour and impressionism.[2]

Turning from generalization to individuals with an unusual appetite for different kinds of knowledge, one might begin with Pythagoras and the Sophists, although we only know about them via the testimonies of disciples or critics, together with a few surviving fragments of their writings.

The interests of Pythagoras of Samos (c.570–c.495 BC), a spiritual teacher or guru who founded something like a sect, ranged from reincarnation to athletics and vegetarianism (though beans were forbidden to his followers). He is remembered as a mathematician, and especially as the author of a famous theorem, although these claims have been challenged. Reactions to Pythagoras, like responses to so many later polymaths, were mixed. Once again, Empedocles and Heraclitus took opposite sides. Empedocles praised Pythagoras as 'a man of immense knowledge', whereas Heraclitus criticized him as 'the prince of impostors' (or 'praters': *kopidōn*).

More wide-ranging than Pythagoras were the so-called 'Sophists', who might be described as walking encyclopaedias. They were itinerant teachers of a wide range of subjects, a whole curriculum (the original meaning of the Greek term *encyklios paideia*, from which our term 'encyclopaedia' is derived). Some of them claimed to be able to answer any question, allowing listeners to consult them just as we consult encyclopaedias in print or online.

One of the most famous of these Sophists was Hippias of Elis (c.460–399 BC), who is supposed to have taught astronomy, mathematics, grammar, rhetoric, music, history, philosophy and the art of memory (an art of obvious use to orators). He is remembered today thanks to a dialogue by Plato, *Hippias Minor*, in which he appears as an arrogant individual whose pretensions are demolished by Socrates. In the dialogue,

Hippias boasts that he is able 'to speak on anything that anyone chooses of those subjects which I have prepared for exhibition and to answer any questions that anyone asks'.[3]

On the positive side, Aristotle (384–322 BC) became famous for his writings on a great variety of topics. In his case breadth does not seem to have led to the charge of superficiality. Aristotle is most often remembered as a philosopher concerned with logic, ethics and metaphysics, but he also wrote on mathematics, rhetoric, poetry, political theory, physics, cosmology, anatomy, physiology, natural history and zoology.[4]

Two versatile scholars were compared to athletes, Posidonius of Rhodes (c.135–c.51 BC) and Eratosthenes of Cyrene (245–194 BC).

Posidonius, nicknamed 'the athlete', wrote on philosophy, astronomy, mathematics, geography and history. Why he should have been given such a nickname is an intriguing question. Athletes were respected in ancient Greece, while the parallel between the discipline necessary for an athlete and for a scholar has already been noted. In the Olympic Games, there was a place for what would later be called the 'all-rounder', especially in the five events held on the same day, the 'pentathlon'. On the other hand, it is not a good sign that the comparison of the polymath with the athlete goes back to the description of Hippias by Plato's Socrates.

The case of Eratosthenes of Cyrene presents a similar ambiguity. Eratosthenes, the librarian in charge of the most famous library in the Greco-Roman world, in Alexandria, was nicknamed 'Pentathlos' for his combination of interests in five subjects. In fact, he studied what by our reckoning would add up to at least seven subjects: grammar, literature, philosophy, geometry, geography, mathematics and astronomy. Eratosthenes was also known as 'Beta', a nickname reminiscent of the description by a British historian of one of his colleagues as 'captain of the second eleven'. In other words, the name 'Pentathlos' is at least as likely to be a criticism as a tribute.[5]

THE ROMANS

In Rome, unlike Greece, we find not only the praises of outstanding intellectual all-rounders but also recommendations to students of particular disciplines to acquire a wide knowledge, perhaps as an antidote to creeping specialization.

Cicero (106–43 BC), one of the most eloquent public speakers of the Roman world, began his treatise on the orator (*De oratore*) by emphasizing the need for wide knowledge (*scientia . . . rerum plurimarum*) as a condition for success in this art. The treatise continues in the form of a dialogue between Marcus Crassus and Mark Antony, in which Crassus claims that 'whatever the topic', the orator will speak better about any branch of knowledge than someone who confines himself to it.[6] Another famous treatise on rhetoric, the *Institutes* of Marcus Fabius Quintilianus (AD 35–100), known as 'Quintilian', also argues that the would-be orator needs to know about all subjects. The author cites the names of eight polymaths, five Greek – including Hippias – and three Roman, including Cicero. The context, ironically enough, is the increasing specialization of rhetoricians, along with grammarians and jurists.[7]

A similar argument to that of Cicero and Quintilian on the orator was put forward in the case of the architect by Marcus Vitruvius Pollio (d. AD 15). Vitruvius claimed that his profession was a 'multidisciplinary' branch of knowledge (*scientia pluribus disciplinis et variis eruditionibus ornata*). According to him, the ideal architect would have a knowledge of literature, draughtsmanship, geometry, history, philosophy, music, medicine, law and 'astrology' (including what we call 'astronomy').[8]

Exemplary polymaths include one expatriate Greek, Alexander of Miletus (Lucius Cornelius Alexander, d. 36 BC), who was taken to Rome as a slave tutor and was nicknamed 'Polyhistor', in other words an individual who enquires into many things. Three Roman polymaths are frequently mentioned in classical texts: Cato, Varro and Pliny the Elder.

Marcus Porcius Cato, otherwise known as Cato the Elder (234–149 BC), was cited by Quintilian for his knowledge of war, philosophy, oratory, history, law and agriculture, and by Cicero's Crassus because 'there was nothing that could possibly be known and learned at that period [a hundred years earlier] that he had not investigated and acquired and, what is more, written about'.[9] In his long life, in which he also held political and military posts Marcus Terentius Varro (116–27 BC) wrote over seventy works on antiquities, language, agriculture, history, law, philosophy, literature and navigation, not to mention his satires. Cicero described Varro as 'a man outstanding for his intellect and his universal learning' (*vir ingenio praestans omnique doctrina*), while Quintilian declared that he wrote on 'many, almost all kinds of knowledge' (*Quam multa paene omnia tradidit Varro!*).[10] Varro's treatise on 'disciplines' in the plural (*Disciplinae*) has been described as 'the first encyclopaedia that is securely attested'.[11] The text has been lost but it is known that it dealt with the seven liberal arts, with architecture and with medicine.

Pliny the Elder (AD 23–79) practised law, commanded a fleet and advised emperors but, as his nephew remarked, 'he thought all time not spent in study wasted'. Some slaves read to him while he dictated to others. Pliny wrote on grammar, rhetoric, military and political history, and the art of fighting on horseback as well as the encyclopaedic *Natural History* which made him famous and which covers much more than what was later understood by 'natural history'. The author boasts in his preface that he had consulted about two thousand volumes and that not a single Greek had written about all parts of his subject single-handed. Although he based some statements on his own observation, Pliny was essentially a compiler. On the other hand, the preface to his *Natural History* denounced plagiarists. He may have guessed that his own work would be plagiarized in later centuries.

CHINA

It would be strange if omnivorous curiosity and wide-ranging knowledge were not to be found outside the Western tradition. In fact, 'Study widely' is a famous phrase from the classic text *Zhongyong* ('Doctrine of the Mean'). The Chinese had a word or words for polymathy, *boxue* ('broad studies') or *bowu* ('broad learning'), while the term for an individual who had mastered these studies was *boshi*, 'broad scholar'. These concepts emerged between the fifth and the second centuries BC.[12]

Like the Greeks, Chinese scholars also engaged in debate about the range of studies, which had important consequences for the famous system of selecting civil servants by competitive examination.[13] During the Song dynasty (960–1279) the examinations required knowledge of classics, poetry, history and politics. In a famous document concerning a failed attempt at reform, 'The Ten-Thousand-Word Memorial', the statesman Wang Anshi (1021–86) complained about the generality of the education of future administrators. The capacity to rule, he asserted, was 'best developed by specialization, and ruined by too great a variety of subjects to be studied'.[14] In later centuries the pendulum swung between specialist and general studies. In his *Instructions for Practical Living*, for instance, Wang Yangming (1472–1529) dismissed broad studies as superficial, preferring the knowledge and cultivation of the self to any kind of knowledge of the outside world.[15] On the other hand, examinations in 'broad scholarship and extensive words' were held in 1679 and 1736.[16]

Comparisons are rendered difficult by differences in terminology – 'there is no term that corresponds to Greek *philosophia* in classical Chinese thought, for example – and also in classification. Chinese 'maps of the relevant intellectual disciplines, theoretical or practical and applied, are very different both from those of the Greeks and from our own'.[17] Differences between the Chinese and the Greek packages of studies also create obstacles to comparison. The theory of music, for instance, the art of divination and the criticism of painting and calligraphy were all important for Chinese scholars.

The life and work of three individual scholars may offer some idea of the range and interests of Chinese polymaths. In the period of the 'Warring States', Hui Shi (370–310 BC) had wide interests. His works have been lost but he is vividly evoked in a famous collection of anecdotes, the Daoist text *Zhuangzi*. According to this text, Hui Shi was 'a man of many devices', while 'his writings would fill five carriages'. On the other hand – a recurrent criticism of polymaths – the text claims that Hui 'abused and dissipated his talents without really achieving anything'.[18]

From the Song dynasty, outstanding figures include two scholar–officials, Su Song (AD 1020–1101) and Shen Gua (AD 1031–1095). Su Song is most famous for the construction of a tower for the use of court astronomers and for describing its mechanical clock, which was driven by a water-wheel, in an illustrated treatise. Su also made maps, including maps of stars. Together with assistants, he produced a treatise on what we know as pharmacology, discussing the medical uses of plants, minerals and animals.[19]

As for Shen Gua, he has been described as 'perhaps the most interesting character in all Chinese science'.[20] He wrote on rituals, *tianwen* (combining astronomy with astrology), music, mathematics, medicine, administration, the art of war, painting, tea, medicine and poetry, as well as making maps (including an early relief map). When he was sent on a mission to Mongolia, he made notes on the customs of the peoples he encountered there. An annalist of the time remarked on Shen's 'vast' knowledge, while in the twentieth century he was described as a Chinese Leibniz (although, unlike Leibniz, he does not seem to have tried to integrate his different kinds of knowledge).[21] Shen's most famous work, produced after he had been forced to retire from the civil service, was a collection of what we might call 'essays', entitled *Mengxi Bitan* ('Brush Talks from the Dream Brook') and organized according to the categories of many Chinese encyclopaedias, including 'Ancient Usages', 'Philological Criticism', 'Strange Occurrences' and 'Calligraphy and Painting'.[22] The miscellaneous genre of 'brush talks' (*bitan*) was ideal for a polymath.

Comparisons and contrasts between polymaths in ancient Greece and in China may be illuminating, along the lines of a classic account of the study of nature in these two cultures.[23] The contributions to knowledge by Greek polymaths are linked to their careers as teachers, something that Pythagoras, Socrates, Plato and the Sophists had in common. The contributions of Chinese polymaths from the Han dynasty onwards developed out of their work as government officials in a culture in which successful candidates in the state examinations were expected to be generalists, not specialists. It was thanks to this shared expectation that British civil servants (required to pass examinations that were originally inspired by the Chinese system) are sometimes described as 'mandarins'.

Among the polymaths already mentioned, Su Song was President of the Ministry of Personnel and, later, Minister of Finance, while Shen Gua was at one time head of the Bureau of Astronomy. He was also active in supervising the draining of rivers, as a financial official and as the commander of an army. Shen's varied interests were 'shaped by his experience as a civil servant'.[24] The opportunity to write his essays came when he was disgraced, after the faction with which he was associated lost power (in Europe, we owe major works such as Machiavelli's *The Prince* and Lord Clarendon's *The History of the Rebellion* to similar circumstances).

EARLY MEDIEVAL EUROPE

Returning to the Western tradition, we find that late antiquity and the early Middle Ages witnessed both a critique and a loss of secular knowledge. Leading Christian writers opposed learning altogether. One was Tertullian (c.AD 155–c.240), who claimed that, ever since Christ, 'we do not need curiosity' (*Nobis curiositate opus non est*). Another, as we have seen, was St Augustine, who criticized a 'vain' curiosity, 'excused in the name of understanding and knowledge' (*vana et curiosa cupiditas nomine cognitionis et scientiae palliata*).[25]

Although the early Middle Ages is no longer viewed as the 'Dark Ages', a time of ignorance, it is difficult to deny the loss of knowledge, or more precisely of certain knowledges, between the years 500 and 1000. The decline of towns was accompanied by the decline of literacy. Libraries shrank. Pliny had had access to two thousand books, but in the ninth century the libraries of the monasteries of Reichenau and St Gall, major intellectual centres in their day, each contained only some four hundred books. Where later polymaths would face the problem of 'too much to know', Early Medieval ones suffered from the problem of 'too little'. In Western Europe, the knowledge of Greek was lost, and together with it the knowledge of much of the classical tradition, condemned as pagan. Many texts, including Varro's survey of ancient knowledge, were no longer copied and so disappeared. Much medical and mathematical knowledge was lost. The correspondence of two eleventh-century scholars, Raginbold of Cologne and Radolf of Liège, shows them discussing what might be meant by the phrase 'the interior angles' of a triangle. As a leading medievalist has remarked, this is 'a forcible reminder of the vast scientific ignorance with which the age was faced'.[26]

In this situation, a major task of scholars was a salvage operation, an attempt to preserve and bring together what remained of the classical tradition, rather than to add to it (the so-called 'barbarian' invaders of the Roman Empire brought their own knowledges with them, but these were usually transmitted orally and so failed to survive the centuries). As the scholars of this period assembled the fragments of ancient Greek and Roman learning, they also classified them, both in the curriculum of the schools attached to cathedrals and in encyclopaedias. The 'seven liberal arts' came to be divided into the *trivium* (grammar, logic and rhetoric, the three subjects concerned with words) and the *quadrivium* (arithmetic, geometry, astronomy and the theory of music, the four subjects concerned with numbers).

It might be said that in these circumstances it would have been easier than it used to be to become a polymath, since there was less to study. On the other hand, finding the necessary books had become more difficult. Wide-ranging scholars who were able to reunite fragments of knowledge were even more necessary than before. Among the most outstanding of these scholars were Boethius, Isidore of Seville and Gerbert of Aurillac.[27]

Boethius (c.480–524) was a Roman senator, consul and *magister officiorum*, in other words head of the officials serving Theoderic, King of the Ostrogoths, who had settled in Italy near Ravenna. Most famous for his book *The Consolation of Philosophy*, Boethius also wrote on logic, rhetoric, arithmetic, music and theology, as well as translating or commenting on texts by Pythagoras, Aristotle, Plato, Archimedes, Euclid, Ptolemy and Cicero. Boethius was described in his own time as 'fat with much learning' (*multa eruditione saginatum*).[28] Aware of the threat to knowledge in his time and the need to preserve it, he salvaged a considerable part of Greek learning by making it available to readers of Latin.[29]

Isidore of Seville (c.560–636) called his encyclopaedia the *Etymologies* because he began his discussion of each topic (the first of which is 'discipline') with the origin of the word for it, beginning with the seven liberal arts and moving on to medicine, law, theology, languages, animals, the cosmos, buildings, ships, food and clothes (his interest in technical knowledges deserves noting). Known as 'the Christian Varro', Isidore actually cites Varro twenty-eight times, but at second hand, a reminder that works by many ancient writers had been lost by the early Middle Ages. It is thought that he had a team of assistants.[30]

Gerbert of Aurillac (c.946–1003) was a French monk who studied in Spain and taught at the cathedral school in Rheims before becoming abbot of the famous monastery of Bobbio in northern Italy and finally pope, taking the name of Sylvester II. His interests ranged from Latin literature, especially the poems of Virgil and the plays of Terence, to music, mathematics, astronomy and what we call 'technology' – he made use of an astrolabe and an abacus and is said to have constructed an organ.

Like Pliny, Gerbert filled his waking hours with study. 'At work and at leisure,' he wrote of himself, 'I teach what I know and I learn what I do not.'[31] His learning became legendary. The chronicler William of Malmesbury, a twelfth-century English monk, wrote that Gerbert absorbed the *quadrivium* with such ease that he made these disciplines appear to be 'below the level of his intelligence', as well as surpassing the Alexandrian scholar Ptolemy in the study of astrology. William also called Gerbert a necromancer, as if no one could know so much without supernatural help, and described his construction of the head of a statue that would answer all his questions, the tenth-century equivalent of Alexa.[32] The story reveals more about normal expectations in the tenth and eleventh centuries than it does about Gerbert, although it should probably be interpreted as an expression of wonder, not so much at his mastery of different disciplines as at his knowing things that no one else knew, at least in Western Europe.

THE ISLAMIC WORLD

Another reason for William of Malmesbury's suspicions about Gerbert was that he learned from the Muslims (*a Saracenis*). When he was studying in Catalonia, Gerbert did indeed do this. By his time, scholars of Arab, Turkic and Persian origin had recovered much more Greek knowledge than was available in Western Europe. Greek texts were translated into Arabic and Pahlevi, either directly or indirectly (via Syriac-speaking Christian scholars). Some of the most learned scholars in the Islamic world between the tenth and the twelfth centuries wrote commentaries on the many works by or attributed to Aristotle and may have been inspired to emulate his breadth of knowledge.

The Arabs had a phrase with a similar meaning to 'polymath': *tafannun fi al-'ulum*, a scholar whose knowledge was 'many-branched' (*mutafannin*). However, although the package of disciplines that scholars needed to master was similar to the western package it was not identical with it. Their *Falsafa* translates well as 'philosophy' – indeed, it is the same word, moving from Greek into Arabic – while *Fikh* translates as 'law', and *Adab* translates more or less as what the Greeks called *paideia*, aimed at producing the *Adib*, 'the gentleman scholar'. The intellectual baggage of such a scholar 'would typically have consisted of a formidable array of the arts and sciences of his age: the web of the religious sciences, poetry, philology, history and literary criticism, together with a solid acquaintance with the natural sciences, from arithmetic to medicine and zoology'.[33]

In similar fashion to Quintilian on the orator and Vitruvius on the architect, the great scholar Ibn Khaldun, whose achievements will be discussed below, wrote that a good secretary 'will have to concern himself with the principal branches of scholarship'.[34] The branches most different from western ones at this point were the interpretation of the Quran (*Tafsir*), the study of accounts of Muhammad's words and deeds (*Hadith*), and what we call 'pharmacology' (*Saydalah*). The classification of knowledge included divisions such as 'rational knowledge' (*al-'ulum al-'aqliyya*) and 'the knowledge of the ancients' (*al-'ulum al-awa'il*).

Another way of praising Islamic scholars was to call them 'complete' (*kāmil*). It has been suggested that 'Many-sidedness was a quality sought by all men of learning.'[35] The education offered in *madrasas*, schools attached to mosques, encouraged this many-sidedness since students could easily move from one teacher (*shaykh*) to another. A study of medieval Damascus argues that 'exposure to many fields and many *shaykhs* was the ideal, rather than specialized training in single subjects'.[36]

The contributions to knowledge made by individual polymaths such as these are difficult if not impossible to evaluate. It was generally believed, both in the Islamic world and in the medieval West, that the function of the scholar was to transmit traditional knowledge rather than to transmit something new. Although some empirical research was carried out and discoveries were made, many learned works took the form of commentaries on the books of earlier scholars. In any case, in manuscript cultures there is generally less emphasis on individual authors than in cultures of print. Works by disciples might circulate under the name of their masters, while copyists often felt free to leave out or even to insert passages in the text that they were transcribing (some treatises cursed scribes who changed the text in this way).

Among the many-sided scholars of the Islamic world, outstanding figures living between the ninth and fourteenth centuries (according to the western chronology) include the following four: Al-Kindi, Ibn Sina (known as 'Avicenna'), Ibn Rushd ('Averroes') and Ibn Khaldun.[37]

Al-Kindi (801–73) came from Basra and studied in Baghdad. He wrote on philosophy, mathematics, music, astronomy, medicine, optics and ciphers, as well as on the manufacture of glass, jewellery, armour and perfume, fields of practical knowledge that make him comparable to the Chinese scholar Su Song, discussed earlier. Al-Kindi was described by a fourteenth-century writer as 'a versatile man' who mastered 'philosophy in all its branches'.[38] A recent study also refers to 'the astonishing range of Al-Kindi's interests'.[39] Appropriately enough, some of his writings were studied by Leonardo da Vinci.

Ibn Sina (c.980–1037) came from Bukhara. When he was still a teenager, he was given permission by Mansur II to use the emir's great library there. Nicknamed 'the prince of physicians', Ibn Sina became well known for his works on medicine and for his critical commentary on Aristotle. At the age of twenty-one he compiled an encyclopaedia, the *Compendium* (*Kitab al-Majmu*), and he went on to write two more encyclopaedic works. The first of these, *The Canon* (*Al-Qanun*), was concerned with medicine. The second, *The Cure* (*Al-Shifa*), was an attempt to cure ignorance by expounding on logic, physics, metaphysics, mathematics, music and astronomy. Ibn Sina also wrote on geography and poetry. He both studied alchemy and criticized it. He was also active as a jurist and as a vizier to an emir in what is now Iran.[40]

Ibn Rushd ('Averroes', 1126–98), who came from Córdoba, was active as a physician and as a judge. Thanks to his commentary on almost all the works of Aristotle, a major enterprise, Ibn Rushd was known as 'the Commentator'. He also produced his own studies of rhetoric, poetics, astronomy, medicine, philosophy, mathematics and music.[41]

Following Ibn Rushd there was something of a hiatus in the list of Islamic polymaths until the appearance of Ibn Khaldun (1332–1406). He was born in Tunis, lived in Fez and Granada, and died in Cairo. He wrote in the intervals between his three careers, a political one as a diplomat and an adviser of rulers, a legal one as a judge and an academic one as a teacher. Ibn Khaldun spent four years in retirement in a castle in what is now Algeria in order to write his masterpiece, the *Muqaddima*, which offers general reflections as an introduction to a history of the Muslim world, the *Kitab al-'ibar*. The *Muqaddima* has been acclaimed as a contribution to sociology and political science, although these disciplines did not exist in the author's time. Thinking with the intellectual categories of his own day, we may say that what made the *Muqaddimah* possible was Ibn Khaldun's knowledge of geography, philosophy, theology and medicine as well as his acute understanding of history and his gift for generalization. It was the West's loss that, unlike some of his predecessors, Ibn Khaldun was not known there until relatively recently. A manuscript of his major work was brought to Leiden in the seventeenth century, but the first translations into European languages were only made in the nineteenth century, while his fame in the West dates from the twentieth.[42]

THE HIGH MIDDLE AGES

The twelfth-century scholar Bernard of Chartres is reputed to have said that he and his colleagues were 'like dwarves standing on the shoulders of giants', in other words ancient Greeks and Romans. It might be more exact to say that medieval western scholars were standing on the shoulders of Muslim scholars who in turn stood on the shoulders of the ancients. In the early Middle Ages, the challenge to scholars had been to save and preserve what remained of the classical tradition. In the later

Middle Ages, it was to recover and to master not only the ancient Greek knowledge that had been lost but also the new knowledge produced in the Islamic world.

A major innovation of this period, from the eleventh century onwards, was the foundation of universities, notably at Bologna and Paris, institutionalizing a package of disciplines. Undergraduates were supposed to study the seven liberal arts, the *trivium* and *quadrivium* described above. The postgraduate disciplines were theology, law and medicine, offering professional training for clergy, lawyers and physicians. Despite these early signs of specialization, some medieval scholars carried on the polymathic tradition. Among the most outstanding of these were the following six: Hugh of St Victor, Vincent of Beauvais, Albert the Great, Robert Grosseteste, Roger Bacon and Ramón Lull.[43]

Both Hugh and Vincent became famous for their encyclopaedias. The monk Hugh of St Victor (c.1096–1141) came from Saxony but worked in Paris. He wrote on theology, music, geometry and grammar but is best known for his *Didascalicon*, an encyclopaedia divided into three types of knowledge: theoretical (philosophy, for example), practical (such as politics) and 'mechanical' (architecture, for instance, and navigation).[44] The Dominican friar Vincent of Beauvais (c.1190–1264) compiled, with the help of assistants, an encyclopaedia known as *The Great Mirror* (*Speculum Maius*), drawing on the writings of Muslim scholars such as Ibn Sina as well as on ancient Greeks and Romans. Like the *Didascalicon*, Vincent's encyclopaedia was divided into three parts, in his case the knowledge of nature, doctrine and history. The liberal and mechanical arts, law and medicine were all included in the section on 'doctrine'.[45]

Two of the polymaths active in this period were Englishmen, Robert Grosseteste (c.1175–1253) and Roger Bacon (c.1214–c.1292). Robert, who became bishop of Lincoln, was doubtless nicknamed 'Big Head' (*Grosseteste*) on account of his many-sided learning. He taught philosophy and theology at Oxford and wrote the first Latin commentary on Aristotle, but is best known for his writings on nature – on the stars, on light, on colour, on the origin of sounds, on the heat of the sun and possibly on the tides. He is also 'the first thinker on record to have identified refraction as the underlying cause of the rainbow'.[46] He learned Greek late in life and was one of the few medieval western scholars to know that language.[47]

Roger Bacon, a Franciscan friar, may have been a pupil of Grosseteste's. He studied and taught philosophy and theology at Oxford but he too is best known for his investigation of nature, ranging from astronomy to optics and alchemy. Like Leonardo later, he attempted to construct a flying machine.[48] Thanks to the first-hand accounts written by three of his Franciscan colleagues, all missionaries, Roger acquired up-to-date knowledge about the Mongols, whose rapid conquests were terrifying Europeans at this time.[49] He also wrote on mathematics and on language. A sign of Bacon's reputation as a polymath in his own time is the story (also attached to Gerbert of Aurillac, as we have seen) that he had a brazen head in his study that answered all his questions. The mythology of polymaths goes back a long way.

The most ambitious medieval polymaths were surely Albert the Great and Ramón Lull. Albert (Albertus Magnus, c.1200–80) should be distinguished from Albert of Saxony (c.1316–90), who contributed to logic, mathematics and physics. Albert the Great was a German Dominican, known in his own day as 'Doctor Universalis' or 'Doctor Expertus', titles that testify to the breadth of his knowledge. One of his students called Albert 'a man so godlike in every branch of knowledge (*vir in omni scientia adeo divinus*) that he can properly be called the wonder and marvel of our age'.[50] Albert studied theology, philosophy, alchemy, astrology and music, commented on all the known works of Aristotle and was familiar with the work of some leading Muslim scholars. He also made his own observations and classification of plants and minerals. He was said to possess a statue, or, as we would say, a robot, that was able to move and say 'Hello' (*salve*), if not to answer questions like the brazen heads of his colleagues Gerbert and Roger.

As for the Catalan friar Ramón Lull (or Llull, 1232–1316), he demonstrated his versatility by writing about 260 different works, including two romances, a book on the art of love and the *Tree of Knowledge* (*Arbor Scientiae*); by learning Arabic in order to work as a missionary in North

Africa; and above all by his *Ars Magna* (*Great Art*), described by Umberto Eco as 'a system for a perfect language with which to convert the infidel'. The *Ars Magna* makes use of logic, rhetoric and mathematics in order to teach readers how to discover, remember and present arguments, employing wheels to allow different ideas to be combined (a technique known as the *ars combinatoria*, apparently borrowed or adapted from the *zairja* of Arab astrologers). Three hundred years later, Lull's art would attract the attention of the greatest polymath of the seventeenth century, Gottfried Wilhelm Leibniz. Needless to say, in an age of computer science, Lull's discussion of the art of combination has been receiving increasing attention.[51]

2

THE AGE OF THE 'RENAISSANCE MAN'
1400–1600

In Europe in the fifteenth and sixteenth centuries, the amount of information in circulation rapidly increased. In the movement now known as the Renaissance, scholars laboured to recover ancient Greek and Roman knowledges that had been lost during the Middle Ages. The exploration and conquest of parts of Europe, Asia and the Americas brought new knowledge in its train, while the invention of printing allowed both old and new knowledges to circulate further and faster. Nonetheless, it was still possible in this period for at least a few scholars to dominate the kinds of knowledge taught and studied in universities, which now included not only the medieval *trivium* and *quadrivium*, mentioned earlier, but also the 'humanities' (*studia humanitatis*), a package of five disciplines – grammar, rhetoric, poetry, history and ethics – that were supposed to make students more fully human.

When we think of the Renaissance, however, we generally call to mind not only scholars but also artists and above all the so-called 'Renaissance Man', a personage who has long made regular appearances in the titles of scholarly books.[1] As we have seen, a number of twentieth-century polymaths, among them Benedetto Croce, Herbert Simon and Joseph Needham, have been described as late examples of the species. This association of versatile individuals with the Renaissance owes much to the great Swiss cultural historian Jacob Burckhardt.

In his famous essay on *The Civilisation of the Renaissance in Italy*, first published in 1860 but frequently reprinted to this day, Burckhardt presented a few individuals of the period – notably Francesco Petrarca, Leonbattista Alberti, Giovanni Pico della Mirandola and Leonardo da Vinci – as examples of what he called the 'all-sided' or at least the 'many-sided' man (*der allseitige Mensch, der vielseitige Mensch*).[2] Of these 'giants', as he calls them, Burckhardt dwelt in particular on Alberti and Leonardo.

Other nineteenth-century writers described major figures of the Renaissance in similar fashion. Before Burckhardt, the French historian Edgar Quinet had characterized Leonardo as 'a citizen of every world . . . Anatomist, chemist, musician, geologist, improviser, poet, engineer, physicist'.[3] After Burckhardt, and perhaps following him, George Eliot praised Alberti in her novel *Romola* for his 'robust universal mind, at once practical and theoretic, artist, man of science, inventor, poet'.[4]

THE IDEAL OF UNIVERSALITY

The ideal of many-sidedness or the 'universal man' (*uomo universale*) was put forward in the Renaissance itself. One of the great teachers of fifteenth-century Italy, Vittorino da Feltre, 'used to praise that universal learning that the Greeks call *encyclopaedia*, saying that to benefit his fellows the perfect man should be able to discuss natural philosophy, ethics, astronomy, geometry, harmony, arithmetic and surveying'. His ideal was knowledge of 'many and various disciplines'.[5] Again, a speaker in a dialogue on 'civic life' (*la vita civile*), written by the Florentine Matteo Palmieri, asks 'how a man might learn many things and make himself universal (*farsi universale*) in many excellent arts'.[6] A famous incarnation of the ideal of universality was the figure of Faust. The hero of the original German *Faustbuch* of 1587 had an 'insatiable desire for knowledge'.[7]

These formulations of the ideal of universality concentrate on academic knowledge, the central topic of this study. Other versions are more ambitious and demand ability in the world of action (the *vita activa*) as well as that of thought (the *vita contemplativa*), a contrast often vividly described at this time as one between 'arms' and 'letters'.[8] Some versions also demand ability in the fine arts. For example, in Baldassare Castiglione's dialogue on the courtier, first published in 1528, one speaker argues that the perfect courtier should not only be skilled in fighting and be 'more than passably learned' (*più che mediocremente erudito*) in the humanities, but also have mastered the arts of dancing, painting and music.[9]

The ideal of universality was also expressed by the emperor Maximilian in his romance of chivalry, the *Weisskunig*, which was written a few years before Castiglione's book. The hero of the romance is presented as skilled in calligraphy, the liberal arts, magic, medicine, astrology, music, painting, building, hunting, fighting and even carpentry, as well as knowing eleven languages.[10] In France, François Rabelais offered a vivid image of a many-sided education in his imaginary biographies of the giants Gargantua and Pantagruel. Gargantua studied not only the liberal arts but also medicine and the art of war, and when it rained he went to see craftsmen at work. He advised his son Pantagruel to study in the same way: liberal arts, law, medicine and natural history, in short 'an abyss of knowledge' (*un abysme de science*).[11]

In England, the idea of universal knowledge goes back to the early sixteenth century, when the printer William Caxton referred to 'an unyversall man almost in all scyences'.[12] The ideal of many-sidedness was formulated in Sir Thomas Elyot's *Book Named the Governor* (1531), a treatise on the education of upper-class males. Elyot not only discusses what he calls the 'circle of doctrine' that students should follow but also suggests that a gentleman should know how to compose music, paint and even sculpt as well as studying academic subjects.[13] However, this vision of the noble amateur, already visible in Castiglione's reference to being 'more than passably learned', should be distinguished from the ideal of the individual who is driven, like Alberti, to excel in everything he attempts.

THE MYTH OF UNIVERSALITY

Despite some of the spectacular examples of versatility already discussed, it may be argued that Burckhardt and some of his contemporaries exaggerated the distinctiveness of the intellectual species they described as the 'universal' or 'Renaissance' man (the case of the 'Renaissance woman' will be discussed later in the chapter). Several of the contemporary testimonies quoted above are less clear-cut than they may appear at first sight. Castiglione, for instance, allows some speakers in his dialogue to challenge many-sidedness, condemning people who 'are always trying to do things they don't know about and neglecting what they do know about', a passage that is generally taken to refer to Leonardo.[14]

Again, the literally 'gargantuan' educational programme described by Rabelais has often been taken seriously as the expression of a Renaissance ideal, but it may also be read as a parody of that ideal. As for Faust, his insatiable thirst for knowledge was condemned in the original *Faustbook* as an example of his spiritual pride. Doctor Faustus was not presented as a hero, but as a warning. The condemnation of curiosity by theologians such as Augustine was still taken seriously in the sixteenth century.

Burckhardt himself was a versatile individual who wrote poetry, sketched and played the piano as well as teaching and writing both history and art history (which had already become separate disciplines in the German-speaking world in his day). As a historian, Burckhardt refused to specialize in a particular period and wrote about the cultural history of Greece, the age of Constantine and (in posthumously published lectures) what he regarded as the world crisis of his own time. No wonder then that he was attracted to many-sided figures such as Alberti and Leonardo and wished to see them as typical of their age, a golden age that preceded an iron age of intellectual and cultural specialization. In this way Burckhardt contributed to what was described earlier as the 'mythology' of the polymath.[15]

There are many definitions of myth. The one followed here has two main features. It is a story about the past which is employed to justify or to criticize a situation in the present, and a story in which the protagonists are larger than life. The story may be completely false, but is not necessarily so. Inside the shell of exaggerations, it often contains a kernel of truth. Let us see whether and to what extent some individuals of this period lived up to the ideal of universality.

ACTION AND THOUGHT

Leon Battista Alberti's combination of abilities was noted by Burckhardt. The anonymous biography of Alberti, generally taken to be an autobiography, described him as an individual so 'versatile' that he mastered all the fine arts, together with physical exercises such as horsemanship, jumping and hurling the javelin.[16] There is no way of verifying his claims to physical feats, but some of his contemporaries were impressed by Alberti's intellectual range. The humanist Cristoforo Landino asked (rhetorically), 'What branch of mathematics was not known to him? Geometry, arithmetic, astronomy, music – and in perspective he did marvels.' In any case, some of Alberti's achievements are still extant: the buildings he designed, his treatises on painting and architecture, his dialogue on the family, his little book on mathematical games and his self-portrait on a bronze medallion.[17]

Thanks to a biography written by one of his pupils, we know that the fifteenth-century Dutch scholar Rudolf Agricola, best known for his studies of logic, was another man of 'many-sided knowledge' (*multiplex scientia*) who emulated Alberti by practising painting, sculpture, music and gymnastics, and who also built an organ.[18]

In the sixteenth century, a number of individuals who lacked the wide range of Alberti and Agricola still combined an active life with a contemplative one, arms with letters. For example, the Spanish noblemen Garcilaso de la Vega and Alonso de Ercilla lived a double life as soldiers and poets. Garcilaso fought in Europe and North Africa and became famous for his lyrics, while Ercilla served in what is now Chile and turned the conflict between the indigenous inhabitants and the Spaniards into an epic. In Elizabethan England, Philip Sidney, a soldier who died in battle in the Netherlands, remains famous for his poetry and his romance *Arcadia*.

Another Elizabethan who combined arms and letters, Walter Raleigh, was closer to the ideal of the *uomo universale*. He described himself on the scaffold, before his execution on a charge of conspiracy against King James I, as 'a soldier, a captain, a sea-captain and a courtier'. He might have added that he was a poet and a scholar, the author of a history of the world. He was also an adventurer in Virginia and what is now Venezuela, while his book the *Discovery of Guiana* (1596) reveals his interest in foreign lands and their inhabitants. Contemporaries described Raleigh as 'An indefatigable reader' and 'a great chemist' (in other words, an alchemist).[19]

As for James Crichton, this young Scottish nobleman was described by a contemporary as 'admirable in all studies' (*omnibus in studiis admirabilis*). The 'admirable Crichton', as he is still known, arrived in Italy in 1579 when he was nineteen and became a kind of intellectual knight-errant, issuing challenges to university professors to debate with him. Crichton made a great impression on at least some Italians before his early death, murdered by the son of his employer, the Duke of Mantua, and was described by one of them as follows: 'He knows ten languages . . . philosophy, theology, mathematics and astrology . . . He has a perfect knowledge of the Cabala . . . improvises verses in all metres . . . makes informed comments on politics', not to mention his prowess as a soldier, athlete, dancer, and as 'a marvellous courtier'.[20]

Other individuals of this period combined learning with a career in public life, including two English lawyers, both of whom occupied the highest post in their profession, that of Lord Chancelllor: Thomas More and Francis Bacon. More was a humanist and a theologian as well as the author of *Utopia*, while Bacon published essays, a biography of King Henry VII and the *Advancement of Learning*, a reflection on the methods by which knowledge might be increased. Bacon carried out experiments in natural philosophy and is said to have met his death from pneumonia following an attempt to preserve chickens by freezing them.[21]

SCHOLARS

Only a few of the 'Renaissance men' described so far count as polymaths in the strict sense, but there was no shortage of many-sided scholars in Europe in this period, described at the time as 'knowing much' (*multiscius*), an adjective used by the Spanish humanist Juan Luis Vives, or as individuals of *multiplex scientia*, the phrase employed by the biographer of the Dutch humanist Rudolf Agricola. To be a humanist, teaching the humanities, required the mastery of five disciplines, as we have seen. Desiderius Erasmus, the most famous humanist of all, also mastered philology and theology. He did not wish to explore further, however, and reminded his readers that Socrates had criticized the interest in 'unnecessary disciplines' such as astrology and geometry, believing that the proper study of mankind is man. In the words of a sympathetic historian, Erasmus only 'aspired to a kind of polymathy'.[22]

Other humanists were more adventurous, following the example of Aristotle rather than Socrates. Philip Melanchthon, for instance, now remembered as a theologian, Luther's right-hand man in Wittenberg, studied or taught not only rhetoric and Greek but also mathematics, astronomy, astrology, anatomy and botany.[23]

Giovanni Pico della Mirandola in particular aimed at universality. Pico is well known for his *Oration on the Dignity of Man*, a kind of manifesto for Renaissance humanism, but his interests were much wider. When he was only twenty-three, in 1486, he proposed to defend 900 theses – 'dialectical, moral, physical, mathematical, metaphysical, theological, magical and cabalistic' – though the proposed defence, in Rome, never took place. Pico argued that mathematics was 'the method for investigating everything that is knowable' (*via ad omnis scibilis investigationem*). He learned Hebrew, Aramaic and Arabic, and was particularly fascinated by the study of the secret Jewish tradition of the Cabala (or Kabbalah), which he 'launched . . . into the Christian world'. He was interested not only in the mystical tradition of the Cabala but also in the use of Hebrew letters and words for magical purposes, a technique that Pico compared to Ramón Lull's art of combination.[24]

Pico was described by a character in a dialogue by Erasmus, the *Ciceronianus*, as an 'all-sided man' (*ingenium ad omnia factum*), while the life of Pico by his nephew referred to him as an example of 'men who are experts in every kind of discipline' (*viri omni disciplinarum genere consumatissimi*). As we shall see, later polymaths and their admirers often referred to Pico as an exemplar.[25]

Pico should not be viewed as an individual who broke with tradition. His 900 theses begin with sixteen conclusions 'according to Albert', in other words the 'Universal Doctor', Albert the Great. They also referred to Ibn Rushd, Ibn Sina and Al-Farabi. The intellectual tournament that Pico proposed at Rome followed a medieval precedent, that of the *quodlibet*, as practised at the university of Prague and elsewhere, in which a university teacher would prepare questions for disputation in all disciplines.[26]

A substantial number of individuals (50 of my 500, all born before 1565) have a good claim to be regarded as Renaissance polymaths. The five examples that follow include a German, two Frenchmen, an Englishman and a Swiss: Heinrich Cornelius Agrippa, Jean Bodin, Joseph Scaliger, John Dee and Conrad Gessner.

Agrippa is believed to have been the model for that symbol of omniscience, Doctor Faustus. In his play on this theme, Christopher Marlowe makes Faustus boast that he will become 'as cunning as Agrippa was' (the word 'cunning' referred at this time to knowledge in general). Before following an academic career, Agrippa served as a soldier, thus joining arms and letters, and he was also employed as a diplomat and a physician. His interests included theology, philosophy, law, medicine, alchemy, magic and the secret Jewish tradition of the Cabala, which also fascinated Pico. Describing himself as 'a glutton for books' (*helluo librorum*), Agrippa made considerable use of the work of Pliny the Elder and wrote a commentary on a work by Lull. His books include *The Vanity of the Sciences* (1527), a general survey of knowledge from a sceptical point of view, and *Occult Philosophy* (1531–3), a treatise on magic (natural, celestial and religious), in which he argued that it could help resolve problems raised by the sceptics. According to rumour, Agrippa's black dog was actually a devil. As in the cases of Gerbert, Roger Bacon and Albertus Magnus, Agrippa was regarded with a mixture of wonder and suspicion.[27]

Jean Bodin was described by the historian Hugh Trevor-Roper as 'the undisputed intellectual master of the later sixteenth century'.[28] He owes much of his fame to his study of the state, *Six Livres de la République* (1576), which argued in favour of absolute monarchy (the word *république* in the title means 'commonwealth', not 'republic' in the modern sense). The book combines political theory with what would be known much later as 'political science', offering a pioneering comparative analysis of political systems. In his *Method for the Easy Comprehension of History* (1566), a guide for students in the form of a bibliographical essay, Bodin had linked the study of history with that of law, recommending the comparison of the laws 'of all or the most famous commonwealths' in order to select the best ones. He described the ideal jurist as 'a living encyclopaedia' and emphasized the need for historians to study geography (including climate) and philosophy, referring to those who did as *Geographistorici* and *Philosophistorici*.[29]

Bodin's other books are known only to specialists. One, the *Demonomania* (1580), describes the activities of witches and their pact with the devil, who, according to the author, tries to persuade judges in witchcraft trials to be lenient. Bodin criticizes Agrippa for studying the occult. Another book, the *Theatre of Nature* (1596), is a kind of encyclopaedia in the form of a dialogue, combining natural history, natural philosophy and natural theology and mobilizing specific examples from astronomy to zoology in order to show that everything in nature has a useful purpose in God's plan. Bodin also contributed to what is now known as economics. He has 'a strong claim to be regarded as the pioneer formulator of the quantity theory of money', put forward in response to the arguments of a royal official concerned with the recent rise in prices.[30]

Bodin was probably the author of the anonymous 'Dialogue of the Seven' (*Colloquium Heptaplomeres*) in which the participants are presented discussing the various virtues of Catholicism, Calvinism, Lutheranism, Judaism, Islam and natural religion. In any case, he was active in attempts to end the wars between Catholics and Protestants in France.[31]

Another Frenchman, Joseph Scaliger, might be considered to be a worthy rival of Bodin for the title of 'intellectual master' of his time. Known in his day as the 'Hercules' of the Republic of Letters, described by Immanuel Kant as a 'marvel' of memory and more recently as a 'titan of learning', Scaliger was essentially a philologist, a peerless example of the scholar's scholar, provoking the emulation of the polymath John Selden, as we shall see.[32] His editions of classical texts, from the Roman polymath Varro to the poets Catullus, Tibullus and Propertius, were marked not only by brilliant emendations but also by innovations in method, notably the reconstruction of the history of the textual tradition.

Scaliger combined the approach of classical philologists with that of lawyers such as Jacques Cujas, with whom he had studied, learning how to fit fragments of evidence together. His edition of an astronomical poem by the ancient Roman Marcus Manilius required him to study the history of that discipline. Scaliger also became an orientalist, learning Hebrew, Aramaic and Arabic. He made use of all these knowledges in his masterpiece 'On the Correction of Chronologies' (*De emendatio temporum*, 1583), supplemented by the 'Treasury of Chronologies' (*Thesaurus temporum*, 1606). In these books Scaliger offered a systematic critique of the sources in different ancient languages and drew on astronomical information, like Isaac Newton a century later, in order to resolve contradictions between Greek, Roman, Babylonian and other chronologies.[33]

The English scholar John Dee is sometimes thought to have served as a model for the protagonist of Christopher Marlowe's play *Doctor Faustus* (like Agrippa in the case of the original German *Faustbook*). He was neglected by historians until relatively recently – again like Agrippa – because his studies included disciplines such as astrology, angelology, magic and alchemy that are no longer taken seriously by mainstream scholars, despite their continuing appeal to enthusiasts of the occult. Dee's interests also extended to mathematics, astronomy, philosophy, law, physics, navigation and geography (which he had studied in the Netherlands with the famous cartographer Gerard Mercator). Dee took a particular interest in some of his polymath predecessors, including Albertus Magnus, Roger Bacon, Ramón Lull and Pico della Mirandola. His library was one of the largest of his day, with some four thousand printed volumes and manuscripts, including treatises on architecture, music, antiquities, heraldry and genealogy as well as the disciplines already mentioned. In short, 'in groping for universal knowledge he was a complete Renaissance man', virtually 'omnidisciplinary'.[34]

In his relatively short life – he died at the age of forty-nine – Conrad Gessner acquired a reputation as a humanist, a physician, a naturalist, and an encyclopaedist. He was variously described as a 'polyhistor', as 'the Pliny of our Germany' (and later as a 'monster of erudition', a phrase to which the following chapter will return).[35]

Gessner was a professor of Greek at Lausanne. He published a number of editions of ancient Greek texts, but he is most often remembered for his massive bibliography cum biographical dictionary, the *Universal Library* (1545). In 1,300 pages, Gessner offered information about 10,000 works by 3,000 authors who wrote in Latin or Greek, producing an invaluable reference work that was intended, at least in part, to help with the discovery and preservation of classical texts.[36] He later produced a comparative study of some 130 languages (*Mithridates*, 1555).

As if this was not enough, Gessner was also active as a physician in Zurich and as a contributor, like other humanists of his generation, to the study of nature as well as of culture. He produced books on animals (*Historiae animalium*, five volumes, 1551–8), baths (*De Germaniae et Helvetiae Thermis*, 1553) and fossils (*De fossilium genere*, 1565), as well as leaving botanical manuscripts that might have become another book had the author lived a little longer. The tradition of Renaissance humanism remains apparent in the interest that Gessner takes in the opinions of ancient writers such as Aristotle and Pliny, but he also relied on his own observation of plants and animals. A genus of flower and a genus of moth have been named after him.

To understand how Gessner was able to publish so much on so many topics in his short life, scholars have recently been focusing on his working methods. Much of his information came from correspondents, whose letters he often cut up and rearranged under topical headings. Other information came from visitors as well as from his wide reading, while the task of organizing the mass of material was delegated in part to assistants and amanuenses. Even so, Gessner's achievement is impressive.[37]

UNITY AND CONCORD

What drove these individuals to study such a wide range of subjects? In Gessner's case it may have been simple fox-like curiosity, though the passion for order and the need to remedy what he once described as the 'disorder of books', doubtless played a part. In the case of other polymaths, the 'hedgehogs', the main aim was the unification of knowledge, a theme that will echo through later chapters of this book. Pico, for instance, offers a clear example of a polymath driven by the desire to reconcile conflicting ideas (those of Plato and Aristotle, for instance) and conflicting cultures (Christian, Jewish and Muslim). No wonder then that he was known in his own day as 'the Prince of Concord', a title all the more appropriate because his family owned the Italian town of Concordia.

Again, Cardinal Nicholas of Cusa, who was active as a philosopher, theologian, lawyer, mathematician and astronomer as well as a diplomat and cardinal, was driven by the idea of reconciling conflicts. His treatise *De Concordantia Catholica* was concerned to heal divisions in the Church.[38] Pico knew about Nicholas and hoped to visit his library in Germany.[39] Another polymath, the Frenchman Guillaume Postel, was also driven by the desire for concord. His book on the subject, *De Orbis Terrae Concordia*, emphasized common elements in the religions of the world.[40]

Bodin too was concerned with harmony, an unsurprising response to the religious wars in France in his day. He viewed nature as a harmonious system, while his book on politics discussed harmonic justice and was in turn discussed by the astronomer Johannes Kepler in his treatise *Harmonies of the World* (1619). It has been suggested that 'the goal of universal synthesis inspires all of Bodin's work on law'; that he had an 'obsession with system'; that the central theme of his *Heptaplomeres* is harmony; and that his *Theatre of Nature* exemplifies the attempt to bring 'order and coherence to ever-increasing quantities of knowledge', an attempt that became more and more difficult from the seventeenth century onwards, as we shall see.[41]

A vision of the whole often underlay the compilation of encyclopaedias, a task that was still performed by individual scholars in this period, despite its increasing difficulty as printed books multiplied. The Spanish humanist Juan Luis Vives wrote about the whole of learning in his book *On Disciplines* (1531). Conrad Gessner produced encyclopaedias of books and animals. Gerolamo Cardano, an Italian physician remembered today for his contributions to mathematics, was also the author of two encyclopaedic works, *On Subtlety* (1550) and *On the Variety of Things* (1558). The Croatian scholar Paul Skalić published his *Encyclopaedia* in 1559, while the Swiss Theodor Zwinger, a professor at the University of

Basel, produced his *Theatre of Human Life* in 1565. The *Theatre* contained example after example of human behaviour arranged under moral categories. By its third edition, the book contained 4,500 pages and over six million words.[42]

ARTISTS AND ENGINEERS

The creativity of participants in the movement now known as the Renaissance has sometimes been explained in terms of what we might call 'de-compartmentalization', in other words the breakdown or at least the weakening of barriers to communication between different groups, bridging 'the gap which had separated the scholar and thinker from the practitioner'.[43]

For example, some humanists, such as Alberti, were on friendly terms with painters and sculptors (in Alberti's case, with Masaccio and Donatello). Alberti advocated a general education for painters and (following the ancient Roman Vitruvius) for architects as well. Another humanist, Georg Agricola, was a physician who worked in the mining town of Joachimsthal (now Jáchymov in Czechia). In his most famous work, 'On Metallurgy' (*De re metallica*, 1556), Agricola drew on the practical knowledge of miners as well as on his own reading and observation.[44]

Academics held no monopoly of many-sidedness at this time. In this period, to be an artist or an engineer was to be a kind of polymath. Alberti's friend Filippo Brunelleschi, for instance, remains famous for two rather different achievements. One was to design and to oversee the building of the dome of the cathedral of Florence, overcoming problems of structural engineering that others had thought insoluble. The other was to rediscover the rules of linear perspective. These rules were illustrated by what was apparently a masterpiece of illusionism, a lost painting of the Baptistery of Florence, intended to be viewed from the back through a spyhole that showed a mirror. It has been suggested that Brunelleschi applied to painting the techniques of surveying that he had learned when measuring the ruins of ancient buildings in Rome. If this was the case, his achievement offers an impressive example of the way in which polymaths contribute to knowledge, transferring ideas and practices from one discipline to another.

Brunelleschi had actually been trained as a goldsmith, a training that led him to sculpture and to participation in a famous competition for the best design for the doors of the Baptistery in Florence (he came second to a more specialized rival, the sculptor Lorenzo Ghiberti). Brunelleschi was also a great inventor of machines, large and small, and the first individual to take out a patent for invention. His brain-children ranged from an early alarm clock to a machine that would hoist the heavy beams essential to the structure of his famous dome. An early biography of Filippo declares that he was not only a mathematician but also 'learned in the Bible' and a student of the works of Dante. In addition, he wrote verse, using the sonnet as a medium for insulting his rivals and critics.[45]

Brunelleschi's friend Mariano 'Taccola', otherwise known as 'the Sienese Archimedes', was active as a notary, a sculptor and a superintendent of roads as well as a military engineer, working for the emperor Sigismund. He is remembered for his two treatises on machines of different kinds, including discussions and illustrations of some of Brunelleschi's inventions as well as of some ingenious weapons of war.[46]

Another Sienese, Francesco di Giorgio Martini, a former pupil of Taccola's, was trained as a painter but revealed a variety of other gifts in the course of his career. He was placed in charge of the water supply in Siena before becoming an architect and a military engineer in the service of the Duke of Urbino and of two kings of Naples. Carrying on the tradition of Brunelleschi and Taccola, Martini wrote on architecture, fortification and machines, including a pump, a saw and a moving chariot that was probably for use in pageants.[47]

In his famous biographies, assembled in *Lives of the Artists*, Giorgio Vasari referred to several artists, including Giulio Romano and Primaticcio, as *universale*, while the Duke of Urbino went one better by describing the architect Bartolomeo Genga by an invented adjective, *omniversale*. In these cases, the terms probably refer to versatility in the arts.[48] In the case of Leonardo, it goes well beyond them.

LEONARDO

The most famous example of the 'Renaissance Man', Leonardo da Vinci, is also one of the least typical.[49] He was not a humanist and, like the engineers mentioned in the previous section, he lacked a humanist education. He may not have gone to school at all, and in later life he was only able to read Latin with some difficulty. Leonardo was trained as an artist in the workshop of the famous Florentine master Andrea Verrocchio, where he learned not only to paint and sculpt but also to design weapons of war, drawing on the Tuscan engineering tradition from Brunelleschi to Francesco di Giorgio (who later became a friend of his). Leonardo is the outstanding example of the extraordinary tradition of innovation in fifteenth- and sixteenth-century Florence, in which masters passed on their knowledge to apprentices in their workshops. It is possible to identify chains of artists, each of whom taught the one before, yet developed his own style. Verrocchio, for instance, taught not only Leonardo but also Ghirlandaio, who taught Michelangelo.

Leonardo left Florence for Milan, bringing himself to the attention of the Duke, Lodovico Sforza, by promising to make bridges, cannon, catapults and mines, and – in the tenth place on his list – to produce works of sculpture and architecture. He was given the post of the Duke's engineer (*ingeniarius ducalis*), concerned not only with canals and fortifications but also with producing 'special effects' for court pageants. At the court of Milan, Leonardo also became known as a skilled musician, playing the lyre and singing, gifts appreciated in the world of Castiglione's courtier. In addition, he invented new musical instruments and carried out research on sound.[50] Leonardo later worked as a military engineer for the Republic of Venice and for the Pope's son Cesare Borgia when Cesare was attempting to conquer the Romagna. Leonardo designed many machines, including a mechanical lion, a giant crossbow, a wheel-lock gun, flying machines and a kind of submarine.[51]

Besides the tradition of painters and sculptors, Leonardo belonged to a Tuscan tradition of artist-engineers that included, as we have seen, Brunelleschi, Taccola and Francesco di Giorgio. Indeed, in the case of some of the machines pictured in his notebooks, it is difficult to say whether they are simply his inventions or whether he was drawing on a common stock of knowledge and ideas. Nevertheless, Leonardo exceeded his predecessors in many ways.

King Francis I of France, according to the sculptor Benvenuto Cellini, 'said that he did not believe that a man had ever been born who knew so much as Leonardo'.[52] There is no need to rely on the king's testimony. The 7,000-odd pages of Leonardo's notebooks, some of which were named 'the Atlantic manuscript' thanks to their volume, bear witness to the breadth of their author's interests, which put even Alberti in the shade.

In most fields, Leonardo was an autodidact who described himself in one of his notebooks as 'a man without learning' (*omo sanza lettere*), although he went on to declare with pride that his knowledge was based on experience rather than texts.[53] In fact, he gradually amassed a library, listing 116 volumes in 1504. He studied the ancient writer Ptolemy on cosmography, for instance, Vitruvius on architecture, medieval texts on optics and anatomy, and the writings of earlier polymaths such as Pliny, Roger Bacon, Al-Kindi and Ibn Sina.[54]

It is likely that Leonardo learned even more from conversation with experts. He wrote notes to himself such as the following: 'Get the master of abacus to show you how to square a triangle . . . Ask Maestro Antonio how bombards are placed on bastions by day or at night. Ask Benedetto Portinari how to run on the ice in Flanders.' When he was living in Milan, Leonardo made friends with a professor of medicine at the nearby University of Pavia, Marcantonio della Torre, and they conducted dissections together.

Leonardo learned most of all by this kind of 'hands-on' investigation and observation. He turned to the study of anatomy, including the practice of dissection, in order to represent both humans and horses more accurately, but he continued to investigate out of curiosity. Anatomy has been described as the field 'in which he made the most far-reaching discoveries'. He seems to have been the first to study the development of arteriosclerosis and he also discovered the function of the aortic valve in the heart.[55] In similar fashion, Leonardo began studying optics as an aid to his art, but went on to discover that, for example, 'The pupil of the eye dilates and contracts according to the brightness and darkness of the objects in view.'[56]

Leonardo was also an enthusiast for geometry, claiming to have found the solution for squaring the circle and writing, 'Let no one read me who is not a mathematician.' He also studied what are now known as the fields of mechanics, hydraulics, chemistry, botany, zoology, geology and cartography. Ironically enough, it now takes many specialists to assess Leonardo's achievements in all these disciplines.

He was fascinated by the movement of water, for example, which he observed by dropping grains or dye into it.[57] He carried out chemical experiments with paint and the preparation of surfaces for painting.[58] His notebooks reveal his careful observation of plants and so does his famous painting *The Virgin of the Rocks* (the version in the Louvre), in which he showed only the flowers that would be found in a moist grotto at a particular season. The Alpine geology as well as the botany is accurate in the Louvre *Virgin*: 'the surfaces of the fractures are weathered in accordance with the respective hardness of each type of rock'.[59] Leonardo also collected fossils, which he viewed as evidence of the history of the earth. He calculated the age of trees by examining their rings.[60] He carefully observed not only horses and birds but also bats, lizards and crocodiles.[61] The maps he made reveal his interest in geography.[62] As the artist Giorgio Vasari remarked in his biography of Leonardo, 'to whatever difficult things he turned his mind, he solved them with ease'.

Vasari was of course exaggerating the achievements of his hero. It is virtually needless to say that Leonardo's wide range of interests had a negative side, the failures. The giant crossbow did not work in practice, the circle was not successfully squared, and the poor condition of the famous *Last Supper*, already visible a few years after it was painted, is the result of failed experiments in chemistry. As Leonardo's contemporaries noted, whether with dismay or glee, he failed to meet many deadlines from his patrons or indeed to finish many of his projects, notably the great equestrian statue of Francesco Sforza (the father of Duke Lodovico) that the artist described simply as 'the horse'. He planned treatises on painting, water, anatomy, optics, flight and mechanics, none of which were completed while some may not even have been begun. One of the greatest artists of his time, if not of all time, Leonardo was described in his late forties as 'out of all patience with his brush' (*impacientissimo del penello*).[63] As we shall see, a number of other polymaths failed to finish projects owing to the dispersal of their interests and energy. It is for this reason that I coined the phrase 'Leonardo syndrome'.

At first sight, Leonardo offers a spectacular example of the fox, the individual interested in almost everything and practising a centrifugal approach to knowledge. Yet, as several scholars have pointed out, to speak of a 'dispersal' of interests in his case is misleading. What appears to be pure curiosity usually turns out to be linked to his main preoccupations. He noted analogies between light and sound, between the branches of trees, rivers and arteries, between flying and swimming, animals and machines, writing for instance that 'A bird is an instrument working according to mathematical law'. Some of his discoveries depended on these analogies. He explained the function of the valves of the heart, for example, by comparing the movement of blood in the human body to the movement of water. In short, Leonardo worked on the assumption that 'all the apparent diversities of nature are symptoms of an inner unity'.[64] In this way, 'invisible threads connect the fragments' that are scattered in the ocean of his notebooks.[65]

THE RENAISSANCE WOMAN

Today, references to the 'Renaissance Man' naturally evoke the question, what about the Renaissance Woman? One question prompts another: what about learned ladies in earlier periods? Late antiquity offers one example of a female polymath, Hypatia of Alexandria, who wrote on philosophy, mathematics and astronomy.[66]

In the twelfth century, the German nun and later abbess Hildegard of Bingen was a visionary, poet and playwright as well as a scholar and a teacher (*magistra*) of other nuns. Drawing on her experiences in the infirmary of her convent, she wrote a guide to healing herbs, the *Physica*, and another to illnesses and their causes and cures (*Causae et curae*). She also studied and wrote on philosophy, theology, music, astronomy and astrology.[67]

On the frontier between the late Middle Ages and the Renaissance, Christine de Pizan, who came from Venice and lived in France, wrote over forty books, including biography and works on morals (*Livre des trois vertus*, 1405), war (*Livre des Faits d'Armes*, 1410), fortune (*Livre de la Mutacion de Fortune*, 1403) and political philosophy, as well as her most famous work, the *Cité des Dames* (1405), which argues for the ability of women by presenting a pageant of famous women in the past.[68]

In Renaissance Europe, women were doubly disadvantaged, since learning was difficult of access while a career as a soldier was out of the question. In order to study, women had to overcome a number of obstacles, notably their exclusion from university, in practice if not in principle, thanks to the common view that learning was not for females. They were expected to confine themselves to careers as housewives, mothers or nuns. Castiglione's famous dialogue discussed the court lady (*gentildonna da corte*) as well as her male counterpart, but limited her knowledge to literature, music, painting, dancing and entertaining men gracefully.[69]

In similar fashion, Burckhardt and other nineteenth- and early twentieth-century writers assumed that the many-sided individuals of the Renaissance were all male, an assumption that has been questioned by later feminist historians. These scholars have pointed out that a small group of women, usually of noble birth and educated by private tutors, overcame the obstacles in their way, studied the humanities and wrote letters, speeches, poems and occasionally treatises in Latin or the vernacular. Not very much is known about any of them, but something is known about a few.

In Italy between 1350 and 1530, according to one historian, three women 'achieved considerable fame' in this respect, while nine more achieved 'some visibility'.[70] The three most famous for their learning were Isotta Nogarola, Laura Cereta and Cassandra Fedele. Isotta, who came from Verona, corresponded with Guarino Veronese, a leading humanist from the same city. She also wrote orations and a dialogue about Adam and Eve.[71] Laura Cereta, from Brescia, studied Latin, philosophy, mathematics and astronomy at a convent. She wrote to male humanists about the education of women and collected eighty-two of her letters into a manuscript volume.[72] Cassandra Fedele, from Venice, studied classics and philosophy, wrote poems, delivered speeches in Padua and Venice in praise of learning, corresponded with leading male humanists and wrote a treatise, now lost, about the order of knowledge, *De scientiarum ordine*.[73]

These scholars were only rarely wide-ranging. A study of Cereta, for instance, notes that she 'expresses no interest in speculative philosophy, dialectic, theology, law or medicine'.[74] Of these and other female humanists, it has been remarked that 'Much of their writing is mediocre; but then much that was written by male humanists is mediocre as well'.[75] Mediocre humanists are not included among the polymaths studied in this book, so if we wish to avoid a double standard, only Cassandra Fedele qualifies.

Outside Italy, learned ladies included Caritas Pirckheimer, elder sister of the humanist Willibald Pirckheimer, who was educated at home before entering the convent of Saint Clare in her native Nuremberg, first as a student, then as a nun and finally as abbess. Caritas was praised for her learning by leading humanists, among them Erasmus.[76] A Spanish contemporary of Caritas, Beatriz Galindo, nicknamed 'La Latina', was able to study at the University of Salamanca, was called to court by Queen Isabella of Castille and taught Latin to the queen and her daughters. She also wrote a commentary on Aristotle.[77]

In England, famous examples of learned ladies included Margaret Roper, daughter of Thomas More, who wrote to his daughter recommending 'humane letters and so-called liberal studies', followed by medicine and sacred literature. Margaret studied Greek as well as Latin and translated Erasmus. Again, the five daughters of the Protestant humanist Anthony Cooke all studied Latin, Greek, Hebrew, Italian and French. Two of his daughters, Anne and Elizabeth, also made translations, Anne from Latin and Elizabeth from French.[78] At this time, translation was considered a more appropriate occupation for women than writing original works.

Perhaps the most remarkable Renaissance woman – although she lived until 1645 – was the Frenchwoman Marie de Gournay. In France, in 1584, Gournay, a young noblewoman who had taught herself Latin, discovered the essays of Montaigne. Her discovery made her so excited that her mother wanted to give her a drug to calm her down. Later, Gournay met Montaigne in person, became a kind of daughter to him and edited later editions of his essays. She wrote poems and a romance, made translations from the classics, practised alchemy and published both a miscellaneous volume, *L'Ombre* (*The Shadow*, 1626), and a polemical treatise on the equality of men and women.[79]

All the same, it has to be conceded that these ladies, who were truly learned, do not qualify as many-sided by the standards of the time. For rivals to Hildegard of Bingen in the Middle Ages, it is necessary to wait until the seventeenth century, as we shall see.

3

THE AGE OF 'MONSTERS OF ERUDITION'
1600–1700

If the Renaissance was the age of the 'universal man', bridging the worlds of thought and action, the following age was that of a more academic ideal, that of the universal scholar, or what the Dutchman Hermann Boerhaave, a polymath himself, described as the 'monster of erudition'.[1]

THE AGE OF POLYMATHS

Retrospectively, the seventeenth century appears to have been the golden age of the many-sided scholar, even if scholars of this kind do not appear to have excelled, like some of their predecessors in the Renaissance, in fencing, singing, dancing, horsemanship or athletics. Ninety-two polymaths on the list in the Appendix were born in the century running from 1570 to 1669, over double the number of the thirty-nine born between 1470 and 1569.

Intellectual curiosity, which had often been condemned by theologians from Augustine to Calvin, was rehabilitated by some influential philosophers, notably Francis Bacon. Noted earlier as an example of the 'Renaissance Man', Bacon made his most important contributions to learning in the seventeenth century. He claimed to take 'all knowledge' as his province, classifying it and discussing problems of epistemology. Hia motto was *Plus Ultra*, in the sense of going 'beyond' what was already known, instead of pausing at the intellectual Pillars of Hercules, represented on the title page of his *Great Instauration* (1620) with a ship sailing between the pillars and the motto, 'many will pass through and knowledge will be increased' (*multi pertransibunt et augebitur scientia*).[2]

It is easy to forget the intellectual range of a number of seventeenth-century scholars because they are mainly remembered today for only a few of their many achievements. The Dutch scholar Hugo Grotius, for instance, remains famous as a jurist, but he was also active as a historian of the Netherlands and as a lay theologian. The German Samuel Pufendorf is remembered as a political theorist, but he was also active as a lawyer, a historian, a philosopher, a political economist and, like Grotius, a lay theologian.

Turning to the natural sciences, the Danish nobleman Tycho Brahe and his former assistant Johannes Kepler are pigeon-holed today as astronomers, although Tycho also practised alchemy and medicine while Kepler made important contributions to mathematics and optics, not to mention what is now known as 'the history and philosophy of science' and even 'science fiction' – his *Dream* (the *Somnium*) tells the story of a visit to the moon.[3] As for Galileo, his interests were far from being confined to the mathematics, physics and astronomy to which he owes his current reputation. Galileo also studied medicine and wrote about the relative merits and defects of painting and sculpture and the poetry of Ariosto and Tasso.[4]

Among the French, René Descartes, remembered today as a philosopher, made important contributions to mathematics and wrote on optics and astronomy. His 'Treatise on the Passions' dealt with what would later be known as psychology.[5] The French scholar Pierre Gassendi, also classified as a philosopher, was active as an astronomer and a mathematician, as well as making contributions to the study of classical antiquity and the theory of music. Indeed, Gassendi was described by an English contemporary as 'the most accomplished general scholar, we have had of late'.[6] Blaise Pascal is relatively fortunate to be remembered not only as a philosopher but also as a theologian, a mathematician and what we call a physicist, thanks to a famous experiment on air pressure.

Despite John Evelyn's eulogy of Sir Christopher's 'Accomplishments . . . thro' all the learned cycle of the most useful knowledge and abstruser sciences', Wren is generally remembered as an architect.[7] He was also a professor of astronomy, first at Gresham College in London and then at

Oxford, improving telescopes, observing comets and offering a new explanation of the rings of Saturn. He dissected fish and dogs. He designed a number of ingenious machines, including one that allowed a writer to produce two copies of a text at the same time. He contributed to the study of mathematics, magnetism, mechanics and meteorology. Had it not been for the Great Fire of London, the greatest English architect might have spent his days as a scholar rather than designing the new St Paul's and (along with another polymath, Robert Hooke) the many 'Wren churches'. He was also the architect of Kensington Palace, the library of Trinity College, Cambridge, and the chapels of Emmanuel and Pembroke in the same university.[8]

As for Isaac Newton, until relatively recently scholars forgot, or more exactly preferred to ignore, the studies of theology, alchemy and chronology that took so much of his time, alongside his more famous contributions to mathematics and natural philosophy.[9] In his *Chronology of Ancient Kingdoms Amended* (1728), Newton made use of astronomical knowledge – as the sixteenth-century polymath Joseph Scaliger had done – as a means of reconciling different chronological systems, arguing that 'The surest arguments for determining times past are those taken from astronomy.'[10] Newton attempted to interpret the prophecies recorded in the Bible and corresponded with some of the leading theologians of his time, while keeping secret his divergences from orthodox Christianity. He certainly qualifies as a polymath, even if, unlike his rival Leibniz, discussed below, he was not a monster of erudition.

FEMALE POLYMATHS

Women as well as men participated in this golden age of wide-ranging scholars. At least eight female polymaths of note were active at this time: Marie de Gournay (discussed in the previous chapter as a 'Renaissance Woman'); Bathsua Makin; Anna Maria van Schurman; Elisabeth, Princess Palatine; Margaret Cavendish; Christina, Queen of Sweden; Elena Corner; and Sister Juana Inés de la Cruz.

The Englishwoman Bathsua Makin (née Reynolds) belonged to the circle of Samuel Hartlib, a friend of Comenius. Described by a contemporary as 'England's most learned lady', her interests included languages, poetry, shorthand, medicine and education. When she was young, Makin published a volume of verse in Greek, Latin, Hebrew, Spanish, German, French and Italian. Towards the end of her life, she published *An Essay to Revive the Ancient Education of Gentlewomen* (1673), arguing for the right of women to receive a good general education.[11]

Bathsua Makin corresponded – in Hebrew – with the Dutchwoman Anna Maria van Schurman, 'the Dutch Minerva'. Schurman was allowed to study at the University of Utrecht, the first female to study at a Dutch university, listening to lectures behind a screen so that the male students would not stare at her. She learned not only Greek and Latin but also Hebrew, Arabic, Aramaic and Syriac, wrote letters on philosophy, theology and education, and produced, though she did not publish, a grammar of 'Ethiopian'.[12] Like Gournay, Schurman might be described as a 'Renaissance woman', given her accomplishments in painting, engraving and embroidery as well as in the humanities.

Elisabeth, Princess Palatine, was the daughter of the ill-starred Frederick V of the Palatinate, the 'Winter King' of Bohemia, who was defeated and forced into exile by the emperor Ferdinand II. She lived in the Netherlands and then in Westphalia, where she became the abbess of a Protestant convent. Elisabeth knew Latin, French, German, Dutch and Italian as well as English. She also studied mathematics, astronomy, history, philosophy and the Bible, and corresponded with several scholars of the day, exchanging ideas with Anna Maria van Schurman and holding her own in arguments with Descartes.[13]

Margaret Cavendish (née Lucas), who became the Duchess of Newcastle, was interested in both political and natural philosophy. She studied anatomy, although what she called 'the modesty of my sex' prevented her from carrying out dissections.[14] She published her best-known book, *Observations upon Experimental Philosophy*, in 1666, claiming – with the modesty of her sex or the false modesty of the noble amateur – to provide 'here a bit and there a crumb of knowledge'. She also wrote a biography of her husband, a number of plays and the utopian romance *The Blazing World* (1666), which has been described, like Kepler's *Dream*, as an early example of science fiction. Eccentric in her dress and manner, she was nicknamed 'Mad Madge'. John Evelyn called her 'a mighty pretender to learning', but some other male scholars took her seriously.[15]

Christina of Sweden, who came to the throne as a child after her father Gustav Adolf was killed in battle in 1632, spent much of her time in study both before and after her abdication in 1654.[16] She liked to be known as the Swedish Minerva, called herself 'versatile', and claimed in her memoirs that 'At fourteen, she knew all the languages, all the sciences and all the accomplishments her instructors thought fit, or were able, to teach her.' According to a contemporary, 'elle sait tout'. The queen was well read in the classics, including the Roman historian Tacitus. In philosophy she was particularly interested in Neoplatonism and Stoicism and compiled a collection of maxims entitled *Les sentiments heroïques*. Brought up as a Lutheran, she became a sceptic and finally converted to Catholicism, taking a particular interest in the ideas of the Spanish mystic Miguel de Molinos. She spoke German, Dutch, Danish, French and Italian, and learned Hebrew in order to read the Old Testament in its original language.

Other polymaths collected books and other objects, but Christina collected scholars. Among the learned men to be found at her court, at least for short periods, were the polymaths Gabriel Naudé, René Descartes, Samuel Bochart, Pierre-Daniel Huet, Hiob Ludolf, Claude Saumaise, Isaac Voss, Herman Conring and Marcus Meibom. She delighted in asking them difficult questions (Huet wrote to his friend Gassendi that the queen was even more intelligent than Anna Maria van Schurman). She had intended to study mathematics and philosophy with Descartes, but when he arrived at her court she was too busy to do so because she was learning Greek.[17] Christina's interests included astronomy, astrology and alchemy. She was particularly interested in comets and subsidized research on them. After her abdication, she practised alchemy herself in a laboratory in her palace in Rome. It seems appropriate that among the paintings she owned was a portrait of Pico della Mirandola.

Elena Corner was the daughter of a Venetian patrician. A child prodigy, she was educated at home by tutors chosen by her father, who realized that her learning might be employed to recover the status of a family that had once been one of the most illustrious in Venice but had fallen into decline. She studied classical literature, modern languages, mathematics, the natural sciences and theology. Refused permission by the bishop to take a doctorate in theology, she took one in medicine instead, at the University of Padua, in 1678. She became a member of several learned academies and was frequently asked to demonstrate her knowledge in public.[18]

Still more famous for her learning was the Mexican Juana Ramírez, known as Juana Inés de la Cruz or 'Sister Juana' after she entered a convent. Juana was described by contemporaries as 'the Mexican Phoenix' and a 'Phoenix of Erudition in all sciences'. She wrote of herself that as a child she had a strong 'desire for learning' and studied in her grandfather's library. Like Schurman, she wished to study at university (which she hoped to attend dressed as a man) but her mother did not allow her to do so. Sister Juana knew Latin (which she apparently mastered after twenty lessons) and also Greek and Nahuatl. As well as writing the poems that are now famous, she studied theology, philosophy (including natural philosophy), law, literature and music theory. She refused offers of marriage and entered a convent in order to be free to study.

In her convent, Sister Juana accumulated an impressive library, some volumes of which appear in the background to the two contemporary portraits of her. Her writings – on music, on philosophy, on the position of women – often quote two earlier polymaths, Pliny and Kircher. She also made references to ancient writers such as Cicero and Tacitus, Fathers of the Church such as Jerome and Augustine, medieval philosophers, Renaissance writers on classical mythology and legal scholars such as Francisco Suarez. Her devotion to learning was criticized by the bishop of Puebla. She was forbidden to publish her ideas and ordered to give away her books.[19]

THE LANGUAGE OF POLYMATHY

The history of language supports the idea that the seventeenth century was a time when polymaths became more important and also more visible. From the late sixteenth century onwards, a set of connected ideas about both knowledgeable people and general knowledge became current in several European languages.

In the case of knowledgeable people, the most common terms were 'polyhistor' and 'polymath' itself. The ancient Roman writer Pliny was described as a *polyhistor* by the Swiss encyclopaedist Theodor Zwinger (possibly implying that his work was disorganized as well as encyclopaedic).[20] Another Swiss encyclopaedist, Conrad Gessner, was himself described as a *polyhistor*, as we saw in the previous chapter.[21] Wide-ranging books were sometimes given the same title, as in the case of a guide to the world of learning by Daniel Morhof, *Polyhistor* (1688). The concept was discussed in an inaugural lecture at the University of Leiden in 1632 and also in later academic dissertations, for instance in Heidelberg in 1660, Leipzig in 1715, Altdorf in 1718 and Jena in 1721.

The Elizabethan scholar Gabriel Harvey coined the term 'omniscians', but his coinage never became common currency. In English, the term 'polymath' came into use a little later. The Oxford don Robert Burton, for instance, referred to 'Polumathes and Polihistors' in his *Anatomy of Melancholy* (1621).[22] All these terms were usually neutral or terms of approval, at least before the eighteenth century. In contrast, the Italian *poligrafo*, like the French *polygraphe*, was pejorative, describing professional writers who wrote a great deal on many subjects because they were paid for piece-work.[23] Another new word that came into use in this period was the Italian term *virtuoso*. It spread into other languages, among them English, to refer to amateur scholars with wide interests that were often expressed not by writing but by collecting a variety of objects – coins, for instance, weapons from different parts of the world, shells, stuffed animals and fish.[24]

Still richer was the vocabulary used to describe the wide-ranging knowledge of these individuals. In Latin, we find a whole cluster of terms, among them *scientia universalis, pansophia* and *polymathia*. Usually neutral, *polymathia* was occasionally used in a pejorative sense to mean 'straying from one's discipline', an early critique of what we call 'interdisciplinarity'.[25] Italians praised individual artists and writers for being *versatile*. The French spoke or wrote of *polymathie* or *science universelle*. Favourite English adjectives to describe scholars were 'curious' and 'ingenious'. As for nouns, the English sometimes used the term 'omniscience' but preferred 'general learning', the title of a treatise by the second-generation scholar Meric Casaubon.[26]

A general discussion of *polymathia* may be found in a treatise published by a well-read and well-travelled scholar from Hamburg, Johannes Wower (1603). 'By perfect polymathy', Wower explains, 'I understand knowledge of diverse things, taken from every kind of study [*ex omni genere studiorum*] and ranging very widely.' The polymath is described as 'wandering freely and with unbridled speed through all the fields of the disciplines' [*per omnes disciplinarum campos*].[27]

Later discussions of the topic include treatises by two Dutch scholars, Gerard Voss and Marcus Boxhorn. Voss wrote a book about the arts and sciences in which he described philosophy, mathematics and logic as *polymatheia* because they were encyclopaedic, while his former student Boxhorn, professor of rhetoric at the University of Leiden, gave his inaugural lecture on polymathy. Boxhorn's own interests extended well beyond rhetoric to include an edition of Tacitus, books on politics and war, an oration on dreams, a history of the world and a comparative study of the history of languages.[28]

As for *pansophia*, the term literally means 'universal wisdom'. In the eyes of some of its adepts, this noble dream was associated with the discovery of the reality behind appearances as well as with attempts to reunite the Christian churches, reform learning, harmonize philosophies and create a universal language, thus reconciling disagreements. *Pansophia* was also associated with an even broader vision that included the end of conflict (in the age of the Thirty Years War), the coming 'universal reform' of all that was wrong with the world, and even the hope of a return to the age before Adam's Fall.[29] The links between *pansophia* and polymathy are particularly clear in the case of two scholars from Central Europe, a German, Alsted, and his Czech student Comenius.

THE POLYMATH AS ENCYCLOPAEDIST: ALSTED

Johann Heinrich Alsted was professor of philosophy and theology at the University of Herborn in Hesse. A prolific scholar, he is best known for an encyclopaedia that he published in 1630. With the help of the binary oppositions popularized by an earlier Protestant scholar, Petrus Ramus, the seven volumes of this encyclopaedia describe and classify not only all the academic disciplines of the time but other knowledges as well, including the mechanical arts, magic, alchemy and the art of memory. Outwardly, Alsted was a good Calvinist who must have been aware that Jean Calvin had condemned curiosity. In private, though, as his letters reveal, he was fascinated by many unorthodox forms of knowledge, including the art of combination expounded by the medieval Catalan friar Ramón Lull.[30]

This art underlay Alsted's encyclopaedic enterprise, one of the last of its kind to be carried out single-handed (an encyclopaedia in a single volume was published in Hungarian in 1655 by János Apáczai Csere, who, like Alsted, made use of the dichotomies of Ramus in organizing his material).[31] Alsted's work encouraged the shift in the meaning of the term 'encyclopaedia' from its original sense of a curriculum (an intellectual track around which students were expected to run) to a book that brought different knowledges together. An encyclopaedia was, at least in theory, both a product of and a means to universal knowledge. Alsted prefaced his book with the claim that, although only God is all-wise, he 'impresses the image of his perfection' on those who embrace 'the whole orb of the disciplines' (*universum disciplinarum orbem*).[32]

THE POLYMATH AS PANSOPHIST: COMENIUS

Alsted may have been a fox, but Jan Amos Komenský, better known as Comenius, was certainly a hedgehog. Comenius came from Moravia (now part of Czechia), studied with Alsted in Herborn, and became a bishop in the church of the Bohemian Brethren. After 1621, when his church was banned in Bohemia, Comenius became a nomad, a refugee in Poland, Sweden, England, Transylvania and the Netherlands. Throughout this time he devoted himself to the reform of education and the critique of natural languages, arguing that 'the meaning of words should be fixed, with one name for each thing'.[33] His reforms were intended as steps towards *pansophia*, which would be attained, together with universal harmony, in the last days of the world, which he, like many people at this time, believed to be near at hand.[34]

Comenius was not the first scholar to use this term. He criticized an older polymath, Peter Lauremberg, for publishing a book called *Pansophia* (1633), describing it as 'unworthy of so sublime a title'.[35] His own 'Introduction to Pansophia' (*Pansophiae Prodromus*, 1639), described it as *sapientia universalis*, a term translated by his follower Samuel Hartlib as 'general knowledge or wisdom' (elsewhere, Hartlib used the phrase 'common learning', while another book by Comenius was translated into English under the title *A Patterne of Universall Knowledge*, 1651).[36] In a third little treatise on the subject Comenius quoted Aristotle, 'the wise man ought to KNOW EVERYTHING, so far as possible' (*sapientem debere OMNIA SCIRE, quantum possibile est*).[37] In the thought of Comenius, *pansophia* was associated with the ideas of *panaugia* or *panergesia* (a universal 'dawn' or 'awakening'), *pampaedia* (universal education), *panglottia* (a universal language) and *panorthosia* (a universal reform, or a reform of the world).[38]

MONSTERS OF ERUDITION

The most important reason for calling the seventeenth century a golden age of polymaths was the presence of a number of what Hermann Boerhaave, himself no slouch in the field of learning, described as 'monsters of erudition': individuals who spanned the disciplines and produced many volumes, all the more impressive when one remembers that their learning was the result of reading by candlelight while their books were produced by writing with a quill. Alsted surely qualifies for the title, while six more monsters will be discussed in what follows: Nicolas-Claude Fabri de Peiresc, Juan Caramuel, Olof Rudbeck the Elder, Athanasius Kircher, Pierre Bayle and Gottfried Wilhelm Leibniz.

THE POLYMATH AS COLLECTOR: PEIRESC

The French magistrate Nicolas-Claude Fabri de Peiresc, *conseiller* in the *Parlement* of Provence, is one of the most famous examples of one type of early modern scholar, often described at the time as a *virtuoso*, an individual with enough time and money to spare to acquire different kinds of learning as a kind of hobby.

Collecting was one of the principal activities of the *virtuoso*, together with the display of items in 'cabinets of curiosities' or *Wunderkammer*, as they were known in German at this time. The cabinets contained both natural objects and the work of human hands, chosen because they were rare, exotic or extraordinary in other ways. Their owners were often individuals of wide interests, such as Ole Worm and Hans Sloane, two scholarly physicians best known for the collections that they assembled in their spare time.

Worm, who was physician to Christian IV of Denmark, was particularly interested in Scandinavian antiquities such as megalithic tombs, urns and ship-burials. His collection, displayed in the *Museum Wormianum*, was immortalized in an engraving that showed human artefacts such as spears and drinking-horns alongside stuffed fish and the skulls of animals.[39] Sloane, who was physician to Queen Anne and her two successors, was able to accumulate a huge and varied collection, thanks to his income from Jamaican plantations and his fees for treating aristocratic patients. He has been described as 'collecting the world'.[40]

However, Worm and Sloane were surpassed by Peiresc, both as collectors and as polymaths. Peiresc's collection, documented from his letters, reveals his enthusiasm for what we call 'material culture': manuscripts in different alphabets, coins, statuettes, vases, amulets, medieval seals, late antique gems and even Egyptian mummies. He was interested in nature as well as culture and owned a crocodile skin, a menagerie of live animals and a botanical garden, which was a kind of outdoor collection and included exotic plants such as papyrus.

Peiresc was described by his friend the painter Rubens as someone who 'possesses in all fields as much knowledge as any one professional in his own' (*possede in tutte le professioni quanto ciascuno nella sua propria*).[41] He studied law, visited Italy, the Netherlands and England, and spent some years in Paris as secretary to the president of his *Parlement* before settling down and spending the last fourteen years of his life in Provence, often in ill health and 'shut up in his study', as his secretary described him, but travelling in his imagination thanks to his library, his collection and his letters.[42]

Peiresc is remembered today for his passion for antiquities (the classical scholar Arnaldo Momigliano once called him the 'archetype of all antiquarians').[43] He was interested in the ancient world, the European Middle Ages (Charlemagne, for instance, or the troubadours), and also in China, in Benin, in the Indians of Canada and especially in the Mediterranean world, past and present, and its many peoples: Etruscans, Phoenicians, Egyptians, Jews and Arabs. Peiresc's knowledge of North Africa, past and present, was unusual for a European of his time.[44] He was fascinated by different manners and customs – shooting arrows while on horseback, drinking from the skulls of enemies and so on.

Peiresc appears to have been an intellectual fox, but religion was a key to some of his diverse interests. He studied the early or 'primitive' Church and its relation to Judaism and paganism, leading him to investigate cults such as Gnosticism and Mithraism from late antiquity. His interest in the Eastern Christians included curiosity about their chants and their musical instruments.[45] He was fascinated by the history of the Bible, which drew him into the study of Hebrew, Coptic, Samaritan (a dialect of Aramaic) and 'Ethiopian' (Ge'ez), while his omnivorous curiosity led him to examine other aspects of these cultures for their own sake. Peiresc's study of different languages led to a concern with the relation between them. He was aware that the spread and mixing of languages could be used as evidence for the migrations of peoples.

Peiresc was interested not only in the 'human sciences' (*scienze humane*, as he was possibly the first to call them), but in the natural sciences as well. He was fascinated by the tides and currents of the Mediterranean. He was especially active in astronomy, observing eclipses, examining the satellites of Jupiter, discovering the nebula of Orion and, with his friend Pierre Gassendi, making a map of the moon. He mobilized a circle of friends to observe Jupiter at the same time in different places in order to correct maps of the Mediterranean.[46] He studied anatomy, reading William Harvey on the circulation of the blood soon after the book was published in 1628 and himself dissecting the eyes of animals, birds and fish. His interests also included fossils and volcanoes.

Peiresc did not publish the results of his researches, whether from lack of time or an aristocratic reluctance to write books that would be exposed for sale. Instead, Peiresc acted as a kind of intellectual broker, soliciting and offering information via his many letters. Some of these letters were addressed to fellow scholars in centres of scholarship such as Rome, Paris and Leiden. Other letters were addressed to individuals beyond the frontiers of Europe where new knowledge – new to Europeans – could be obtained. Peiresc's network included many agents and informants, among them merchants in Cairo and friars in Sidon and Istanbul. To the agents who bought items for his collections, Peiresc sent detailed wish lists, and, to the informants, elaborate questionnaires.[47]

THE POLYMATH AS SCHOLASTIC PHILOSOPHER: CARAMUEL

The Spaniard Juan Caramuel y Lobkowitz was a Cistercian monk who lived a nomadic life, spending ten years in the Spanish Netherlands and ten years in Prague before becoming a bishop in Italy, first in Campania and then in Vigevano in Lombardy. An eighteenth-century biographer called him 'omniscient', while he was known in his own day as 'the phoenix of Europe'.[48] The comparison with the phoenix was intended to imply uniqueness, as the poet John Donne explained in his *Anatomy of the World*: 'Every man alone thinks he hath got/To be a phoenix, and that there can be/None of that kind, of which he is, but he.' All the same, the term was applied to one scholar after another, from Erasmus to Benito Feijoo, who will be discussed in the following chapter.[49]

Caramuel, a child prodigy in mathematics, is said to have known twenty-four languages (including Hebrew, Arabic and even some Chinese, learned from a native speaker whom he met in Vienna in 1654). Well known in later life for his sermons, he was also active as a diplomat and an amateur architect. In Prague, he became a friend of two more polymaths, the Italian Valeriano Magni and the Czech Jan Marcus Marci. Caramuel criticized Descartes, corresponded with Kircher and befriended Gassendi.

Caramuel wrote more than sixty books, including a life of St Benedict, a history of Gregorian chant, an unpublished encyclopaedia of music and a treatise on architecture, as well as studies of grammar, poetry, oratory, mathematics, astronomy, physics, politics, canon law, logic, theology and philosophy (carrying on but also modernizing the tradition of scholasticism). One of his books, the *Apparatus Philosophicus* (1665), offered a brief account of 'all the sciences and arts'. Caramuel was commissioned by Philip IV of Spain to prove his right to the Portuguese throne, using genealogical, historical and legal arguments, and by the emperor Ferdinand III to justify the negotiations with Protestants that ended the Thirty Years War. In his last years as a bishop in Vigevano, Caramuel found the time to write not only religious and political works but also a paper on river management, with special reference to embankments on the Po.[50]

In his *Theologia rationalis* (1654), Caramuel tried, like Thomas Aquinas, to reconcile theology with reason. In moral philosophy, he tried to apply mathematical rules, but he also defended the doctrine of 'probabilism', in other words the idea that since certainty is unattainable, we are allowed to follow a probable opinion (he was also one of the first mathematicians to study probability).[51] Like Alsted, Caramuel was interested in the ideas of Ramón Lull, recommending his art of memory to intending preachers, though he also noted that Lull often promised what he could not perform. Like other polymaths, from Lull to Neurath, whose work will be examined later, Caramuel was driven by a vision of the unity of knowledge. Linking many of his endeavours, from logic to music and architecture, was 'the dream of mathematics as a unifying language for the universe'. This dream of *mathesis universalis* was shared by other seventeenth-century polymaths, including Descartes and Leibniz.[52]

THE POLYMATH AS PATRIOT: RUDBECK

The Swede Olof Rudbeck, rector of Uppsala University, was a figure larger than life. A big man with a loud voice and enormous self-confidence, Rudbeck's projects were on an appropriately grand scale. He contributed to the study of anatomy, languages, music, plants and antiquities (including what we now call 'archaeology'). He began with anatomy. His dissection of around four hundred animals such as cats and dogs led him to the discovery of the lymphatic system, as well as generating a dispute over priority with another polymath, the Danish scholar Thomas Bartholin. Sent to study medicine in Leiden, Rudbeck discovered botany. As professor of theoretical medicine at the University of Uppsala, he lectured on anatomy, botany and chemistry but he also taught music, mathematics, physics and astronomy. Rudbeck designed an anatomy theatre for the University of Uppsala and an aqueduct for the city. He wrote music. He was an active cartographer. He headed a team that attempted both to describe and to illustrate all known plants, thus associating the University of Uppsala with advances in botany almost a century before Linnaeus. In fact, Linnaeus was a student of Rudbeck's son Olof Rudbeck the Younger, whose interests included medicine, ornithology and linguistics as well as botany.[53]

For better or worse, however, Rudbeck senior is most widely known today as the author of the *Atlantica*, a huge unfinished treatise on northern antiquities.[54] Thanks to this project, on which he embarked late in his career, he is often viewed as an eccentric, but his interest in the civilization of the North in the remote past may be located in a Swedish tradition, known as 'Gothicism' because it included the belief that the Swedes were the descendants of the Goths as well as the idea that civilization began in Sweden.[55] The polymath Johannes Bureus, for instance, who was tutor to the young king Gustav Adolf, searched for the lost wisdom of the Goths.[56] A colleague of Rudbeck's at the university, Olaus Verelius, professor of Swedish antiquities, identified a site in old Uppsala with a temple of the 'Hyperboreans', a people that, according to Herodotus and other ancient Greeks, lived 'beyond the North Wind' (the Bora).

Rudbeck took these claims much further, identifying the Swedes not only with the Goths but also with the Scythians and the Trojans. He argued that civilization (including writing, calendars and astronomy) arose in the North and that Plato's Atlantis was located in Sweden. He might be described as both obsessive and ethnocentric in his grand claims for the North, for Sweden and even for Uppsala – he located the capital of Atlantis in the village of old Uppsala, not far from his university.

In order to support his assertions, Rudbeck attempted to synchronize different chronologies, ancient and modern. He compared the myths and customs of ancient peoples with those of modern Scandinavians, arguing, for instance, that sun worship began in Northern Europe. Inventive in his methods, Rudbeck also drew on the evidence of nature, according to him 'the wisest and most certain of books'. For instance, his method of dating was based on a careful study of the humus, an approach that archaeologists would develop centuries later. 'He cut a trench through barrows in Old Uppsala and drew the vertical sections, noting the characteristics of each layer,' and measured each stratum in order to calculate its age.[57]

Rudbeck even practised a kind of experimental archaeology, reminiscent of a later Scandinavian scholar, the Norwegian Thor Heyerdahl, who took the raft *Kon-Tiki* from Peru to the Tuamotu Islands in 1947 in order to support his claim that Polynesia was settled by immigrants from South America. In similar fashion, in order to show that Jason's famous ship the *Argo* could have been transported from the Black Sea to the Baltic, Rudbeck supervised an attempt to transport a ship over land.

Rudbeck combined wide learning with many original ideas, but he often found what he wanted to find, especially when Sweden was concerned. Some criticisms of his work will be discussed later.

THE POLYMATH AS PANSOPHIST: KIRCHER

Even more monstrously wide than Rudbeck's was the learning of the German Jesuit Athanasius Kircher, described by the German writer Philipp von Zesen as 'easily the phoenix of the learned of this century'. Kircher wrote thirty-two books and has been described, as we have seen, as 'the last man who knew everything', or, somewhat more modestly, as 'a Renaissance man' and 'the last of the polymaths'.[58] His works include studies of China and Egypt, the geography of Tuscany and Latium, magnetism, mathematics, mining and music. In his studies of acoustics and optics, Kircher drew analogies between the propagation of light and sound. He also wrote on *scientia universalis* itself, in a book entitled, in honour of Ramón Lull, the 'Great Art of Knowledge' (*Ars Magna Sciendi*).

Kircher knew twelve languages, studied medical chemistry, observed eclipses, and attempted to break codes and to decipher the Egyptian hieroglyphs, presenting his interpretation, thanks to a subsidy from the emperor, in sumptuous folio volumes entitled *Oedipus Aegyptiacus* (1652–4).[59] He was also an inventor who constructed a sunflower clock, a water organ, a perpetual-motion machine, a magic lantern and a box (the *arca musarithmica*) to assist the composition of music for a given text. He wrote a story about a visit to the moon, the *Ecstatic Heavenly Journey*, surely an attempt to surpass a similar but shorter story by Johannes Kepler.

It remains difficult not to be impressed by the way in which Kircher was able to marshal masses of information in his enormous folios and to draw on sources in many languages, 'writing in Latin, Italian, Spanish, German, Dutch, Greek, Hebrew, Armenian, Arabic and Coptic, and reading in many more'.[60] He made serious contributions to knowledge and some of his synthetic works were also valuable, notably the book about China.

There was, however, a downside to these achievements. Kircher was prone to errors and he was often criticized by scholars in particular fields – by Marcus Meibom on the history of music, for instance, by Marin Mersenne on magnetism, and by Hiob Ludolf on language. Ludolf, a major figure in what we would call comparative linguistics, warned a colleague, 'Please keep your distance from Kircher. He does not have as scholarly a command of languages as he claims.'[61]

Kircher sometimes promised more than he could perform, as in the notorious cases of his claims to square the circle and to interpret Egyptian hieroglyphs, which (like Renaissance humanists) he viewed not as a form of writing but as emblems with a hidden meaning.[62] More serious than his failures was his continued belief in his success, a case of hubris that is not unparalleled among polymaths and that probably led (together with the common prejudice against Jesuits) to accusations of fraud. It might be said that, compared with his leading scholarly contemporaries, Kircher possessed a surplus of curiosity, enthusiasm, energy and ingenuity (a quality much prized in his time), but that his critical faculty was relatively weak, as some contemporaries were aware.[63] His career illustrates the risks already involved in attempting polymathy at this time.

Kircher's interest in Pico della Mirandola and especially in Ramón Lull place him in a polymathic tradition. So does his belief in the unity of knowledge, discussed in the previous chapter. This belief led Kircher to draw analogies between different phenomena (light and sound, for instance). It also encouraged or drove him to attempt to produce a synthesis between knowledges – pagan and Christian, Eastern and Western. If Comenius had not been a Protestant, Kircher would doubtless have admired him. In any case he practised a kind of *pansophia*, even if it was not associated with plans for the reform of the world.[64]

THE POLYMATH AS CRITIC: BAYLE

Less wide-ranging than Kircher, but still extremely broad, was the learning of Pierre Bayle, a French Protestant pastor who became a refugee in the Dutch Republic in the 1680s. Bayle once confessed to being 'hungry to know everything' (*affamé de savoir tout*).[65] He taught at Protestant academies, first in France (in Sedan) and then in Rotterdam, but gave up an academic career when he was invited to become the editor of a scholarly journal, *Nouvelles de la République des Lettres*, which appeared once a month and lasted for three years (1684–7). He wrote most of the 'news' (mainly book reviews) by himself. Bayle was far from the only Protestant exile to produce a cultural journal, and some of his colleagues might also be described as polymaths – Henri Basnage, for instance, wrote on history, theology, language and even mechanics. However, Bayle's interests were even wider than those of Basnage. They are revealed by his famous *Dictionnaire Historique et Critique* (1697).

This 'dictionary' was a historical encyclopaedia, designed to replace an earlier reference book, *Le Grand Dictionnaire Historique*, published by a Catholic priest, Louis Moreri, in 1674 and, in Bayle's view, insufficiently critical. Bayle's dictionary was much larger than Moreri's, and it has become famous for its footnotes or 'remarks', occupying more space than the text and offering opportunities for the author to express his own ideas and to cast doubt on much that others had presented as reliable information. The dictionary, like the journal that Bayle edited, was concerned not only with history, philosophy, theology and literature, but also with the study of nature. Bayle seems to have been well informed about recent developments in what we call the natural sciences. The *Nouvelles* discussed medicine, anatomy, physics, chemistry and natural history, while the *Dictionnaire* includes famous 'remarks' on the rationality of animals ('Rorarius'), and on the ideas of Galileo and Newton ('Leucippus').[66]

Bayle's vast correspondence (now becoming available online, like the letters of Peiresc and Kircher) offers more clues to his interests and also to his informants.[67] For example, for news about the English branch of the Republic of Letters, Bayle relied on French exiles there, including his friend Daniel de Larroque, the surgeon Paul Buissière and the librarian Henri Justel (who translated publications of the Royal Society for him). For German news, he obtained information from another friend, the pastor and scholar Jacques Lenfant. For natural philosophy, Bayle turned to two leaders in the field, Christiaan Huygens in physics and Antonie Leeuwenhoek, a pioneer in the use of the microscope, in what is now known as microbiology. Skilled in networking himself, it is no surprise to find that Bayle admired his predecessor Peiresc, devoting an article in his *Dictionnaire* to him and describing him as 'Procurator-General' of the Republic of Letters, an allusion to Peiresc's knowledge of the law and also, perhaps, to his ability to procure information.[68]

THE POLYMATH AS SYNTHESIZER: LEIBNIZ

The most famous example of a seventeenth-century polymath is of course Gottfried Wilhelm Leibniz. He is usually remembered today – like Aristotle – as a philosopher.[69] Once again, this label is little more than a symptom of our own propensity to squeeze scholars into single fields. In his own day, Leibniz was active not only as a philosopher but as a mathematician and a theologian. He was a linguist, interested in families of languages and showing an early awareness of the analogies between the grammars of Finnish and Hungarian.[70] He was also a historian, a jurist, a writer on politics and an expert on China who once described himself as a one-man 'office of address' for information on the subject.[71]

Leibniz was aware of the importance of Peiresc's researches and hoped for the publication of his many letters.[72] All the same, he himself was reluctant to publish, so much so that, as he once wrote to a friend, anyone who knew only his published work did not know him. His papers reveal his interest in 'botany, psychology, medicine and natural history' as well as 'astronomy, physics, chemistry and geology'.[73]

As if this were not enough, Leibniz was also engaged in many practical activities – diplomacy, the reform of the law, the foundation of learned academies (the Berlin Academy in 1700, the Academy of Sciences of St Petersburg in 1725) and the management of libraries.[74] His interest in technology led him to the invention of a calculating machine, a cipher machine, and improved lenses, pumps and watches. His visits to mines were concerned not only with the study of geology but also with improving the efficiency of production. He had ideas for the reform of coinage, for a dye factory and for the organization of archives.

As one of his patrons put it in a moment of semi-exasperation, Leibniz was a man of 'insatiable curiosity', a phrase that has been repeated more than once by students of his work.[75] He was described by one contemporary as 'deeply versed in all sciences', and by another as 'so comprehensive and universal a genius'.[76] Posterity agreed. The French polymath Bernard de Fontenelle compared him to someone driving an eight-horse carriage, since 'Leibniz could manage all the sciences simultaneously'.[77] In a dictionary of scholars published in 1733, Leibniz appeared as 'a famous polymath', while a well-known nineteenth-century German scientist, Emil Du Bois-Reymond, called him a scholar with 'knowledge of everything and of the whole' (*All- und Ganzwisser*).[78]

Combining as he did acute curiosity with a desire for order, Leibniz was an obvious choice for the post of librarian. In fact, he catalogued a private library, that of Baron von Boineburg, before becoming librarian to the Duke of Brunswick in Hanover, and then, for a quarter of a century, in Wolfenbüttel. He was offered similar appointments at the Vatican and in Paris and he himself applied for the post of imperial librarian at Vienna. Plato claimed that for an ideal state to come into existence, either philosophers would have to become kings or kings would have to become philosophers. In similar fashion, one might suggest that, for an ideal library to be established, philosophers would have to become librarians or librarians would have to become philosophers. The link between the classification of books and the classification of knowledge is indeed clear in Leibniz's practical and theoretical work.[79]

What drove Leibniz was more than curiosity, insatiable as this was. In the tradition of Lull, Alsted and Comenius (to whom he once addressed a poem), he had a dream of reforming all the sciences. Aware that the task was too great to carry out single-handed, Leibniz both preached and practised collaboration, from consulting fellow scholars to founding learned journals and academies and attempting to organize a collective 'Thesaurus' or encyclopaedia. The dream of reform underlies projects of his such as a universal language that would eliminate misunderstandings between scholars who spoke in different tongues; the logical calculus, reducing complex arguments to simple calculations; and the *scientia generalis*, defined as 'the science which contains the principles of all the other sciences'.[80]

MINOR POLYMATHS

In the art of the Italian Renaissance, the outstanding achievements of Leonardo, Raphael and Michelangelo were linked to those of an unusual number of relatively minor artists. In similar fashion, the age of the seven 'monsters' was also the age of many lesser polymaths (some of whom are listed in the Appendix), who provide yet another reason for calling this century a golden age.

Many of these individuals were professors, including Samuel Pufendorf, who lectured on law at the University of Lund and wrote on history, philosophy and what he called the 'discipline' of natural law; Isaac Barrow, a colleague of Newton's at Cambridge, who has been described as 'one of the last Renaissance universal scholars', and Daniel Morhof, a professor at the University of Kiel, whose *Polyhistor* (1688) was long used as an introduction to scholarship.[81] However, four of the most remarkable minor polymaths of this period – 'minor', relative to the seven monsters – followed careers outside the academic world. They were respectively a bishop, a lawyer, a soldier and an administrator: Pierre-Daniel Huet, John Selden, Luigi Marsili and Nicolaes Witsen.

The diversity of the interests and achievements of Pierre-Daniel Huet, who became bishop of Avranches in Normandy but resigned this position to have more time to study, offers a remarkable example of an intellectual fox. As he wrote of himself in old age, he 'flew' from discipline to discipline and read 'immoderately'. A later polymath, Charles de Sainte-Beuve, called him 'the man of the widest reading who ever existed'.[82] Unsurprisingly, Huet accumulated a library of more than eight thousand volumes. The range of his contributions to knowledge is not so different from that of the seven 'monsters' described earlier, even if he is less well known today and sometimes regarded as a scholar of the second rank.[83]

Although he only became a priest at the age of forty-six, Huet's interest in theology began much earlier. He studied with the polymath biblical scholar Samuel Bochart, who took his pupil with him when he was invited to Stockholm by Queen Christina. Discovering in the queen's library a manuscript commentary on the Gospel of St Matthew by the Greek scholar Origen, Huet edited it and translated it into Latin. He learned Hebrew and Syriac to help in his biblical studies.

These studies led Huet, like his teacher Bochart, to examine myths from a comparative point of view. Bochart argued that the story of Noah was a prototype for later myths, while Huet offered a similar argument in the case of the story of Moses, making use of accounts by missionaries of myths current in Canada, Peru and Japan. Biblical studies also led Huet towards geography, with one study of the terrestrial paradise and another of the voyages of King Solomon. He wrote on philosophy, notably a critique of Descartes (1689) and a treatise, *The Weakness of Human Understanding* (posthumously published, 1723).[84] He published an essay titled the *Origin of Romances* (1670), the first history of this literary genre, and wrote a romance himself, *Diane de Castro*.[85] Huet was later active as a historian, producing a history of his native city, *Les origines de la ville de Caen* (1702), and a pioneering study in what we call economic history, *Histoire du commerce et de la navigation des anciens* (1716).

Like other *virtuosi* of his day, Huet was also interested in mathematics and the natural sciences. His enthusiasm for geometry is evident in his *Demonstratio Evangelica* (1679), presenting a proof of the truth of Christianity in the form of deductions from axioms. He was the co-founder of the Académie de Physique in Caen (1662), concerned with the study of nature in general and anatomy in particular. Huet himself carried out many dissections, especially of fish. His other interests included astronomy, natural history and chemistry. His original contributions to science include a discussion of sound waves and precise descriptions of the snail, the leech and the salamander. Huet also invented an instrument to measure the humidity of the atmosphere and another to measure the speed of wind.[86]

After Bacon, the seventeenth-century lawyer with the most remarkable range of learning was surely another Englishman, John Selden, despite competition from the Dutchman Hugo Grotius. Selden and Grotius were involved on opposite sides in a controversy over the freedom of the seas, but they respected each other as scholars.

A contemporary, Lord Clarendon, noted Selden's 'stupendous learning in all kinds and in all languages'.[87] His interests included medieval English history and oriental studies. His pursuit of the history of law (common law, civil law, canon law, maritime law and natural law) led him in a number of directions, including the English Middle Ages and ancient Israel (much of his late career was spent studying the Talmud and writing on Jewish law). His lively curiosity took Selden still further, into the study of ancient religions and the publication of a book, *On the Syrian Gods* (1617). In it he emulated the famous study of chronology by Joseph Scaliger, a sixteenth-century scholar whom Selden described as the 'mighty prince' of the commonwealth of learning.

Selden built up a library of about eight thousand books and manuscripts. His learning was combined with analytical power, shown in his comparisons between different systems of law and between different gods (Baal and Jupiter for instance, or Astarte and Venus). His penetrating intelligence is also revealed, together with his wit, in his posthumously published *Tabletalk*.

Despite the breadth of his interests, Selden insisted on going back to the sources. As he wrote with pride in his treatise *Titles of Honour* (1614), 'I vent to you nothing quoted at second hand, but ever loved the fountain'. For his oriental studies, Selden learned Hebrew, Aramaic and Arabic. For his studies of medieval England, he learned Anglo-Saxon and examined official records in the Tower of London. He also made use of the evidence of inscriptions and coins. His critical approach to texts was sharpened by a keen sense of anachronism and a concern with chronology. A versifier himself on occasion, he made friends with the poets John Donne, Michael Drayton and Ben Jonson. It was Jonson who best summed up Selden's combination of broad interests with specialized knowledge by comparing him to a compass: '. . . keeping one foot still/ Upon your centre, do your circle fill/Of general knowledge.'[88]

As we have seen, Renaissance writers often combined arms and letters. In the seventeenth century, by contrast, Luigi Marsili (or Marsigli) offers a rare example of a military polymath. A professional soldier in imperial service, he combined this activity with a wide range of studies, becoming a leading *virtuoso* of his time. He was an individual with a strong dose of curiosity. Captured by the Turks at the siege of Vienna in 1683 and put to work in a coffee house, Marsili put the knowledge he acquired in captivity to good use on his release by publishing a treatise on coffee, *Bevanda Asiatica* (1685).

Following his retirement (in disgrace, following the surrender of the fortress of Breisach in 1703), Marsili had more time for reading, writing and accumulating an extensive collection, which he later presented to the University of Bologna. His publications include an account of the armed forces of the Ottoman Empire and studies of phosphorus, coral, mushrooms and the sea. His masterpiece, *Danubius* (1726), presents observations on the river – as the title page claims – from geographical, astronomical, hydrographic, historical and physical points of view.[89]

Nicolaes Witsen was another man of action, several times burgomaster of Amsterdam and one of the administrators of the Dutch East India Company. However, the 'many-sided' Witsen lived a 'second life' as a scholar.[90] He found the time to collect curiosities, study natural history and publish books on ancient and modern shipbuilding and also on what he called 'North and East Tartary' (especially Siberia), including a map of that territory.[91] Witsen's interest in geography extended to South Africa, Australia and New Zealand. He was a friend of the polymaths Isaac Voss and Nicholas Steno, corresponded with Leibniz and, thanks to his extensive network, was able to help his friend Hiob Ludolf, yet another polymath, acquire texts in languages from many parts of the world, including Khoekhoe, spoken by the so-called 'Hottentots' of southern Africa.

Witsen's extensive collection of curiosities included shells (some of them from Australia), plants, stuffed animals, ancient coins and statues, Scythian ornaments from Siberia, a *kris* from Java, an ancient Chinese mirror, many Chinese landscape paintings and statues of Hindu gods from Kerala. His network was of great service in this respect: the statues from Kerala, for instance, came to Witsen via the Dutch governor of Ceylon.[92]

CONCORD

The previous chapter mentioned the desire for intellectual and especially for religious harmony as one motive driving polymaths of the Renaissance, from Pico to Bodin. This drive, like the conflicts to which it responded, continued to be a powerful one in the seventeenth century.

Comenius, as we have seen, hoped and worked for universal harmony. Caramuel attempted to reconcile faith and reason. Kircher hoped that his work would reveal the harmony underlying the apparent conflict between traditions, which he described as *discors concordia*. Huet wrote a book about the concord between faith and reason. Samuel Pufendorf was interested in reconciling the religious views of Catholics and Protestants in the divided Germany of his day.

Leibniz, who was born just before the end of the Thirty Years War, was also preoccupied with conflicts and ways of ending them. The point of his logical calculus, like the universal languages devised by scholars such as the English polymath John Wilkins, was to make it unnecessary for philosophers to disagree. He attempted, like Pico, to reconcile

71

conflicts in philosophy, in his case between Cartesianism and scholasticism. He also tried by means of natural theology (a kind of lowest common denominator of belief) to reconcile conflicts between religions (Protestantism and Catholicism) as well as between cultures (China and the West). In this sense he may be described as the last of the pansophists.

ORIGINALITY VERSUS PLAGIARISM

The flourishing of polymaths in the seventeenth century appears all the more remarkable when we remember that the bar over which they had to jump was raised at this time. In the Renaissance, as in the Middle Ages, scholars could make a reputation for wide-ranging knowledge even if they failed to make discoveries or to offer original ideas. In the seventeenth century, by contrast, scholars were increasingly expected to make fresh contributions to knowledge.

Evidence for this assertion includes the priority disputes and accusations of plagiarism that proliferated from the late sixteenth century onwards. They did not begin at that time: in the fifteenth century, Filippo Brunelleschi was the first individual to protect his intellectual property by taking out a patent, for a new design for a ship, in 1421, 'in order that the fruit of his genius may not be harvested by another'. In conversation with his friend Taccola (Mariano di Jacopo), Brunelleschi told him, 'Do not share your inventions with many people' because rivals will steal them and attribute the credit to themselves.[93] What was new in the seventeenth century was the frequency of accusations of plagiarism.

John Dee, for example, was accused by Tycho Brahe and Johannes Kepler of stealing their information and ideas, and in his turn Dee accused others of theft. Olof Rudbeck and Thomas Bartholin both claimed to have been the first to discover the lymphatic system. Newton's followers accused Leibniz of stealing their master's ideas about the calculus, while Newton was in his turn accused by the polymath Robert Hooke of stealing his ideas about the refraction of light and about the inverse square law of gravitational attraction.[94]

In order to safeguard their priority, some natural philosophers announced their discoveries in a coded manner by means of anagrams, a favourite literary device of the period. For example, when Galileo, looking through his new telescope, found that the planet Saturn was formed from three different bodies, he communicated this discovery by means of the mysterious message *SMAISMRMILMEPOETALEUMIBUNENUGTTAUIRAS*.[95] When Christiaan Huygens observed that Saturn was surrounded by a ring, he announced this discovery in the Latin anagram, AAAAAA CCCCC D EEEEE G H IIIIIII LLLL MM NNNNNNNNN OOOO PP Q RR S TTTTT UUUUU.[96] Robert Hooke produced the anagram *CEIIINOSSSSTTUV* to reveal his law that the tension in a solid is proportional to the force applied to it.[97]

As schoolboys used to know, in classical Latin the term *plagiarius* originally referred to someone who kidnapped a slave, but it was applied by the poet Martial to literary theft, from which he, like Horace and Virgil, claimed to suffer. At the Renaissance, terms such as 'stealing' were current in literary circles. What was relatively new in the seventeenth century was the extension of the idea to scholarship. Between 1673 and 1693 at least four treatises were devoted to this subject.[98] Once again, the history of language offers precious evidence of the history of consciousness. In French, *plagiaires* is a seventeenth-century word. In English, the term 'plagiary' is first recorded in 1601; 'plagiarism' in 1621; 'plagiarist' in 1674; and 'plagiarize' in 1716.

EXPLAINING THE GOLDEN AGE

What made the seventeenth century into a golden age of polymaths? Answers to big questions such as this are necessarily speculative, but a few points may be worth making. They suggest that the achievements described above were not the result of the miraculous birth of giants (or monsters), but were encouraged by social and cultural change. In the first place, seventeenth-century Europeans enjoyed an extended moment of freedom from the traditional suspicion of curiosity on one side and from the rise of the division of intellectual labour, which produced another climate that was – and remains – unfavourable to many-sidedness, on the other.

In the second place, the ongoing discovery of the New World by Europeans and their increasing contacts with Asia and Africa – whether by trade, missions or conquest – was a powerful stimulus to curiosity, revealed by the formation of many 'cabinets of curiosities' displaying exotic objects from these parts. Some Europeans became familiar with many new plants, trees, animals, birds, fish, insects, peoples and their languages and customs. New knowledge was arriving at a rate that excited the curiosity of scholars without overwhelming them. For example, the five hundred species of plants described by the ancient Greek physician Dioscorides had expanded by 1623 to the six thousand described by Caspar Bauhin.

Another kind of new world was revealed in the course of the so-called 'Scientific Revolution' of the seventeenth century by the use of new instruments, the telescope and the microscope, revealing objects that were very far away, such as the planets, and a world of living things that were near but very small, like the louse famously illustrated in Robert Hooke's *Micrographia* (1665). Hooke's contemporary, the Dutchman Antonie van Leeuwenhoek, was the first to observe and describe bacteria with the aid of a still more powerful microscope.

Other fields of knowledge were explored by new methods, notably systematic experiment. Amateurs were able to make original contributions to the study of nature as well as culture at a time when new discoveries were still described in a language close to that of everyday life, while many experiments were simple enough to carry out at home. Many discoveries within the reach of individuals using relatively simple instruments were still waiting to be made at this time. In its turn, the accumulation of information was a stimulus to scholars to turn it into knowledge by verifying and classifying it.

A third relevant point concerns the reorganization of what contemporaries called the 'Commonwealth of Learning' or the 'Republic of Letters' (*Respublica litterarum*), an imagined community held together by correspondence between scholars living in different countries and on occasion divided by religion. The seventeenth century was a time of increase in the density of the postal networks in Europe.[99] This revolution in communications underlay the expansion of the personal networks of individual scholars. Four of the seven monsters (Peiresc, Bayle, Leibniz and Kircher) maintained large networks of correspondents, providing information that would have been difficult to find in Aix-en-Provence, Rotterdam, Wolfenbüttel and even Rome.

Peiresc's correspondence, for instance, runs to 10,000 letters, including letters to fellow polymaths such as Selden, Gassendi, Grotius and Kircher.[100] Bayle's own letters, recently edited, fill fourteen printed volumes.[101] Leibniz too kept in regular contact with other scholars by letters, of which more than 15,000 survive. Still wider was the network of Kircher, who corresponded with his fellow polymaths Peiresc, Gassendi and Caramuel as well as drawing on the resources of Jesuit missionaries. He was even able to assemble a team of Jesuits to observe magnetic variation in different parts of the globe.[102] Just as Roger Bacon had derived his information about the Mongols from three Franciscan missionaries, so Kircher, thanks to the Jesuit network, had access to first-hand knowledge of China.

Some polymaths are best known as intellectual brokers. Samuel Hartlib, for instance, a Pole who studied in Germany and lived in England, was a disciple of both Bacon and Comenius who devoted his life to diffusing their ideas, as well as other kinds of information. His vast correspondence made Hartlib what a colleague of his, John Dury, called 'the hub of the axletree of knowledge'. Hartlib was known at the time as an 'intelligencer', gathering information in order to spread it by means of a newsletter. In similar fashion, Henry Oldenburg, a German who lived in England and had joined Hartlib's circle, owed his extensive knowledge to his activities as secretary of the Royal Society.[103] Another networker was the Florentine librarian Antonio Magliabechi, a passive polymath who made no original contribution to any discipline but was widely consulted by scholars on a variety of subjects – as the 20,000 letters to him that survive testify.[104]

The expansion of the postal system also underlay the rise of newssheets and journals in the seventeenth century, including, in the second half of the century, learned journals such as the *Philosophical Transactions* of the Royal Society of London (1665), edited by Oldenburg, the *Journal des Savants* (1665) in Paris, the *Giornale de' Letterati* (1668) in Rome, the

Acta Eruditorum (1682) in Leipzig and the *Nouvelles de la République des Lettres* in Amsterdam (1684). This new form of communication included learned articles, obituaries of scholars, accounts of experiments and – a new literary genre – book reviews, thus making it possible for readers to keep up to date with events in the world of learning.

In short, the seventeenth century was a time of relative equilibrium between the conflicting demands for wide knowledge and for original contributions. The increasing pressure to make discoveries, together with the ever-increasing proliferation of books, would make it increasingly difficult to become a polymath after the year 1700. The delicate equilibrium was already perceived by a few observers as tipping into a crisis of knowledge.

THE CRISIS OF KNOWLEDGE

The laborious lives of the scholars described in this chapter have suggested that the seventeenth century was the apogee of the general scholar.[105] However, there was also a dark side to the intellectual history of that century. The seventeenth century was also an age of doubt. The years around 1650 reveal what has been called a 'crisis of consciousness' or a 'crisis of the European mind', forming part of what historians have christened the 'general crisis of the seventeenth century'.[106]

The term 'crisis' has been used about too many changes, devaluing the intellectual currency. In what follows I shall therefore try to use the word in a relatively precise sense, close to its origins in ancient Greek medicine, when a 'crisis' was the moment when a patient hovered between recovery and death. Let us think of a crisis as a moment of turbulence leading to a change of structure. In other words, it is a 'tipping point' or 'critical threshold', often reached after a long period of gradual change.[107]

The intellectual crisis of the seventeenth century had a number of aspects. One was the transition from an organic image of the world – the world as alive, as an 'animal' – to the view of the universe as a huge machine.[108] A second aspect of the crisis was the rise of scepticism, or, as it was often called at this time, 'Pyrrhonism', after the ancient sceptical philosopher Pyrrho of Elis. Doubts were aired about the knowledge both of nature and of the past.[109] Some thinkers argued in favour of cultural relativism, notably the polymath Pierre Bayle, who famously wrote that 'History is dished up very much like meat . . . Each nation and religion takes the same raw facts and dresses them in a sauce of its own taste, and each reader finds them true or false according to whether they agree or disagree with his prejudices.'[110]

INFORMATION OVERLOAD

A third aspect of the crisis, the one most relevant to the subject of poly-maths, was the increase in the amount of knowledge available, a collec-tive benefit but also a reason for individual anxiety because there was 'too much to know'.[111] Following the invention of printing (with moveable type, in Europe) in the mid-fifteenth century, the production of books increased, at first relatively slowly but then at a vertiginous rate. According to a recent calculation, around 345,000 titles had been printed by the beginning of the seventeenth century.[112]

Anxiety about this explosion of knowledge – 'explosion' in the sense of expansion combined with fragmentation – was expressed more and more frequently. Complaints that there were too many books multiplied and so did metaphors such as the 'flood' of books in which readers feared drowning or the 'forest' in which they felt themselves to be lost.[113]

The English polymath Robert Burton made the point in his vivid way when he wrote, in a much-quoted passage, of the 'vast *Chaos* and confu-sion of Bookes'; 'we are oppressed with them, our eyes ache with reading, our fingers with turning'. Another well-known complaint came from the French librarian Adrien Baillet, who feared the return of barbarism as a result of 'the multitude of books which grows every day in prodigious fashion', making it increasingly difficult to identify what was really worth reading.[114] Even the widely read Leibniz wrote of the 'horrible heap of books that is constantly increasing' (*horrible masse de livres qui va toujours augmentant*).[115] Printing, once viewed as a solution to the problem of information scarcity, had become a problem itself.

In order to cope with the overload, scholars became more concerned with the organization of knowledge, writing the information they needed or expected to need on paper slips that were arranged in boxes or pasted into volumes. One polymath, Vincent Placcius, published a book titled *The Art of Taking Notes* (*De arte excerpendi*, 1689), recommending storing the slips on hooks organized by topic and hanging from metal bars in a 'closet'.[116]

The proliferation of books was not the only reason why scholars felt that there was now too much to know. Another reason was the very discovery of new worlds of knowledge that was noted earlier as a stimulus to broad learning. The glamour of these new knowledges may have inspired scholars to expand their interests, but the downside of this 'advancement of learning', as Francis Bacon memorably described it, was an increase in what is now known as 'information anxiety'. Discoveries were being made too rapidly for individuals to digest. The six thousand plants described by Caspar Bauhin in 1623 had multiplied by 1682 to the eighteen thousand described by John Ray.[117] It may even be the case that the seventeenth century is remembered as a golden age of polymaths precisely because it became more difficult for later generations to live up to the ideal of universal knowledge.

The challenge was to incorporate the new information into intellectual systems, old and new, without those systems breaking apart.[118] The problem of fragmentation was already being perceived as serious by some scholars by the middle of the seventeenth century.

FRAGMENTATION

The spread of new words such as 'polymath' in the seventeenth century was not necessarily a good sign. Indeed, the more frequent use of the terms is more likely to be an indication of the growing consciousness of a problem. In his play *Philosophaster*, Robert Burton distinguished the true scholar *Polumathes* from the arrogant individual 'Polupragmaticus', who claims, like ancient Greek sophists, to be 'omniscient'.

Among the best-known discussions of the problem are two treatises mentioned earlier, *Polymathia* (1603) by Johannes Wower and *Polyhistor* (1688) by Daniel Morhof.[119] Wower and Morhof presented *polymathia* as a concern with the connections between different disciplines, *scientiarum cognatio et conciliatio*.[120] To some seventeenth-century polymaths, these connections seemed to be at risk. Looking back at Alsted's encyclopaedia, we may view it as an attempt not so much to express as to restore the unity of knowledge at a time when this unity was under threat. Alsted's student Comenius was worried by what he called 'the tearing apart of the disciplines' (*scientiarum laceratio*).[121] He complained in vivid language that 'Metaphysicians sing to themselves alone, natural philosophers chant their own praises, astronomers dance by themselves, ethical thinkers make their laws for themselves, politicians lay their own foundations, mathematicians rejoice over their own triumphs and theologians rule for their own benefit'.[122]

' 'Tis all in pieces, all coherence gone.' The awareness and the fear of intellectual fragmentation was memorably expressed by John Donne in his poem *An Anatomy of the World*.[123] Scholars expressed a similar concern. The polymath John Selden noted that different fields of learning had become severed, although, as his own intellectual itinerary showed, 'every one hath so much relation to some other, that it hath not only use often of the aid of what is next it, but through that, also of what is out of ken to it'.[124] Again, the Puritan divine Richard Baxter complained that 'We parcel arts and sciences into fragments, according to the straitness [narrowness] of our capacities, and are not so pansophical as *uno intuitu* to see the whole.'[125] There is, of course, a danger of taking this remark out of context. Baxter was making a point about the human condition and contrasting 'us' with God and perhaps the angels. All the same, the date of his comment, the mid-seventeenth century, is surely significant, and so is his reference to *pansophia*, a movement that should be interpreted as – among other things – a response to fragmentation.

The need to see the whole was emphasized by other scholars such as the English divine Thomas Fuller and the polymath Isaac Barrow. Fuller declared that learning 'hath so homogeneal a body, that the parts thereof do with a mutual service relate to, and communicate strength and lustre each to other'.[126] In his treatise *Of Industry*, Barrow wrote that 'he can hardly be a good scholar, who is not a general one'. General knowledge was made necessary by what Barrow called the 'connection of things, and dependence of notions', so that 'one part of learning doth confer light to another'.[127]

Comenius offered *pansophia* as a solution to this problem. For Morhof, on the other hand, *pansophia* was the problem, or at least part of it. His solution was not only to reject it altogether but polymathy as well, which he viewed as too ambitious and too vague, given 'the limitations of the human mind' (*mentis humanae angustia*). He was particularly critical of scholars who tried to 'inhabit' all disciplines at the same time and he warned his readers against exaggerated ambitions. 'Those who wish to live everywhere will live nowhere and dominate nothing, or at best visit many places superficially' (*qui nusquam habitabunt, nusquam dominerunt, si ubique habitare volent, aut levi percursatione plurime attingent*). Morhof's ideal was more limited: *historia literaria*, in other words the history of scholarship, or, more exactly, scholarship approached through its history.[128]

Another Anglican clergyman, Meric Casaubon, the son of the famous scholar Isaac Casaubon, and himself a polymath who wrote on theology and natural philosophy, edited classical texts, and studied antiquities and medicine, was the author of an essay, written in 1668, on what he called 'generall learning' in which he admitted to a 'sad apprehension . . . of the decay of learning, and great danger of approaching barbarism'. Casaubon dated this decay from the beginning of the seventeenth century, in other words his father's time, on the grounds that it had become much more difficult than before to become a good scholar: 'for a man to make himself considerable . . . soe much labour, soe much industrie was required, as is enough to fright any, whom God hath not endowed with extraordinarie courage, and strength of bodie withal'.[129] It is possible that the son was projecting his sense of inferiority to his father onto the whole century. All the same, the younger Casaubon was not alone in his worries.

POLYMATHS UNDER FIRE

At this point it may be illuminating to return to the polymaths discussed earlier in this chapter, looking this time not at their achievements but at their weaknesses. A critique of polymathy is as old as ancient Greece, as we have seen, but criticisms cluster in the late seventeenth and early eighteenth centuries, so many signs of crisis.

Gilbert Burnet wrote to Leibniz that 'Very often those who deal in many things are slight and superficial in them all' (he exempted Leibniz himself from this generalization). Burnet was criticized for the same fault. He 'stayed no longer upon a science than after he had got some view of it', preferring 'the appearance of knowing many things rather than any one perfectly'.[130] Again, Newton criticized Hooke because he 'does nothing but pretend and grasp at all things' rather than providing proof for his hypotheses.[131]

The *virtuosi*, like the more specialized 'antiquaries', were sometimes criticized for missing true knowledge in their passion for detail. Hans Sloane, for instance, a successful London physician who owned a huge and varied collection (including 32,000 medals and 50,000 volumes), was called a 'a master of only scraps, pick'd up from one and from another, or collected out of this book and that, and these all in confusion in his head'.[132] In other words, Sloane collected bits and pieces of knowledge in the way that he accumulated material objects.

LEONARDO SYNDROME

A number of polymaths have been diagnosed as suffering from what might be called the 'Leonardo Syndrome'. Leonardo was and is notorious, as we have seen, for beginning many projects but bringing few to completion. In principle he was a hedgehog, with a vision of connections between different kinds of knowledge, but in practice he was a fox, dispersing his energies. A similar point might be made about Peiresc. Gassendi noted that the variety of his friend's interests and his drive to learn more and more prevented him not only from finishing particular projects but even from beginning to write. Leibniz criticized another polymath, Johann Joachim Becher, as 'concerned with too many things' (*polypragmon*).[133] Kircher too tried to do too much, complaining on one occasion that he was so busy that 'I don't know which way to turn' (*ut quo me vertam nesciam*).[134]

Even Leibniz seems to have felt the strain of keeping up his different knowledges. The downside of his enthusiasm for different projects was their tendency 'to snowball into things of unmanageable proportions'.[135] His history of the Guelphs, for instance, did not confine itself to the Middle Ages, as originally intended, but expanded backwards into what were later known as 'prehistoric' times. As Leibniz wrote wearily to another polymath, Placcius, answering a question about his projects, 'I have pursued many but perfected and completed none'. Writing to Placcius again, nearly twenty years later, he declared that 'I often don't know what to do next'. To another correspondent, he complained about 'the division of my concerns among too many things'.[136]

Lesser figures faced the same problem. The *virtuoso* John Evelyn, for instance, planned but did not finish a history of trades and an encyclopaedia of gardening. Robert Hooke has been called 'London's Leonardo' in a positive sense of the phrase, but it may also be argued that he suffered from the syndrome. Even a sympathetic biographer describes Hooke as someone who 'habitually took on too much' and 'whose versatility condemned him to miss the mark by a whisker'.[137]

Hooke's friend Christopher Wren certainly had solid achievements to his credit – St Paul's Cathedral among them – but he too began projects without finishing them, among them a treatise on architecture. A study of his contribution to mathematics calls him a 'dabbler' whose 'diversity of interest prevented him from attaining the heights which his ability allowed'.[138] The Mexican polymath Carlos de Sigüenza y Góngora, despite or because of his intellectual ambitions, 'failed to publish anything other than occasional pamphlets'. The biographer of Luigi Marsili remarks on 'the amazingly broad span of Marsili's interests', but also notes that on occasion he 'abruptly lost interest in one piece of work to turn to something different'.[139]

Despite their remarkable achievements, the giants of the seventeenth-century scholarly world may be viewed as a kind of human litmus paper, revealing problems that would become more and more acute as the years passed. In response to these problems, a more limited ideal of general learning became dominant in the eighteenth century and the first half of the nineteenth: the ideal of the 'man of letters'.

4

THE AGE OF THE 'MAN OF LETTERS'
1700–1850

In his old age, one of the leading scholars mentioned in the previous chapter, Pierre-Daniel Huet, reflected on what he believed to be the decline of learning: 'I hardly know anyone today who can be described as a true scholar.' Indeed, he continued, 'some people pride themselves on their ignorance, ridicule erudition, and describe learning as pedantry'.[1] In similar fashion, a scholar from a later generation, Giambattista Vico, to be discussed below, complained in a letter written in 1726 about the 'exhaustion' of European scholarship in all departments of knowledge (*per tutte le spezie delle scienze gl'ingegni d'Europa sono già esausti*). To support his complaint he noted that in his time in his native city of Naples, the price of learned works in Latin had fallen by more than half.[2]

Scholars often complain about the decline of learning, but in this case there is other evidence of a major change in the intellectual climate at the beginning of the eighteenth century. It was becoming less favourable to polymaths.

THE EIGHTEENTH CENTURY

One such sign was the decline in the reputations of two of the 'monsters' discussed in the previous chapter, Olof Rudbeck and Athanasius Kircher, whose intellectual edifices turned out to have serious flaws, like the 'feet of clay' of the statue described in the *Book of Daniel*. Leibniz, for instance, declared that, although he admired Rudbeck's intelligence and learning, 'I cannot approve of many of his opinions'. He argued that Rudbeck's etymological conjectures were often unfounded and joked that he was afraid that the French scholar Paul-Yves Pezron, who wrote about the origins of the Celts, 'might Rudbeckize somewhat' (*nonnihil Rudbeckizet*).[3] Rudbeck's ideas in the *Atlantica* were also criticized by colleagues in Sweden in his own day, while his reputation declined after his death. His ideas about Sweden as Atlantis became the object of satire.[4]

As for Kircher, his supporters, including two fellow monsters, Peiresc and Leibniz, became increasingly suspicious of his scholarship as time went by. Peiresc, initially enthusiastic about Kircher's contribution to the study of ancient Egypt, came to suspect fraud, as well as complaining that some of his protégé's interpretations were based only on intuition, as if they had 'come to him through the spirit'.[5] Leibniz, who had expressed admiration for Kircher's book on China in 1670, confessed to doubts about the *Ars Magna Sciendi* in 1680, while by 1716, commenting on Kircher's Egyptian studies, he concluded that 'he understands nothing'.[6] According to another polymath, Isaac Voss, 'even his friends' wished that Kircher 'had not written his *Oedipus*', with its claims to be able to read Egyptian hieroglyphs.[7]

Kircher's declining reputation was in part the result of a major change in the world view of educated people around the beginning of the eighteenth century, the transition from the view of the universe as animate, one that he shared, to the view that was coming to supplant it, that of the universe as a vast machine. There was also a transition from the idea of objective 'correspondences' (between microcosm and macrocosm, for instance), to that of subjective analogies. As the American intellectual historian Marjorie Nicolson put it, 'Our ancestors believed that what we call "analogy" was *truth*, inscribed by God in the nature of things.'[8] Kircher shared this belief, and he was left behind by the new trends.

PEDANTS AND POLYHISTORS

In the eighteenth century, the term 'polyhistor' shifted from compliment to criticism, at least in the German-speaking world. For Kant, polyhistors were no more than 'supermen of memory' (*Wundermannen des Gedächtnisses*). Their achievement was simply to provide the 'raw material' for philosophers to work on.[9] Criticisms of the polyhistor even spread to encyclopaedias. In Johann Heinrich Zedler's *Universal-Lexikon* (1731–54) the article on 'Polyhistorie' declared that 'the greatest polymaths did not do such a great service to the world, simply because they were polymaths and therefore occupied themselves with trifles'. The famous *Encyclopédie* (1751–72) delivered a similar verdict: 'Polymathy is often nothing but a confused mass of useless knowledge' which is offered 'to put on a show'.[10] The polyhistor was becoming associated with the acquisition of trivial information for its own sake, contrasted with what came to be known as *Politisch-galante Wissenschaft*, the kind of knowledge that was relevant to a man of the world and a gentleman.[11]

The jurist Ulrich Huber delivered an oration against pedantry in 1678, printed ten years later by the philosopher Christian Thomasius, who was himself a fierce critic of what he called *Scholastische Pedanterey*. Two plays from the first half of the eighteenth century – both of them written, as it happens, by polymaths – vividly evoke the image of a pedant: *Erasmus Montanus* (1723) by Ludvig Holberg, and *Der Junge Gelehrte* (1748) by Gotthold Ephraim Lessing.

Lessing, who went on to become a famous playwright, declared that he was not a scholar (*Ich bin nicht gelehrt*) and that 'to be a professor is not my thing' (*das Professoriren meine Sache nicht ist*). In fact, he was a learned man who tried to wear his learning lightly. As a child, he wanted his portrait painted together with 'a huge, huge heap of books (*einem grosse, grosse Haufen Bücher*). Lessing loved knowledge, planned to contribute to the fashionable genre of the history of learning, became the director of the famous library at Wolfenbüttel (like Leibniz before him), and wrote a daring study of the evangelists as 'merely human historians'.[12]

The increasing suspicion of many-sidedness is also revealed by the rise of the term 'charlatan' and its synonyms. In ancient Greece, Plato's *Phaedrus* had already condemned the sophists who only 'appear to be wise'. In the seventeenth century, it became commonplace to compare scholars who promised what they could not perform to the notorious sellers of fake medicines in public places such as Piazza San Marco. Kircher was described by Descartes as a 'charlatan', by the scholar–archbishop

James Ussher as a 'Mountebank', and by Christopher Wren as a 'juggler' (probably in the sense of an impostor).[13]

In the eighteenth century, Descartes's pejorative term was popularized by the Leipzig professor Johann Burckhardt Mencke. Mencke's book 'On the Charlatanry of the Learned' (*De charlataneria eruditorum*, 1715) is a hilarious description of the techniques used to promote themselves by the scholars of his time (though most if not all of these techniques may still be observed today).[14] The idea of the pseudo-scholar or charlatan has been described as 'central to the social workings of the eighteenth-century republic of letters'.[15] Even the Comte de Buffon, who dominated the extensive field of natural history, was called a char-latan by a fellow polymath, the Marquis de Condorcet.[16]

Aspiring polymaths were increasingly considered to suffer from hubris. Samuel Johnson, himself an individual of broad interests, told his readers that 'The circle of knowledge is too wide for the most active and diligent intellect' and that 'Even those to whom Providence has allotted greater strength of understanding, can expect only to improve a single science. In every other part of learning, they must be content to follow opinions, which they are not able to examine.'[17] In similar fashion, the biographer of James Tytler, editor of the supplement to the *Encyclopaedia Britannica*, remarked in 1805 that 'No man, however astonishing his talents and intense his application, can ever reasonably expect to be a walking encyclopaedia.'[18]

A NEW IDEAL

The ideal of many-sidedness was not abandoned at this time but it was limited, lowering the bar over which candidates for the title had to jump. Since 'universal knowledge is no longer within the reach of man' (*la science universelle n'est plus à la portée de l'homme*), as the *Encyclopédie* put it, it was replaced by a new ideal, dominant in the eighteenth and early nineteenth centuries. This new ideal was put into practice by the *gens de lettres*, culti-vated people (usually but not always male) who avoided pedantry and showed their knowledge in sparkling conversation in *salons* or in essays written in the vernacular and addressed to general educated readers.

The importance of the *salons* in eighteenth- and early nineteenth-century culture, most famously in Paris but also in Milan, Berlin, London and elsewhere, has long been noted. This form of institutionalized sociability for both sexes helped to shape the written style as well as the style of speaking of the participants. Some cultural journals reproduced this conversational tone. An early example is Bayle's *Nouvelles de la République des Lettres*, aimed at an upper-class public that the author described as *gens du monde*. The *Nouvelles* were imitated by Lessing, an admirer of Bayle and his light touch, in a periodical with a similar name, *Critischen Nachrichten aus dem Reiche der Gelehrsamkeit* (*Critical News from the Republic of Letters*), 1751.

Cultural journals proliferated in the eighteenth century, among them the *Spectator* (founded in 1711), the *Gentleman's Magazine* (1731) and the *Allgemeine Deutsche Bibliothek* (1765), which all tried to be accessible to what would later be called a 'middlebrow' readership. Joseph Addison declared in the first issue of the *Spectator* that 'I shall be ambitious to have it said of me, that I have brought Philosophy out of Closets and Libraries, Schools and Colleges, to dwell in Clubs and Assemblies, at Tea-tables, and in Coffee houses.' In similar fashion, the preface to another of these cultural journals observed that 'The public demands to be taught in an agreeable manner and finds a dry analysis boring.'[19] Voltaire was of course one of the masters of such an 'agreeable manner'. These periodicals helped to create the public that in turn made the careers of 'men of letters' possible.

MEN OF LETTERS

The term 'man of letters' was ambiguous at this time, since 'letters' often meant 'learning', as the phrase *Respublica Literaria*, 'the Republic of Letters', reminds us. However, its meaning was slowly shifting in this period towards *belles-lettres*, 'literature' in the modern sense, while scholars were increasingly expected to present their work in a clear and elegant form to the general educated public.

The phrase *uomo di lettere* had already been used in Italian in the title of a book by the Jesuit Daniele Bartoli as early as 1645. Two Italian polymaths of the seventeenth century, Francesco Redi and Lorenzo Magalotti, already deserved to be described in this way. Redi's fame depends partly on his research on parasites and partly on his poem in praise of the wines of Tuscany, *Bacco in Toscana*. Magalotti wrote poems and stories as well as publishing accounts of experiments and letters on 'scientific and learned' subjects.[20]

Despite such early examples, it was the period from the early eighteenth to the later nineteenth century that was the true age of the man of letters, in other words, an individual who (besides writing poems, plays or novels) made contributions to the humanities and showed an interest in the natural sciences.[21]

WOMEN OF LETTERS

As the gender-free phrase *gens de lettres* suggests, the new learning offered women a more important role than before or, more exactly, two roles, one as an animator and the other as a scholar.

Mid-eighteenth-century Paris witnessed the great age of the *salons*, organized by cultivated ladies such as Madame Dupin, Madame Geoffrin, the Marquise du Deffand and her niece and former assistant Mademoiselle de Lespinasse, known as the 'Muse of the *Encyclopédie*'. The polymaths Montesquieu, Voltaire, Buffon, Diderot and d'Alembert could often be seen and heard on these occasions. Breadth of interests was essential for a hostess to be successful, while the *salons* widened the education of both the men and the women who frequented them.[22]

Salons of this kind were organized in other countries and continued to play an important role in intellectual life for several generations. In London in the 1760s, for instance, the term 'bluestockings' was applied to the people who frequented the *salons*, first to both sexes and then to intellectual women alone. The most famous *salon* was that of Elizabeth Montagu, 'Queen of the Bluestockings', whose regular guests included the polymath Samuel Johnson together with Joshua Reynolds, David Garrick, Edmund Burke and Horace Walpole.[23] In Berlin in the 1780s, the brothers Humboldt, not yet polymaths, were introduced to the *salon* of Henriette Herz and Rahel Levin.

Some women of the time demonstrated a wide range of knowledge. Lady Mary Wortley Montagu, who established a *salon* in Venice in her old age in the 1750s, knew Latin as well as several modern languages, wrote poems, novels and literary criticism, introduced inoculation for smallpox to Western Europe, discussed education and the position of women, and planned to turn her letters describing the Ottoman Empire, where she lived from 1716 to 1718, into a book.[24]

Women were also active, and increasingly so in this period, as scholars in their own right. Among the best-known examples, discussed later in the chapter, are Émilie du Châtelet in France, Maria Gaetana Agnesi in Italy, the cosmopolitan Germaine de Staël (originally Swiss), the German Dorothea Schlözer, the Scot Mary Somerville and the Englishwomen Harriet Martineau and Mary Ann Evans, better known as George Eliot, a versatile essayist before she found a second vocation as a novelist.

THE FRENCH ENLIGHTENMENT

The obvious place to look for wide-ranging *gens de lettres* in the Enlightenment is France, since the French were trendsetters not only in the worlds of art and fashion but also in the intellectual world of Europe. Leading French polymaths in this period include Montesquieu, Voltaire, Châtelet, d'Alembert, Diderot and Condorcet.

A biographer of Montesquieu has noted the problem of writing about 'a man of many interests' in that it requires 'a multiplicity of competences, scientific, philosophical, legal, historical and literary' from anyone who writes about him.[25] His most famous contribution to literature, the *Persian Letters* (1721), reveals his interest in the Orient as well as his ability to imagine how France might appear to a visitor from another culture. Besides his masterpiece of comparative social and historical analysis, *L'esprit des lois* (1748), Montesquieu wrote on political economy and ancient history.

Although he 'disliked and knew nothing about mathematics and physics', Montesquieu's interest in the natural sciences is shown by his notebook on anatomy, his projected geological history of the earth and a paper, read to the Academy of Bordeaux in 1721, describing his experiments on animals and plants. The full range of his interests is revealed by his library of nearly four thousand volumes, still to be seen in the municipal library of Bordeaux, including the many travel books from which, together with his own visits to Italy, England and Central Europe, he learned to appreciate the variety of human customs. Montesquieu took a particular interest in China, not only reading about it but also questioning a Chinese convert to Christianity, Arcadius Huang, and a Jesuit missionary, Jean-François Fouquet.[26]

A biographer of Voltaire has commented on 'the universality of his interests' and described him as an 'omniscient polymath'.[27] On purely academic criteria, Voltaire might not pass muster as a polymath, but it is impossible to deny such a many-sided man a place in this study. Voltaire thought of himself as a man of letters and also as a *philosophe*, more or less what we mean by the phrase 'public intellectual', active in the debates and conflicts of his time, including the case of Jean Calas, a Protestant tortured and executed on a charge of murdering his son because he believed that son was about to turn Catholic. Many of Voltaire's poems, plays and stories, notably his satire *Candide* (1759), were vehicles for his subversive ideas. His *Letters on the English* (1734) was more than a simple travelogue or a guide to English culture, since its praise of England implied a critique of France. Voltaire was particularly productive as a historian, with books on Charles XII of Sweden, Peter the Great of Russia and Louis XIV of France, as well as his famous *Essay on Manners* (1756), a pioneering work in what is now known as social and cultural history.[28] Voltaire also wrote on philosophy, criticizing Descartes and Leibniz. He was a popularizer of science, especially Newtonian science, an activity that gained him a Fellowship of the Royal Society. He published an essay on geology and carried out experiments in physics and biology, cutting off the heads of snails, for example, to see whether they regenerated.[29]

Voltaire wrote that *Essay* for his mistress, the Marquise Émilie du Châtelet, who was a woman of letters in her own right. She was particularly well known as a mathematician and a natural philosopher, submitting a dissertation on fire in a competition organized by the Académie des sciences and discussing topics such as kinetic energy and dynamics with leading natural philosophers such as Pierre Maupertuis. Her book *Institutions de Physique* offered readers a synthesis of the ideas of Newton and Leibniz. Du Châtelet wrote a discourse on happiness and a treatise on biblical exegesis, and translated Newton's *Principia* and selections from Bernard Mandeville's *Fable of the Bees*. She contributed to the *Journal des savants* and was elected a member of the Academy of Bologna.[30]

The editors of the *Encyclopédie*, Jean d'Alembert and Denis Diderot, were themselves encyclopaedic in their interests. D'Alembert is most famous as a mathematician but he also made important contributions to physics (notably to the study of the movement of solids and fluids) and to the theory of music. He wrote a history of the suppression of the Jesuits and published five volumes of essays on literature and philosophy. D'Alembert's articles for the *Encyclopédie* ranged from religion to mathematics. He also wrote the celebrated 'preliminary discourse' to the work, surveying all the arts and sciences.[31]

As for Diderot, his interests included philosophy, psychology, natural history, chemistry and music, discussed in his *Letter on the Blind* (1749) and in other works that were only published posthumously, such as *Rameau's Nephew*. He made an important contribution to the anonymous collective work the *Histoire des deux Indes* (*History of the Two Indies*, 1770) attributed to another *philosophe*, Guillaume-Thomas Raynal. Like Voltaire, Diderot sometimes expressed his ideas through fiction, notably in *Jacques le fataliste*, which discusses the problem of determinism.

In addition to his work as editor, Diderot wrote several hundred articles for the *Encyclopédie* on philosophy, literature, acoustics, biology, art, music and the crafts. Himself the son of an artisan, Diderot respected technical knowledge. Thanks to him, know-how has an important place in the *Encyclopédie*, not only in the text but in the many illustrations of technical processes.[32] Among the 137 remaining contributors to the *Encyclopédie*, at least one, Louis de Jaucourt, was even more polymathic than the editors. Jaucourt, who had studied theology in Geneva, natural sciences at Cambridge and medicine at Leiden, contributed about eighteen thousand articles on subjects that ranged from history to botany, chemistry, physiology and pathology.

The *philosophes* just mentioned belong to a larger group, some of whom regularly met one another for conversation in the *salons*. Two members of this group had particularly wide interests, Buffon and Condorcet. The Comte de Buffon is best known for his contribution to the sciences, but he prided himself on his literary style and wrote for the general educated public. His *Histoire Naturelle*, published in thirty-six volumes between 1749 and 1788, ranged over the fields of geology, botany, zoology, palaeontology and ethnology (presented as the natural history of man). The book emphasized the action of climate – Buffon was an admirer of Montesquieu – and what the author called the 'epochs of nature', estimating the age of the world at 100,000 years. Buffon was also active as a mathematician (working on probability theory) and as a physiologist, as well as conducting experiments on trees in his private forest in response to the government's concern with improvements in the wood used in shipbuilding.[33]

The Marquis de Condorcet has been described as 'remarkable, even in an encyclopaedic age, in the range of his interests and activities'.[34] He studied mathematics with Jean d'Alembert, published an essay on calculus, and began to frequent the *salon* of Mademoiselle Lespinasse, who noted his interest in 'philosophy, belles-lettres, science, the arts, government, jurisprudence'. Condorcet was a friend of the statesman and political economist Anne Robert Jacques Turgot, who placed him in charge of the French mint. He applied the mathematics of probability to the analysis of voting, an enterprise that he viewed as an element of a science of human behaviour that he described as 'social mathematics'.

As Secretary of the Academy of Sciences, Condorcet wrote the obituaries of its members, a task that required a broad knowledge of the topics that they had studied. Condorcet's interest in history, including, as in Voltaire's case, the history of civilization, is apparent in his most famous work, the posthumously published *Esquisse d'un tableau historique des progrès de l'esprit humain* (*Sketch for a Historical Painting of the Progress of the Human Mind*), 1795. This essay divided human history into nine epochs defined not by politics or war but on technological criteria, the ages of agriculture, for instance, of writing and of printing.

The outstanding figures discussed so far were part of a larger cluster of writers and thinkers active in this period, including René de Réaumur, best known for his thermometer; Antoine Lavoisier, famous for his contribution to chemistry; and Turgot, remembered for his political career and his writings on political economy. All three of them ranged much more widely. Indeed, a friend of the family described the young Lavoisier as someone whose 'natural taste for the sciences leads him to want to know all of them before concentrating on one rather than another'.[35]

THE SCOTTISH ENLIGHTENMENT

As in France, a cluster of wide-ranging men of letters can be found in eighteenth-century Scotland. Where the French men of letters met one another in mixed company in the *salons*, the sociability of their Scottish equivalents centred on male clubs such as the Select Society of Edinburgh, founded in 1754. Its original fifteen members included David Hume, Adam Smith, Adam Ferguson, William Robertson, Lord Kames and Lord Monboddo. All six were individuals of wide interests and achievements, an example supporting the idea of the importance of small groups in the history of scholarship as in other kinds of innovation.[36]

David Hume spent some time in Paris, frequenting the *salons* of Madames Lespinasse, Geoffrin and Deffand and striking up a friendship with Turgot. He is usually remembered as one of the leading British philosophers, although the catalogue of the British Library used to describe him as 'David Hume, historian', a reminder that his achievements were not limited to philosophy and that his *History of England* (1754–61) made him famous as well as wealthy (he received £4,000 from the publisher). The breadth of interests of a man who wrote in his autobiography of his passion for 'general learning' is even more visible in his *Essays Moral, Political and Literary* (1741–2) concerned with a variety of topics, some 'light' – impudence, love, avarice and so on – and others 'serious' – taste, for instance, superstition, demography, the coalition of parties, a perfect commonwealth, the study of history and the rise of the arts and sciences. His notebooks also bear witness to Hume's interest in natural philosophy. It is not difficult to see why one of his biographers emphasizes his role 'not as a specialist' but as a 'man of letters', writing in an informal, accessible style for a general educated public that included women as well as men.[37]

Just as Hume is remembered as a philosopher, his friend Adam Smith is remembered as an economist, thanks to his masterpiece *The Wealth of Nations* (1776). However, this famous book is considerably more than a treatise on 'economics' in the specialized sense of the term current today. It demonstrated the relation of that subject to moral philosophy, law and politics. As Smith's friend William Robertson wrote to the author, 'You have formed into a regular and consistent system one of the most important parts of political science'.[38] The book also includes a good deal of history, notably the chapter 'On the Rise and Progress of Cities and Towns after the Fall of the Roman Empire'.

In any case, Smith did not begin his academic career as a political economist. He was first a professor of logic and then a professor of moral philosophy at the University of Glasgow, publishing a *Theory of Moral Sentiments* (1759). He also lectured on rhetoric, theology and jurisprudence. After he turned his attention to political economy, he did not abandon his wide interests. For example, he wrote an article on the origin of language, a topic that was attracting a good deal of interest in the later eighteenth century. While writing the *Wealth of Nations*, Smith confessed in a private letter that he had been 'studying botany' and 'some other sciences to which I had never given much attention before'.[39] The results of these studies can be seen in his posthumously published *Essays on Philosophical Subjects* (1795) concerned with the history of astronomy, ancient physics, logic and metaphysics, and the affinities between music, dance and poetry and between English and Italian verse.

Other members of the Select Society were not exactly narrow in their interests either. Robertson was a minister of the Church of Scotland and Principal of Edinburgh University as well as a famous historian of both the ancient and the modern worlds. The rival law lords Kames and

Monboddo did not confine themselves to the study that launched their careers. Kames produced essays on education, history, farming, religion and morality, while Monboddo published multi-volume treatises on language and metaphysics.[40] Adam Ferguson, professor of natural philosophy and then of moral philosophy at the University of Edinburgh, published *History of the Roman Republic* but is most famous for his *Essay on the History of Civil Society*. Sociologists still treat him as a distinguished ancestor.[41]

Another constellation of versatile Scots centred on the *Edinburgh Review*, founded in 1802. Besides the editor, the polymath Francis Jeffrey, who actually lived in Edinburgh, they included the expatriates Thomas Carlyle, who spanned philosophy, literature, history and mathematics; Thomas Macaulay, poet and politician, who wrote history and essays on a variety of subjects; and Henry Brougham, a lawyer who wrote on physics, fossils, biography and natural theology and supported general education.

THE ENGLISH ENLIGHTENMENT

In eighteenth-century England, Samuel Johnson offers an example of a man of letters who was also a polymath, and Joseph Priestley that of a polymath who was also a man of letters.

Johnson, the son of a bookseller in Litchfield and so familiar with a wide range of books from an early age, was a poet (in English and Latin), the author of a play, *Irene*, and a romance, *Rasselas*. He was also a literary critic and an editor of Shakespeare. However, his interests were much wider. He is known as 'Dr Johnson' because he was awarded two doctorates in law, one at Trinity College Dublin and the other at Oxford. He wrote a series of biographies of scholars for the *Gentleman's Magazine* and planned to write a history of 'the Revival of Learning in Europe'.[42] Johnson confessed to his biographer, James Boswell, that he was a great browser in an 'irregular manner' and had 'looked into a great many books which were not commonly known at the Universities'. He took to heart the advice of his cousin: 'learn the leading praecognita of all things – no need perhaps to turn over leaf by leaf, but grasp the trunk hard only and you will shake all the branches'.[43] He claimed that 'All knowledge is of itself of some value. There is nothing so minute or inconsiderable, that I would not rather know it than not.'[44]

A contemporary expressed his admiration for 'the expanse of matter which Johnson had found room for in his intellectual storehouse'.[45] This store of knowledge came in handy, to put it mildly, when Johnson embarked on his major project, the *Dictionary of the English Language* (1755). Although he described this project as 'drudgery' which did not require 'the light of learning', it was based not only on wide reading but also on knowledge of the various languages from which English borrowed. It also required an understanding of the technical terms used in the professions (the Church, medicine, the law, the army and navy) and (although the preface notes the omission of 'many terms appropriated to particular occupations') such practical arts as brewing, coining and tanning.[46]

Joseph Priestley was a scholar of a very different style, 'a self-taught man hostile to the notion of increasing specialization'.[47] He made original contributions to both physics and chemistry. He discovered oxygen and six other gases and published the *History and Present State of Electricity* (1767) and *Experiments and Observations on Different Kinds of Air* (1774–86). In the humanities, he was a gifted and wide-ranging popularizer. As a Dissenter from the Church of England he was excluded from Oxford and Cambridge, but he taught modern languages and rhetoric at Warrington Academy. His biographer refers to his publications on 'language study, English grammar, philosophy of education, rhetoric, politics, history, religion and biblical criticism, as well as the science for which he is best known'.[48] For example, Priestley's *Lectures on History* (1788) became a widely used textbook, thanks in particular to its use of memorable biographical and chronological charts.[49]

Like their French and Scottish counterparts, both these English polymaths participated in discussion groups. Together with his friend the painter Joshua Reynolds, Johnson founded The Club (1764), also known as The Literary Club, which met once a week in the London tavern the Turk's Head to dine and converse on various subjects. As for Priestley, he was, like another polymath, Erasmus Darwin, a leading member of the Lunar Society of Birmingham, so-called because the members met once a month when the moon was full so that they could ride to and from meetings without danger. Members discussed new discoveries in the natural sciences, the nature of electricity, for example, and also the application of science to medicine, manufactures and other practical activities.[50]

The achievements of these English polymaths, remarkable as they may seem, were eclipsed by those of a Welshman, Sir William Jones, known as 'Oriental Jones'. He more or less confined his interests to the humanities, but ranged over Asia as well as Europe. Jones was learned not only in the common law dominant in Britain but also in Roman law, ancient Greek law and, after his appointment to the Supreme Court in Bengal, in Hindu and Muslim law as well. Jones was also a polyglot who was said to know thirty languages. As well as writing poetry himself, he discussed and translated Arabic, Persian and Sanskrit literature, including a Sanskrit play, *Shakuntala*, which became famous in Europe in the age of Romanticism. Jones played an important role in the identification of the family of what are now known as the Indo-European languages, noting analogies between Greek, Persian and the Romance, Germanic and Celtic languages. He also studied Indian chronology and wrote a history of chess. No wonder then that he has been described, with only a little exaggeration, as 'one of the greatest polymaths in history'.[51]

FROM SPAIN TO RUSSIA

The ideal of the many-sided man of letters was also personified by individuals in other countries at this time: in Spain, for instance, Italy, Sweden and Russia. In Spain, three rather different individuals come to mind: Lorenzo Hervás y Panduro, Gaspar Melchor de Jovellanos and Benito Jerónimo Feijoo.

Hervás, described by one of his biographers as 'the great forgotten figure of the Spanish Enlightenment', was a Jesuit. He studied philosophy, theology, mathematics and astronomy at the University of Madrid. After the expulsion of the Jesuits from Spain and its Empire in 1767, he moved to Italy, where he published his encyclopaedic *Idea del Universo* in twenty-one volumes between 1778 and 1787. Hervás was and is best known as a linguist. His encyclopaedia included a catalogue of the languages of all known peoples, a task in which he was assisted by missionary colleagues who had learned Amerindian languages. Hervás also published a comparative study of the origin, formation, working and harmony of languages. His interest in language led him to write about methods of teaching deaf mutes. Like an earlier Jesuit polymath, Kircher, Hervás made an early contribution to science fiction in his 'Ecstatic Voyage to the World of the Planets' (*Viaggio estatico al mondo planetario*). His unpublished manuscripts include studies of palaeography, chronology and the history of the first colonies in the New World.[52]

In his working hours, Jovellanos, a leading figure in the Spanish Enlightenment, was active as a lawyer, a judge and minister of justice, while in his moments of leisure he was a poet, a playwright and a scholar. He offers a fine example of practical reason, interested in applied rather than pure knowledge and employing it in the reform of the law, education, commerce, industry and the constitution. Much of his thinking went into 'reports' (*informes*), arguing against the use of torture, in favour of the liberty of industry, supporting technical education and discussing agriculture and mining. He saw connections between disciplines and pleaded for a historical approach to the study of law and a geographical approach to the study of history. Jovellanos also wrote on language, theology, architecture, geology, botany and medicine. He was a pioneer in the revaluation of the Gothic and Moorish styles in Spain, while his contribution to political economy would later be praised by Joseph Schumpeter.[53]

Feijoo was a Benedictine monk and a professor of theology at the University of Oviedo for nearly thirty years. In some ways he appears an old-fashioned scholar, and he was indeed praised by contemporaries in a manner appropriate to the previous century, as 'the phoenix of the intellects of his age' and as 'a monster of learning' (*monstruo de sabeduría*).[54] Feijoo's forte was high-level popularization, combined with criticism. His *Teatro crítico universal* (nine volumes, 1726–40) included essays, according to the title page, on 'every kind of subject' (*todo genero de materia*). In his prologue, the author explained that he had planned to arrange the essays by discipline (*facultad*) but desisted 'either because they did not belong to any discipline, or because they participated equally in all of them'.

Feijoo might be described as a man of letters in monk's clothing who wrote for the general public, criticizing 'experts' and adopting a conversational style in the manner of Montaigne (whom he admired), enlivened by epigrams and vivid metaphors. He was an Anglophile, an empiricist and an admirer of Francis Bacon, praising this 'great and sublime genius' for removing the obstacles to the study of natural science (*la ciencia de las cosas naturales*). Feijoo neither made nor claimed to make an original contribution to knowledge. His aim was, in true Enlightenment fashion, to combat ignorance, prejudice and what he called 'common errors'. To this end he wrote on theology, philosophy, philology, history, medicine, natural history, alchemy, astrology, mathematics, geography, law, political economy, agriculture, literature and hydrology, ranging from earthquakes and fossils to the ideas of the medieval polymath Ramón Lull.[55]

In Italy, wide-ranging scholars included Maria Gaetana Agnesi, mainly in the sciences, and Giambattista Vico, mainly in the humanities. Agnesi was a child prodigy. Educated at home in Milan (where her father was a professor), she defended 191 theses on logic, mechanics, chemistry, botany, mineralogy and other subjects at a meeting there and published them in 1738. A French scholar who visited her described Agnesi as 'a walking polyglot' (she knew Latin, Greek, Hebrew, French, Spanish and German), and compared her 191 theses with the ones that Pico had been expected to defend in 1486. Agnesi wrote but did not publish a critical comment on a treatise on conic sections by a French mathematician. She did publish a study of calculus, which modestly claimed to be 'for the use of young Italians' as if it was simply a popularization, but also offered new ideas. Agnesi was appointed professor of mathematics at Bologna but did not take up the appointment, turning instead to the study of theology and to charitable work.[56]

As we saw at the beginning of this chapter, Vico was a scholar of the old type. His great ambition, according to his autobiography, was to unite all human and divine wisdom (*tutto il sapere umano e divino*). In practice, Vico, like Jones, more or less limited himself to the humanities. He was trained as a scholastic philosopher and then as a lawyer. He hoped to become a professor of jurisprudence but had to content himself with the chair of rhetoric at the University of Naples and the post of historian to King Charles III. He was more familiar with Latin than with French or English and habitually cited seventeenth-century scholars (including the polymaths Bacon, Grotius, Selden, Pufendorf and Huet) rather than later ones. His writings may seem old-fashioned and even provincial, at least on occasion, but they also reveal a vivid imagination and some extremely original ideas. Posthumously famous for his critique of Descartes, it might be suggested that it was easier for Vico than for some of his contemporaries to become a post-Cartesian because he had been trained as a pre-Cartesian.

Vico's most important work, the *Scienza Nuova* (*New Science*; 1725, enlarged edition 1744) drew on the disciplines of philosophy, philology, literature and law as well as on the descriptions of exotic societies by European travellers to other continents. Like Montesquieu, Vico viewed law as part of what we call 'culture'. It is a pity that the two scholars remained ignorant of each other's work. (When Montesquieu visited Italy, someone recommended him to read the *Scienza Nuova*, but he seems not to have taken this advice.)

Vico viewed himself as the Galileo or the Newton of history, and described his book as an attempt to provide the principles of a new science. He argued the case for the existence of a recurrent sequence of changes in customs and mentalities that he described as the three ages of the gods, heroes and men, distinguished by different kinds of law, language and mentality. His most profound and original observations concerned the first age and its 'poetic mode of thought', concrete and metaphorical like the thought of children. In a section of his book entitled 'the discovery of the true Homer', Vico presented the *Iliad* and the *Odyssey* as histories of ancient Greek customs, precious evidence of what would later be described as 'primitive' thought. He supported his views with a new interpretation of myths or 'fables' (*favole*), as he called them, treating them as evidence for the history 'of the oldest customs, orders and laws'.[57]

Sweden was the home of two remarkable scholars who are remembered today for only a small part of their many achievements. Carl Linnaeus, now classified as a botanist, was 'a jack-of-all trades' who 'worked in medicine and natural history' and classified not only plants but also animals, minerals and diseases as well as writing on political economy and producing a description of Lapland that combined geography with what we would call ethnography.[58] Emanuel Swedenborg, now remembered for his second career as a visionary and mystic, following his midlife crisis in 1743, had a first career as a polymath and was active as a hydraulic engineer as well as investigating metallurgy, chemistry, astronomy, anatomy, physiology and physiognomy, designing machines and writing a report on trade and industry for his patron, King Charles XII.[59]

In Russia, Mikhail Lomonosov combined a career as a professor of chemistry at the Academy of Sciences with studies of mathematics and oceanography, while his manuscripts reveal his interest in mineralogy and in many aspects of physics. He was also a man of letters, a poet in the vernacular, and the author of a grammar of Russian and a history of Russia. Before Lomonosov, German expatriates had dominated the field of learning in Russia, having been invited by the tsars, from Peter the Great to Catherine the Great, in order to help Russians catch up with Western European scholarship. For example, the polymath Peter Simon Pallas was invited to Russia by Catherine, appointed professor of natural history at the Academy of St Petersburg, and spent forty-three years in Russia, contributing to the knowledge of Russian geography, geology, botany and zoology, as well as collecting information on world languages for the empress. Another polymath, August von Schlözer, who only spent six years in Russia, produced a report to the Academy of St Petersburg, two years after his arrival, about the way in which Russian history should be written. Thanks to Lomonosov, however, the St Petersburg Academy, once almost entirely composed of foreigners, was gradually Russianized and a native tradition of scholarship developed.[60]

Another Slav polymath, born in the same year as Lomonosov, 1711, was Rudjer Bošković, a Jesuit from Dubrovnik. Like Lomonosov, Bošković was not only a natural philosopher who made original contributions in a number of fields, but also a poet (in Latin in his case). He was an archaeologist, excavating mosaics in Frascati, a diplomat, a cartographer, making a new map of the Papal States at the request of Pope Benedict XIV, and an inventor of scientific instruments. Nonetheless, the fame of Bošković is mainly due to his studies of astronomy and optics, together with his masterpiece, *Theory of Natural Philosophy* (1758), a kind of theory of everything in which he introduced the idea of atoms that are no larger than points and used it to reduce natural philosophy, so he claimed, to a single law.[61]

THE NEW WORLD

In Spanish America, Pedro de Peralta carried on the tradition of Sister Juana and Carlos Sigüenza y Góngora. This polymath was professor of mathematics at the university of Lima and later its rector, while his publications include an epic on the conquest of Peru as well as studies of music, metallurgy, astronomy, fortification and the history of Spain.[62]

In North America, two leading polymaths were active in politics, Benjamin Franklin and Thomas Jefferson. They were both inspired by Joseph Priestley. Besides his political career as a member of Congress and as a diplomat in England, France and Sweden, Franklin, who had been trained as a printer, was an inventor of the lightning rod, bifocal lenses and a stove that was designed to produce more heat and less smoke than an ordinary open fireplace. He also made contributions to the study of electricity, meteorology and oceanography.[63]

As for Jefferson, he was not only one of the founding fathers of the United States and its third President, from 1801 to 1809, but also a practising lawyer and a farmer who introduced innovations in agriculture. This is to say nothing of his inventions (including an improved mould-board for ploughs, the 'dumb waiter' and a revolving bookcase), his excavation of an Indian burial mound near his house in Monticello, Charlottesville, Virginia, his architectural designs and his interests in natural history, linguistics and art. No wonder then that Jefferson has been called a 'Renaissance Man' (and even, like some later polymaths, 'the last Renaissance Man').[64]

The late eighteenth and early nineteenth centuries was the time of two remarkable clusters of polymaths, one in England and the other in Germany.

ENGLAND

Two men of letters of this period, Samuel Coleridge and his friend Thomas De Quincey, were particularly wide-ranging. Coleridge, remembered today mainly for his poems, has been described as 'Romantic England's quintessential polymath'.[65] In a letter of 1796 he wrote that he had 'read almost everything – a library cormorant – I am *deep* in all out of the way books'. He declared that he meant to be 'a tolerable Mathematician' and 'would thoroughly know Mechanics, Hydrostatics, Optics, and Astronomy, Botany, Metallurgy, Fossilism, Chemistry, Geology, Anatomy, Medicine then the mind of Man – then the Minds of Men – in all Travels, Voyages and Histories'.[66]

As for De Quincey – who dropped out of Oxford, took drugs and is remembered today for his *Confessions of an Opium Eater* (1821) – he made a living as a popularizer of knowledge in *Blackwood's Magazine* and other journals. His essays 'covered an astonishing range of topics: German philosophy, political economy, literary history and biography, murder, the history and philosophy of ancient Greece and Rome, political commentary on current affairs, physiology'.[67]

Other polymaths made original contributions to a number of disciplines. Thomas Young, a Fellow of Emmanuel College, is the second individual to be described by a biographer as 'the last man to know everything'. Somewhat less dramatically, Young's tombstone in Westminster Abbey calls him 'eminent in almost every department of human learning'. Early in his career, at the end of the eighteenth century, Young was attracted by oriental languages and learned Hebrew, Syriac, Samaritan, Arabic, Persian and Turkish. He was trained as a physician, practised this profession and pursued medical research. He also published important papers calculating life insurance and describing his experiments in acoustics and optics (he was a prominent early supporter of the wave theory of light).

Young also lectured on physiology, chemistry and the theory of the tides, acted as secretary to the Commission of Weights and Measures (taking a particular interest in the pendulum), and contributed articles to the *Supplement* to the fourth edition of the *Encyclopedia Britannica* on – among other topics – Annuities, Egypt, Hydraulics and Languages. The article on languages divided them into five main families, including the 'Indo-European', which Young was the first to name, although, as we have seen, an earlier polymath, William Jones, had already discussed affinities between Sanskrit, Greek and the Latin, Germanic and Romance languages.[68] Turning to the study of Egyptian hieroglyphics, which were attracting renewed attention at the time of Napoleon's invasion of Egypt in 1798, Young was making good progress on their decoding, but was overtaken in this task by a more specialized French rival, Jean-François Champollion.[69]

In the next generation, John Herschel has been described as 'one of the last of the great universalists'. He was not only an astronomer, first assisting and then carrying on the work of his father, William, but also a mathematician and a chemist. He made contributions to the study of magnetism, botany, geology, acoustics, optics and photography, putting him in a good position to produce what he called, following d'Alembert, a 'Preliminary Discourse' concerning 'the study of natural philosophy'. In addition to all these interests, Herschel translated Schiller, Dante and Homer.[70] As a student at Cambridge in the early 1810s, he made friends with two future polymaths, William Whewell and Charles Babbage, who founded what they called a 'philosophical breakfast club'.[71] The friendship of these three individuals at an impressionable age is another example supporting the idea of the creativity of small groups.

Herschel's friend Whewell, who became Master of Trinity College, Cambridge, is another individual with a good claim to be regarded as a universal scholar.[72] Herschel himself wrote of Whewell that no one else had gathered 'a more wonderful variety and amount of knowledge in almost every department of human inquiry'.[73] Whewell wrote on mathematics, mechanics, mineralogy, astronomy, philosophy, theology and architecture. He confessed to a 'desire to read all manner of books at once', and was said, like Aldous Huxley later, to have read his way through the *Encyclopaedia Britannica* 'so as to have the whole of it at his fingers' ends'.[74] He invented a machine to measure wind velocity, went on geological expeditions, revised the classification of minerals, went further than Young in what he called 'tidology', and published a *History of the Inductive Sciences* (1837) and *Philosophy of the Inductive Sciences* (1840).

As for Babbage, he is best known for his construction of two ancestors of the computer, the 'analytical engine' (complete with punched cards) and the 'difference engine', an enterprise in which he was assisted by Ada, Countess of Lovelace (daughter of Lord Byron). Besides his activities as a mathematician and a physicist, Babbage published papers on chess, statistics, geology, ciphers, eclipses and lighthouses. In addition, he wrote on natural theology and 'the decline of science in England' as well as helping to found the Astronomical Society.[75]

GERMANY

An even more remarkable cluster of polymaths active in the late eighteenth and early nineteenth centuries was to be found in Germany, a cultural nation although not yet a political one. German-speaking polymaths could of course be found earlier in the eighteenth century. Lessing, for instance, has already been mentioned. The Swiss Albrecht von Haller, professor of medicine, anatomy and botany at Göttingen, was also active as a literary critic, poet and novelist. Immanuel Kant might be included here as well, since his interests were not confined to philosophy. It is true that what we call psychology and anthropology, disciplines to which he contributed, still formed part of philosophy in his time, but Kant also wrote on cosmology and physical geography.

A group that flourished around the year 1800 included Johann Gottfried Herder, his friend Johann Wolfgang von Goethe and Goethe's friends the Humboldt brothers, Wilhelm and Alexander.

Herder, who died in 1803, made important contributions to the study of language, literature and culture. Early in his career, he won the annual essay competition organized by the Berlin Academy of Sciences with a study of the origins of language. He also argued that each language had its own character. 'In the language of a nation,' he wrote, 'dwell its entire world of tradition, history, religion, principles of existence: its whole heart and soul.' Hence his publication of folk songs, which he viewed as the 'voices of the people' in the sense of the whole nation.[76] Herder's concept of *Volksgeist* ('the spirit of the people') implied the existence of autonomous cultures in the plural, in contrast to earlier ideas of progress towards a single standard of 'civilization'. *Volksgeist* would later play an important part in the development of new disciplines such as folklore and cultural anthropology, where it would be taken up by another German polymath, Franz Boas, discussed later.

Herder's interests were still wider. One of his most famous works, *Ideas on the Philosophy of the History of Humanity*, contributed to what is now known as 'Big History', discussing the state of the earth before humans made their appearance. He also made a contribution to what is now known as the philosophy of science, emphasizing the role of analogy in scientific discovery and the importance of the prototype (*Hauptform*), which is only visible in its variations.[77]

Herder's younger friend Goethe, remembered today as the greatest German writer, saw himself as a scholar and a scientist as well. The choice of Dr Faustus as the protagonist of his most famous drama was no accident, for Goethe himself had a Faustian desire for knowledge of many kinds.[78] He studied languages with enthusiasm – Latin, Greek, French, Italian, English and some Hebrew and Arabic as well. His literary interests extended to world literature, to Persian poetry, for instance, and to Chinese romances. He was interested in philosophy, studying Kant but disagreeing with him.[79] 'Development' was one of Goethe's central ideas, expressed in his use of the term *Bildung* ('self-formation') and in his novel *Wilhelm Meister* (later described as a *Bildungsroman*), which focuses on the development of Wilhelm's personality.

In the natural sciences, Goethe made original discoveries and put forward original ideas. He made contributions to anatomy (the discovery of the intermaxillary bone in the human jaw), botany (criticizing the system of classification devised by Linnaeus) and mineralogy (he was at one time director of a silver mine). He criticized Newton's optics and developed his own theory of colour (*Farbenlehre*, 1810). He was fascinated by what he called 'morphology', the study of the development and transformation of natural forms, a development from Herder's idea of the *Hauptform*.[80]

Among Goethe's friends from the 1790s were the brothers Wilhelm and Alexander von Humboldt, forming a creative small group that also included the poet, historian and philosopher Friedrich Schiller. Wilhelm spent more than a decade on his personal *Bildung*, studying and trans-lating ancient Greek writers as a form of self-development as well as carrying out experiments either alone or with his brother Alexander. Wilhelm then followed an active career as a diplomat and an educational reformer, but retired in 1819, aged fifty-two, to devote his time to the study of language.

Humboldt was also a philosopher and a theorist of general education, which he defined in Goethe's terms as *Bildung*, emphasizing the cultiva-tion of the self rather than the acquisition of knowledge and skills. He wrote on history (including another seminal essay on 'The Task of the Historian'), politics (on the limits of state action) and literature (discussing the work of Goethe, for instance). He was interested in the natural sciences, especially anatomy, as well as taking enough interest in chemistry to write an introduction to his brother's treatise on gases.[81]

As a linguist, or to use the term current in his day, a philologist, Wilhelm von Humboldt was interested, like Herder, in the distinctive character of different languages, as revealed in their structure as well as their vocabulary. He wrote two pioneering monographs, one on Basque and the other on Kavi (the ancient language of Java). Of all the polyglot polymaths mentioned in this book, Humboldt surely holds the record for the number of languages that he learned, from Hungarian to Japanese, allowing him to take a global view of his subject and write his famous essay on variation in linguistic structures. Humboldt's achievement in this field has been described as a 'Copernican revolution'.[82]

The supreme example of the nineteenth-century polymath, however, is surely Wilhelm's younger brother Alexander von Humboldt, a monster of erudition on a Leibnizian scale. His contemporaries were well aware of his range. In the United States, the President of Harvard, John Kirkland, described Humboldt as 'at home on every subject', while the philosopher–poet Ralph Waldo Emerson made a speech to commemorate his centenary in which he declared that 'HUMBOLDT was one of those wonders of the world, like Aristotle, like Julius Cæsar, like the Admirable Crichton, who appear from time to time, as if to show us the possibilities of the human mind, the force and the range of the faculties – a universal man'.[83]

Humboldt began his career as an expert on mines and mining. A five-year expedition to Spanish America (1799–1804) with his friend the botanist Aimé Bonpland allowed him to investigate the geology, botany, zoology and meteorology of the New World. It might be said that he arrived at the right moment, when there were many new plants and animals (new to Europeans, at least) waiting to be discovered in that part of the world. Humboldt was familiar with the latest scientific methods, including the measurement of natural phenomena, and carried some forty different measuring instruments with him on the expedition. He was also known as the intrepid traveller who climbed Mount Chimborazo in what is now Ecuador and later, in 1829, when he was sixty, explored Siberia.

Humboldt's fertile imagination suggested new fields of study such as the geography of plants. He measured the temperature of the ocean and studied ocean currents, one of which was named after him. He launched the study of geomagnetism, in other words the investigation of the magnetic field of the earth, not only by his own papers on the subject but by organizing the work of others. Late in his long life, Humboldt published a general book on the cosmos, which originated as lectures delivered to the general public in Berlin. *Cosmos* extended his interest in physical geography to what he called the 'perhaps too boldly imagined' programme of 'a physical description of the universe, embracing all created things in the regions of space and in the earth'.

Humboldt was also a man of letters in the nineteenth-century sense of the phrase. Like his brother Wilhelm, Alexander was a polyglot who shared Wilhelm's interest in philology.[84] His book *Cosmos* described not only the natural world but also the history of its study and the emotions felt when contemplating nature. It ranges from Arab poetry to Chinese chronology, from the archaeology of ancient Egypt to Titian's landscapes, and from Columbus to Copernicus. In the introduction to the book, Humboldt suggested that scientific description 'is not wholly incompatible with a picturesque animation of style', an animation found in many of his writings.

Like Goethe, Alexander von Humboldt bridged the cultures of the humanities and natural sciences, as well as the worlds of action and contemplation.[85] His *Political Essay on the Kingdom of New Spain* (soon to become independent under the name of Mexico) described the economy, the social structure and the political system. His concern with the geographical milieu included its influence on different civilizations as well as on plants. His habit of measurement was extended to the pyramid of Cholula, while his interest in precise figures included statistics on the population of Spanish America, its density in different places and its division into whites, blacks and indigenous peoples. If his many interests make Humboldt seem like a fox, his concern for connection (*Zusammenhang*) reveal his hedgehog side. The point of all his measurements was to help establish general laws of nature that would transcend its different domains.

Although he expressed anxiety about falling into what he called 'the superficiality of the encyclopaedist', Humboldt's career shows that it was still possible for an individual to make original and important contributions to a wide range of disciplines, combining breadth with depth. He has been described – like the 'last men who knew everything' but with more reason – as 'the last of the polymaths'.[86]

There was only one Alexander von Humboldt, an individual who was still able in the 1850s to match both the range and the discoveries of the seventeenth-century monsters of erudition. In the next generation, though, a few individuals attempted to create intellectual systems that would contain all or at least most of human knowledge, defying the mountain of information that continued to accumulate. These individuals included Auguste Comte, Herbert Spencer and Karl Marx.

SYSTEM BUILDERS

Comte's career was spent on the margins of the academic world, as he complained, making his living as an examiner and a lecturer outside the university.[87] He was a pioneer in the history of the sciences who asked the minister of education to create a chair for him in that subject at the Collège de France (the minister, François Guizot, refused). Comte was one of the most versatile scholars of his time. His public lectures ranged from astronomy to the history of humanity. He was particularly interested in classifying different kinds of knowledge, distinguishing between what he called the more 'abstract' sciences, such as mathematics, from the more 'concrete' ones. He also contrasted 'simple' sciences such as physics, producing general laws, with more complex sciences, such as biology and sociology, the laws of which were more specific. In order to create his classification, Comte studied mathematics, mechanics, astronomy, acoustics, optics, 'thermology' (the physics of heat), chemistry, biology, political economy and a new discipline for which he chose a new name, 'sociologie', describing it as the study of 'the fundamental laws pertaining to social phenomena'.[88]

For a British equivalent to Comte – who always denied his debt to Comte – one might nominate Herbert Spencer, who also made his name as a system builder.[89] Spencer wrote on phrenology, biology, physiology, psychology and sociology as well as presenting what he called a 'synthetic philosophy'. Spencer claimed that the social sciences should be modelled on the natural sciences and that society should be viewed as an organism that evolved from relatively simple forms to more complex ones. He combined wide reading – or rather, browsing, since he rarely read books from beginning to end – with a propensity to react against the ideas of the author. Spencer was an intellectual outsider, an autodidact who did not go to university. His training was that of a civil engineer, who worked for the railways before becoming a journalist (at *The Economist*) and then a freelance writer, living on the royalties from his books and the fees for articles in the reviews that formed such an important part of the intellectual landscape in Victorian Britain.[90] However, Spencer's remarks about social 'equilibrium' in his *Social Statics* (1851) suggest that the habit of mind he formed as an engineer never left him.

Karl Marx's system has lasted longer than those of Comte and Spencer, although his range was narrower than theirs.[91] This system, expounded and illustrated most fully in *Das Kapital* (*On Capital*), 1867–93, offered a synthesis of political economy, philosophy, history and the new discipline of sociology. Marx's interest in history would now be described as 'global'. He studied India and China in pursuit of a general theory of historical evolution that included the 'Asiatic mode of production'. He also wrote over thirty articles on India for the *New York Tribune* around the time of what the British call the 'Indian Mutiny' of 1857 (Indians describe it as a war for independence). Late in life, the author discovered the new discipline of anthropology, notably the work of the American scholar Lewis Morgan on the Iroquois.[92]

Marx's interests went well beyond the social sciences. At the University of Berlin, he wrote his doctoral thesis on the Greek philosopher Epicurus. Like other educated men of his time, Marx was familiar with the Greek and Latin classics, while his knowledge of the masterpieces of modern European literature was exceptional. He took part in the philosophical debates of his own day, for and against Hegel. During his long exile in England (1850–83), Marx spent much time studying in the famous circular Reading Room of the British Museum, plunging again and again, as his friend, colleague and later opponent Arnold Ruge put it, into 'an infinite ocean of books'.[93] When 'utterly incapable of work', as he said himself, Marx liked to read books on anatomy and physiology.[94]

THE SURVIVAL OF THE MAN OF LETTERS

The tradition of the wide-ranging man of letters remained a strong one in the nineteenth century. Whether they concentrated on fiction or fact, or published books or articles, it was becoming easier for writers to live by their pens. For polymaths, cultural journals such as the *Edinburgh Review* or the *Revue des Deux Mondes* offered the opportunity to make a living by writing critical reviews of new books on a variety of subjects. Long reviews turned into independent essays that could be collected into volumes. A new role was emerging for men of letters at this time, that of a critic, not only in the sense of someone who evaluates works of art and literature but an individual who points to what is wrong with contemporary culture and society.

FRENCH CRITICS

Four leading men of letters of this type were active in France in the nineteenth century: Charles Sainte-Beuve, Alexis de Tocqueville, Ernest Renan and Hippolyte Taine.

Sainte-Beuve is remembered as a literary critic, but he had broader interests. He wrote poetry, a novel and a five-volume history of the monastery of Port-Royal, which was a centre of the Jansenist movement in the seventeenth century, sometimes described as a kind of Catholic Puritanism. In any case, his critical essays were not confined to literature in a narrow sense but extended to a discussion of the ideas of Bayle and Rousseau, for instance. For Sainte-Beuve, the first stage in criticism was 'to understand everything that has lived' (*comprendre tout ce qui a vécu*). He described his essays, many of which appeared in the journals *Le Constitutionnel* and *Le Moniteur*, as 'Chats' (*Causeries*) because they were written in an accessible style, close to spoken French. This style owed something to the author's frequentation of the *salons* of Juliette Récamier and other leading hostesses of the time, who were continuing the great tradition of the eighteenth century.[95]

In his relatively short life, the French aristocrat Alexis de Tocqueville followed a political career, but in his memoirs he stationed himself between 'men of letters who have written history without taking part in public affairs, and politicians who have concerned themselves with producing events without thinking about them'. He travelled widely and wrote two masterpieces of political and social analysis, *De la démocratie en Amérique* (*Democracy in America*), 1835–40, and *L'Ancien Régime et la Révolution* (*The Old Regime and the Revolution*), 1856. Tocqueville also wrote about poverty in England and Ireland, visiting poorhouses to see how the system worked, and about colonialism in Algeria, which he studied at first hand a century before the sociologist Pierre Bourdieu, although he reached opposite conclusions, supporting both conquest and colonization.[96] Tocqueville studied religion, especially Islam and

Hinduism, and planned a book about the British in India. His contribution to knowledge has been described as 'polymorphic'.[97] It went well beyond political science. His book on democracy in America has been described as containing 'an important and original analysis of the United States economy', thanks to its emphasis on the cultural dimension, that of social customs (*moeurs*).[98]

Ernest Renan followed a more turbulent career, or more exactly three careers, the first as a priest, the second as a scholar and the third as a critic and what might be described as a public intellectual. At the seminary he studied philosophy, theology and Hebrew. Approaching the Old Testament as a philologist, he began to have doubts about his vocation to the priesthood and abandoned it. As a lay scholar, Renan published a book about Averroes, the medieval Arab philosopher discussed in chapter 2, and a comparative study of the Semitic languages. He was invited to lead an archaeological mission to 'Phoenicia' (now the Lebanon) and elected to a prestigious chair at the Collège de France. Renan once described himself as 'the least literary of men'.[99] All the same, he became a man of letters. He wrote for both the *Revue des Deux Mondes* and the *Journal des Débats*. His controversial and best-selling *Life of Jesus* (1863) launched him as a public figure who lectured on many subjects and a cultural critic who argued that France needed both intellectual and moral reform. It was said of him that 'No brain has been more universal, more comprehensive.'[100]

Hippolyte Taine offers a still more spectacular example of a mid-nineteenth-century polymath.[101] As a young man, Taine wished to become a philosopher but he was also attracted to both the social and the natural sciences, especially physiology, medicine and natural history. A fellow student described Taine's mind as 'a prodigious sponge'.[102] He hoped for an academic career, but this hope was frustrated by his failure in a major examination, thanks to his heterodox philosophical ideas, and the rejection of his proposal for a doctoral thesis. He turned to a career as a critic, writing for the *Revue des Deux Mondes* and the *Journal des Débats* and then publishing his articles in book form in *Essais de critique et d'histoire* and *Histoire de la littérature anglaise* (1863), launching the idea that literature, like culture in general, was shaped by three factors that he called *race, milieu* and *moment*.

Writing for journals and for the popular publisher Hachette and frequenting *salons* encouraged Taine to write, like Sainte-Beuve, in an accessible style (with more than a shade of malice, the Goncourt brothers noted Taine's 'great fear of being a pedant').[103] Taine also wrote on the philosophy of art and the psychology of intelligence. In reaction to the shock of French defeat by the Prussians in 1870, he turned to history. His *Origines de la France contemporaine* (1875–93) presented French history from 1789 onwards from a psychological point of view, inspired by the experience of the Paris Commune. In short, Taine spanned the humanities, the natural sciences and the social sciences that were emerging in the space between the two. No wonder then that the Danish critic Georg Brandes described him as a 'Renaissance Man'.[104]

ENGLISH CRITICS

In England, leading cultural critics included John Stuart Mill, John Ruskin, William Morris and Matthew Arnold.

Mill's main interests were philosophy, politics and economics. The son of another polymath, James Mill, he was educated at home and became an infant prodigy. When he was still a teenager, he studied mathematics and natural science in Montpellier and corresponded with Comte. Mill studied law but gave this up to spend thirty-five years as an administrator at the India Office of the East India Company as well as acting as research assistant to the reformer Jeremy Bentham for his work on judicial evidence. Mill's publications include books on logic, representative government and (together with his wife Harriet Taylor) liberty, political economy and the subjection of women.[105] He also published essays on subjects such as civilization, religion, the spirit of the age and fellow polymaths such as Coleridge and Taine.[106]

Ruskin began his career as a critic of art and architecture. An artist himself, he defended the work of Turner in the first volume of *Modern Painters* (1843) as he did the work of the Pre-Raphaelites later. He wrote about what he believed to be the decline and fall of Venetian architecture from the Middle Ages onwards and placed this decline in historical context in *The Stones of Venice* (1851–3). In later life, Ruskin turned from aesthetic to social criticism. He lectured on what he called 'the political economy of art' and, later, on political economy in general, criticizing the industrial society of his day. Although he was opposed to Darwinism, Ruskin was no enemy of natural science. He had a lifelong interest in geology, botany and zoology, even if he did not contribute to these disciplines.[107]

To the young William Morris, Ruskin's writings were a 'revelation', and he followed a similar itinerary from art to politics. Strictly speaking, according to the definition employed in this book, Morris was not a polymath because he took little interest in academic disciplines (though he knew the Middle Ages as well as any historian of his day). Yet he was so versatile – I would call him a 'Renaissance Man' if he had not hated the Renaissance – that it is impossible to exclude him. His disciple Walter Crane once described Morris as having six personalities, five of them public: author, artist, businessman, printer and socialist.[108] He began by working as an architect, turned to sculpture and painting, found his vocation as a designer but also insisted on practising a number of crafts, including weaving, dyeing and calligraphy. He loved 'hands-on' activities in the most literal sense of the term, his hands turning indigo blue during his dyeing phase. He might be described as an experimental archaeologist, since he took medieval textiles to pieces to discover how they were made.

Morris was also active as a translator, from Homer and Virgil to Beowulf and Icelandic sagas, as a poet and as a writer of romances. When he entered politics, he expressed his socialist ideals in the form of fiction, notably in his utopian novel *News from Nowhere* (1890). Like Ruskin, he was a critic of his own society from both an aesthetic and a moral point of view, calling it ugly, 'shoddy' and unjust.[109]

Matthew Arnold combined the role of critic with those of a poet and an inspector of schools. He believed that assessing the influence of books on what he called the 'general culture' was the most important function of literary criticism.[110] 'Criticism' was a word that often flowed from his pen, as it did from the pens of Renan and Taine in France. Arnold described Sainte-Beuve as 'the first of living critics'. His *Essays in Criticism* (1865) was mainly concerned with literature but included an essay on Spinoza, while his most famous book, *Culture and Anarchy* (1869), was subtitled 'An Essay in Political and Social Criticism'. It pointed to the cultural weaknesses of the British upper class (whom Arnold described as 'barbarians'), the middle class (the 'philistines') and the working class (the 'populace'), and called for more 'sweetness and light', his version of the German term *Bildung* (elsewhere he wrote of the need to become 'more humane'). Literature was at the centre of Arnold's interests, but he related it to religion (*Literature and Dogma*, 1873), to language (studying philology) and to culture more generally, taking an interest in the emerging discipline of ethnology as well as ranging beyond texts in English to discuss Homer, for instance, Dante, Goethe and even Celtic literature, 'although he was not fluent in any Celtic language'. His wide reading included the *Bhagavad Gita* and Wilhelm von Humboldt's essay on it, an inspiration for Arnold's own poem *Empedocles on Etna*.[111]

THE NEW WOMEN OF LETTERS

In the early to mid-nineteenth century, the age of Jane Austen, the Brontë sisters and George Sand, some women were able to follow a literary career and a few deserve to be remembered as polymaths.

Germaine de Staël, for instance, who came from Switzerland, was a precocious child who made an appearance at the age of five in the *salon* hosted by her mother – Suzanne Courchod, the girl whom Edward Gibbon had once wished to marry. Germaine later frequented the *salons* of Madame Geoffrin and Madame du Deffand in Paris as well as founding her own. Besides her novels and plays, Madame de Staël wrote on philosophy, the passions, suicide, translation and politics (on the trial of Marie Antoinette, on peace and on the French Revolution). Her best-known works are a study of what has come to be known as the sociology of literature, *De la littérature considérée dans ses rapports avec les institutions sociales* (1800), and *De l'Allemagne* (1813), which combined a description of German society, including religion and the position of women, with a presentation and assessment of the achievements of Germans in literature, philosophy and the natural sciences.[112]

Another precocious child was Dorothea Schlözer, the beneficiary – or the victim – of an educational experiment by her famous father, the historian August Schlözer. She was already learning the alphabet at eighteen months, moving on to modern languages and – at the age of five – mathematics. She was the first female to be awarded a Ph.D in a German university (at Göttingen in 1787). She knew ten languages and studied botany, zoology, mineralogy, optics, religion and art, distinguishing herself from her father by her concern with the natural sciences.[113]

In Britain, female polymaths included Harriet Martineau and Mary Ann Evans, better known under her pen-name of George Eliot. Martineau wrote of herself that 'She could popularize while she could neither discover nor invent.' All the same, her range was impressive. She was said to be able to converse on almost any subject. Having decided to support herself by writing, she published books on religion (*Devotional Exercises*, 1823); political economy (*Illustrations of Political Economy*, 1832); *Society in America* (1837), the fruit, like Tocqueville's *Democracy in America*, of a visit to the United States; education (*Household Education*, 1848); *Eastern Life, Present and Past* (1848), following a tour of the Middle East; and *The Thirty Years' Peace* (1849), a history of the period 1816–46. Martineau also wrote for newspapers and produced essays, novels and an abridged translation of Comte's *Positive Philosophy* (1853).[114]

George Eliot once declared that 'I enjoy all subjects'.[115] Her description of Maggie Tulliver, the heroine of *The Mill on the Floss*, as 'thirsty for all knowledge' surely applies to her creator. Her non-fiction has long been overshadowed by her famous novels, but her career began as the unofficial editor of what became a leading periodical of her time, the *Westminster Review*, and as a contributor of long articles on subjects such as 'Woman in France', 'Church History of the Nineteenth Century', 'The Future of German Philosophy', translation and ethnography, as well as sketches of the lives of (among others) Mary Wollstonecraft, Goethe, Milton, Tennyson and Wagner. She knew seven foreign languages and translated Spinoza's *Ethics*, Ludwig Feuerbach's *Essence of*

Christianity and David Strauss's controversial life of Jesus. In the 1850s, when she met George Henry Lewes, her main interests were in the humanities and in the social sciences (notably the ideas of Auguste Comte and Herbert Spencer). After going to live with Lewes, she accompanied him on scientific expeditions and 'read with him works on medical science, zoology, anatomy and marine biology'.[116]

Now best known as George Eliot's partner, Lewes was a remarkable polymath himself. He edited the *Fortnightly Review* and published two novels as well as *A Biographical History of Philosophy*, a study of Spanish drama and an analysis of Comte's philosophy of the sciences and biographies of Robespierre and Goethe. Lewes then turned to the natural sciences, producing a study of marine biology, a book on physiology and an unfinished treatise on psychology, *Problems of Life and Mind*, which Eliot completed after his death.[117] Incidentally, this highly educated man did not go to university.

Eliot's interest in science is visible in her essays, letters and notebooks, which reveal a familiarity with geology, biology, physics, astronomy and anatomy. Indeed, her imagination has been described as 'permeated by scientific ideas and speculations', so much so that she was sometimes criticized by reviewers for the number of learned allusions in her fiction.[118] Her notebooks bear witness to the careful research that she carried out in preparation for her novels. For *Middlemarch*, she studied the political history of England in the decades before the Reform Bill of 1832. For *Romola*, whose heroine was a woman of the Renaissance who wished to become as learned as Cassandra Fedele (discussed in chapter 2), Eliot carried out research in Florence, the British Museum and the London Library.[119] For *Daniel Deronda*, focused on the Jewish community in London, she learned Hebrew and became, according to Lewes, 'as profoundly versed in Jewish history and literature as any rabbi'. She is best remembered for her unflattering portrait of the scholar Edward Casaubon in *Middlemarch*, but once admitted that 'the Casaubon tints are not quite foreign to my own complexion'.

The Scotswoman Mary Somerville was a scientist who was compared by a leading English colleague to Maria Agnesi (discussed earlier).[120] She grew up 'a wild creature', as she wrote much later, in a small town in Scotland and was mainly self-taught, since a woman of her generation was not allowed to attend a British university. She studied Latin, Greek, mathematics, astronomy, mineralogy and geology, carried out experiments (on the effects of solar radiation, for example) and published papers in the *Transactions* of the Royal Society. Moving to London, Somerville made the acquaintance of the polymaths Young, Herschel and Babbage (whom she praised for his 'extensive knowledge on many subjects').[121]

Unable, as a wife and mother, to find the time for systematic research, Somerville made a virtue, or at least an opportunity, of necessity, concentrating on the synthesis of information and ideas. Her life changed, she wrote later, when she was invited to translate a book on 'the mechanism of the heavens' by Jean-Pierre Laplace. The essay that she wrote as an introduction to this book led to her major work, *On the Connection of the Physical Sciences* (1834). This book was written in a clear and accessible style to appeal to general readers and offers a fine example of what polymaths do best, viewing the big picture and pointing out connections that specialists had missed. Somerville also published a successful textbook on physical geography. Her work was praised not only by Whewell but also by Alexander von Humboldt, who appreciated her ability to see connections.[122]

SCIENTISTS

By the time that George Eliot and Mary Somerville were studying the natural sciences, the term 'scientist' (coined by the polymath William Whewell in the 1830s) was coming into use, an early sign of the gradual split between what would be known, more than a century later, as 'the two cultures' of science and the humanities.[123] At this time, however, individuals who made a reputation as scientists, often in several fields, also participated in the culture of the humanities and sometimes contributed to it.

In France, for example, Antoine Cournot began his career in mechanics, moved on to mathematics, applied mathematics to the study of wealth in a pioneering study of political economy, and ended his career as a philosopher, the author of an essay on the foundations of knowledge. He also took a lively interest in astronomy. Georges Cuvier dominated the related fields of zoology, comparative anatomy, paleontology and geology but he also wrote on the history of science. Cuvier's friend, collaborator, rival and opponent Étienne Geoffroy Saint-Hilaire worked in the first three of these fields and was also active in experimental embryology.[124]

GERMAN SCIENTISTS

German examples of the polymathic scientist from this period include Rudolf Virchow, Hermann Helmholtz and Ernst Haeckel. Virchow was active in politics as well as working not only as a physician, pathologist and biologist but also as an ethnologist and prehistorian. In fact, he claimed that 'medicine is a social science and politics is nothing more than medicine on a grand scale'.[125] He certainly took politics seriously, participating in the revolution of 1848 and later becoming a Liberal deputy and an opponent of Bismarck, who described him as an individual who has 'amateurishly stepped out of his field and into mine'.[126] Besides his contributions to the natural sciences, notably to the theory and the pathology of cells (explaining the origin of cancer and identifying leukemia), Virchow studied physical anthropology and directed a survey of the hair, skin colour and eye colour of nearly seven million German schoolchildren, concluding that the idea of an Aryan race was a fantasy. He edited a journal of ethnology and wrote on Goethe as a student of nature. He also supported the businessman Heinrich Schliemann's excavation of Troy and carried out his own archaeological investigations in Pomerania (in those relatively unspecialized times it was not necessary to be a card-carrying archaeologist in order to conduct excavations).[127]

Helmholtz has been described as a 'universal genius' and as 'the last scholar whose work, in the tradition of Leibniz, embraced all the sciences, as well as philosophy and the fine arts'.[128] The normally laconic *Dictionary of Scientific Biography* credits him with contributions to 'energetics, acoustics, physiological acoustics, physiological optics, epistemology, hydrodynamics, electrodynamics'.[129] As an adolescent, Helmholtz was fascinated by physics but followed his father's advice to study medicine. At the University of Berlin, he took up chemistry, mathematics and philosophy. Helmholtz was appointed a professor of anatomy and physiology, first at the University of Bonn and then at Heidelberg, working on the physiology of sight and hearing. Returning to his first enthusiasm, he moved back to Berlin as professor of physics. Helmholtz was particularly interested in the perception of art and in the theory of music. He lectured to art students and corresponded with the ancient and modern historians Theodor Mommsen and Heinrich von Treitschke. Like Virchow, he wrote about Goethe and science.[130]

In the next generation, Virchow's student Ernst Haeckel spanned the fields of anatomy, zoology and ecology (a discipline that he was the first to name), as well as writing on the philosophy of science. He was concerned with the unity of science and founded the League of German Monists (*Deutsche Monistenbund*) to further the cause as well as to offer a secular religion for his age. Haeckel was also an artist who illustrated his own books and an athlete who won a prize for the long jump, making him the first polymath to distinguish himself in this field since the Renaissance, the age of Leonbattista Alberti, Rudolf Agricola and James Crichton. He loved travel and exploration, including mountaineering. His role model, appropriately enough, was Alexander von Humboldt.

Humboldt also inspired the American polymath George Marsh. Marsh was active as a lawyer, diplomat and social reformer, but in his spare time this 'versatile Vermonter' was an art collector, archaeologist, linguist, geographer and a pioneering environmentalist, described by his biographer David Lowenthal as 'the broadest scholar of his day'.[131]

BRITISH SCIENTISTS

In Britain too, the Victorian age was a time of some many-sided scientists, who contributed to several disciplines and combined a scientific culture with a literary one.

Charles Darwin, for example, was, among other things, a Victorian man of letters. His father wished him to become a doctor and sent him to Edinburgh, but Charles discovered that he hated anatomy. He was sent to Cambridge to train for a career in the Church, but discovered natural history. He was an admirer of Alexander von Humboldt, confessing that 'my whole course of life is due to having read and reread as a youth his *Personal Narrative*'.[132] Like Humboldt's expedition to Spanish America, Darwin's long voyage on *The Beagle* (1831–6) changed his life. On his travels, 'Everything seemed to interest him, people, places, creatures, plants, climate, the structure of the rocks, the politics, the indigenous tribes.'[133] Darwin eventually published six books on botany, three on geology and one on 'the expression of the emotions in animals and man'.

His *On the Origin of Species* (1859), which made him famous, can be and has been analysed as a work of literature, presenting its argument in the form of a narrative and both supporting and enlivening it with examples that are precisely observed and vividly described.[134] The book owes important ideas to the author's wide reading, illustrating the way in which a polymath can make a contribution to one discipline by borrowing ideas from its neighbours and adapting them to the new situation. His friend Charles Lyell's *Principles of Geology* led Darwin to think of the evolution of different species as a process extending over the very long term, while *The Principle of Population* by Thomas Malthus gave him the idea of the struggle for survival.[135]

Thomas Henry Huxley, best known for his public defence of Darwin, was another polymath who once thanked the gods for his 'diversity of tastes', declaring that 'if I had as many lives as a cat, I should leave no corner unexplored'. Like Darwin, Huxley studied medicine, but did not take a degree. Like Darwin, his life was changed by an expedition, in his case to the Torres Straits and Australia between 1846 and 1850, as surgeon on HMS *Rattlesnake*. Huxley became interested in zoology, carrying out research on sea anemones, jellyfish and sea urchins. On his return to Britain, Huxley taught geology as a lecturer at the School of Mines in London. Geology and a concern with evolution led him to palaeontology, studying dinosaurs and the skull of a Neanderthal man. Following a meeting with Herbert Spencer, Huxley was introduced into the circle of the *Westminster Review* and came to write for it regularly, discovering a gift for lucid and vivid popularization. He also gave public lectures on a wide variety of topics, including the famous lecture, 'On a Piece of Chalk', delivered to the working men of Norwich in 1868. Huxley's collected essays and lectures run to nine volumes and include a debate with Matthew Arnold over the relative place in education of literature and science.[136]

Another versatile scientist was Francis Galton, now famous – or notorious – for his advocacy of eugenics. He too began his career as an explorer, in his case in the Middle East and in parts of Southwest Africa previously unknown to Europeans, and he published a book on the art of travel. A cousin of Charles Darwin, Galton was particularly interested in heredity, studying both humans and sweet peas. He was also a mathematician, a statistician, a physical anthropologist who founded an anthropometric laboratory, an experimental psychologist interested in intelligence tests and visual memory, and a meteorologist who discovered and named the anti-cyclone. He also classified fingerprints, building on the work of William James Herschel, son of the polymath John Herschel.[137]

William Henry Fox Talbot offers a spectacular example of a many-sided individual who is known today almost entirely for one form of knowledge and skill, in his case a contribution to the development of photography. Even if he had not invented a camera and written about photography in *The Pencil of Nature* (1844), Talbot would have a secure place in history as a Victorian polymath. He was a distinguished mathematician: 'Talbot's curve' is named after him. After meeting John Herschel, he began working on optics and formulated 'Talbot's law'. Optics led him via the spectroscope to chemistry, demonstrating that the different elements could be identified from their spectra. His interests in optics and chemistry converged on photography, but Talbot's range was wider still. In botany, he identified two new species. He published three papers on astronomy and several on the theory of numbers. He also wrote on etymology and he was one of the first individuals to decipher Assyrian cuneiform texts. Thinking like a natural scientist, he proposed what he called an 'experiment' to test the reliability of translations from these texts, in which a few scholars translated a newly discovered inscription without communicating with one another (happily, their versions did not differ very much). Talbot was also active as a Member of Parliament and his many books include *Thoughts on Moderate Reform in the House of Commons*.[138]

TOWARDS A NEW CRISIS

As the amount of information gradually increased throughout this period, both the idea and the practice of the division of intellectual labour began to gain ground. From the middle of the eighteenth century, specialization, including specialized knowledge, became the subject of public discussion. In 1748, Denis Diderot had already noted the development of specialization in surgery and predicted – correctly – a similar tendency in the case of medicine.[139]

In his lectures on jurisprudence in 1763, Adam Smith preceded his famous discussion of the division of labour in the *Wealth of Nations* by remarks on intellectual work, remarking that 'Philosophy' (meaning what we call 'science') 'becomes a separate trade and in time like all others, subdivided into various provinces' or into 'a great number of branches, each of which affords occupation to a peculiar tribe or class of philosophers'. One might have thought that Smith was being sarcastic, but he continued by remarking that 'Each individual becomes more expert in his own peculiar branch, more work is done upon the whole, and the quantity of science is considerably increased by it.'[140]

Immanuel Kant, writing in 1785, agreed with Smith about the division of labour in general and also about philosophy, especially the division between empirical and rational approaches. According to Kant, it was worth asking 'whether pure philosophy in all its parts does not require each its particular man, and whether it would not stand better with the learned trade as a whole if those who, catering to the taste of the public, are accustomed to sell the empirical along with the rational, mixed in all sorts of proportions unknown even to themselves, if they were warned not to carry on simultaneously two enterprises that are very different in their mode of treatment, each of which perhaps requires a particular talent, and the combination of which in a single person produces only bunglers.'[141]

In England, Charles Babbage, despite his own wide range of interests, welcomed what he called the division of 'mental labour'.[142] Again, a major theme in Herbert Spencer's theory of society was the tendency towards specialization, or 'differentiation', which according to him contributed to progress or social 'evolution'.[143] Other English scholars were less happy with the tendency. The polymath William Whewell was particularly eloquent, noting 'an increasing proclivity of separation and dismemberment' among the sciences. 'The mathematician turns away from the chemist; the chemist from the naturalist; the mathematician, left to himself, divides himself into a pure mathematician and a mixed mathematician, who soon part company,' and so on.[144] Adopting a political metaphor that has often been employed since his time, Whewell expressed his fear that what he called the 'commonwealth of science' might disintegrate like 'a great empire falling to pieces'.[145]

Specialization was encouraged by the foundation of new institutions. In France, for instance, the old regime of non-specialized regional academies gave way in the nineteenth century to local agricultural, archaeological, antiquarian and scientific societies. In Paris, the Académie Celtique (founded in 1804) was followed by the Société Asiatique and the Société de Géographie (both founded in 1821), the Société Géologique (1830), the Société Anthropologique (1832), the Société Ethnologique (1839) and the Société d'Économie Politique (1842). In Berlin, new foundations included the Society for German Language and Antiquities (1815), the Geography Society (1828), the Physics Society (1845), the Geological Society (1848) and the Anthropology Society (1869).[146]

In London, the foundation of the Geological Society (1807) was followed by the Astronomical Society (1820) and the Royal Society of Literature (both 1820), the Political Economy Club (1821), the Royal Asiatic Society (1823), the Zoological Society (1826), the Entomological Society (1833), the Botanical Society (1833) and the Ethnological

Society (1843). Joseph Banks, President of the Royal Society of London, found a vivid metaphor for fragmentation in his comment on this trend, writing that 'I see plainly that all these new-fangled Associations will finally dismantle the Royal Society, and not leave the Old Lady a rag to cover her'.[147]

In France, Comte expressed ambivalence. He believed that the price of specialization was an inability to see what he called 'the spirit of the whole', but also that specialization was necessary to progress and that a group would emerge who would specialize in generalities. The story told in the following chapter suggests that Comte was right on all three counts.

5

THE AGE OF TERRITORIALITY
1850–2000

By the late nineteenth century, the cultural climate was becoming less favourable to wide-ranging scholars. As we have seen, a few monsters of erudition, notably Athanasius Kircher and Olof Rudbeck, had been criticized for excessive ambition in the seventeenth century, but such criticisms became more and more frequent in the nineteenth.

POLYMATHS IN A COLD CLIMATE

Alexander von Humboldt, for instance, was criticized by his friend Friedrich Schiller because he 'dabbled in too many subjects', while Humboldt himself complained that 'people often say that I'm curious about too many things at once'.[1] It was said of William Whewell (by the wit Sidney Smith) that 'omniscience is his foible'. The essayist William Hazlitt wrote of Coleridge that 'There is no subject on which he has not touched,' but also 'none on which he has rested'.[2] Coleridge featured in the novelist Thomas Peacock's satirical novel *Headlong Hall* (1816) as 'Mr Panscope', who 'had run through the whole circle of the sciences, and understood them all equally well'.

Thomas Young was another polymath who was criticized for attempting too much. An Italian scholar wrote to Young about the 'universal regret that your versatility is so widely engaged in the sciences . . . that you are unable to press on with your discoveries and bring them to that pitch of perfection which we have the right to expect from a man of your conspicuous talents'. On his death the President of the Royal

Society combined praise of Young's achievements with the warning that the Society 'rather recommends the concentration of research within the limits of some defined portion of science, than the endeavour to embrace the whole'.[3]

Another sign of change in the intellectual climate was the shift in the meaning of the term *dilettante*. When it was coined (in Italian, spreading to English by the eighteenth century), the word was positive, meaning someone who 'delighted' in something, just as the French term *amateur* originally referred to anyone who 'loved' art or learning. In the course of the nineteenth century, these terms became pejorative, denoting not enthusiasm but the superficial understanding associated with non-specialists. For example, Georg Waitz, a specialist on medieval Germany, criticized what he called *Dilettantismus* in the first number of the first journal for professional historians, the *Historische Zeitschrift* (1859). In similar fashion, Goethe's studies of the natural science were dismissed by a leading German physiologist, Emil Dubois-Reymond, as the pastime (*Spielerei*) of 'a self-taught dilettante'.[4]

OVERLOAD

Why was the climate changing? In a word, 'overload'. As in the seventeenth century, there was an explosion of knowledge, in the double sense of expansion and fragmentation. The invention of the steam press, together with the use of cheaper paper made from wood pulp, reduced the price of books and journals and so encouraged them to proliferate, leading to what has been called the 'second revolution of the book' or 'the flood of cheap print'.[5] The popularization of knowledge, especially scientific knowledge, was increasingly important at this time.[6] One of the British polymaths mentioned in the previous chapter, Thomas De Quincey, vividly expressed his anxiety in a vision or nightmare about 'a procession of carts and wagons' that kept unloading piles of books outside his house.[7]

Overload was not simply the result of cheap print. More knowledge was being produced, thanks to research that included experiments in physics and chemistry; the observation and description of an increasing variety of rocks, plants and animals; and historical research in the official archives that were gradually opening to the public. New stars and new elements were among the many discoveries of this period, thanks to more powerful telescopes and microscopes. Scientific expeditions, many of them funded by governments for strategic and economic purposes, brought back thousands of mineral, botanical and zoological specimens and vastly increased western knowledge of other parts of the world, notably Africa, Oceania and the Arctic – their natural resources, their peoples and their languages.[8]

Academic knowledge was not the only kind of knowledge to expand in this way. A 'revolution in government' was taking place in the nineteenth century, the rise of the 'information state' in which the systematic collection of data, often by means of surveys, preceded important decisions.[9] Much of the data collected took the form of statistics and a good deal of it was published. There was an 'avalanche of printed numbers' in this period, much of it generated by bureaucracies.[10]

The rise of empires – the British in India, the French in North Africa, the Belgians in the Congo and so on – made it necessary for the rulers and their officials to learn something about the geography, the resources and the peoples under their rule. Territories were surveyed and mapped and reports were written about the propensity of their inhabitants to obey or rebel against the imperial regimes.[11] At home, police forces were accumulating more and more information. In 1879 the British Criminal Investigation Department, the CID, dealt with more than 40,000 official letters and special reports.[12] Business gradually followed the model of government, with American railways in the lead, increasing the demand for information, first of all in order to avoid accidents and later, like other companies, to manage an expanding enterprise.[13]

All this information had to be organized. In the seventeenth century, as we have seen, one response to the first crisis of knowledge was to develop new methods of taking and filing notes. In the eighteenth century, reference books on an increasing variety of subjects proliferated, books that were designed to be consulted or skimmed rather than read. There were so many of them that a dictionary of these dictionaries was published in 1758.[14]

Writing in 1819, the Scottish polymath Francis Jeffrey, editor of the famous *Edinburgh Review*, expressed the fear that 'if we continue to write and rhyme at the present rate for 200 years longer, there must be some new art of *short-hand reading* invented – or all reading will be given up in despair'.[15]

In the later nineteenth century the German polymath Hermann von Helmholtz noted improvements in what he called 'appliances', such as 'catalogues, lexicons, registers, indexes, digests', that made knowledge 'immediately accessible'.[16] He may have been thinking of the card indexes pioneered by the polymath–librarian Melvil Dewey, whose standardized cards appealed not only to other librarians but also to scholars and businesses ('Card indexing has become nowadays an essential requirement of modern business').[17] Helmholtz may also have been thinking of the filing cabinet, first produced in 1875, a piece of furniture that came to take up more and more space in offices and libraries.

SPECIALIZATION

The principal response to this explosion of knowledge was to specialize, thus reducing the amount of information that needed to be mastered. Specialization may be regarded as a kind of defence mechanism, a dyke against the deluge of information. In 1979 a distinguished American historian noted the need for what he called 'a still unwritten general history of specialization'.[18] The gap has not yet been filled, perhaps because writing such a general history would itself require a team of specialists. All that can be offered here is a brief summary. The early stages of the process were noted in the previous chapter, but the trend became more and more powerful between the 1850s and the millennium.

New words once again reveal the consciousness of the problem. As we have seen, the term 'scientist' was coined in the 1830s, an early sign of a growing split between men of letters and investigators of nature. In France in the 1830s and 1840s the term *spécialité* came into use, followed by *spécialiste*, once again in a medical context, in 1848. It was, paradoxically, the polymath Auguste Comte who coined the abstract noun *spécialisation*.[19] In English, the term 'specialist' is first recorded in 1856, 'specialism' in the same year and 'specialization' in 1865. New words were necessary to describe new trends.

The debate initiated by Kant and Adam Smith continued to reverberate. On one side, the sociologist Émile Durkheim argued that the division of labour made society more cohesive because it made individuals more dependent on one another. Despite the breadth of his own interests, Durkheim extended his praise of the division of labour to the academic world and held a 'consistently positive view of disciplinary specialization'.[20] He supported specialization in sociology itself, on the grounds that it allowed the study of society, all too often 'a form of philosophical speculation', to become more precise and more objective.[21]

On the other side, Karl Marx's vision of a future communist society was one where it would be 'possible for me to do one thing today and another tomorrow, to hunt in the morning, fish in the afternoon, rear cattle in the evening, criticize after dinner, just as I have a mind'. William Morris was another critic of a society where the majority of workers were 'always doing one minute piece of work and never being allowed to think of any other'. In his ideal society, an artisan 'shall put his own individual intelligence and enthusiasm into the goods he fashions. So far from his labour being "divided" . . . he must know all about the ware he is making and its relation to similar wares.'[22]

The polymathic social scientist Max Weber expressed his ambivalence in a famous lecture delivered in 1917, *Wissenschaft als Beruf* (a phrase translatable as either 'Science as a Vocation' or 'Learning as a Profession'), in which the lecturer discussed the tension between many-sidedness and specialization.[23] Weber felt this tension himself. It may even have contributed to his nervous breakdown in 1897.

THE DIVISION OF INSTITUTIONS

It is no accident that terms such as 'specialist' were first used in a medical context, since medicine, as Diderot noted in the mid-eighteenth century, was becoming divided into doctors focusing on particular diseases or parts of the body.[24]

Universities, on the other hand, were concerned with knowledge in general. One reason for the survival of the polymath in the age of the man of letters was the relatively unspecialized nature of the western system of higher education at that time. German students, for example, regularly moved from one discipline to another just as they migrated from one university to another before taking their degree. In Scotland, where the first degree was the four-year MA (in contrast to the three-year BA elsewhere in Britain), the traditional curriculum was a general one that included compulsory philosophy.[25] In Cambridge before the 1870s, undergraduates were examined either in classics or mathematics, but there were optional lectures in other disciplines that sometimes led on to informal tuition. Charles Darwin, for instance, who arrived as an eighteen-year-old student in 1828, plunged into the study of natural history with the help of two professors, John Henslow in botany and Adam Sedgwick in geology.

In the later nineteenth century, however, the example of the medics was followed by the new research universities in Germany, the United States and elsewhere. These institutions were followed in their turn by universities in general, divided into more and more departments in order to accommodate new disciplines.[26]

As an American academic who had studied in Germany noted in the book about German universities that he published in 1874, the German professor 'is not a teacher in the English sense of the term; he is a specialist'.[27] In Germany and the United States in particular, new academic specialties proliferated, often claiming the title of disciplines and taking institutional form in separate departments. The increasing emphasis on research, in other words on original contributions to knowledge, encouraged if it did not force individuals who hoped for an academic career to focus on limited fields. An American classicist who studied in Germany in the 1850s later remembered many seminar topics as 'hopelessly microscopic'.[28]

Declarations of independence became frequent, turning fields into autonomous disciplines. The year 1872, for instance, marks the establishment of both the École Libre des Sciences Politiques in Paris and the chair of Political and Social Sciences at Yale. Émile Durkheim fought passionately, with eventual success, for the autonomy of sociology, with its own object and its own 'right to exist', separate not only from law but also from philosophy and psychology.[29] Experimental psychology became independent from philosophy at the University of Leipzig in 1879, at Johns Hopkins in 1884 and at the University of Geneva in 1891.

Like philosophy, the old discipline of philology, which had been defined in broad cultural and historical terms as late as the mid-nineteenth century, lost territory to rising subjects such as the study of vernacular literatures (German, Romance, Slavic, English and so on). Even in the case of the ancient Greek and Roman world, the rise of classical archaeology and art history reduced the field of the philologists to the study of language.[30]

New disciplines, like some new nations, rapidly fragmented. History was divided into periods (ancient, medieval and modern). It was also divided into economic history, which acquired its own chairs (at Harvard in 1892, for instance) and the history of science (with a chair at the Collège de France, founded in the same year). Geography was divided into physical and human geography, while the latter soon split into economic geography and political geography (otherwise known as 'geopolitics', named in 1899).

In England, the later nineteenth century marks a turning point. At Oxford, after the reform of the university in 1871, it became possible for students to take degrees in modern history, law, theology, mathematics and natural sciences (all from 1872), English literature (1894), modern languages (1903) and so on.[31] The Scots resisted for a time: compromises were reached in 1858, when better students could follow general studies with a course in one discipline for 'honours', and in 1889, when the old general degree coexisted with the alternative of specialized courses.[32]

The frontiers between disciplines became more difficult to cross, producing a landscape of 'academic tribes and territories'.[33] Among the signs of this territorialization of knowledge was the growing use of phrases such as 'my field' or (for historians) 'my period'. Some academics became extremely conscious of the need to defend their fields from competitors. At a meeting of the American Economic Association in 1894, one participant declared that the sociologists 'had no right to stake off for themselves a portion of the field of social science without consulting the economists'.[34]

The fragmentation of knowledge was also encouraged by the development of technical terms, for example in physical anthropology, 'dolicocephalic' (long-headed); in social psychology, 'de-individuation' (loss of self-awareness); in zoology, 'zoosemiotics' (the study of forms of knowing in animals); in anthropology, 'schismogenesis', the process of cultural differentiation. They were useful shorthand for insiders, but incomprehensible jargon for everyone else – creating more definite boundaries between disciplines and also between professionals and amateurs. They were also encouraged by the employment of methods that were not immediately intelligible to the laity.

In the eighteenth century, scientific experiments were still close to everyday observation and could be replicated by amateurs such as Voltaire, who would cut off the heads of snails to see if they grew back like the tails of lizards. Even in the nineteenth century, hands-on science was still available to amateurs, looking through microscopes, hammering rocks, collecting dried plants or using a relatively simple piece of apparatus such as a Bunsen burner. However, scientific progress became increasingly dependent on large and expensive instruments. Amateurs are in no position to replicate the experiments that led to the discovery of the structure of DNA or Higgs' boson in particle physics. As the philosopher Alfred Whitehead observed in the 1920s, 'scientific theory is outrunning common sense'.[35]

In short, the university campus became a kind of archipelago, containing many islands of knowledge, separated from one another by the walls of 'departments', as they were called in Britain, or 'institutes', as they were known in Germany and elsewhere.[36]

MUSEUMS, SOCIETIES, CONGRESSES

Outside the university, knowledge institutions also became increasingly specialized from the later nineteenth century onwards. New museums often confined themselves to a particular field – natural history, for instance, archaeology, anthropology, Asia or even, in the case of a museum in Vienna, 'war economy'. Like academic departments, older museums sometimes fragmented. In London, the Natural History Museum became independent from the British Museum in 1881. Four years later, the Science Museum became independent from the South Kensington Museum (now known as the Victoria and Albert Museum). The British Museum itself was gradually divided into departments such as Prints and Drawings, Coins and Medals, Oriental Antiquities and so on.

The rise of specialized societies at the expense of the Royal Society was noted in the previous chapter. The Royal Society itself was becoming more specialized. Until 1847 it had elected its Fellows in the fields of 'learning and science', including 'archaeologists, numismatists and antiquaries', but after that date the candidates were expected to be natural scientists. In 1887 specialization went further, and the society's *Philosophical Transactions* were divided into two series, known as A (mathematical and physical sciences) and B (biological sciences).[37] It is true that a few archaeologists and anthropologists were still able to join the Royal Society after 1847 (John Lubbock in 1858, Edward Tylor in 1871, Augustus Pitt-Rivers in 1876, Arthur Evans in 1901 and James Frazer in 1920).[38] However, archaeology was regarded as a science at that time, while anthropology, despite the emphasis on culture in the work of Tylor and others, was widely viewed as concerned with the natural history of humans.

At the professional level, interaction with colleagues in other countries was increasing, thanks to the rise of the international congress in the later nineteenth century, made possible by the spread of the railway network in Europe. These congresses were usually confined to a particular discipline. For example, the first international congress of anthropology and prehistoric archaeology was held in 1865, followed by the geographers in 1871, the orientalists in 1873 and the art historians in the same year. Some congresses were even devoted to sub-disciplines such as 'criminal anthropology' (first congress, 1885) or dermatology (1889). These congresses surely helped forge specialist identities by making individuals more aware of colleagues with similar interests.[39]

JOURNALS

If the early nineteenth century was the great age of journals concerned with general knowledge, such as the *Edinburgh Review* or the *Revue des Deux Mondes*, the late nineteenth century was the age of the specialized academic journal. It has been suggested that one reason why the *Revue des Deux Mondes* lost subscribers after the 1870s was that specialized journals began competing with it for readers.[40] Famous examples in their various fields include the German *Historische Zeitschrift* (1859), the *Revue Historique* and the *Revue Philosophique* in France (both 1876), the British philosophical journal *Mind* (1876), the *American Journal of Philology* (1880), the *Political Science Quarterly* (1886), the *Quarterly Journal of Economics* (1887), the *Annales de Géographie* (1891), the *Année Psychologique* (1894), the *American Journal of Sociology* (1895) and the *Année Sociologique* (1898).

In the natural sciences, the development of specialization went further and faster. Disciplinary periodicals such as the *Journal de Physique* (1872) or the *American Journal of Mathematics* (1878) were soon joined by sub-disciplinary ones such as the *Zeitschrift für physiologische Chemie* (1877), *Beiträge zur Geophysik* (1887) and the *Journal of Tropical Medicine* (1898). The rapid differentiation of scientific journals in the 1880s and 1890s has been noted. It has been estimated that there were already 1,258 such journals in existence by the year 1900.[41]

In order to make an original 'contribution to knowledge', articles in these journals had to become increasingly specialized, while their language became more technical. A comparison between issues of the same journal, such as the *American Journal of Sociology*, when it was founded in 1895 and a hundred years later, reveals this process at work. The 1895 volume included articles such as 'The Relation of Anthropology to the Study of History', 'Business Men and Social Theorists' and 'Local Alliances'. In the 1995 volume we find 'Statistical Methods for Comparing Regression Coefficients between Models', 'Shifting Currents in Critical Sociology of Education' and 'Social Capital and the Control of Right-Wing Extremism among East and West Berlin Youth'.

TWO CULTURES

In a famous – or notorious – lecture delivered in Cambridge in 1959, the physical chemist turned novelist C. P. Snow distinguished between what he called the 'two cultures' of the natural sciences and the humanities. He lamented the fact that by the middle of the twentieth century, a formerly unified intellectual culture had split, that the two groups had 'almost ceased to communicate', and that educated individuals on the humanities side lacked even a superficial knowledge of science.[42]

The debate that followed Snow's lecture, and that was renewed much later, should not be understood in a parochial way as merely part of the history of the University of Cambridge, or even as part of the history of English culture in the middle of the twentieth century. As became obvious from later comments on Snow's thesis in Germany, The Netherlands, Italy, Sweden and elsewhere, the Cambridge debate was simply a local example of a much more general phenomenon.[43]

Today, nearly seventy years after the original lecture, it may seem odd that the lecturer noted a division into no more than two cultures. A third culture, 'social science', has often been mentioned (originally by Snow himself), while the assumption that all scientists (or all scholars in the humanities) form a single culture now seems extremely questionable. Fragmentation was already visible in the nineteenth century, as the examples of societies, congresses and journals suggest, and it has gone much further since the 1950s.

In a famous study of nineteenth-century nationalism, Benedict Anderson launched the phrase 'imagined community', presenting the nation as one such community, held together by the national press, since individuals not only read the same news at the same time as their compatriots but were aware of doing so.[44] If reading a particular journal regularly and knowing that others do so too, like joining a society or attending an international congress, helps form an 'imagined community', such disciplinary communities have proliferated at the expense of the old Republic of Letters and the later Commonwealth of Science.

TEAMWORK

In order to manage increasing amounts of information and turn them into knowledge, the labours of individual scholars were increasingly supplemented by those of teams, as in the case of scientific expeditions, encyclopaedias, laboratories and observatories.

More and more scientific expeditions were launched from the later eighteenth century onwards, and scholars who joined these expeditions were often chosen on the basis of specialist qualifications. On his expedition to the Pacific in 1785, for instance, the Comte de La Pérouse took ten specialists, including an astronomer, a geologist, a botanist, a physicist and three naturalists. When Nicolas Baudin was sent by the French government on an expedition to Australia in 1800, for research on geography (especially hydrography) and natural history, he set out with 'three botanists, five zoologists, two mineralogists . . . two astronomers and two geographers', although he lost some of these researchers on the way.[45] The more specialized British expedition on *The Challenger* (1872–6), concerned with the depths of the ocean, included two marine biologists, two naturalists and a chemist.

As was noted earlier, the famous French *Encyclopédie* (1751–72), edited by Jean d'Alembert and Denis Diderot, drew on the knowledges of at least 139 individuals.[46] The multiplication of contributors has continued ever since. The famous eleventh edition of the *Encyclopedia Britannica*, for instance, published in 1911, called on the expertise of 1,507 contributors, while by 1937 the *Enciclopedia Italiana* had 3,272.[47] In the age of Wikipedia, even these numbers have come to seem tiny.

Teamwork was not confined to expeditions and encyclopaedias. By the beginning of the twentieth century, it was already a feature of 'Big Science' (*Grosswissenschaft*), especially in Germany. The chemist Emil Fischer complained in 1902 that the 'mass production methods which dominate modern economic life have also penetrated experimental science'. In Russia at the same time, Ivan Pavlov's physiology laboratory, in which about a hundred people worked, was compared to a factory.[48]

The division of labour has gone much further since that time, as the increasing number of names attached to scientific papers testify.

The social sciences were moving in a similar direction. In France around the year 1900, Durkheim advocated teamwork (*travail en commun*) and established the practice in the group of sociologists that he led.[49] In the case of history, Lucien Febvre advocated teamwork in the 1930s, at least in the weak sense of individuals agreeing to study similar problems and ask similar questions, while carrying out research and writing up the results by themselves. Today, this form of teamwork has become common in the humanities, driven by the need to attract grants from bodies such as the European Science Foundation, with rules requiring a given project to include scholars from a number of different countries.

THE DEPARTMENTALIZATION OF THE UNIVERSITIES

Even more important, since it affected many more people and at a younger, more impressionable age, was the trend towards the increasing specialization of university teaching. In early modern universities, as in medieval ones, a division of intellectual labour already existed, especially in the graduate faculties of theology, law and medicine. Within these faculties, new chairs were founded, mainly in the seventeenth and eighteenth centuries. Professors of Hebrew joined faculties of theology, professors of natural law joined the lawyers, while the faculty of medicine came to include professors of pharmacology and 'iatrochemistry' (in other words, chemistry for medical purposes).

The arts faculty traditionally offered a more general education. It was this faculty, later known as the faculty of philosophy, which saw most changes. One specialist chair was 'practical philosophy', including ethics, politics and 'economics' in the sense of the management of a household. Ethics (or 'moral philosophy') had its own chair in some places, and so did politics (or 'political philosophy'), and finally, in the eighteenth century, 'political economy', known today as 'economics'. Natural philosophy, now known as the 'natural sciences', became independent from philosophy in general and then split into specialties such as chemistry and natural history. In its turn, natural history came to be subdivided into geology, botany and finally zoology. The trend continued in the early nineteenth century. For example, chairs of mineralogy were established in Moscow, Cambridge and Montpellier between 1804 and 1809. At the University of Berlin, chairs of *Germanistik* (German language and literature), geography, Sanskrit, medical history and art history were all founded before 1850.

EXPLAINING SPECIALIZATION

A specialist in the history of education has identified an 'iron law' of specialization.[50] Why was there such a powerful – and some would say, irresistible – trend in this direction at this time? It is surely an oversimplification to account for the process in terms of one element alone, the explosion of knowledge. Several different answers, or kinds of answer, can be given and indeed have been given to this question, each offering its own insights.

Sociologists, for example, have argued that 'internal differentiation' into different specialties led to the emergence of a system of disciplines.[51] Behind this approach to the history of knowledge stands the Victorian polymath Herbert Spencer, who famously argued that societies and their institutions evolved from homogeneity to heterogeneity by a process of differentiation. The use of the term 'evolved' makes the process seem at once inevitable, irresistible and impersonal.

A second answer has been given by historians, noting that the trend was particularly strong in certain periods. It was the expansion of higher education in Europe and the United States that made specialization possible. One study speaks of the emergence of a 'mass market for education' around the year 1800, while others date expansion to the second half of the nineteenth century.[52] In France, the population of university students grew rapidly between 1876 and 1914, especially in faculties of letters.[53] In Germany, it grew even more rapidly, from 20,000 in 1871 to 68,000 in 1910.[54]

Increasing the size of departments allowed a greater variety of specialized courses. At Harvard University in 1870, for instance, '32 professors taught 73 courses; by 1910, 169 professors taught 401 courses'.[55] Expansion was sometimes rapid: the Faculty of Letters at the Sorbonne had about 120 students in 1887, but by 1902 (following the opening of new buildings) the number of students had risen to 1,830.[56] Looking back from the 1990s, it has been suggested that 'The runaway expansion of the university system worldwide ... created a structural pressure for increased specialization simply because scholars were in search of niches.'[57]

A third explanation of specialization brings people – individuals and groups – into the story. For students and scholars alike, specialization allowed them to keep their heads above water in the flood of information. For ambitious professors or would-be professors, working in a competitive environment, the creation of new specialties was a form of what Pierre Bourdieu famously called 'distinction'.[58] Market researchers speak of 'product differentiation' as a means to success in the struggle for market share. The ideal was to find a new problem, turn it into a sub-field and then into an autonomous discipline.

SPECIALIZATION BECOMES THE PROBLEM

Specialization was a response to the problem of overload, but it was sooner or later perceived as a problem in itself. Hence the rise of a movement aimed at restoring the lost unity of knowledge. In 1864 the polymath scientist Lothar Meyer declared the need to reunite 'the now severed sciences'. This ideal attracted a number of twentieth-century polymaths, examples of the hedgehog, among them the Scotsman Patrick Geddes, the Belgian Paul Otlet and the Austrian Otto Neurath. It is surely significant that all three turned to diagrams and other visual aids that allow the viewer to absorb in a moment information that might take several minutes to read when presented in words.

Geddes liked to use the word 'synoptic', and his ambition to see the whole was expressed by his reconstruction of the Outlook Tower in Edinburgh as a museum in which visitors could see the relation between Edinburgh, Scotland, Europe and the world. It offered a general view of knowledge in visual form. Otlet's desire to classify knowledge included a project for a storehouse of images. Neurath developed what he called an 'International System of Typographic Picture Education' (ISOTYPE).

Geddes described himself as 'a comprehensive, synthesizing gener-alist' and was described by a contemporary as someone who 'specialized in omniscience'.[59] He began his career as a biologist but discovered soci-ology by reading the work of an earlier polymath, Frédéric Le Play. Although he never took an academic degree, Geddes became a professor of botany at the University of Dundee. He was described by an acquaint-ance as 'a most unsettling person, talking, talking, talking – about anything and everything'.[60] According to one of his disciples – he was a charismatic figure who attracted disciples – he was 'too integral for the specialists to understand . . . They have to dub him a little mad – or else think that of themselves.'[61] A fellow Scot, the poet 'Hugh MacDiarmid' (Christopher Murray Grieve), declared that Geddes 'knew that water-tight compartments are useful only to a sinking ship, and traversed all the boundaries of separate subjects'.[62]

Geddes began his career in botany, but his eye problems made the use of the microscope impossible and he turned to marine biology. He wrote two books on biology together with one of his students, but, while carrying out research in France, he was diverted into sociology and social reform. His concern with slum improvement in Edinburgh expanded into an interest in town planning, and he moved in 1919 from his chair in botany in Dundee to a chair of 'Civics and Sociology' at the University of Bombay. Geddes would not have seen this step as a big one, since he practised what he called 'bio-sociology', attempting to see the city as a whole, as an organism that was related to its region and gradually evolved.[63]

Like Francis Bacon, the Belgian Paul Otlet took the whole of knowl-edge as his province. Trained as a lawyer, he is often described as a bibli-ographer, and he did indeed plan a universal bibliography stored on index cards. He was also what he called a 'documentalist', using micro-fiches (a technology that became available in the 1920s) for storing and retrieving documents and planning an encyclopaedia stored on micro-film that would be accessible from anywhere. To hold this archive he founded what he called the Mundaneum, an institution in Brussels that still exists, though not on the original site.

Otlet has been described, like the eighteenth-century collector Hans Sloane, as a man who tried to classify and catalogue the world.[64] His schemes for information retrieval were part of a wider vision that included world peace and world government. In this respect Otlet resembles Comenius and other adepts of *pansophia*. So does Geddes, who shared Otlet's views on peace and corresponded with him. Even if Otlet's political dreams remain unrealized, his technological dream came true following the digital revolution. What he called his *réseau mondial*, and his contemporary H. G. Wells, the English pioneer of science fiction, called the 'nervous network' of a 'world brain', became reality in the World Wide Web. If Tim Berners-Lee is the father of the web, we might say that Paul Otlet was one of its grandfathers.

Otto Neurath's life work was to restore the 'unity of science', as he called it, after taking refuge in Britain in 1940 (earlier, writing in German, he had referred to *Einheitswissenschaft* and included sociology and psychology as well as the natural sciences). People who met him remarked on Neurath's 'all-embracing knowledge', and also on his bookshelves, 'filled with works by scientists, philosophers, poets, fathers of the church'.[65] He 'estimated that on the average he read two books a day'.[66]

While writing a thesis on the economic history of the ancient world, Neurath was also editing the works of a German Romantic poet. He was active in politics (a member of the short-lived Bavarian Soviet in 1919), as a philosopher (a member of the famous Vienna Circle); as an economist, particularly interested in war economics; as an empirical sociologist, interested in housing; as a museum curator; and as a theorist of the social sciences. He was the inventor of a cable railway and 'an aiming-device for aircraft' at the time of the First World War.

Neurath is best known as an organizer, founding an institute and a journal, arranging congresses and editing an encyclopaedia.[67] He shared Otlet's vision of international co-operation and indeed briefly co-operated with him, opening a branch of the Mundaneum in The Hague.[68] He was conscious of the place of his movement in an intellectual tradition. His *Encyclopedia*, he once wrote, 'continues the work of the famous French *Encyclopédie*'.[69] The tradition included Comenius, who also believed in the use of pictures in education. Indeed, Neurath's crusade for the unity of science is rather like an adaptation of the vision of *pansophia* to the world of the twentieth century, placing more emphasis on organizations.

THE SURVIVAL OF THE POLYMATH

How did polymaths survive in the new world of specialists, departments and teams? One role that was open to them was to fight for the unity of science, like Geddes, Otlet and Neurath. Another was to become a generalist, in other words, paradoxically enough, a specialist whose role was to correct the increasing narrowness or myopia of other specialists.

Take the case of the American Lewis Mumford. A follower – at least for a time – of Geddes (after whom he christened his son), Mumford also described himself as a 'generalist', whose 'Master' Geddes had 'saved' him 'from becoming "just another specialist"'.[70] His friend the writer Van Wyck Brooks regarded Mumford as a hedgehog, declaring that 'Lewis was one of the few men who have not *ideas* but *an idea*, and he was to spend his life working this out'.[71]

As a young man, Mumford studied geology, economics and anthropology, besides the disciplines to which he later contributed, literature, architecture, history and sociology. Later in life, when students at Dartmouth College asked Mumford about his field, he replied that he was *Professor der Allerlei Wissenschaften* – 'Professor of Things in General'. Appropriately, Mumford loved bridges. He wrote a play about Brooklyn Bridge, and another about Leonardo da Vinci. 'Only by forfeiting the detail can the general pattern be seen,' he explained, reassembling fragments that had been separated 'because specialists abide too rigorously by a gentleman's agreement not to invade each other's territory'.[72] Again, 'The generalist has a special office, that of bringing together widely separated fields, prudently fenced in by specialists, into a larger common area, visible only from the air' (or, one might add, from Geddes' Outlook Tower).[73]

Mumford, who has been described as 'America's last man of letters', was a serial polymath who began his career as a literary critic.[74] From literary criticism, including a book on Herman Melville, he turned to architectural criticism and so to the roles of cultural critic (like Ruskin, another of his heroes) and public intellectual.

Mumford had once hoped to become an engineer and continued to take an interest in technology, publishing *Technics and Civilization* (1934). His interest in architecture and his love of New York led Mumford to the study of cities and so to the social and technological changes that had transformed them over the centuries – in Mumford's view, for the worse – at least since the Industrial Revolution. In this way he combined an interdisciplinary approach, architectural, historical and sociological, with a concentration on a single (large) object of study, producing *The Culture of Cities* (1938) and *The City in History* (1961), which is surely his masterpiece.

PASSIVE POLYMATHS

Distinctions were drawn earlier between three types of polymath, passive, clustered and serial. These distinctions became clearer than before in the age of territoriality.

H. G. Wells, Aldous Huxley and Jorge Luis Borges are remembered as creative writers, but they were also passive polymaths. Wells used to read encyclopaedias in his youth while working in a draper's shop, and in later life planned an encyclopaedia in which he would contribute 'the plan and prefaces'.[75] Huxley and Borges (curiously enough, both of them individuals with weak eyesight) read the *Encyclopaedia Britannica* (like William Whewell earlier) rather than merely consulting it.

Huxley carried volumes of the *Britannica* on journeys in a special case, while Bertrand Russell remarked that it was always easy to discover which volume Aldous was reading, because his conversation would revolve around topics beginning with a particular letter of the alphabet.[76] Huxley used to write for periodicals such as *The Athenaeum* and *Harper's*, the equivalents of the famous nineteenth-century reviews that were discussed earlier. His articles ranged over a wide variety of topics – art, literature, philosophy, politics, psychology, music, sociology, religion and so on. He described his essays as 'moderately erudite, but not pedantic, as I don't know enough to do the professor stunt with confidence'. He later declared that 'By profession I am an essayist who sometimes writes novels and biographies.'[77] Huxley also appeared on 'The Brains Trust', a BBC programme of the 1940s and 1950s in which a group of intellectuals answered questions from the public. 'Few figures in the twentieth century have so insistently laid claim to the title of "polymath".'[78]

Borges told an interviewer that 'As a youngster, I used to come here to the library [the Biblioteca Nacional, Buenos Aires] quite frequently, and since I was very shy and didn't dare ask the librarian for books, I would take a volume of the *Britannica*, any volume, from the shelf myself . . . and read it.'[79] Borges had a love affair with encyclopaedias, not only reading them but also writing about them, as in the famous case of the imaginary Chinese encyclopaedia described in his essay on the seventeenth-century English polymath John Wilkins.

Borges might be considered an equivalent of Huxley in the Spanish-speaking world, combining his fiction with essays and reviews on a great variety of topics.[80] Indeed, if he had died in 1940, at the age of forty-one, Borges would be remembered today only as a poet and as an essayist (with five volumes of essays already published at that time). He described himself at the age of forty-seven, travelling 'up and down Argentina and Uruguay, lecturing on Swedenborg, Blake, the Persian and Chinese mystics, Buddhism, *gauchesco* poetry, Martin Buber, the Kabbalah, the *Arabian Nights*, T. E. Lawrence, medieval Germanic poetry, the Icelandic sagas, Heine, Dante, expressionism and Cervantes'.[81] The range of topics seems almost unbelievable.

The major interests of Borges – philosophy, language, mathematics, history, orientalism and the occult – surface in his fiction, which often deals with epistemological questions, notably the relation between representation and reality, the problem of classifying knowledge (approached via the Chinese encyclopaedia), and the method of 'abduction' (a particular kind of inference associated with the polymath Charles Peirce) in 'The Garden of the Forking Paths'. The stories are especially concerned with the idea of total knowledge. The library of Babel is infinite, Funes remembers everything, and a map is described as the same size as the territory it represents.[82]

CRITICS

In the twentieth century, as in the nineteenth, a number of polymaths became cultural critics. Among the leading players of this role were Johan Huizinga, José Ortega y Gasset, Edmund Wilson, George Steiner, Susan Sontag and Umberto Eco. Let us focus for a moment on Steiner and Sontag (Eco will make his appearance later).

George Steiner has been described as 'the best generalist reviewer of books since Edmund Wilson'.[83] He has also been called 'a late, late, late Renaissance man' and 'This monster who knows everything' (Boerhaave's metaphor remains current).[84] Steiner spent some formative years at the University of Chicago, taking courses in physics, chemistry, biology, anthropology, literature and philosophy and discovering Heidegger by listening to a lecture by Leo Strauss. He has written about philosophy, theology, linguistics, history and chess as well as trying his hand at fiction. Much of his work consists of essays originally published in the *New Yorker* and other journals.

Steiner has played the role of a cultural critic with gusto, denouncing the 'barbarism' of our time and, more constructively, advocating the extension of the idea of cultural literacy to include the sciences as well as the arts.[85] He has described himself as engaged in intellectual 'border-crossing' and offers an especially vigorous critique of specialization, which according to him 'has reached moronic vehemence'.[86] Despite the variety of topics on which he has expressed opinions, at times with over-confidence, his reputation rests most firmly on his studies in comparative literature, especially European literature of the nineteenth and twentieth centuries.

The hat of a cultural critic also fits Susan Sontag, who built up a library of 10,000 books and was described by a friend as 'an intellectual marathon runner, always trying to better her time'. She once declared that 'I do not want to be a professor and I do not want to be a journalist. I want to be a writer who is also an intellectual.'[87] As a child, Sontag 'used to like to read encyclopaedias'.[88] Like Steiner, she enrolled at the University of Chicago, attracted by the interdisciplinary 'core curriculum' (discussed in chapter 8), and studying science as well as philosophy and literature. When she married Philip Rieff, she worked with him on *Freud: The Mind of the Moralist* (1959). She registered as a graduate student in English literature at Harvard but became a teaching assistant in philosophy. She went to Paris to study contemporary philosophy but spent much of her time at the cinema.

Sontag wrote novels and plays and directed two films, but she confessed to an 'addiction' to essay writing as well as to smoking. In fact, she produced no fewer than nine collections of essays, including *Against Interpretation* (1966), *On Photography* (1977) and *Illness as Metaphor* (1978). Like Steiner, she became a cultural critic – unafraid, when still in her thirties, to offer confident generalizations and to point out the weak points of celebrated figures such as Ingmar Bergman ('callow pseudo-intellectuality'), Georg Lukács ('crude') and C. P. Snow ('shallow knowledge of the arts').[89] Her interests took a political turn from 1968 onwards with visits to North Vietnam and Cuba. She first supported the Left but later criticized it. Her comments on 9/11 took an unpopular line, refusing to call the terrorists 'cowards' and viewing them as responding to US foreign policy.

Sontag's essays concentrated on the arts and humanities, ranging over painting (from Mannerism to modern art), literature, theatre, dance, philosophy, psychoanalysis, anthropology, history and especially photography and film, an area in which she became an expert.[90] Her greatest achievement was probably to construct bridges between two cultures, not the sciences and the humanities this time but between 'high' and 'low' culture, confessing an interest in 'David Bowie and Diderot' and giving interviews to both *Rolling Stone* and *Tel Quel*.[91]

CLUSTERED POLYMATHS

Some polymaths may be described as 'clustered' in the sense that their achievements are concentrated in related fields, following what the polymath Donald T. Campbell, a critic of 'the ethnocentrism of disciplines', called the 'fish-scale model' of overlapping enterprises.[92] Where generalists such as Patrick Geddes and Otto Neurath built bridges between distant disciplines, the clustered polymaths built bridges that were shorter but carried more traffic. The transfer and domestication of concepts between neighbouring disciplines is at once less difficult and less spectacular than transfers between distant ones, but, because it is more frequent, it has probably played a more important role in the history of knowledge.

Max Weber, often described, like Durkheim, as one of the 'founding fathers' of sociology, once quipped that 'I now happen to be a sociologist according to my appointment papers'.[93] He began his career as a historian and his thesis on Roman agrarian history impressed the great ancient historian Theodor Mommsen, so much so that he regarded the younger man as his destined successor. Weber also contributed to the disciplines of philosophy, law and economics. He effectively gave up his chair of sociology in 1903 in favour of 'a future career conducted along interdisciplinary lines'.[94] Historians still argue about Weber's explanation of the rise of capitalism; philosophers of social science still discuss his notion of the 'ideal type' or model; and sociologists and political scientists still make use of his categories of traditional, bureaucratic and charismatic rule (Weber borrowed the term 'charisma' from the theologian Rudolf Otto, adapting it to his purposes).

In economics, Kenneth Boulding described himself as 'a fairly pure economist' until 1949 and 'a rather impure social philosopher' after that, explaining that 'The pursuit of any problem in economics always draws me into some other science before I can catch it.' He also declared that there is 'no such thing as economics, only social science applied to economic problems', viewing the economy (like another polymath, Karl Polanyi) as embedded in a larger whole. An Englishman by birth, Boulding was attracted to the University of Michigan because 'Ann Arbor looks like a good place to integrate the social sciences if they are integrable'. Besides economics, Boulding's 40-odd books and 800 articles were concerned with society, knowledge, conflict, peace, the history of the nineteenth and twentieth centuries and what he called 'eco-dynamics'.[95]

The American political scientist Harold Lasswell studied philosophy and economics at the University of Chicago but turned to political science, writing his doctoral dissertation on propaganda during the First World War. He discovered psychoanalysis, was himself analysed, and became widely known for his book *Psychopathology and Politics* (1930). In the course of his career, Lasswell collaborated with a lawyer, a philosopher and a sociologist.[96] The American Council of Learned Societies declared him to be 'master of all the social sciences and a pioneer in each: rambunctiously devoted to breaking down barriers between the social studies, and so acquainting each with the rest; filler-in of interdisciplinary spaces between political science, psychology, philosophy and sociology'.[97] The declaration not only honours Lasswell but also offers a vivid summary of the social role of polymaths.

Still more difficult to classify is Michel Foucault. Although his father, a surgeon, wanted his son to study medicine, Foucault began his career as a philosopher, but developed interests in different kinds of psychology, from experimental psychology to psychoanalysis. His doctoral dissertation, on madness, arose from these interests but led him further afield to the cultural and historical context of changing attitudes to patients. Published in 1961 as *Histoire de la Folie* (*The History of Madness*), it made the author famous.

While he was writing the dissertation, Foucault was teaching French language and literature in Sweden. On his return to France he began to publish studies of writers, including Gustave Flaubert, Alain Robbe-Grillet and Raymond Roussel. In the same year – actually, on the same day – that he published the book on Roussel, in 1963, Foucault also published a better-known book, *The Birth of the Clinic*, finally responding to his father's wish that his son would study medicine, but in a typically unexpected way. The study focused on institutions and on spaces, thus making a contribution to sociology or social geography.

Three years later came Foucault's *Les Mots et les Choses* (*The Order of Things*), a study in intellectual history focused on three disciplines, linguistics, economics and biology. The book began in dramatic fashion with a close analysis of a painting by Velázquez, a first foray into the history of art (Foucault later wrote, but did not publish, a book on Manet). In the 1970s his interests expanded to include law, crime and punishment. He published a dialogue on popular justice with a Marxist intellectual, a study of a nineteenth-century parricide (in collaboration with members of his seminar) and one of his most famous books, *Surveiller et Punir* (*Discipline and Punish*, 1975), which focused on the history of prisons. A year later Foucault published the first volume of an ambitious history of sexuality, *La Volonté de Savoir* (*The History of Sexuality*, 1976), continuing to work on it until his early death but also lecturing on other topics such as governmentality and biopolitics.

Foucault's various interests were in fact connected, with the history of knowledge at their centre. The author described his history of madness as a study of knowledge 'invested' in institutions and his history of prisons as part of the background to the formation of knowledge in modern society. He defended his approach to intellectual history in a book entitled *L'Archéologie du Savoir* (*The Archaeology of Knowledge*, 1969). He discussed the relation between knowledge and power (*savoir* and *pouvoir*) in a famous interview given in 1975 and began his history of sexuality with an essay on the 'will to knowledge'.[98]

NEW DISCIPLINES

Paradoxically enough, the foundation of new disciplines in an age of specialization offered a new role for polymaths, at least in the short term, since a new discipline is necessarily taught in the first generation by professors who have been trained in something else. The discipline needs serial polymaths, nomads in an age of territoriality. It also attracts them, offering the freedom associated with a frontier of knowledge. This kind of opportunity for polymaths comes only once, since the second generation is trained in the new discipline and so reinforces specialization.

A few polymaths have christened new disciplines, successful or unsuccessful. Auguste Comte christened 'sociology', Charles Peirce 'semiotics', Norbert Wiener 'cybernetics', Constantinos Doxiadis 'ekistics', Félix Guattari 'ecosophy', Ray Birdwhistell 'kinesics' and Hans Blumenberg, 'metaphorology'. At the beginning of the twentieth century the development of biometrics, a form of mathematical biology, owed a good deal to a single polymath, Karl Pearson.

Pearson, a disciple of Galton who was appointed to a chair in applied mathematics at University College London in 1884, wrote some important papers on 'mathematical contributions to the theory of evolution'. However, Pearson's interests were much wider. One of his first publications, at the age of twenty-six, was an article on Spinoza's debt to Moses Maimonides, an article that revealed Pearson's knowledge of Hebrew, Latin and Dutch. He was particularly interested in German culture and gave lectures in London on Martin Luther and also, as he remembered later, on Ferdinand Lassalle and Karl Marx 'on Sundays at revolutionary clubs around Soho'. He later became a professor of eugenics.[99]

Polymaths also played an important role in the early development of biochemistry. Linus Pauling, for instance, carried out research in physics and chemistry (for which he won a Nobel Prize) before he turned to molecular biology, a field that the 'knowledge manager' Warren Weaver was supporting in the 1930s. Weaver studied civil engineering and taught mathematics before becoming Director of the Division of Natural Sciences at the Rockefeller Foundation in 1932, where he was appointed in order to launch a new programme on biochemistry 'described at the time as 'vital processes'. Weaver adopted a hands-on approach, approving projects personally and staying at home on Wednesdays so that he could catch up with new publications in the field. Weaver's wide interests inform his collaboration with Claude Shannon on the mathematical theory of communication, his involvement with the Green Revolution in the third world, his work on computer translation and his book, *Lady Luck*, on probability theory.[100]

THE SOCIAL SCIENCES

In the social sciences, which were emerging as autonomous disciplines from the later nineteenth century onwards, the role of polymaths is particularly visible. Some recruits to these new disciplines came from medicine, such as Paolo Mantegazza, who exchanged a chair in pathology at the University of Pavia for one in anthropology. He published articles on a wide range of topics as well as a novel set in the future.[101] His compatriot Giuseppe Pitrè was trained in medicine before becoming a historian of popular traditions and finally, at the age of seventy, professor of 'popular psychology' (*demopsicologia*) at the University of Palermo.[102] A third Italian, Cesare Lombroso, was originally a surgeon who moved into psychology (and parapsychology) before becoming famous as the founder of the anthropology of criminals.[103]

A fourth Italian, Vilfredo Pareto, began his career as a civil engineer, working on the railways. He moved into economics (becoming professor of political economy at Lausanne in 1893), and then into political and social sciences. When he moved disciplines, Pareto took the idea of equilibrium with him, illustrating once again the contribution that serial polymaths can make to innovation.[104] So do the early histories of the disciplines of sociology, psychology and anthropology, and more recently the fields of computer science, general systems and semiotics.

SOCIOLOGY

Sociology, a discipline named by Auguste Comte, owes its emergence to polymaths. In France, Frédéric Le Play, whose book inspired Geddes, was an engineer and a professor of metallurgy before turning to the sociology of the family, or, as he called it, *économie sociale*. In Belgium, Adolphe Quételet began his career as a mathematician but moved into astronomy and meteorology. His interest in the mathematics of probability led him into the study of statistics and so into what he called 'social physics', contributing to anthropometry and to what we call 'criminology'.[105] Much later, the statistical turn in North American sociology was encouraged by the Austrian refugee Paul Lazarsfeld, who was originally an applied mathematician.

One of the most famous sociologists, Émile Durkheim, began his academic career teaching philosophy and education. His rival Gabriel Tarde was a magistrate who became a professor of philosophy at the Collège de France. Tarde was not only the author of a book on social 'laws' such as imitation, but also a criminologist who adopted anthropological and psychological approaches to criminals. Like Mantegazza, Tarde wrote a novel set in the future.[106] In Germany, Georg Simmel, who was, like Durkheim, concerned to establish sociology as an independent discipline, was also known as an individual of 'extensive and many-sided knowledge'.[107] He published essays on a wide variety of subjects that included Rembrandt and Goethe as well as psychology and philosophy.

In the United States, the story is a similar one. Lester Ward, who was appointed professor of sociology at Brown University in 1906, at the age of sixty-five, had worked for the Bureau of Statistics as a librarian and for the US Geological Survey as a botanist, geologist and paleontologist. No wonder, then, that he had the confidence to entitle one of his courses 'A Survey of All Knowledge'.[108]

In Britain, despite the foundation of a department of sociology at the London School of Economics in 1904, the discipline was slow to develop. Hence the German polymath Norbert Elias was able to make a major contribution to this development as late as the 1950s. Elias studied medicine, philosophy, history and psychoanalysis as well as sociology, and all these disciplines shaped his social theory. He knew enough about embryology to discuss the theoretical implications of research carried out by his friend Alfred Glucksmann.[109] From medicine, Elias turned to philosophy, writing a doctoral dissertation on the philosophy of history at the University of Breslau. Moving to Heidelberg, he discovered sociology. As an exile in Britain after Hitler's rise to power, Elias discovered psychoanalysis. His most famous book, *Über den Prozess der Zivilisation* (*The Civilizing Process*, 1939), combined history, psychology and social theory.

Appointed a lecturer in sociology at the University of Leicester in 1954 – at the age of fifty-seven – Elias played a major role in building up the department. He disliked being classified as a historical sociologist, arguing that all sociology should have a historical dimension and criticizing his colleagues for what he called their 'retreat into the present'. Elias also studied society in his own time and he was, above all, an original theorist. He never forgot his medical training, and the relation between the body and society remained an enduring theme in his work, from the early studies of good manners to the later ones on sport. Developing the sociology of knowledge associated with Karl Mannheim (whose assistant he had been at the University of Frankfurt in the early 1930s), Elias analysed the process of specialization and the rise of what he called 'scientific establishments', comparing their rivalry to the competition between firms and nation states.[110]

PSYCHOLOGY

As psychology became independent from philosophy in the later nine-teenth century, it attracted serial polymaths. Wilhelm Wundt, for instance, began his career in medicine and physiology, moving into experimental psychology, a field of which he was one of the founders, and on to philos-ophy and the 'psychology of peoples' (*Völkerpsychologie*).[111] William James, who accused Wundt of aiming to become 'a sort of Napoleon of the intel-lectual world', followed a similar itinerary. James studied medicine at Harvard, becoming an instructor in anatomy and physiology and then founding what is said to be the first laboratory for experimental psychology in the world in 1875. He remains best known as a philosopher and as the author of *Varieties of Religious Experience* (1902).[112]

In France, Gustave Le Bon, who had also been trained in medicine, wrote travel books and popular science before making his reputation in psychology, especially the psychology of crowds, an interest triggered – as in the case of Taine, discussed earlier – by his observations during the Paris Commune of 1871.[113]

The founder of psychoanalysis was another polymath. Freud began his career in the Faculty of Medicine at the University of Vienna, followed by the study of marine biology in Trieste. He turned to physiology, studying the nerve cells of fish. Indeed, for twenty years, Freud 'was primarily a neurologist and anatomist'. His first book, *Aphasia* (1891), has been described as 'a solid contribution to conventional neuro-pathology'.[114] When he moved into psychology and developed the method of psychoanalysis, his genetic approach was inspired by biology. An admirer of Darwin, Freud has been called the 'Darwin of the psyche' and 'the biologist of the mind'.

Freud's interests were not limited to the natural sciences. His classical education left traces on his later work, most obviously in his concept of an 'Oedipus Complex'. He was well read in modern literature and wrote on Shakespeare and other authors. He studied history, including the history of art, and wrote on Leonardo da Vinci and on a case of posses-sion by the devil in the seventeenth century. He collected ancient Egyptian artefacts. He discovered anthropology and published *Totem and Taboo* (1913), discussing what he called 'resemblances between the psychic life of savages and neurotics' (though leading anthropologists such as Franz Boas were not convinced).[115]

ANTHROPOLOGY

The first generation of teachers of anthropology (or ethnology) and writers on the subject came from a broad span of disciplines, including former medics, zoologists, classicists and theologians.

In France, Paul Broca, the founder of the Société d'Anthropologie de Paris, came from medicine and was particularly interested in physical anthropology. On the other hand, Durkheim's nephew and intellectual heir Marcel Mauss was a pioneer of cultural anthropology whose *Essay on the Gift* (1925) remains a fundamental work in that field. Mauss had even wider interests than his uncle. He studied oriental philology and taught both ethnography and the history of religions. He also made studies of law, economics and history. No wonder, then, that his students used to say that Mauss knew everything. He wrote and published relatively little, spending his time learning new things. His reputation rests on a few seminal essays that would have been impossible to write had the author not read so widely.[116] In the United States, Franz Boas, an emigrant from Germany and another pioneer of cultural anthropology, had been active as a geographer and a museum curator before becoming professor of anthropology at Columbia in 1899. His pupils and disciples would become major figures in the new discipline.[117]

The Englishman Alfred Haddon was a zoologist who became interested in the culture of rural western Ireland in the course of his research on sea anemones there. He was invited to join an expedition to the islands of the Torres Straits (now part of Queensland) in 1898 as a zoologist, but there too he studied the local culture. He was appointed a lecturer in ethnology at Cambridge in 1900.[118] Another member of the expedition to the Torres Straits was William Rivers who, encouraged by Haddon, added anthropology to a portfolio of intellectual interests that already included medicine, neurology and psychology. His study *The Todas* (1906) made a major contribution to the ethnography of India.[119]

Another route to anthropology was through classics, as in the case of James Frazer, who became interested in comparative mythology and religion and wrote *The Golden Bough* (1890), thanks to which he is regarded as an ancestor, if not exactly a founder, of social anthropology.[120] Some of the many publications of another classicist (and another Scot), Andrew Lang, were concerned with anthropology and folklore, disciplines that were not yet clearly differentiated at the beginning of the twentieth century. Lang has been described as 'a raider, a free-lance, crossing all men's frontiers'.[121] He wrote on mythology, psychical research and Scottish history.[122] Bronisław Malinowski studied mathematics and physics at Cracow before Frazer's *Golden Bough* inspired him to make his famous anthropological turn. The same book inspired Jack Goody, who began by reading English at Cambridge, to move into anthropology (he later wrote on history and sociology as well).

Like Lang, the most remarkable of the British polymaths involved with anthropology in its early years never held a post in that discipline. William Robertson Smith, another Scot, was for a time the editor-in-chief of the *Encyclopedia Britannica* in the 1880s. A fellow scholar remarked on the 'rare versatility' of his knowledge, while an obituary declared that 'Professor Smith, in the depth and range of his knowledge, had no equal among living men.'[123] Smith's intellectual trajectory went from mathematics to theology and a chair in biblical exegesis in Aberdeen, from which he was removed for 'heresy'. He became Professor of Arabic at Cambridge and published a study on *Kinship and Marriage in Early Arabia* (1885). It was Smith's friendship with Frazer that encouraged the latter's anthropological turn.[124]

COMPUTER SCIENCE

In the middle of the twentieth century a number of polymaths came together in the new and fast-developing field of computers and artificial intelligence. They included, in order of seniority, Norbert Wiener (born in 1894), John von Neumann (1903), Alan Turing (1912) and Claude Shannon (1916). Other polymaths attracted to this field were Herbert Simon, Allen Newell and Marvin Minsky.

Wiener gained a degree in mathematics at the age of fourteen, wrote his Ph.D dissertation on logic and tried out a number of occupations, from engineer to journalist, before settling down as a professor of mathematics at MIT. His research on the automatic aiming of anti-aircraft guns during the Second World War led him into the field that he christened 'cybernetics', participating in the annual conferences on the subject organized by the Macy Foundation from 1946 onwards and exchanging ideas with John von Neumann.[125]

Neumann, another child prodigy in mathematics, went on to study chemistry and to carry out research on hydrodynamics and meteorology. An acquaintance testified that 'von Neumann's mind was all-encompassing. He could solve problems in any domain.'[126] At the Institute of Advanced Study in Princeton, he worked on mathematical economics, including a famous application of game theory to economic behaviour. Making use of computers to assist his calculations, Neumann became interested in improving them, developing what he described as 'an obscene interest' in these machines, including their viruses.[127] From 1946 onwards, he too attended the Macy conferences on the subject.[128]

Claude Shannon graduated from the University of Michigan with two degrees, one in mathematics and the other in electrical engineering, and wrote his Ph.D dissertation on the uses of mathematics in the study of genetics. His article 'A Mathematical Theory of Communication' (1948), which drew in part on the work of Wiener, laid the foundations of information theory. It developed into a book he wrote with Warren Weaver, the 'knowledge manager' discussed earlier, *The Mathematical Theory of Communication*, 1949. Shannon was also an inventor of (among other things) a machine that explained how computers worked.[129]

During the Second World War, Shannon worked on code-breaking. It was in this capacity that he met the only Englishman in this group, Alan Turing, a serial polymath who was in turn a mathematician, philosopher, cryptanalyst, engineer and theoretical biologist. In 1936 Turing invented what he called a 'universal machine', now known as the 'Turing machine', which was able to do the work of all other machines. The most famous episode of Turing's career was during the Second World War, when he was sent to Bletchley Park to assist with breaking the German 'Enigma' code, designing a machine to do so. After the war, before his career came to a tragic end (probably suicide) following his arrest for homosexuality, Turing worked on what he called the 'imitation game', in other words the construction of a computer that would be able to respond to questions in a manner indistinguishable from humans.[130]

The careers of this quartet of extraordinary men illustrate two recurrent themes of this study. One is the attraction of an emerging field of study to individuals with wide interests. The other is the role of the outsider as innovator, examining problems in one discipline with the habit of thought of an individual trained in another.

GENERAL SYSTEMS

Towards the end of his short life, Turing moved into mathematical biology, viewing the analogies between living creatures and machines from the opposite perspective. In similar fashion, working with computers led Neumann to think of the nervous system as digital and so to contribute to the rise of neuroscience. His book *The Computer and the Brain* was published posthumously in 1958.

Among biologists, systems were already a central interest of polymaths such as Lawrence Henderson, Ludwig von Bertalanffy and Anatol Rapoport. Henderson was active as a chemist but is better known for his work in physiology. While working in the chemistry laboratory at Harvard, he attended the seminars in philosophy led by Josiah Royce. Henderson later organized a seminar of his own on the sociology of Vilfredo Pareto and published a book on Pareto written from a physiologist's point of view and discussing the idea of systems across the disciplines.[131]

Biologists, like engineers, form a group that think with, as well as about, systems. The Austrian Ludwig von Bertalanffy, for instance, was both a biologist and a founder of general systems theory. He began his academic career by studying philosophy and art history and wrote his Ph.D dissertation on the work of another polymath, the philosopher–psychologist–physicist Gustav Fechner. Turning to theoretical biology, he adopted a mathematical approach (the 'Bertalanffy equation' describes the growth of an organism in mathematical terms). He went on to contrast the 'closed systems' of physics, subject to the laws of thermodynamics, with the 'open systems' of living things, moving outwards still further to include psychology and the social sciences in his *General Systems Theory* (1969) or GST.[132]

The Russian-American Rapoport was a third scientist of wide interests that included music and psychology but centred, like Bertalanffy's, on mathematical biology, the behavioural sciences and general systems theory (he helped to found the Society for General Systems Research in 1954). He declared himself to be fascinated by what he called 'the fundamental interconnectedness of everything with everything else'.[133]

The polymathic economist Kenneth Boulding dated the birth of GST to Palo Alto in California in 1954, when Bertalanffy, Rapoport, Ralph Gerard and Boulding himself met and realized that they were 'converging on something like General Systems from different directions'.[134]

SEMIOTICS

Semiotics is a crossroads rather than a field or a discipline, so it is particularly appropriate that polymaths have played a large part in the development of this 'science of signs'. They include Charles Peirce, Roman Jakobson, Juri Lotman, Roland Barthes, Charles Morris, Jacob von Uexküll, Thomas Sebeok, Giorgio Prodi and Umberto Eco, an international group who arrived at this destination from some very different points of departure.

Peirce, now best known as a philosopher, studied chemistry and zoology and carried out his own research on gravity and the mathematics of probability. Working on logic, he distinguished a kind of inference that was neither deduction nor induction, and coined the term 'abduction' to describe it. He also studied psychology and economics. Like other polymaths, from Bacon to Comte, Peirce was interested in the classification of the sciences. He studied what he called 'semiotics' from the point of view of a logician, distinguishing between three kinds of sign that he called an 'icon', which resembles its object; an 'index', which is connected to its object; and a symbol.[135]

Roman Jakobson liked to describe himself as 'a Russian philologist', words that are inscribed (in Russian) on his tombstone, but the interests of this polyglot scholar were much wider. Colleagues called him a 'polyhistor' and 'one of the most far-ranging scholars of the 20th century'.[136] If language was at the centre of his interests, there was also plenty of periphery.

Jakobson was a friend of the Russian folklorist Petr Bogatyrev, 'who', so he wrote later, 'initiated me into the delights and arduous tasks of ethnographic field work'.[137] Together they published a seminal article about folklore, comparing and contrasting it with literature. The authors argued that folklore corresponds to what linguists call *langue*, in the sense of a system of resources for speech, whereas literature corresponds to *parole*, a particular selection from those resources.[138] The article offers a typical example of the recurrent use of binary oppositions in Jakobson's work, a legacy of his early study of Hegel's dialectic.[139]

His interest in language also led Jakobson towards psychology, including neuropsychology.[140] He studied the acquisition of language by children and in 1956 published a famous article on aphasia. Jakobson noticed that two types of this impairment of language ran parallel to two well-known figures of speech, metaphor (based on similarity), and metonymy (based on contiguity).[141] This article illustrates once again how serial polymaths can make original contributions to their second or third disciplines by approaching them with the mental habits acquired in their first one.

Jakobson's ideas have made an impact on even more disciplines than the ones to which he contributed in person. The psychoanalyst Jacques Lacan's approach to the unconscious in terms of language was indebted to his work.[142] Claude Lévi-Strauss, who first met Jakobson in New York in 1941 and later collaborated with him, acknowledged a debt to his ideas about the importance of binary oppositions in language. In this way, Jakobson contributed to structuralist anthropology and so to the more general rise of structuralism (a term that he had already used as early as 1929 to refer to an emphasis on the relations between things rather than on things themselves).[143]

Another Russian, Juri Lotman, an admirer of Jakobson who founded the Tartu school of semiotics, coined the term 'semiosphere' to describe a field in which different systems of signs meet. Roland Barthes preferred the term 'semiology' and focused on literature, but also applied this 'structuralist' approach to language, advertising, wrestling, food and especially fashion. Even his account of a visit to Japan presented the author as an observer engaged in reading signs.[144]

The American Charles Morris studied engineering and psychology and took a Ph.D in philosophy before moving into semiotics. He also belonged to the movement for the unity of science. His former student Thomas Sebeok was active as a linguist and an anthropologist before helping to found biosemiotics, a field that owes much to the Estonian aristocrat Jakob von Uexküll. Uexküll was a physiologist, biologist and ecologist who became interested in the way in which different animals perceive their environment (their *Umwelt*, a concept that was taken up by Lotman). He studied living organisms as examples of information processing, since they respond to signs. The Italian Giorgio Prodi, whose principal field was medicine, was another leader in the field of biosemiotics. He was also a friend of Umberto Eco, one of the leading polymaths of recent years, described by Prime Minister Giulio Andreotti as 'a polyhedric personality'.[145]

Eco was a philosopher, a literary critic, a semiotician and an essayist on an extraordinary variety of subjects – serial music, *candomblé*, the Red Brigades, the Middle Ages and so on. The essays, often articles in newspapers such as *L'Espresso*, offered lucid and accessible summaries of difficult subjects for a wide range of readers, and also arguments that often contradicted the conventional wisdom about the individuals and the topics discussed. Like Susan Sontag, Eco bridged the divide between high culture and popular culture, using semiotic theory to write about Superman and James Bond, juxtaposing Heidegger to the sports press and discussing the Middle Ages as evoked both by the French historian Georges Duby and by what Eco called the 'pseudo-medieval pulp' of *Conan the Barbarian*.

Eco followed a mainly academic career, writing a dissertation on the aesthetics of Thomas Aquinas (1954). His friendship with the composer Luciano Berio led him to produce a general study of the avant-garde in the arts and sciences, drawing analogies between different 'disciplinary universes', as he called them. Eco moved from a chair of visual communication at the University of Florence to a chair of semiotics at the University of Bologna. He combined his academic career with work in television, publishing, journalism and finally fiction, beginning with his best-selling novel *The Name of the Rose* (1980), which linked several of the author's interests. It is a murder story in which the detective follows Peirce's method of abduction, it is set in the Middle Ages, and the solution of the mystery depends on the correct reading of a sign.[146]

SIX SERIAL POLYMATHS

More polymaths were active in the twentieth century than can possibly be fitted into this chapter, but it is equally impossible to leave out six individuals whose range is reminiscent of the seventeenth-century 'monsters' who were discussed earlier. In chronological order of birth, they are Pavel Florensky (1882), Michael Polanyi (1891), Joseph Needham (1900), Gregory Bateson (1904), Herbert Simon (1916) and Michel de Certeau (1925).

Pavel Florensky has been described as 'Russia's unknown da Vinci'. After studying mathematics and philosophy at university, he went on to become an Orthodox priest, to lecture on theology and to publish studies in that discipline as well as in philosophy and the history and theory of art. Studying icons, he focused on the representation of space (revealing the habitus of a geometrician). Less predictably, Florensky collected popular songs and carried out research in electrodynamics, describing this as compensation for 'the cultural barrenness' of self-sufficient mathematics. At this time, the 1920s, electrification was a major project of the new Soviet Union and Florensky participated in electrification commissions (addressing one conference on the topic while wearing his cassock, to the surprise of another participant, Leon Trotsky). Even after he had been arrested, in the course of Stalin's purges, Florensky continued to study topics as various as the Orochen language and the production of iodine from seaweed.[147]

Michael Polanyi came from Hungary and was originally trained in medicine. He turned to chemistry, carrying on research in Germany before fleeing to England in 1933 after the Nazis' rise to power and becoming Professor of Physical Chemistry (C. P. Snow's discipline) at the University of Manchester. Already in his German days, Polanyi was extremely interested in economic and social studies, stimulated by debates with his elder brother (Karl defended socialism, whereas Michael opposed it). He later left the Department of Chemistry to become a philosopher. Polanyi began his new career at the age of fifty-seven, enquiring into 'the nature and justification of scientific knowledge', as the preface to *Personal Knowledge* (1958) described his book, and going on to analyse what he called 'implicit knowledge', in other words the practical knowledge that individuals do not know that they know. Polanyi's remark to a friend that 'I have been a vagabond all my life' applies to his intellectual itinerary as well as his successive displacements from Hungary to Germany and from Germany to Britain.[148]

Joseph Needham, who has been described, like Lasswell, as a '20th-century Renaissance Man', began his career as a biochemist. He became interested not only in embryology but also in its history.[149] His passion for China was awakened in the late 1930s and reinforced by his years in that country during the Second World War. Needham found his vocation as a historian of Chinese science, producing, together with a number of collaborators, a book that is still in progress (despite the main author's death in 1995) and now runs to twenty-seven large volumes published over more than sixty years. Like James Frazer before him, Needham was elected a Fellow of both the Royal Society (in 1941) and the British Academy (thirty years later). For a short period, on his return to Cambridge after the war, he was working on *Science and Civilisation* while 'at the same time he was still holding his Readership in biochemistry and teaching three special courses'. Needham was able to devote the rest of his life to his enthusiasm, the history of Chinese science (as a student at Oxford, I once heard him lecture on water-clocks and can testify that his enthusiasm was infectious).[150]

Needham believed that the 'rising tide of specialization' had encouraged people to forget that many problems 'cannot be understood in terms of one subject'. He liked to ask big questions, most famously the

'Needham Question': why did the Scientific Revolution happen in Europe and not in China? He was aware of the dangers of rashness and superficiality and described his essays as 'exciting reconnaissances, never saying the last word on anything, but opening up mines of treasures which other scholars can develop later'.[151] His remark offers a good description of one of the distinctive contributions of polymaths to the common store of knowledge.

The biologist William Bateson christened his son 'Gregory' in homage to Gregor Mendel, whose work he had helped to rediscover. Gregory Bateson began his career by studying zoology at Cambridge, but switched to anthropology in order, as he confessed, to make 'a break with ordinary, impersonal science' and also to escape the role of 'the son of William Bateson'.[152] He carried out fieldwork among the Iatmul in New Guinea and later in Bali, working with and subsequently marrying the anthropologist Margaret Mead. Following his divorce from Mead in 1950, Bateson underwent psychotherapy and then began to study it, introducing the idea of the 'double bind' to describe the irreconcilable demands on individuals that lead to what used to be called a 'nervous breakdown'. When Harvard did not renew his appointment in anthropology, Bateson began working with the psychiatrist Jürgen Ruesch at the University of California's Medical School in San Francisco.

Bateson's active interests also included ecology and ethology (studying the behaviour of otters and dolphins). He has been described as 'an intellectual nomad'.[153] However, he did not simply move from one discipline to another, while keeping his various interests in different compartments. On the contrary, he engaged in the typically polymathic enterprise of using concepts from one discipline to study others. He called his interest in ideas an 'ecology of mind' and borrowed the concept of self-regulation from computer science, employing it to analyse the emotions and the behaviour of individuals and groups.

Bateson's interests may seem dispersed, but a concern with communication was at the heart of most if not all of them.[154] In Bali in the 1930s he photographed gestures. In the 1940s he was one of the pioneers of cybernetics, and spoke at the famous Macy conferences on the subject along with Norbert Wiener and John von Neumann, commenting later that 'membership in those conferences . . . was one of the great events of my life'.[155] His interest in psychology focused on schizophrenic communication, and together with his colleague Ruesch he published a book entitled *Communication: The Social Matrix of Psychiatry* (1951). When he studied dolphins, it was to find out how they communicate with one another. As Bateson wrote of himself, he wanted to find a 'bridge between all branches of the world of experience – intellectual, emotional, observational, theoretical, verbal and wordless'.[156]

Herbert Simon studied at the University of Chicago at a time (the age of Robert Hutchins, discussed below) when it was necessary to pass exams in humanities, social sciences and natural sciences. He began his career as a political scientist, particularly interested in the process of making decisions. He turned to public administration, business administration and so to economics, winning a Nobel Prize in the subject without ever having worked in a department of economics. His own comment on the situation was that 'Psychologists think that I am an economist, but economists think I am a psychologist. In fact, I feel allegiance to none of these academic tribes, but regard myself as a citizen of the world – a behavioral scientist.'[157] Simon's particular interest was behavioural economics, linking up with his earlier work on decisions.[158] This serial polymath saw 1955–6 as a turning point in his intellectual life, 'when the maze branched in a most unexpected way', transforming him into 'a cognitive psychologist and computer scientist'. Together with a younger colleague, Allen Newell, another polymath who began his career as a mathematician, he set up a laboratory to study artificial intelligence at Carnegie-Melon University, making use of computers to simulate human problem-solving.[159]

Simon might also be described as a philosopher, given his study of what he called 'bounded rationality', midway between the poles of conventional rationality and irrationality. He claimed to read more than twenty languages and used them to read fiction as well as behavioural science. After reading a story by Borges, 'The Garden of Forking Paths', he visited the author in Buenos Aires in order to discuss it, seeing links with his own habits of thought.

The last of the six modern monsters, the French scholar Michel de Certeau, liked to describe himself as a historian, but he moved in and out of nine different disciplines (history, theology, philosophy, sociology, anthropology, linguistics, literature, geography and psychoanalysis). Certeau was trained by the Jesuits in philosophy and theology. While working on a doctorate in the field of religious studies, he attended the seminars directed by a historian of religion (Jean Orcibal) and a political and social historian (Roland Mousnier). Certeau was fascinated by the history of mysticism, an interest that links his early work to the book *The Mystic Fable* (1982), which he published towards the end of his career.

So far his intellectual trajectory seems a normal one, but Certeau went on to participate in the seminars of the dissident psychoanalyst Jacques Lacan. His book *La Possession de Loudun* (1970) studied the nuns in that convent, who were supposed to have been possessed by devils, from a psychoanalytical as well as a historical and a theological point of view (Aldous Huxley had written a book about the same episode, but in a more conventional manner).

The French student revolt of 1968, which Certeau interpreted as a *prise de parole* (a phrase with the double meaning of 'speaking out' and 'a capture of speech'), stimulated his interest in politics, culture and society. He published an essay on the significance of the 'events' of '68, as well as a study of the politics of language in the French Revolution.[160] Thanks to the former essay, the Ministry of Culture invited Certeau to organize a seminar on the prospects for culture in France. This request led in turn to a collective survey of the culture of the working class and so to Certeau's best-known work, *L'Invention du Quotidien* (1980), an essay in which he argued, against the Marxists, that ordinary individuals still retain a certain degree of freedom in contemporary society and that consumption should be regarded as a form of production.

GIANTS OR CHARLATANS?

Despite the achievements described above, criticisms of polymaths continued. Even a sympathetic account of Otto Neurath remarked that his many projects gave him 'no time for him to work them out'.[161] A sharper criticism of polymaths, only to be expected in an age of special-ization, has been to describe them as dilettantes, amateurs or even, reviving the seventeenth-century term, as charlatans.

Émile Durkheim, for instance, expressed anxiety 'that sociology might be invaded by charlatans' and criticized his rival the polymath Gabriel Tarde as an 'amateur'.[162] Kenneth Boulding was once described as 'much admired as an economist – by non-economists'.[163] Isaiah Berlin described Michael Polanyi as a 'great scientist' who gave up science to write 'mediocre works of philosophy'.[164] Alan Turing described his fellow polymath Warren McCulloch as a 'charlatan'.[165] Lewis Mumford dismissed his fellow polymaths Buckminster Fuller and Marshall McLuhan as 'charlatans'.[166] Sitting in a café in Paris, the British historian Edward Thompson once remarked to Carlo Ginzburg that 'Foucault is a charlatan'.[167] Noam Chomsky called the French psychoanalyst Jacques Lacan 'a total charlatan'.[168] Isaiah Berlin, asked about Jacques Derrida and unable to resist an oxymoron, replied that 'I think he may be a genuine charlatan, though a clever man'.[169] Similar criticisms have been made (sometimes by journalists) about George Steiner and Slavoj Žižek.[170] The term has the advantage of concentrating in a single word a wide range of criticisms – arrogance, superficiality, unfulfilled promises and 'playing to the gallery'.

What Chomsky disliked most about Lacan was his 'posturing before the television cameras' in an age when a few intellectuals, including Steiner, Sloterdijk and Žižek, stand in this new kind of limelight.

Peter Sloterdijk, who wrote his doctoral dissertation in German liter-ature, has extended his interests to philosophy, geography, ecology and media theory, and writes for the newspapers on contemporary issues such as the welfare state, terrorism and globalization. He courts contro-versy, notably in his attacks on living members of the Frankfurt School, dismissing them as mere academics. As for his learning, even a friendly critic has called Sloterdijk 'an intellectual magpie'. Like Susan Sontag, he has discussed social and political problems in a literary way and from a literary point of view, focusing on narrative and metaphor and illus-trating his arguments by quoting novels.[171]

Žižek, who began his career with two doctoral dissertations, one on structuralism and the other on psychoanalysis, also writes on sociology, politics and film. Like Eco and Sontag, he delights in juxtaposing high culture and popular culture.[172] In his case, as in that of Jacques Derrida, a playful style of writing has encouraged critics to call him a charlatan, a 'comedian' or a 'Marx Brother'.[173]

Some of these criticisms may be fair but others are not. It is scarcely possible to be a public intellectual these days without appearing on television. Behind the criticisms lurks the assumption that any claim to wide-ranging knowledge must be fraudulent, an assumption that seems increasingly obvious as the process of specialization accelerates.

What may have been new in the twentieth century is the occasional expression of regret for their wide range on the part of polymaths themselves. Andrew Lang was often described as 'versatile', but 'there was nothing he less liked to hear'. He said once that 'if I had stuck to one thing . . . I should have been a really big swell at anthropology'.[174] Among the various tensions in Max Weber's life and work was the one between the generalist and the specialist. He pursued his wide-ranging projects, but told the audience of one of his most famous lectures that 'Limitation to specialized work, with a renunciation of the Faustian universality of man which it involves, is a condition of any valuable work in the modern world.'[175]

Despite possible flaws, the achievement of all or at least most of these polymaths commands admiration. They prompt the question: how were they able to do it? This problem will be explored in the following chapter.

6

A GROUP PORTRAIT

Is the polymath a particular kind of individual? What encourages or drives them to follow this career? It is time to attempt to identify some general characteristics of the species, summarizing the analysis in earlier chapters and attempting a synthesis. Such a synthesis will necessarily be tentative, since polymathy, unlike creativity, does not seem to have been the subject of systematic investigation by cognitive psychologists. In any case, information about the early years of polymaths is all too often lacking.

Nevertheless, the recurrent references to a series of qualities in their autobiographies and in the reminiscences of their friends and relatives is suggestive, to say no more. Many of these qualities are shared in some degree with other scholars, but some are particularly important for polymaths, who might be described as scholars who possess these traits to a superlative degree. A number of these qualities will be discussed in what follows, offering a group portrait in a *pointilliste* style, a collective image created by juxtaposing many small items of information. Some of these qualities, such as curiosity, a good memory or exceptional creativity, may be genetic, one of the genes being what is known as the 'brain-derived neurotrophic factor' (BNDF).

The interests, abilities and achievements of polymaths are also shaped by their upbringing and by the milieu and the epoch in which they live, discussed in the next chapter on 'Habitats'. It is virtually needless to say that the line between the psychological and the social is difficult to draw, being not so much a line as a border zone with features of its own. In any case, my central argument is that polymaths do not succeed by virtue of their individual gifts alone. They also require an appropriate niche.

CURIOSITY

There may be a gene for curiosity – in the case of a bird, the great tit, a team of researchers at the Max Planck Institute have indeed discovered what they termed a 'curiosity gene', Drd4.[1] In the case of humans, the question cannot yet be answered. Besides, an overdose of curiosity, long known as the *libido sciendi* and described by the polymath Francis Bacon as 'inquisitive appetite', is surely the most general as well as the most obvious characteristic of the species.

Modern studies of Leonardo da Vinci, based on his voluminous notebooks, often refer to his curiosity, describing it as 'omnivorous', 'passionate', 'obsessive' and even 'relentless'. Polymaths have often described themselves in this way. In the seventeenth century, Sister Juana de la Cruz, for instance, explained to the bishop of Puebla her need to acquire knowledge. Peiresc noted 'the excess of my curiosity'.[2] Pierre Bayle described himself as 'hungry to know everything' (*affamé de savoir tout*). Pierre-Daniel Huet recalled his 'infinite desire to learn' (*infinitum discendi desiderium*) and remembered the time when 'I believed that I had learned nothing, when I saw there was something left to learn'.[3] In his puritanical youth, Isaac Newton apologized to God for 'setting my heart' on learning more than on Him.[4] Benjamin Franklin described his 'thirst for knowledge' when he was a child.[5] Alexander von Humboldt confessed his 'irresistible impulse toward knowledge of various kinds'.

Despite the rise of intellectual specialization in the nineteenth and twentieth centuries, some individuals were still driven by wide-ranging curiosity. Alexis de Tocqueville described himself when young as 'given up to insatiable curiosity' (*livré à une curiosité insatiable*).[6] At the age of twenty-one, Hippolyte Taine wrote to a friend that he studied not for practical reasons but driven by 'the need for knowledge' (*besoin de savoir*).[7] Sigmund Freud studied medicine at the University of Vienna, 'moved,' so he confessed, 'by a sort of greed for knowledge'.[8] Bertrand

Russell listed 'the search for knowledge' as one of his three main passions.[9] The Cuban sociologist Fernando Ortiz confessed to 'restless curiosity' (*inquietas curiosidades*).[10]

Some friends and acquaintances of polymaths tell a similar story. One of the patrons of Leibniz referred to his 'insatiable curiosity'.[11] A friend of the young Samuel Johnson described him as 'uncommonly inquisitive'.[12] Lewis Mumford, who observed his hero Patrick Geddes with care, described his 'all-devouring curiosity' that 'matched Leonardo's'.[13] Klári, the second wife of John von Neumann, remembered that 'Johnny's most characteristic trait was his boundless curiosity about everything and anything'.[14] An acquaintance of Karl Polanyi remarked on his 'endless curiosity'.[15] The biographer of Edmund Wilson, who knew his subject personally, described him as 'intensely curious'.[16] One of the teachers at Michel Foucault's school later testified that 'you could feel a formidable intellectual curiosity in him'.[17] A colleague of the Jesuit Michel de Certeau noted 'the passionate interest' that he took 'in everything'.[18] His 'immense, omnivorous curiosity' is also noted in a study of David Riesman, who became a famous sociologist without undergoing any formal training in sociology.[19]

CONCENTRATION

Another important quality of at least some polymaths is the power of concentration, at an unconscious as well as a conscious level. Giambattista Vico described himself as 'reading, writing and thinking while conversing with friends and during the shouts of his children'.[20] John von Neumann was said to wake up in the morning with the solution to a problem he had been thinking about the night before. When he was awake, he was able to work 'in crowded railway stations and airports, trains, planes, ships, hotel lobbies, lively cocktail parties'. Indeed, he preferred a background of noise.[21]

Such a resistance to distraction was and is particularly necessary in the case of female polymaths who are also mothers. Mary Somerville's daughter inserted a note in her mother's autobiography about what she called Mary's 'singular power of abstraction', allowing her to be 'so completely absorbed' in her work as not to hear either conversation or music – a gift all the more valuable because this scholar did not have a 'room of her own', but read and wrote in the drawing room.[22]

As in the case of more specialized scholars, the ability of a polymath to concentrate was often perceived as 'absent-mindedness', although that mind was present elsewhere, detached from everyday life while focusing on a particular problem. Celebrated cases, which include John Selden, Isaac Barrow, Isaac Newton, Montesquieu, Immanuel Kant, Samuel Johnson, Adam Smith, Henri Poincaré and Norbert Wiener, have generated a number of anecdotes, not always reliable.

According to Anthony Wood, the Oxford scholar and gossip, when Selden left his books to the Bodleian Library, 'in opening some of the books they found several pair of spectacles that Mr Selden had put in, and forgotten to take out'.[23] According to the equally gossipy John Aubrey, Barrow was 'so intent' on his studies that he did not notice when his bed was made (presumably with him in it), 'and would sometimes be going out without his hat on', and at least once with his cloak 'half on and half off'.[24] Newton would forget to eat and when he was living in Trinity College, Cambridge, he would sometimes go to dinner in hall wearing his surplice, as if he was going to chapel.[25] Adam Smith is supposed to have walked for fifteen miles on one occasion without realizing that he was still wearing his dressing gown.[26]

According to his nephew, Poincaré 'thought at the table, at family reunions, even in the *salons*', while a friend described him as 'almost permanently distracted'. There is a story that Poincaré once went for a walk and found he was carrying a birdcage that he must have picked up without noticing it.[27] As for Norbert Wiener, a well-known anecdote presents him on one occasion as failing to recognize his own daughter. Compared to examples such as these, Karl Polanyi's propensity to forget his gloves, a scarf or even his passport becomes a minor eccentricity.[28]

MEMORY

Curiosity and concentration are not sufficient to make polymaths. A good memory is another great advantage. Kant was surely right to discuss polymaths as examples of what he called 'marvels of memory' even if it was rather unkind of him to emphasize that particular quality at the expense of others. At all events, people who knew polymaths personally often remembered this quality. Blaise Pascal's niece, Marguerite Périer, for instance, remarked on his extraordinary memory. A friend of Thomas Browne remarked that 'His memory was capacious and tenacious', while two contemporaries of Gilbert Burnet referred to his 'prodigious memory'. A friend of Dr Johnson remembered that his memory was 'so tenacious, that whatever he read or heard, he never forgot'.[29] A friend of Condorcet declared that 'his memory is so prodigious, that he has never forgotten anything'.[30] Georges Cuvier was 'blessed with a memory that retained everything he saw and read, and which never failed him in any part of his career . . . long lists of sovereigns, princes, and the driest chronological facts, once arranged in his memory, were never forgotten'.[31] Macaulay too was famous for his memory, which allowed him to recite whole texts by heart, among them *Paradise Lost, The Pilgrim's Progress,* and *The Lay of the Last Minstrel.*[32] According to a friend, Sainte-Beuve had 'a prodigious memory *of everything*'.[33]

More recently, Wiener boasted about his memory. A friend of John von Neumann marvelled at his ability, 'on once reading a book or article, to quote it back verbatim'. Another eyewitness remembered that Neumann's memory 'was just beyond conception, a photograph for everything he ever learned or saw' (Neumann will recur in this chapter because he seems to have ticked almost all the boxes of its imagined questionnaire).[34] Joseph Needham's wife Dorothy and some of his collaborators commented on his 'photo-memory' or 'fantastic memory'.[35] Fernand Braudel was known for what he called his 'elephantine' memory, allowing him to write most of his major work on the Mediterranean world far away from his books and files, in prisoner-of-war camps.

SPEED

The ability to assimilate new kinds of information, preferably at high speed, is something that all polymaths need and some are said to have possessed. A contemporary of Gilbert Burnet remarked on his 'quick apprehension', while Burnet himself remarked that his memory 'took things soon'.[36] A fellow student of Louis Agassiz at the University of Zurich wrote that 'Agassiz knew everything. He was always ready to demonstrate and speak on any subject. If it was a subject he was not familiar with, he would study and rapidly master it.'[37] In similar fashion, Macaulay's biographer noted his 'capacity for taking in at a glance the contents of a printed page'. 'He read books more quickly than other people skimmed them, and skimmed them as fast as anyone else could turn the leaves.'[38] A friend of Robertson Smith remarked on 'the extreme quickness of his mind, which rapidly acquired knowledge on almost any kind of subject'.

The polymath Kenneth Boulding said of another polymath, Anatol Rapoport, that he was 'a man of unusually quick learning ability'.[39] Walter Pitts was 'known to master the contents of a textbook in a field new to him in a few days'.[40] Joseph Needham had 'a special gift of learning a new subject' rapidly.[41] A former classmate of Linus Pauling said of him that 'it just seemed like all he had to do was sit down at a table, look at a book, and he'd absorb the knowledge without reading it'.[42] The ability to learn new things is associated with the desire to do so. It was said of George Evelyn Hutchinson, whose interests ranged from zoology and ecology to art history and archaeology, that he liked to learn something new every year.[43] One of the pioneers of artificial intelligence, Marvin Minsky, declared in an interview that he liked 'learning new things', whereas 'most people don't like learning something new'.[44]

IMAGINATION

A vivid imagination forms an important part of a polymath's psychological equipment. Charles Darwin noted in himself a tendency to daydream, while Herbert Simon described himself as 'a terrible daydreamer', who 'seldom can keep a coherent line of thought'. It may be argued that it is through daydreaming (viewed by others as 'absent-mindedness') and the unconscious association of ideas that these individuals reach at least some of their insights. One of their leading qualities is the capacity to make what Darwin called 'linkings of facts', in his case facts about different species and their different environments.[45] They perceive connections that others miss. For example, the 'breakthroughs' of Shen Gua, who was discussed earlier, 'frequently came from juxtaposing insights that did not conventionally fit together'.[46] In the language of Pierre Bourdieu, polymaths bring the 'habitus' acquired in one discipline to bear on the problems of another. In the language of Michel de Certeau, they have a special gift for the 're-employment' of ideas in new contexts.

Like poets and other creative writers who think with metaphors, polymaths constantly draw analogies, engaging in what Aristotle famously called the 'perception of the similarity in dissimilars'. As we have seen, the notebooks of Leonardo da Vinci offer many examples of this practice, comparing birds and bats to flying machines, for instance. Herder once described Newton, Leibniz and Buffon as poets because they reached their discoveries via analogy, while later philosophers of science have pointed out that scientific theories or models have something important in common with metaphors.[47] A number of Thomas Young's contributions to knowledge depended on his perception of analogies: between waves of light and sound, for instance, and between different Indo-European languages.

A similar point might be made about the social sciences. Vilfredo Pareto's transfer of the idea of equilibrium from engineering to economics has already been noted. Max Weber borrowed the idea of charisma from theology and used it to discuss politics. Pierre Bourdieu employed a number of analogies in his social theory, taking the idea of 'field' from social psychology, 'habitus' from art history, 'capital' from economics and 'consecration' from theology.

It is not surprising, then, to find that polymaths have played leading roles in the development of the comparative method, defined as a search for both similarities and differences. Contributions to comparative mythology were made by (among others) Samuel Bochart, Pierre-Daniel Huet, Giambattista Vico, James Frazer and more recently by Georges Dumézil, who studied myth in a long tradition from India via Greece and Rome to Northern Europe.[48] A number of polymaths, among them

Conrad Gessner, Leibniz, Hiob Ludolf, Wilhelm von Humboldt and Roman Jakobson concentrated on comparative linguistics, and yet others on comparative studies of law (Montesquieu, for instance) or religions (Selden and Robertson Smith). Cuvier's fame rests on his comparative anatomy, which underlay his famous reconstructions of extinct animals (his genius for analogy was noted by Balzac). Darwin's theory of the evolution of species drew on analogies with the work of Charles Lyell on rocks and Malthus on human populations. Alan Turing's work on artificial intelligence depended on analogies between people and machines.

For these reasons it seems illuminating to speak of a scientific imagination, or more generally still of a scholarly imagination, particularly strong in innovators in their fields. In drawing analogies, polymaths have the advantage of personal acquaintance with different disciplines. If innovation consists, as has been argued, in the displacement of concepts, polymaths are among the leading displacers.[49]

The idea that polymaths in particular are endowed with fertile and creative imaginations is supported by the fact that a number of them have, among other achievements, published poems. In the early modern period, the twenty-one examples are not so surprising, since writing poetry was a common pastime, at least among the social elite.[50] However, at least fourteen polymaths from the nineteenth and twentieth centuries did the same: not only Goethe, Coleridge, Matthew Arnold and Thomas Macaulay but at least ten others as well.[51]

Besides three novelists who were also polymaths (George Eliot, Aldous Huxley, Vladimir Nabokov), over forty of the polymaths listed in the appendix published romances or novels. 'Science fiction', in a broad sense of the term, is represented by the *Discovery of a World in the Moon* by John Wilkins, the *Blazing World* by Margaret Cavendish, the *Heavenly Journey* of Athanasius Kircher and the *Ecstatic Voyage* of Lorenzo Hervás, as well as by the images of the future offered in works by Tommaso Campanella, Paolo Mantegazza, Gabriel Tarde, William Morris, Alexander Bogdanov, H. G. Wells, Aldous Huxley and the Austrian biologist Karl Camillo Schneider. Umberto Eco's *The Name of the Rose* became a global bestseller.[52]

ENERGY

A good memory and a lively imagination would be of little use to a polymath if he or she did not work hard to employ these qualities. Also necessary is the physical energy to do this work, a quality that is often noted by observers. A former collaborator described John Wilkins as 'indefatigable'.[53] Pierre Bayle's friend Jacques Basnage described him as 'a tireless worker' (*infatigable au travail*) and noted that on the eve of his death, despite his poor health, Bayle worked until eleven at night.[54] Burnet remarked on his own 'very happy constitution', making him 'capable of much labour and hard study'.[55] Buffon was known for his ability to rise at dawn and work 'with prodigious energy' for fourteen hours a day.[56] So was Émilie du Châtelet. The 'indefatigable energy' of Alexander von Humboldt was noted by his brother.[57] The biographer of Louis Agassiz notes his 'amazing store of physical energy'.[58]

One observer noted William Morris's 'immense energy'. To another, he seemed 'overcharged with energy'.[59] When Max Weber lectured, listeners were impressed by his explosive energy, sometimes compared to a volcano. In similar fashion, an acquaintance of Herbert Simon described him lecturing: 'The intellectual energy pours out of him, as if it could light the city tonight.'[60] A friend of the many-sided political scientist Harold Lasswell noted his 'high level of physical energy'.[61] Visitors to Henri Berr, a veteran campaigner for historical synthesis, were impressed by his *élan*.[62] A number of acquaintances remarked on the 'vitality' of Otto Neurath. Mumford bore witness to the 'intellectual energy' and 'immense vitality' of Patrick Geddes.[63] One colleague of Joseph Needham called him 'a fountain of physical and intellectual energy', while another remarked on 'his titanic energy and enthusiasm'.[64] Susan Sontag's son David called his mother 'a person with truly boundless energy'.[65]

Multitasking was a quality of at least a few polymaths. Buffon was said to work 'in several directions at the same time'.[66] William Morris was observed translating Homer in his head while standing at an easel painting, and he once said that 'if a chap can't compose an epic poem while he's weaving tapestry he had better shut up'.[67] Joseph Needham was supposedly able to lecture and read proofs at the same time. Otto Neurath 'liked to do three things at the same time', according to his wife Marie.[68] Linus Pauling was another polymath who 'ranged over several problems at once'.[69]

RESTLESSNESS

A surplus of energy often leads to restlessness, which may be viewed either as a positive trait that encourages serial polymathy or as the downside of curiosity. Leibniz criticized Becher as 'restless'.[70] Alexander von Humboldt was also criticized for being 'restless' (*rastlos, unruhig*). Henry James described the 'nervous restless manner' of William Morris.[71] August Strindberg was notoriously restless. Umberto Eco described his friend the polymath Giorgio Prodi as always 'in a hurry'.[72]

Other polymaths gloried in the nomadic condition. Robert Burton told his readers about his 'roving humour'. Georg Simmel was described by a former student (Siegfried Kracauer, another polymath) as 'a wanderer'. Gilbert Chinard, an expatriate professor of literature who wrote biographies and historical studies, sent a book to a former student with the inscription remembering half a century of 'vagabondage littéraire'. Michael Polanyi remarked to a friend that 'I have been a vagabond all my life', moving from chemistry to philosophy as well as from Hungary via Germany to England.[73] Julian Huxley was described by his wife as 'escaping from one activity by diving into yet another'.[74]

Gregory Bateson has been described as an 'intellectual nomad', 'traveling from place to place, and from one field to another, without ever settling into the safety of a secure niche'.[75] George Steiner described himself as 'a grateful wanderer', experiencing the sorrows (and benefits) of what he called 'unrootedness' (since he lacked a place to be uprooted from).[76] Edward Said saw himelf as a nomad, 'out of place' everywhere.[77] Bruce Chatwin, a travel writer and novelist who has a good claim to be considered a polymath, given his interest in art, archaeology and anthropology, was restless himself. No wonder that he was attracted to the life of nomads or that one of his last books was *Anatomy of Restlessness*.

Serial polymaths move from one discipline to another and another. Herbert Simon described himself as having 'wandered . . . from political science and public administration, through economics and cognitive psychology, to artificial intelligence and computer science'.[78] The anthropologist Gregory Bateson and the physiologist Henry Murray were both drawn to the study of psychology as a result of their own psychological problems. A few polymaths were forced to wander. Gustav Fechner, Patrick Geddes, Aldous Huxley and Herbert Fleure all suffered from eye problems that drove them out of their original field, physics in the case of Fechner, botany for Geddes, medicine for Huxley and zoology for Fleure.

A few polymaths tried various occupations before embarking on an academic career. The geographer Friedrich Ratzel and the sociologist Robert Park were professional reporters, the anthropologist Adolf Bastian was a ship's doctor, while Elton Mayo worked as a journalist and as a clerk in an African gold mine before finding his vocation as an industrial psychologist and settling down at Harvard.[79]

The link between crossing two kinds of frontier, national and disciplinary, provokes further thought. In the twentieth century, at least seven leading polymaths were active in the international peace movement: Wilhelm Ostwald, Paul Otlet, Patrick Geddes, Bertrand Russell (who established the Peace Foundation), Kenneth Boulding, Linus Pauling (recipient of the Nobel Peace Prize for 1962) and Noam Chomsky (who received the Sean McBride Peace Prize in 2017). It may not be a coincidence that these scholars supported both internationalism and interdisciplinarity. Some earlier polymaths, notably Comenius and Leibniz, had also worked for peace between nations.

WORK

If any readers of these lines harbour the ambition to become a polymath, they should be warned that for success, long hours of work are needed. Their energy allows some polymaths to sleep less than ordinary mortals and to devote the time saved to study. The philologist Franciscus Junius worked a sixteen-hour day, normally from 4 a.m. to 8 p.m.[80] Pierre-Daniel Huet claimed in his autobiography that he allowed himself to

1. Some scholars think that this drawing in red chalk of a handsome old man represents Leonardo, as the inscription claims. It certainly matches other possible portraits of the artist, as well as descriptions of him by contemporaries.

2. Here is one of Leonardo da Vinci's illustrations to a book by his friend the friar Luca Pacioli, *On Divine Proportion*, published in 1509. It testifies to Leonardo's fascination with mathematics, an important discipline for Renaissance artists, whether they were concerned with the laws or perspective or the vital statistics of an ideal human figure. In his notebooks, Leonardo wrote, 'Let no one read me who is not a mathematician'.

3. Today, Nicolaus Copernicus is generally remembered for one achievement: his argument that the sun and not the earth was the centre of the universe. However, he was also active as a physician, studied law and put forward pioneering theories in what is now known as economics. This sixteenth-century diagram shows the sun, not the earth, in the centre of the universe. Copernicus wrote that 'In the middle of all sits the sun on his throne, as upon a royal dais ruling his children the planets which circle about him'.

4. Private museums of 'wonders' (remarkable works of both art or nature) were fashionable in the sixteenth and seventeenth centuries. The museum illustrated here belonged to the Danish physician Ole Worm, a polymath who was particularly interested in 'curiosities' from Scandinavia, from weapons to stuffed animals, birds and fish.

5. Juan Caramuel y Lobkowitz, a Spanish monk who lived in Vienna and Prague before becoming a bishop in Vigevano, is said to have known twenty-four languages. He published more than sixty books on a variety of subjects, from theology to music, besides his activities as a diplomat and an architect.

6. Known as the 'Swedish Minerva', Queen Christina of Sweden was said to 'know everything'. Her interests included languages, philosophy, astronomy and alchemy. She invited a number of scholars to her court to give her tutorials, look after her library or dispute in public with one another.

7. The most famous of the scholars at Christina's court, the philosopher René Descartes, is shown here standing at the table of the queen, who seems to be presenting her arguments while the courtiers listen. Unfortunately, Descartes did not survive a Swedish winter, dying in Stockholm in February 1650.

8. Of all the so-called 'monsters of erudition' who flourished in the seventeenth century, Gottfried Wilhelm Leibniz was surely the greatest. He is remembered today mainly as a philosopher and a mathematician who competed with Newton in the discovery of calculus, but he also made important contributions to the study of history, languages and law, took an interest in all the natural sciences and was known in his own day as an expert on China.

9. This portrait gives viewers some sense of the flamboyant style of Madame de Staël, a Swiss intellectual who wrote on philosophy, the passions, suicide, translation, politics and society (including the position of women), not to mention her novels and plays.

10. This painting portrays a meeting of the *salon* of Madame Geoffrin, which met on Mondays and Wednesdays in mid-eighteenth-century Paris. Montesquieu and Rousseau are represented here, while a bust of Voltaire observes the proceedings. *Salons* of this kind, in which men and women of letters displayed their knowledge with elegance and wit, had a particularly important role in intellectual life in France in this period.

11. Voltaire was, among many other things, a popularizer of science and together with his mistress Émilie du Châtelet, he wrote an introduction to the theories of Isaac Newton. In this engraving, Voltaire is shown as a poet, wearing a crown of laurel, while Émilie is not shown at all.

12. Today, the Swede Emanuel Swedenborg is remembered almost exclusively for the religious writings he produced in later life, including the book in the portrait, *Apocalypse Revealed*. It comes as something of a surprise to learn that the younger Swedenborg was celebrated as an engineer as well as for his contributions to metallurgy, chemistry, astronomy, anatomy, physiology and physiognomy.

13. Thomas Young, a Cambridge don, was known as 'Phenomenon Young' thanks to his many interests. Trained in medicine, he made experiments in optics and acoustics, lectured on physiology, learned six oriental languages and was working on the decoding of Egyptian hieroglyphs when he was overtaken by his French rival, Champollion.

14. Described as 'one of the last of the great universalists', John Herschel, best known as an astronomer, also made important contributions to mathematics, chemistry, magnetism, botany, geology, acoustics, optics and photography. In his spare time, Herschel translated Homer, Dante and Schiller.

15. Not content with ranging widely over the natural sciences, the independent scholar Alexander von Humboldt took an informed interest in literature and art. He looked at landscape with the eyes of an artist, as well as practising drawing himself.

16. The Scottish scientist Mary Somerville was mainly self-taught, since a woman of her generation was not allowed to attend a British university. Unable, as a wife and mother, to find the time for systematic research, she concentrated on synthesis, publishing her major work, *On the Connection of the Physical Sciences*, in 1834. Somerville College Oxford is named in her honour.

17. Pavel Florensky, shown here in his white cassock, was an Orthodox priest who wrote on philosophy, theology and religious art, and was also, less orthodox in this respect, an electrical engineer. Accused in Stalin's time of attempts to overthrow the Soviet system, he was successively exiled, sent to a labour camp and shot. Florensky has been described as 'Russia's unknown da Vinci'.

18. Herbert Simon's academic career ranged from political science to computer science via cognitive psychology. He was awarded a Nobel Prize for Economics without having officially worked in that discipline. It is no surprise to learn that Simon did not take the differences between what he called 'academic tribes' very seriously.

19. The Belgian scholar Paul Otlet has been described as 'the man who tried to classify the world'. His schemes for information retrieval, inspired by Dewey's decimal system for the classification of books, formed part of a wider vision that included world peace and world government. The Mundaneum, an institution that Otlet founded to bring together the whole of knowledge, still exists, although it has been moved from Brussels to Mons.

20. Susan Sontag is probably best described as a cultural critic, who once declared that 'I do not want to be a professor and I do not want to be a journalist. I want to be a writer who is also an intellectual.' A regular writer for the *New Yorker* and the *New York Review of Books*, Sontag collected her work into nine volumes of essays, concerned with painting, literature, theatre, dance, philosophy, psychoanalysis, anthropology, history and especially photography and film.

21. The Princeton Institute for Advanced Study was founded in 1930 to offer selected scholars the leisure necessary for research, thought and writing. Its first director, Abraham Flexner, was an educationalist, famous for an essay on 'The Usefulness of Useless Knowledge'. Early members of the Institute included Albert Einstein and the polymath John von Neumann.

22. The programme of the University of Sussex, the first of seven new universities founded in Britain in the 1960s and photographed here in 1964, was 'to redraw the map of learning' by emphasizing interdisciplinary research and teaching. Particularly successful in this respect were the seminars led by teachers in neighbouring disciplines, among them history and literature.

sleep for only three hours a night in order to have more time for study. Alexander von Humboldt was said, like Napoleon, to need only four hours sleep a night, and John von Neumann, three or four.[81] Émilie du Châtelet 'could function with four or five hours' sleep a night' and was capable of getting up at four in the morning and working a fourteen-hour day.[82] A life of Thomas Jefferson describes his 'amazing readiness' to work long hours, sometimes from five in the morning until midnight, and his advice to a student to work for eleven hours a day. John Theodore Merz, who earned his living as a manager and director of industrial enterprises, wrote his four-volume history of nineteenth-century European thought from five till eight in the morning, before beginning his normal work. Lester Ward was educated in evening classes and went on to write a book on sociology at night, at a time when his day job was working for the United States Geological Survey.[83]

The biographer of Joseph Leidy, asking how he found the time for his multifarious activities, noted that he was 'working until 2 a.m. every night and most Sundays, leaving only one evening a week free', and on occasion working from 8 a.m. until 8 p.m. without even a drink.[84] Karl Pearson attributed his success to 'a capacity for hard work'.[85] John Maynard Keynes 'was always inclined to overwork' according to Bertrand Russell.[86] Herbert Simon presented himself, apparently with pride, as a 'workaholic', at his desk 'for sixty to eighty hours a week, sometimes more'.[87] Linus Pauling explained that he developed 'the habit of working' when he was young.[88] Klara, the wife of John von Neumann, remembered that 'His capacity for work was practically unlimited.'[89] A collaborator of Joseph Needham described him as 'working non-stop', even at breakfast, and as liking boiled eggs because he could work while they were boiling.[90] Michel Foucault worked hard and took few breaks, from his years in school until shortly before his death. The very day in 1974 that he finished one book, *Discipline and Punish*, he began writing another, *The Will to Knowledge*.[91]

Without such habits of work, it is difficult to imagine how some polymaths could have been as prolific as they were. Henri Poincaré, for instance, produced over 30 books and some 500 articles, but was overtaken by Kenneth Boulding's 40 books and about 800 articles. Niklas Luhmann published some 70 books, Benedetto Croce over 80, while Salomon Reinach published 90.

Long hours at the desk sometimes exacted a price. The autobiography of Leonbattista Alberti describes him as suffering what a much later generation would call a 'nervous breakdown', in which the words he was reading would turn into scorpions. Darwin worked so hard as to damage his health. William Robertson Smith is said to have given up lunch in order to have more time for research and his early death may have been the result, at least in part, of overwork.[92] The same was probably true of Karl Lamprecht, who believed that 'he could drain inexhaustible amounts of energy from his body by sheer will power'. His friend Wilhelm Ostwald remembered warning Lamprecht, who died at the age of fifty-nine, that he was working too hard.[93]

Herbert Spencer's habitual overwork led to a nervous breakdown in 1855. T. H. Huxley's breakdowns in 1871 and 1884 seem to have had a similar cause. Leslie Stephen compared himself to a hoop – 'When I'm not going at full speed, I drop.'[94] According to Bertrand Russell, it was overwork that led to the death of John Maynard Keynes. Max Weber's breakdown followed the death of his father, but overwork may have made him more vulnerable.

MEASURING TIME

The sense of a duty not to waste time but to put it to good use was inculcated in a number of polymaths at an early age. It is a form of what Weber called 'worldly asceticism' (*innerweltliche Askese*). The polymath Mark Pattison, an Anglican clergyman, preached sermons suggesting that education is, or should be, a form of asceticism.[95] In his autobiography, John Stuart Mill described his father as someone who 'vigorously acted up to the principle of losing no time' and so 'was likely to adhere to the same rule in the instruction of his pupil'.

The diary of the Calvinist scholar Isaac Casaubon vividly reveals his 'preoccupation with time and the lack of it'.[96] The motto of his fellow Calvinist Hugo Grotius was 'Time is running out' (*Ruit Hora*). Thomas

Browne was described in his own day as 'so impatient of Sloth and Idleness, that he would say he could not do nothing'.[97] Newton's amanuensis described him as 'Thinking all hours lost, that was not spent in his studies . . . I believe he grudged that short time he spent in eating and sleeping'.[98] Montesquieu associated idleness not with the joys of heaven but with the torments of hell. Benjamin Franklin declared that 'leisure is time for doing something useful'. In his retirement, Wilhelm von Humboldt told a friend that 'I never go to bed before one o'clock' and 'most of my life is spent in my study'.[99] Thomas Young declared with pride at the end of his life that he had never spent an idle day. The young John Herschel wished he had 'that enviable capacity of husbanding every atom of time'.[100] Darwin's opinion was that 'A man who dares to waste one hour of time has not discovered the value of life.'[101]

A few polymaths were driven by the need to make up for lost time. Although Darwin was able to study on board the *Beagle*, as well as to make many precious observations whenever he landed, by the end of his five-year expedition he was looking forward 'with a comical mixture of dread and satisfaction to the amount of work that remains for me in England'.[102] The philosopher Hans Blumenberg, who lived in Nazi Germany during the war, was not allowed to attend university at that time because he was half-Jewish. After the war, he gave up sleep for one night a week in order to study longer.[103]

Weber's 'work mania' is discussed by a recent biographer, together with his sharp sense of the passing of time. His 'compulsive haste' was 'apparent in his impossible handwriting'.[104] H. G. Wells worried about wasting time, writing to his mother that, at seventeen, he had spent 'more than a quarter of my life already'. He later suffered from overwork.[105] An even more extreme case of preoccupation with time is that of Melvil Dewey, a fanatic for efficiency who required his staff to be well prepared when speaking to him, 'so that without loss of a moment, you can present the case in [the] fewest possible words'.[106] He is said to have scolded a library receptionist for greeting him with 'Good Morning, Dr Dewey!' because this was a waste of valuable time. There would seem to be a pathology as well as a psychology of the polymath.

COMPETITION

The passion for work is often driven by competition. It has been noted that John Selden wrote two of his treatises in emulation of scholars that he admired, Joseph Scaliger in the case of *Syrian Gods* and Hugo Grotius in that of *Natural Law*.[107] A school friend of Samuel Johnson remembered 'his ambition to excel'.[108] Herbert Simon confessed that 'I have been, and am, a competitive person', while George Homans remembered his schoolboy self as 'always the great little competitor'.[109] This quality is obvious enough in other polymaths, from Isaac Newton to Karl Mannheim, who wrote a famous article on 'competition as a cultural phenomenon' and was himself described as extremely competitive by his former assistant, Norbert Elias.[110] Thomas Young believed that 'scientific investigations are a kind of warfare . . . against all one's contemporaries and predecessors', a statement borne out by his relations with Jean-François Champollion, his rival in the decipherment of hieroglyphics.[111] Competition encourages the desire to succeed and what Needham called 'a certain ruthlessness in pursuing objectives'.[112] Sibling rivalry helps explain the achievements of the Humboldt brothers, the Polanyi brothers and the Huxley brothers. Each pair developed a division of labour but did not always respect it. Michael Polanyi moved from chemistry to economics, while Julian Huxley wrote science fiction.

THE PLAY ELEMENT

It would surely be a mistake, though, to see the achievements of polymaths as purely Apollonian, all work and no play. There is also a Dionysian aspect to their achievements, the pleasure taken both in acquiring knowledge and in solving problems. In an interview, Carlo Ginzburg, a historian of unusually wide interests, has compared the pleasure of learning about a new topic to that of skiing on fresh snow.[113] Some polymaths love wordplay, among them Jacques Derrida, who coined the term *différance* to include both 'difference' and 'deferral', Slavoj Žižek, who has published a collection of jokes, and Gilberto Freyre, who shocked some readers with a pun (in Portuguese) on civilization and syphilis. Kenneth Boulding had the habit of writing humorous verse about his many interests. Umberto

Eco, who imagined a treatise on laughter by Aristotle and wrote a percep-
tive essay about Johan Huizinga's *Homo Ludens*, a study of the play
element in culture, was himself a playful scholar. Well known for his
battute ('witticisms'), the man who entitled a serious study of philosophy
Kant and the Platypus was certainly able to wear his learning lightly. So
was the sociologist David Riesman, who wrote playfully as well as writing
about play.

In the sixteenth century, Girolamo Cardano was known for his practical as well as his theoretical interest in games of chance, while different
forms of play seem to have been an important element in the culture of
the first computer scientists. Constructing machines that played chess
was itself a game, though one with serious consequences.

Claude Shannon has been called 'the playful inventor'. One of his
devices was a juggling machine. Alan Turing enjoyed a variety of games.
Warren McCulloch valued what he called 'fun', while his collaborator
Walter Pitts enjoyed 'inventing all kinds of word games'.[114] John von
Neumann, who made use of the theory of games in his work, was himself
described as 'a playful man'. The computer scientist and cognitive
psychologist Allen Newell, who published a book on *The Chess Machine*,
was remembered by an interviewer as 'playful' and as calling science a
'game'.[115] Newell's colleague Herbert Simon seems to have written his
articles on physics as a form of relaxation (along with playing the piano
and reading Proust in French). Solving scientific problems was the equivalent for him of solving crosswords for ordinary mortals.

HEDGEHOGS AND FOXES

As we have seen, polymaths have sometimes been divided into two opposite groups, foxes versus hedgehogs.[116] I began research for this book
expecting to find that most polymaths would belong to the group of
foxes, drawn in centrifugal fashion towards many different kinds of
knowledge. Some polymaths have indeed viewed themselves as foxes.
Gilbert Chinard confessed to his *vagabondage*, as we have seen, and so
did Michael Polanyi, while Gregory Bateson admitted his fondness for
what he called 'detours'.[117]

On the other side, what to outsiders looks like a dispersal of interests may be viewed very differently by polymaths themselves. Of Herman Conring it has been suggested that 'His writings have seemed bewilderingly disparate, but in his mind they were united.'[118] The father of Pavel Florensky (the 'Russian Leonardo') worried about young Pavel's regular changes of direction, but Pavel himself wrote to his mother that 'Mathematics is the key to a world view', in which there would be 'nothing so unimportant as not to be worth studying and nothing that was not linked to something else'. He wrote of himself, as we have seen, that his 'life's task' was to continue along 'the path toward a future integral world view'.[119] In similar fashion, the father of Joseph Needham, noting the variety of his son's reading, used to warn him, 'Don't dissipate your energies, my boy.' Needham himself, however, looking back on his life, saw himself as a bridge-builder or a syncretist.[120]

With interests that included all the social sciences, as well as mathematics and computer science, Herbert Simon looks like an extreme case of a fox, but, according to him, 'what appeared to be scatteration was really closer to monomania', focused on the logic of decision-making.[121] Jacob Bronowski wrote about himself that 'All that I have written, though it has seemed to me so different from year to year, turns to the same centre: the uniqueness of man that grows out of his struggle (and his gift) to understand both nature and himself.'[122] The number of polymaths involved in projects for the unification of knowledge also testifies to the importance of the hedgehog ideal.

Some polymaths see themselves or are seen by others in a way that confuses or transcends the original distinction. In the essay that launched the dichotomy, Isaiah Berlin described Tolstoy as a fox who thought that he ought to be a hedgehog. Paul Lazarsfeld (according to Marie Jahoda, his former wife), was a fox 'by talents and interest', attracted to mathematics, psychology, sociology and the study of the media, although 'historical accidents forced him to masquerade as a hedgehog'.[123] George Steiner has been described as 'two Steiners', both fox and hedgehog.[124] The historian Carlo Ginzburg has described himself as 'becoming more and more a fox, but ultimately I regard myself as a hedgehog'.[125]

The cases of Leonardo, Alexander von Humboldt and Michel de Certeau also highlight difficulties with this dichotomy. Leonardo has often been described as an individual of centrifugal interests, but it has been noted that what appears to be undirected curiosity is usually linked to his main preoccupations: 'These invisible threads connect the fragments.' Leonardo worked on the assumption that 'all the apparent diversities of nature are symptoms of an inner unity'.[126] Alexander von Humboldt also appears to be a spectacular example of a fox, but he believed that 'all forces of nature are interlaced and interwoven'. His scientific achievement was, above all, to show connections 'between climate and vegetation, between altitude and fertility, between human productivity and property relationships, and between the animal and plant kingdoms'.[127] In his *Cosmos* (1845–62), originally lectures delivered to a lay public, Humboldt presented an account of connections on a literally global scale.

To pursue the question in more detail, it may be illuminating to return to Michel de Certeau.[128] Certeau's intellectual itinerary from a historian of mysticism to a sociologist of consumption was certainly an unusual one. He practised as well as preaching what he called interdisciplinary 'poaching' (*braçonnage*).[129] However, in his forays into different disciplines, Certeau worked with the same fundamental concepts. Some central themes link his explorations, among them the idea of alterity – the 'otherness' of other cultures, other periods, of mystics and of individuals possessed by the devil. Certeau's language of analysis also remained constant when its objects changed. He had a remarkable gift for perceiving analogies and some of his sociological concepts turn out to be transformations of theological ones. To use his own favourite term, he 're-employed' them. Belief, *la croyance*, and the production of belief, *faire croire*, are major themes in Certeau's work, first in a religious context and later in a political one, noting for instance that the capacity to believe was in retreat in the political domain. His later discussion of social practices, from shopping to reading, echoes his earlier articles on religious topics, using phrases such as *pratique sacramentelle*, *pratique chrétienne*, *pratique de l'amour* and so on.

Again, absence and related themes such as invisibility and silence play an important role in Certeau's political and social analyses: the significance of absence, the need to listen to silence, and so on. These themes had emerged earlier in his studies of mysticism. 'Otherness' or *altérité* is another major theme in Certeau's work. This key term is an adaptation to secular contexts, such as the colonial encounter, of a concept that Certeau had begun to use when studying religious experience in general and mysticism in particular. Finally, the very idea of re-employment has religious origins. It is explicit in some of the Fathers of the Church, especially Augustine, discussing whether Christians can make use of classical culture and comparing this practice to the 'spoils of Egypt' taken by the Israelites at the Exodus. In short, Certeau may be described as a hedgehog in fox's clothing.[130]

This point about the centripetal drive of apparently centrifugal scholars such as Humboldt and Certeau may be generalized. Rather than make a sharp distinction between two groups of polymaths, it may be more useful to place them along a continuum between these poles. It may be even more illuminating to think of many polymaths as tugged back and forth between centrifugal interests and the desire to make connections.

True foxes seem to be rare, and hedgehogs much more numerous, although it is surely necessary to distinguish between individuals who want to see connections, those who claim to have seen them, and those who actually demonstrate links between different domains of knowledge. In any case, the fox element has not infrequently led to what I have called 'Leonardo syndrome'.

LEONARDO SYNDROME

A recurrent theme in the life of polymaths is a dispersal of interests that has sometimes prevented them from producing books, completing investigations or making the discoveries to which they were close.

Leonardo is surely the most famous example of this dispersal, but he has rivals in this respect. Lucas Holstenius, a German scholar best known for his editions of classical and medieval texts, embarked on a number of ambitious projects such as collecting inscriptions and writing a history of the popes, but left them unfinished. Peiresc, as we have seen, did not publish, although he contributed more to the circulation of knowledge through his letters than many other scholars did through their books. Leibniz never finished his pioneering investigation of medieval German history. A modern admirer of Robert Hooke also notes his 'failure to carry things through', a weakness that contributed to the failure of posterity to recognize his importance.[131]

Examples of the syndrome can also be found in the nineteenth and twentieth centuries. Thomas Young admitted, as we have seen, that his forte was 'acute suggestion' rather than taking an enquiry to its conclusion. Although he worked for a long time, on and off, at deciphering Egyptian hieroglyphics, it was his French rival Champollion who was finally successful.[132] In similar fashion to Young, Thomas Huxley wrote of himself that his intellect was 'acute and quick' rather than 'grasping or deep'. The German philosopher Arnold Ruge remarked that, because of his many interests, Karl Marx 'never finishes anything' (in fact, Marx almost finished *Das Kapital* before his death, leaving his friend Friedrich Engels the task of making it ready for the press).[133]

As for Alexander von Humboldt, he intended to publish his account of his expedition to the Americas soon after he returned in 1804, but its final section was only published thirty-five years later, while the introduction to the book was never finished. If he had died at seventy, instead of eighty-nine, Humboldt's most famous book, *Cosmos*, presented in the form of lectures between 1825 and 1827, would never have appeared in print at all (its five volumes were published between 1845 and 1862). This book, too, remained incomplete.

Freud, according to his friend and biographer Ernest Jones, 'narrowly missed world fame in early life through not daring to pursue his thoughts to their logical – and not far-off – conclusion', notably in the case of the medical uses of cocaine.[134] It has been said of Patrick Geddes that he 'rapidly became bored and was always more interested in the next idea than in following the last one to the point where he could write a monograph about it'.[135] A study of Otto Neurath notes 'the enormous fertility and suggestiveness of his ideas', but also that there was 'no time for him to work them out'.[136] According to sympathetic biographers, Michael Polanyi's record, even in his main discipline, chemistry, was 'dotted with near misses'.[137] Linus Pauling, who combined careers as a physicist, chemist and biologist, was on the track of the structure of DNA but failed to reach his goal, perhaps because he was distracted by his other interests.

On other occasions, though, fear of Leonardo syndrome turned out to be unjustified. One of Certeau's Jesuit colleagues worried about 'his perpetual attraction to new topics of research, the passionate interest that he shows in everything (in the manner of an extremely gifted adolescent) and the virtual impossibility for him to make a choice and to settle down'.[138] In fact, as we have seen, Certeau went on to produce an important and coherent body of work.

HABITATS

A good memory and abundant energy belong to the realm of nature rather than nurture. So, perhaps, does curiosity, although in order to be effective it needs to be awakened and allowed to flourish, conditions that only some societies offer. Other characteristics of polymaths also require a cultural or social explanation. Where the previous chapter concentrated on the psychology of polymaths, this one is concerned with their habitat, from their early environment, geographical and social, to the niches that they later found for themselves.

In his autobiography, Vico declared that he became a scholar because he was born in Italy 'and not in Morocco'. If he had known of the existence of Ibn Khaldun, who lived in Fez for a time, Vico might not have chosen this example, but his general point about the geography of scholarship is surely valid.[1] Western polymaths were not distributed equally either in Europe or the Americas.

Of the 500 polymaths listed in the appendix to this book, 84 were German and 81 British (including a Welshman, William Jones, and a Channel Islander, Herbert John Fleure), 76 were French, 62 North American, 43 Italian. From other parts of the West the numbers are much lower: 21 Scots, 18 Austrians, 17 Spaniards, 15 Netherlanders (including Belgians), 14 Swiss, 11 Russians, 10 Hungarians, 6 Swedes, 5 Danes, 5 Czechs, 4 Poles, 4 Mexicans, 3 Argentinians, 3 Brazilians, 3 Irish, 2 Canadians, 2 Romanians, and one each from Algeria (Jacques Derrida), Australia (George Elton Mayo), Bulgaria (Tristan Todorov),

Croatia (Rudjer Bošković), Cuba (Fernando Ortiz), Estonia (Jacob von Uexküll), Greece (Constantinos Doxiadis), Malta (Themistocles Zammit), Peru (Pedro de Peralta), Venezuela (Andrés Bello) and Portugal (Fernáo de Oliveira).

The place of some small nations is particularly impressive. The Swedes include two individuals who remain famous for only one of their many achievements: Emanuel Swedenborg, discussed earlier, as a visionary, and August Strindberg as a dramatist – he also wrote on (among other things) history, photography, alchemy, linguistics, China and Japan.[2] The relatively high score of a small population in the Swedish case may be linked to the country's literacy rate, already approaching 90 per cent of adults by the end of the seventeenth century.[3] In the eighteenth century, Scotland produced a remarkable cluster of polymaths, notably David Hume, Adam Smith, Adam Ferguson, Lord Kames, Lord Monboddo and the brothers John and William Playfair. The Swiss score high from the sixteenth century (Conrad Gessner and Theodor Zwinger) to the twentieth (Carl Gustav Jung and Jean Piaget), with Leonhard Euler, Albrecht von Haller, Germaine de Staël, Louis Agassiz and Jacob Burckhardt in between.

The Dutch contribution, concentrated in the seventeenth century with nine polymaths, looks particularly spectacular and this success story may help in the search for general explanations. The Dutch Republic in the seventeenth century was a densely populated country with good internal communications by canal, and good connections with much of the world thanks to its many ships. It was an urban culture with one of the biggest cities in Europe (Amsterdam), a high literacy rate and four universities (Leiden, Utrecht, Harderwijk and Franeker), the first of these being a major centre of learning with a good library, some famous professors and many foreign students. In addition, an important educational institution, the Athenaeum, was located in Amsterdam, together with a Stock Exchange, the headquarters of the East and West India Companies, and other 'centres of calculation' or 'sites of knowledge'.[4]

Access to knowledge via schools, universities, libraries and so on is obviously important for would-be polymaths, so it was a great advantage to be born in a major city such as Amsterdam or Hamburg, a commercial city that either produced or offered niches to six early modern German polymaths, thanks in part to a famous school, the Johanneum, founded in 1529. A history of the scholars of Hamburg was published as early as 1783.[5] In the nineteenth and twentieth centuries, Paris, London and Berlin were major centres of polymathy.

Twelve of the polymaths listed came from Latin America.[6] The number is not high relative to the total population of the region, or indeed to the United States, where opportunities were greater, but nonetheless it is striking. A possible explanation may be late specialization and the survival of the idea of the 'man of letters'. It has often been noted that social theory has been produced mainly in Western Europe and North America and that theorists have tended to generalize on the basis of those parts of the world. Two major exceptions to this rule, examples of what is known as 'Southern Theory', are the Cuban Fernando Ortiz and the Brazilian Gilberto Freyre.

Both men taught in universities on occasion but they were primarily men of letters who wrote poems and stories as well as reading widely in sociology, anthropology, geography, history and psychology, and developing their theories from their investigation of their own societies. Both of them emphasized the importance of cultural mixing (rejecting the idea of 'race'). Ortiz compared Cuban culture to the local stew (*ajiaco*) and wrote about what he called 'transculturation', while Freyre wrote in similar terms about the 'interpenetration' of cultures, especially in Brazil.[7]

THE WORK ETHIC

The geography of religion is also relevant to the distribution of polymaths. In the long debate about the causes of the Scientific Revolution of the seventeenth century, it has sometimes been argued that what Max Weber called 'The Protestant Ethic' was important for the rise of science as well as the rise of capitalism.[8] This argument certainly needs to be qualified. Rather than referring to all Protestants, it should concentrate, as Weber did, on the 'Puritan' variety, with its ethic of frugality and hard work. Conversely, what is often called the 'Protestant' work ethic is found among other groups as well, including Confucians and Jews (discussed below) as well as some Catholics, including Umberto Eco, whose 'work ethic' (*etica lavorativa*) has been emphasized by one of his former students.[9] The presence of ten Jesuit polymaths in the group undermines any simple appeal to a Protestant ethic.

Despite these necessary qualifications to his thesis, there remains a kernel of truth in Weber's argument and it is tempting to extend it to scholars in general and polymaths in particular, encouraged by the fact that one of Weber's favourite examples of the Protestant ethic was the polymath Benjamin Franklin, whose 'Plan for Future Conduct' (1726) shows his concern at the age of twenty with frugality and industry.

The argument is supported by the number of polymaths who were Protestant ministers, nineteen altogether, whether Lutheran, Calvinist or Anglican. In Central Europe, they included Philipp Melanchthon, Johann Heinrich Alsted, Johannes Comenius and Johann Gottfried Herder. In Scotland, they included Gilbert Burnet, John Playfair (a mathematician, geologist and astronomer) and William Robertson Smith. In mainly Catholic France, ministers included Samuel Bochart, Pierre Bayle and Comte's mentor Daniel Encontre (who was successively a professor of literature, mathematics and theology). Other polymaths expected, or were expected by their parents, to follow this career, including the biologist–psychologist James Miller; Warren McCulloch, a pioneer in the field of artificial intelligence; the economist–historian Harold Innis, whose family were Baptists; and Melvil Dewey, another Baptist, who thought of becoming a missionary.

Twenty-nine polymaths, including Olof Rudbeck, Pierre Bayle, Carl Linnaeus, Emanuel Swedenborg, Adam Ferguson, Jacob Burckhardt, John Stuart Mill, Louis Agassiz, Carl Gustav Jung, Harold Lasswell and Robert Hutchins, were the sons of Protestant ministers and so particularly likely to have the 'Protestant ethic' inculcated in them at an early age.[10] Friedrich Nietzsche, himself the son of a Lutheran clergyman, once wrote that 'The Protestant pastor is the grandfather of German philosophy', a remark that might be extended to scholarship in general.[11] Grandchildren of pastors include Johann Albert Fabricius, Madame de

Staël and Jürgen Habermas. Habermas, who spends long hours at his desk, is the grandson of a pastor 'who upheld the Prussian virtue of a strict work ethic'.[12]

An outstanding example of such an ethic is Max Weber himself, whose mother, like the mothers of Benjamin Franklin and Warren McCulloch, was a devout Protestant. Max once said to his wife, Marianne, that for him, uninterrupted work was a 'natural need'. John Maynard Keynes (another workaholic, as we have seen) was the son of 'an earnest Nonconformist' and, according to Bertrand Russell, 'Something of the Nonconformist spirit remained in his son'.[13]

THE VEBLEN QUESTION

To place the Weber thesis in perspective, it may be juxtaposed to an argument by another polymathic sociologist, Thorstein Veblen. In a famous essay published in 1919, Veblen discussed what he called 'The Intellectual Pre-Eminence of Jews in Modern Europe', attempting to explain why the Jews have contributed 'a disproportionate number of the men to whom modern science and scholarship look for guidance and leadership', 'the pioneers, the uneasy gild of pathfinders and iconoclasts'. Rejecting a racial explanation of the phenomenon on the grounds that 'the Jewish people are a nation of hybrids', Veblen adopted a social one, claiming that it is only when Jews join 'the gentile republic of learning' that they become creative, poised between two worlds and therefore regarding both with a certain degree of detachment or scepticism.[14]

The prosopography of polymaths on which this book is based also suggests that individuals of Jewish origin (whether they were practising Jews, Catholics, Protestants or atheists) have punched well above their weight, at least from the mid-nineteenth century onwards, beginning with Marx. Among the individuals listed in the appendix who were born in 1817 or later, 55 out of 250 were Jewish. This figure confirms Veblen's idea in one way yet it undermines it in another. The problem is that, if Veblen was right, as Jews left the ghettoes and became assimilated into European and American culture, what he called 'the supply of Jewish renegades' should have dried up early in the twentieth century. It has conspicuously failed to do so in the case of polymaths. Alternative explanations for Jewish 'intellectual pre-eminence' are therefore necessary in order to supplement if not to replace Veblen's insight.

As in the case of other minorities such as the Quakers, exclusion from politics will have encouraged intelligent young men to move into another domain, such as trade or scholarship. Jewish parents traditionally respected learning and becoming a scientist or a scholar was a kind of secularization of the tradition of studying the Tanakh and the Torah. It is not surprising to find some parents who pushed their children hard in this direction, as in the case of Norbert Wiener, who later joked that he had been 'brought up in a doubly Puritan environment', in a Jewish family in Protestant New England.[15] The importance of exile is also worth noting, as Veblen surely would have done if he had been writing in the 1930s rather than in 1919. The polymaths of Jewish origin discussed in this book were usually either exiles themselves or the children of exiles, living between the culture of their homeland and that of their 'hostland' and so viewing both with a certain degree of detachment, allowing these refugees to escape the provinciality of scientists and scholars who are rooted in one particular environment and the ways of thinking that accompany it.[16]

EDUCATION

Did a particular kind of upbringing encourage polymathy? It is plausible to suggest, though difficult to prove, that education at home rather than school encourages a lack of respect for formal academic boundaries or even a lack of awareness of their existence. At any rate, some leading polymaths were educated at home. For a long time this was necessarily the case for women, for Anna Maria Schurman, for instance, for Sister Juana de la Cruz, for Mary Somerville and for Lady Mary Wortley Montagu, who studied Latin by herself when 'everyone thought I was reading but romances'. Among the males, polymaths who were educated at home, at least in their early years, include Christiaan Huygens, Nicolaes Witsen, Christopher Wren, Gilbert Burnet, the Humboldt brothers, Thomas Young, John Stuart Mill, Mark Pattison, William Robertson Smith, Karl

Pearson, Karl and Michael Polanyi, John von Neumann, Bertrand Russell, Jorge Luis Borges and Ludwig von Bertalanffy.

A number of polymaths were child prodigies: Blaise Pascal, for instance, Juan Caramuel, Maria Agnesi, the Swiss physiologist Albrecht von Haller, Thomas Macaulay, John Stuart Mill, Dorothea Schlözer, Manuel Menéndez y Pelayo, Jean Piaget (who published several scientific articles while he was a teenager), John von Neumann, Norbert Wiener (whose autobiography was entitled *Ex-Prodigy*), his friend William Sidis (who went to Harvard at the age of eleven) and Walter Pitts.

Some of these, notably Mill, Schlözer, Wiener and Sidis, all three of whom were the children of intellectuals, felt the pressure of the 'great expectations' of their fathers. Mill began Greek at the age of three, Dorothea Schlözer began geometry, French and Latin at the age of five, while Wiener studied physics and chemistry aged seven, went to university aged twelve and took his BA aged fourteen. He remembered his father's 'hard and unceasing work' and the fact that 'what Father expected of himself, he expected of me as well'. Ralph Gerard, whose background was similar to Wiener's, was fifteen when he went to university and described his father as 'a master teacher, a demanding prod, and a tyrant'.[17] Kenneth Boulding did not view his parents as tyrants, but remembered that they too had 'extremely high expectations' of their precocious son.[18]

Other polymaths attended conventional schools but went their own way. Vico called himself an autodidact. Alan Turing, who went to Sherborne, a public school in Dorset, 'always preferred his own methods to those supplied by the text-book', while Herbert Simon claimed that when he was a schoolboy in Milwaukee, he 'kept his education entirely in his own hands, seldom asking for advice'. Simon followed the same 'strategy of self-instruction', as he called it, when learning mathematics and languages in later life.[19] He was not the only polymath to praise this method. Daniel Morhof defended the autodidact.[20] David Hume declared that 'there is nothing to be learnt from a professor, which is not to be met with in books'. Thomas Young agreed that there was 'very little' that 'a person who is seriously and industriously disposed to improve may not obtain from books with more advantage than from a living instructor'.[21]

Access to a well-stocked library at home or nearby encouraged self-education in parallel with school. Christiaan Huygens, for instance, had access to the extensive collection of books accumulated by his father. Giambattista Vico and Samuel Johnson had the advantage of being the sons of booksellers. Thomas Young discovered the natural sciences by browsing in the library of a neighbour.[22] H. G. Wells was allowed to borrow books from the library of the country house of Uppark when his mother was a servant there, and in middle age he remarked on 'the wonders of self-education'.[23] George Homans believed that 'much of what I learned from books I learned not at school but at home, from our excellent library'.[24] Jorge Luis Borges also lived in a house with many books in it, and later said that 'if I were asked to name the chief event in my life, I would say my father's library'.[25] Walter Bagehot, Norbert Wiener, John von Neumann and Joseph Needham all developed their wide interests by browsing in their father's libraries, while Otto Neurath, the son of a professor who owned about 13,000 books, confessed that 'I made my first mathematical estimates counting the number of books in the library'.[26]

Some polymaths dropped out of university, among them Robert Hooke, Denis Diderot, David Hume, Thomas De Quincey, T. H. Huxley, August Strindberg, Patrick Geddes, Elton Mayo, Kenneth Burke, H. G. Wells (who began studying at the Normal School of Science in London) and Lewis Mumford. Mumford later taught at colleges on occasion, but avoided permanent attachments and once described being read by academics as 'a second burial'. A few never studied at university at all, among them Leonardo, Joseph Priestley (unable to enter Oxford or Cambridge because he was not an Anglican), Herbert Spencer and Jorge Luis Borges.

In more than the first two-thirds of the period examined in this book, more or less 1400–1800, formidable obstacles were placed in the way of female scholars. They were not forbidden to go to university but it was generally assumed that higher learning was not for them. If they developed intellectual interests, these were expected to be in *belles-lettres* rather than learning, just as their publications, if any, were expected to be translations rather than original work. In these circumstances it is little short of miraculous that a few female polymaths emerged in the early modern period, twelve of them between 1450 and 1800.[27]

The removal of some of these obstacles in the way of intellectual women led to a slight rise of female polymaths, six of them in the nineteenth century: Germaine de Staël, Dorothea Schlözer, George Eliot, Mary Somerville, Harriet Martineau and Harriet Taylor. They have been succeeded in the twentieth and the twenty-first centuries by a larger cluster of versatile scholars who were able to take advantage of the expansion of female education and of occupations for educated women, especially for the generation born in the 1930s, such as Susan Sontag and Clara Gallini, who was active as a classicist, historian of religion and cultural anthropologist, and their successors.

Living women with a good claim to be considered as polymaths include Gayatri Chakravorty Spivak, active in philosophy, literary theory and postcolonial studies; Luce Iragiray (philosophy, psychoanalysis and linguistics); Hélène Cixous (philosophy, psychoanalysis, literature); Juliet Mitchell (literature, psychoanalysis and gender studies); Julia Kristeva (literature, philosophy, psychoanalysis, semiotics); Griselda Pollock (art history, cultural theory, psychoanalysis); Aleida Assmann (literature, cultural history, anthropology); Judith Butler (philosophy, linguistics, politics); Margaret Boden (philosophy, psychology and cognitive studies); Mieke Bal, a theorist of literature, art and the media who also practises as a video artist, and Jacqueline Rose, who writes on literature, psychoanalysis, gender studies, politics and history (not to mention a novel).[28]

INDEPENDENCE

Curiosity, energy and the drive to make a productive use of time are still not enough. Polymaths also need the leisure to do their own work. This was sometimes provided by life in community in Oxford and Cambridge colleges or as members of religious orders – Benedictines (Johannes Trithemius and Benito Feijóo), Carmelites (Bodin for a time, and Sister

Juana), Cistercians (Caramuel), canons regular (Erasmus, for a time, and Copernicus), Franciscans (Rabelais and Sebastian Münster, both for a time), Dominicans (Fernão de Oliveira, Giordano Bruno, for a time, and Tommaso Campanella), Servites (Paolo Sarpi) and especially Jesuits (the ten mentioned earlier). Princess Elisabeth became a Protestant abbess. Celibacy and the freedom from concern with food and lodging allowed these scholars to concentrate on acquiring and transmitting knowledge, while Athanasius Kircher in particular made good use of his order's global network. His book on China drew on the first-hand knowledge of colleagues who were missionaries. Kircher was even able to assemble a team of Jesuits to observe magnetic variation in different parts of the globe.[29]

A few lay polymaths never married. In some cases, from Leonardo to Alan Turing, this was probably because they were homosexual, but in other cases the likely reason was to avoid distraction from their studies. The group includes Filippo Brunelleschi, Joseph Scaliger, Franciscus Junius, Nicolas-Claude Peiresc, Leibniz, Pierre Bayle, René de Réaumur, Gaspar Melchor de Jovellanos, Alexander von Humboldt, Thomas Macaulay, Herbert Spencer, Charles Sainte-Beuve, William Robertson Smith and Charles Ogden. When Charles Darwin made his famous list of the case for and against marriage, one of the arguments for remaining single was 'Loss of time – cannot read in the Evenings' (nevertheless, he married Emma Wedgwood).[30]

A substantial number of polymaths were members of a 'leisure class' with an income that did not depend on employment: Pico della Mirandola, for instance, John Dee, Tycho Brahe, Christiaan Huygens, Scipione Maffei, Montesquieu and Buffon. Alexander von Humboldt had enough not only to live on but also to finance his famous expedition to Latin America. In Britain, Charles Babbage, Charles Darwin, Francis Galton, John Lubbock and William Henry Fox Talbot were all gentleman scholars with private incomes. Aby Warburg, the son and brother of a banker, was able to live comfortably and buy all the books he needed for his studies.[31] Walter Benjamin was supported, not always willingly, by his wealthy parents. Henry Murray was 'independently wealthy'.[32]

Inheriting a fortune allowed a number of polymaths to indulge their wider interests in later life –Thomas Young, for instance, Charles Peirce, Herbert Spencer, Georg Simmel and Vilfredo Pareto, who gave up teaching at the age of sixty-one in order to devote more time to his books. Bertrand Russell inherited £20,000 from his father, although he still needed to write books and make lecture tours in the United States in order to support his various wives and children.

ENFORCED LEISURE

A few polymaths made good use of enforced leisure, among them Walter Raleigh, who, according to Aubrey, 'studied most in his Sea-Voyages, where he carried always a trunk of books along with him'.[33] Darwin, who spent five years at sea on the *Beagle*, reading and writing in his hammock, wrote to his father that 'a ship is singularly comfortable for all sorts of work. Everything is so close at hand, and being cramped makes one so methodical, that in the end I have been the gainer.' One of the books he read in this way was Charles Lyell's *Principles of Geology* (1830–3), which helped shape his theory of evolution.[34]

Raleigh's second bout of enforced leisure was as a prisoner in the Tower of London, where he wrote his *History of the World*. John Selden wrote a study of Jewish legal history in the Marshalsea prison, where he was confined for political reasons in 1629. He later remarked wryly on 'the abundant leisure of prison'.[35] Thomas Campanella spent twenty-seven years in Neapolitan prisons and indeed wrote some of his most important books in these circumstances. Samuel Pufendorf, who was employed as a tutor in the family of a Swedish diplomat, was imprisoned in Copenhagen when war broke out between Denmark and Sweden. According to his own testimony, Pufendorf employed his time in prison to write his *Elements of Jurisprudence* – from memory, since he had no access to books.[36] The Spanish statesman Jovellanos, in prison in the castle of Bellver in Mallorca, used his leisure to study the geology of the region, to produce a historical description of the castle, and to write up his notes on the buildings of Palma. Bertrand Russell, who was imprisoned for five months for supporting the refusal of 'conscientious objectors' to fight in the First World War, 'read enormously' in gaol and, like Pufendorf, he was able to write a book before he was released.[37]

FAMILIES

Families linked a number of the individuals discussed in this study, whether (as one of them, Francis Galton, claimed) because 'genius' is hereditary, or whether it is the early environment that encourages the development of many-sidedness. Famous examples of polymathic families include the brothers Wilhelm and Alexander von Humboldt; John and William Playfair, the elder focusing on mathematics and natural philosophy and the younger on engineering and political economy; Julian and Aldous Huxley, dividing the natural sciences and the humanities between them; and the French scholars Joseph, Salomon and Théodore Reinach (it was remarked that the initials of the three, J, S and T, stood for 'je sais tout').

As for the brothers Karl and Michael Polanyi, they were only the best-known members of what a friend called 'the most gifted family I have ever known or heard of', including their sister Laura. They seem to have taken after their mother, Cécile, who 'penned unpublished texts on a miscellany of cultural and political topics, from graphology to jewellery, pedagogy to pyjamas, romance to the Russian revolution'.[38] Another remarkable example of a gifted family is that of the six Prodi brothers, all of whom followed academic careers, including at least two polymaths, Giorgio (in medicine, biology and semiotics) and Paolo (in church history and political thought). Of the remaining four, Giovanni was a mathematician, Franco and Vittorio were physicists, while Romano, an economist, later became Prime Minister of Italy.

Fathers and sons include three examples from the seventeenth century, one Swedish and two Dutch. Olof Rudbeck the Younger did not match his father's range, but his work in medicine, botany, ornithology and what we call 'linguistics' surely merits the title of polymath. The leading mathematician and natural philosopher Christiaan Huygens was the son of Constantijn, whose wide interests were mainly in the humanities. Another Dutchman, Isaac Vossius, was the son of an equally well-known scholar, Gerard Vossius.

The polymaths studied here also include a pair of fathers and daughters. August von Schlözer was not only one of the leading historians of his time but also wrote on what he was one of the first to call *Völkerkunde* (the comparative study of different peoples) and on *Statistik*, which included the description of political systems as well as tables of figures. His daughter Dorothea, the first German woman to take a Ph.D, knew nine languages and studied mathematics, botany, zoology, optics, religion, mining, mineralogy and art. Jacob Bronowski and his daughter Lisa offer another example. Jacob's straddling of the two cultures was discussed earlier, while his daughter, better known as Lisa Jardine, was a mathematician turned literary critic and cultural historian as well as a public intellectual.

NETWORKS

Polymaths include groups of friends as well as relatives. Despite rivalries, members of the species are often drawn to one another. After his migration to America, Joseph Priestley became a friend of his fellow polymath Thomas Jefferson. The young Goethe was a friend of Herder and the middle-aged Goethe was a friend of the Humboldt brothers.

John Herschel, William Whewell and Charles Babbage became friends when they were students at Cambridge. James Frazer's friendship with William Robertson Smith began when Smith arrived at the same university. Yet another Cambridge friendship, between Charles Ogden and Ivor Richards, began when the two men were students at Magdalene College. Ogden, who studied classics, turned to psychology and later invented and advocated Basic English. Richards studied 'moral sciences', taught philosophy and English literature, and became a professor of education.[39]

In Germany, the so-called 'Frankfurt School', discussed in the following chapter, included friends who knew one another from their schooldays: Theodor Adorno, Max Horkheimer and Siegfried Kracauer. In France, Georges Bataille and Roger Caillois were friends who founded the so-called 'College of Sociology' together. They shared interests in literature (Bataille wrote poetry and Caillois a novel), but both are best known for ambitious studies that drew on anthropology while offering broader conclusions. Bataille's *La part maudite* (1949) offered a theory of consumption, while Caillois presented a theory of play, *Les jeux et les hommes* (1958).[40] Another productive friendship was that between Gilles Deleuze, a philosopher and critic who wrote on literature, art and the cinema, and the psychologist, philosopher and semiologist Félix Guattari.

The relation between William Robertson Smith and James Frazer might also be described as that of master and disciple, another recurring theme in the history of polymaths.[41] Karl Pearson was a disciple of Francis Galton. Lewis Mumford described himself as a rebellious disciple of Patrick Geddes, recognizing that Geddes 'changed my whole life' and 'gave me a new view of the world' but also that, as he grew older, 'my own way of thinking had departed from his'.[42] Henry Murray was one of Lawrence Henderson's students, and Ernst Haeckel a pupil of Rudolf Virchow. In his turn, Haeckel became a master for whom Friedrich Ratzel expressed 'unqualified admiration'.[43]

Wider networks of correspondents have often been mentioned in earlier chapters. Some of these networks are well known. They run from Erasmus to Charles Darwin via Peiresc, Kircher, Leibniz, Bayle and Alexander von Humboldt. Face-to-face contacts are not always documented but they are probably even more important. For example, Gregory Bateson saw himself as part of a common enterprise involving at least four other polymaths whom he knew personally: Bertalanffy, Wiener, von Neumann and Shannon.[44]

Family and friends form what might be called a lateral network of individuals living at the same time or at least overlapping for several decades. Also important for polymaths is what might be called their vertical network or their intellectual genealogy, which often includes earlier polymaths such as Ramón Lull, Pico della Mirandola, Johannes Comenius and Francis Bacon. Pico, Heinrich Cornelius Agrippa, Kircher, Caramuel, Leibniz and Benito Feijoo were all fascinated by Lull's art of combination. Johannes Bureus admired Pico, while Queen Christina owned a portrait of him. Leibniz and Kircher were both interested in Comenius. Bacon was a hero for d'Alembert, Feijoo and

Jovellanos, and later for Comte, Spencer and Melvil Dewey. Even some relatively recent polymaths had this sense of genealogy. Both Geddes and Neurath found Comenius inspiring. Borges expressed interest in Lull (writing an essay on his 'thought machine'), Pico (reviewing a book about him), Kircher, Leibniz, Coleridge, De Quincey ('essential for me'), and 'The Huxley dynasty' (including Aldous's brother Julian and their grandfather T. H. Huxley).

To flourish, polymaths need a niche that will allow them to make a living. Among the most common of these niches have been courts, schools, universities, libraries and journals.

COURTS AND PATRONAGE

In early modern times an important niche for polymaths, as for other scholars (not to mention artists, poets and musicians), was the court, royal or aristocratic. Leonardo left Florence for the court of Lodovico Sforza in Milan, and ended his life in France supported by King Francis I. Charles IX of Sweden and his successor Gustav Adolf were patrons of Johannes Bureus, who has been described as 'the great polyhistor of the age of greatness' and is best known for his studies of the occult sciences and of Swedish antiquities.[45] Particularly important for scholars, as we have seen, was the court of Gustav's daughter Christina of Sweden.

Leibniz lived at the courts of Hanover and Wolfenbüttel. Lorenzo Magalotti and Francesco Redi lived at the Medici court in Florence. Samuel Pufendorf was employed as a historian at the court of Charles XI of Sweden and then at the court of the Elector of Brandenburg in Berlin. Peter Simon Pallas and August Schlözer were supported by Catherine the Great and Denis Diderot spent a few months at her court in St Petersburg, like Voltaire at the court of Frederick the Great in Potsdam. As late as the nineteenth century, Alexander von Humboldt served as chamberlain at the Prussian court.

The attitude of polymaths to courts was often ambivalent. For scholars who lacked a private income, the salaries paid by monarchs and aristocrats were often tempting. One reason for the nomadic life of Agrippa, in Cologne, Turin, Metz, Geneva, Fribourg, Lyon and Antwerp, was the search for patrons, among them the emperor Maximilian, Louise of Savoy and Margaret of Austria. Patrons might pay for books to be printed. Without the financial aid of the Emperor Ferdinand III, the massive illustrated folios of Kircher's *Oedipus Aegyptiacus* might never have been published. Again, powerful patrons offered protection. In his conflicts with academic colleagues, Swedenborg was supported by King Charles XII.

On the other hand, scholars often resented the distraction from their studies entailed by the need to play the courtier. In Rome, Kircher complained about spending his time answering questions from Pope Alexander VII.[46] When Leibniz was serving as historian to Ernst August, the Elector of Hanover, his patron regularly asked him to attend to other matters. As for Humboldt, he was required to read to King Friedrich Wilhelm III at meals and deal with his correspondence, and later to answer Friedrich Wilhelm IV's many questions on a variety of subjects, using him like an encyclopaedia.[47]

Today, the patronage of monarchs and aristocrats has been taken over by foundations. Their role in some enterprises involving polymaths will be discussed below.

SCHOOLS AND UNIVERSITIES

In early modern Germany, a number of polymaths taught in schools, especially in the academically oriented gymnasia in Hamburg and elsewhere. A few individuals preferred this niche to a place in a university, as if they were uncomfortable with the need to restrict their teaching to a single discipline.[48]

All the same, many polymaths did gravitate to universities, which have often offered more freedom for scholars than is customary today. Before the second half of the twentieth century, the administration of academic departments was not yet too demanding, while teaching loads might be light. At Johns Hopkins, where he was a professor from 1910 to 1938, Arthur Lovejoy 'refused to teach undergraduates' and 'never taught more than four hours per week' and only small groups of graduate students.[49] In addition, many professors were able to leave domestic affairs to their wives and servants. Of Friedrich Ratzel it has been remarked that 'It was still possible in the last quarter of the nineteenth century for a professor, especially a German professor, untrammelled by administration, welfare work and domestic chores, to acquire an extraordinary sweep of knowledge'.[50]

Academic freedom included opportunities for switching disciplines, a form of freedom particularly important for polymaths. At the University of Helmstedt, Hermann Conring moved between law, history and medicine.[51] At Uppsala, Olof Rudbeck, originally appointed to teach medicine, lectured on a wide range of natural sciences. At the University of Leiden, Herman Boerhaave, professor of botany and medicine, was allowed to hold the chair of chemistry as well. In the nineteenth century, Hermann Helmholtz moved from a chair in physiology to one in physics.

Even in the twentieth century, some universities showed themselves to be flexible in this respect. At the University of Graz, in 1924, a special chair in meteorology and geophysics was created for Alfred Wegener, whose interests also included astronomy. At Oxford, R. G. Collingwood was given the made-to-measure post of University Lecturer in Philosophy and Roman History. In Cambridge, after the Second World War, Joseph Needham, Reader in Embryology, retained his post at the university after he had given up biology in order to write the history of Chinese science.

Three serial polymaths were able to remain professors in their respective universities despite their dramatic shifts between academic fields, simply moving across the campus from one department to another. At the University College of Aberystwyth, Herbert Fleure, formerly head of the department of zoology, became the first (indeed the only) professor of anthropology and geography. At the University of Manchester, as we have seen, Michael Polanyi exchanged a chair in chemistry for one in 'social studies'. At the University of California at Los Angeles, Jared Diamond, a former professor of physiology, moved to the Department of Geography.

DISCIPLINES

A few disciplines in particular appear to have provided trampolines for polymaths. Philosophy is an obvious example, via its tradition of concern with the foundations of knowledge. Durkheim, Foucault and Bourdieu, for instance, were all trained as philosophers. Medicine was another springboard, offering training in precise observation that proved to be of use in other disciplines as well. In the early modern period physicians often studied botany and chemistry in the search for cures, while Miguel Servet was also interested in astronomy and geography. Among the early modern virtuosi who were famous for their cabinets of curiosities were the Danish physician Ole Worm and the Irishman Hans Sloane. Later, a few physicians were drawn to physical and also to social anthropology. The Frenchman Paul Broca migrated from medicine to anthropology, like his compatriots Gustave Le Bon and Paul Rivet and the Italian Paolo Mantegazza.[52]

In the nineteenth and twentieth centuries, engineering was yet another route to polymathy. Léon Walras and Vilfredo Pareto moved into economics, for instance, Frédéric Le Play and Herbert Spencer into sociology, Warren Weaver into the study of agriculture and the theory of communication, Vannevar Bush into computer science, John Maynard Smith and Robert May into biology, Benjamin Whorf into linguistics and anthropology, and Buckminster Fuller into architecture and what he called 'the principles governing the universe'. It seems that the sense of system necessary to be a good engineer is capable of adaptation to other disciplines, just as John Playfair's training as an engineer's draughtsman helped him to invent graphs and charts.

New disciplines emerge as part of the process of specialization. Paradoxically, they also offer particular opportunities for polymaths, at least in the short term, since the first generation of teachers of new disciplines is necessarily trained in something else. Freud's move from medicine and zoology to psychoanalysis offers a famous example of what might be described as the creative 'renegade'.[53]

In the case of anthropology, migrants came from geography (Franz Boas), zoology (Alfred Haddon) and psychology (William Rivers) as well as from medicine. In sociology, Frédéric Le Play came from engineering, Émile Durkheim from philosophy and pedagogy, Max Weber from law, Robert Park from philosophy and journalism, and Lester Ward from geology and palaeontology.

LIBRARIES AND MUSEUMS

The post of librarian is an obvious niche for polymaths, beginning in the third century BC with Eratosthenes in Alexandria. Pierre Bayle thought at one time of becoming a librarian because that would provide him with 'sufficient books', together (so he thought) with 'the time to study'.[54] In our period, at least twenty polymaths occupied this position at some time in their careers. They include Benito Arias Montano at the Escorial, Hugo Blotius in Vienna, Gabriel Naudé in Paris, Stockholm and Rome, Leibniz and Lessing in Wolfenbüttel, Antonio Magliabecchi in Florence, David Hume and Adam Ferguson in Edinburgh, William Robertson Smith in Cambridge, Marcelino Menéndez Pelayo in Madrid and Jorge Luis Borges in Buenos Aires.[55] Classifying books is obviously linked to classifying knowledge, as in the cases of Leibniz, Melvil Dewey and Paul Otlet.[56]

Museums too used to offer the curators the time and the opportunity to study. The Muséum d'histoire naturelle in Paris, which was in the early nineteenth century 'the world's largest establishment dedicated to scientific research', was the base for the many activities of Georges Cuvier.[57] Adolf Bastian founded the Museum für Völkerkunde in Berlin. Franz Boas worked there, and it was in the course of cataloguing exhibits that he became interested in artefacts produced in the North West Coast of the United States, a region that he continued to study throughout his career. After his arrival in the United States, Boas was active in the Field Museum at Chicago and the American Museum of Natural History in New York before moving to Columbia University.

Other polymaths studied and wrote in the intervals afforded by their employment, intervals that were often more generous in the eighteenth and nineteenth centuries than they became later. John Stuart Mill had the good fortune to work in an office in the East India Company, where his duties were light enough to allow him to write his books. John Lubbock was able to write his books on prehistory while active as head of the family bank and a Member of Parliament. When Borges was cataloguing books in a public library in Buenos Aires, his occupation for nine years, what he described as a light workload gave him the opportunity to continue his wide reading.

ENCYCLOPAEDIAS AND JOURNALS

On the edge of the academic world, a number of polymaths have written, edited or contributed to encyclopaedias – appropriately enough, given their encyclopaedic interests. As we have seen, Johann Heinrich Alsted compiled a massive encyclopaedia single-handed, while Diderot and d'Alembert managed a team of contributors. Thomas Young contributed over sixty articles to the fifth edition of the *Encyclopedia Britannica*. Robertson Smith was chief editor of the ninth edition of the *Britannica*, while Andrew Lang contributed nineteen articles to that edition. For a time, the young Norbert Wiener made a living by writing articles for the *Encyclopedia Americana*.

Another niche for polymaths, from the age of Bayle until today, has been the cultural journal or the newspaper, especially for those who prefer the freedom of a freelance worker to the relative security of an institution such as the university. Samuel Johnson, for instance, founded *The Rambler*, which, like his *Dictionary*, allowed him to support himself outside what he called 'the shelter of academic bowers'.[58] Macaulay earned £200 a year (a reasonable income at that time) from his famous essays for *The Edinburgh Review*.[59] George Eliot wrote for the *Westminster Review*, Ernest Renan and Hippolyte Taine for the *Revue des Deux Mondes*, Siegfried Kracauer for the *Frankfurter Zeitung*, Lewis Mumford, George Steiner and Susan Sontag for the *New Yorker*, Sontag, Steiner and Oliver Sacks for the *New York Review of Books*, Michel Foucault for *Le Nouvel Observateur* and Umberto Eco for *L'Espresso*.

A few polymaths edited or founded journals as well as writing for them. Francis Jeffrey edited the *Edinburgh Review*, Lewis Mumford and Kenneth Burke edited *The Dial*, Benedetto Croce founded *La Critica*. Editing a series, as a kind of midwife of books, has been another role for polymaths, among them Gustave Le Bon, who edited the *Bibliothèque de Philosophie Scientifique* for the publisher Flammarion; Henri Berr, who edited the historical series *L'Évolution de L'Humanité* for Albin Michel; and Charles Ogden, who edited the International Library of Psychology, Philosophy and Scientific Method for Routledge, a series that eventually reached 201 volumes.

COLLABORATION

Even in the 'golden age' of polymaths, they did not work alone but depended on a network of friends and informants. As the difficulty of mastering different disciplines has grown, later polymaths have collaborated at least some of the time. Alexander von Humboldt, who employed assistants for his observations, was also devoted to international scientific collaboration, especially in geophysical research, encouraging the setting up of a network of observation posts in different countries to measure the magnetism of the earth.[60] H. G. Wells collaborated with Julian Huxley on *The Science of Life* (1929). Karl Polanyi had a number of assistants in his studies of anthropology and ancient history.

Throughout his long career, Paul Lazarsfeld carried out research in collaboration with colleagues. Joseph Needham's assistants and collaborators enabled the many volumes of *Science and Civilization in China* to continue to appear long after the death of the senior author.[61] Ernst Gombrich worked with the neuropsychologist Richard Gregory (on eye and brain) and the biologist Robert Hinde (on non-verbal communication). Herbert Simon participated, by his own count, in 'more than 80 research partnerships'.[62]

Famous collaborations include Charles Ogden with Ivor Richards on *The Meaning of Meaning* (1923), a book about philosophy and language; John von Neumann with Norbert Wiener on cybernetics and with Oskar Morgenstern on *The Theory of Games and Economic Behaviour* (1944); Claude Shannon with Warren Weaver on *The Mathematical Theory of Communication* (1949). Yuri Lotman and Boris Uspensky were partners for decades in their studies of the semiotics of culture.

Michel de Certeau wrote his study of the politics of language together with two young historians, Jacques Revel and Dominique Julia. Michel Foucault carried out one study, on the history of the family, together with the historian Arlette Farge, and another, on the parricide Pierre Rivière, with the members of his seminar at the Collège de France, including the anthropologist Jeanne Favret and the historian of medicine Jean-Pierre Peter.[63]

It would be easy to add to these examples. Projects for multidisciplinary or interdisciplinary collaboration, whether formal or informal, are the subject of the following chapter.

8

THE AGE OF
INTERDISCIPLINARITY

As the position of 'lone ranger' among the fields of knowledge is becoming increasingly untenable, it is necessary to shift attention to attempts to achieve collectively what some polymaths have achieved individually, an overview of a territory that extends well beyond the boundaries of a single discipline.[1] Attempts of this kind have been made by small, informal, face-to-face groups and also by formal institutions founded for the purpose.

The story begins well before the adjective 'interdisciplinary' came into common use in the 1950s, in French and German as well as in the Anglophone world. Before that time, attempts at interdisciplinary work, whether by individuals or by teams, were described as intellectual 'co-operation' or 'cross-fertilization'.[2] Since then, a confusing variety of terms has come into occasional use, among them 'adisciplinary', 'anti-disciplinary', 'cross-disciplinary', 'multi-disciplinary', 'non-disciplinary'. 'omni-disciplinary', 'pluri-disciplinary', 'post-disciplinary', 'pre-disciplinary' and 'trans-disciplinary'. What follows will avoid most of these terms, retaining the word 'interdisciplinary' to describe studies on the borders – or in the gaps – between disciplines, and 'multidisciplinary' to refer to teams that draw their members from different disciplines in order to work on a common project.

As we have seen, the encyclopaedias and the scientific expeditions of the eighteenth century already depended on such teams. So did industrial research laboratories in the late nineteenth century, financed by firms such as General Electric, Standard Oil, Eastman Kodak and Bell Telephone.[3] So did projects funded by governments in the First and Second World Wars and beyond.

The polymath Herbert Simon criticized teamwork in the social sciences, describing it as 'bringing unlike social scientists together'. What was needed, according to him, was a polymath, 'bringing unlike social sciences together in one man'.[4] If everyone was like Simon himself, he would surely have been right. However, the central theme of this chapter is that the explosion of knowledge has made it impossible for all but a few energetic and dedicated individuals to keep up with what is happening in even a few disciplines. Hence the many collective attempts to solve the problem, at the level of general education as well as that of problem-oriented research.

A number of the polymaths who starred in earlier chapters will appear once again, viewed this time as participants in collective attempts to combat specialization. Thomas De Quincey discussed 'superficial knowledge'; José Ortega y Gasset denounced the 'learned ignoramus' and claimed that specialization led to barbarism; Lewis Mumford was proud to call himself a 'generalist'; George Steiner has called specialization 'moronic'; and Robert Heinlein, a former engineer best known as a writer of science fiction, asserted that 'specialization is for insects'.

A more balanced view was expressed by the British journalist and sociologist L. T. Hobhouse, who wrote in 1901 that 'To specialization . . . we owe the efficiency and accuracy of modern science. To it we also owe a loss of freshness and interest, a weakening of the scientific imagination, and a great impairment of science as an instrument of education.'[5]

A notable feature of the debate over specialization is the recurrence of a few metaphors. The metaphor of territory is rather worn by now but it remains irresistible, not least because the idea of 'fields' of knowledge has passed into common academic use. It is associated with fences and frontiers. A writer in the *New Yorker* once commented on the polymath Beardsley Ruml's 'creative ignorance', 'which prevents him from seeing the No Thoroughfare, Keep Off the Grass, Don't Trespass and Dead End Street signs in the world of ideas'.[6]

Conversely, interdisciplinary enterprises are presented as opening doors or windows, building bridges and knocking down walls. At Yale, President Angell described his interdisciplinary project, whether grandiloquently or wryly, as dismantling the 'Great Wall of China'.[7]

Alternatively, the critics of specialization make use of political metaphors. In the early nineteenth century, William Whewell was already referring to the danger that the 'commonwealth of science' would disintegrate 'like a great empire falling to pieces'. Specialization has been described as 'balkanization' or 'disciplinary chauvinism'. Norbert Elias remarked that 'The departments of scientific knowledge, as constituted today, have some of the characteristics of sovereign states.' According to Herbert Simon, 'disciplines play the same role in academe as nations in the international system'.[8]

The aims of the critics of specialization have varied from the modest to the ambitious. Some, like Otto Neurath, have been visionaries (the vision was that of the unity of science, or of knowledge more generally). Others were pragmatists. Ortega y Gasset did not reject specialization entirely but favoured an equilibrium between specialist knowledge and 'culture', which 'is necessarily general' (*no puede ser sino general*).[9] The polymath social scientist Donald T. Campbell offered what he called a 'fish-scale model' of overlaps between disciplines, implying that scholars should pay particular attention to what is happening in fields neighbouring their own.[10]

The methods of the supporters of interdisciplinarity also varied. Some favoured the foundation of new institutions, whereas others preferred informal arrangements. It may be useful to distinguish six overlapping phases, with older forms of co-operation coexisting with new ones.

The first phase, from the middle of the nineteenth century onwards, was one of informal or semi-formal discussion groups in *salons*, clubs and cafés. It was followed in turn by the international movement for unified science; by the foundation of interdisciplinary centres for research, especially in the social sciences, in the United States, together with a revival of the idea of general education; by government support for research in the natural sciences and 'area studies', again in the USA;

by the rise of new universities committed to interdisciplinary teaching in Europe and elsewhere; and by the rise of interdisciplinary journals and the proliferation of institutes for advanced study.

In other words, we have moved from an age of institutionalized specialization in the second half of the nineteenth century to an age of institutionalized anti-specialization in the second half of the twentieth century and beyond.

SEMI-FORMAL ARRANGEMENTS

Informal discussion groups were and are one way to encourage interdisciplinarity. The term 'informal' is not easy to define, and it may be more illuminating to think in terms of 'semi-formal' groups that met outside academic departments and often outside the university altogether. Some met in a fixed place and at a regular time and had a fixed membership, sometimes by election. Others met in cafés, including peripheral members around a central core. They all focused on common themes and problems viewed from the standpoints of different disciplines, fuelling discussions and encouraging freedom of speech by means of coffee, wine and beer.

These forms of intellectual sociability were situated between the traditions of the traditional Spanish *tertúlia* (more sociable than intellectual, combining conversation with cards and music) and the academic seminar (more intellectual than sociable, although discussion might continue in the café or the pub).[11]

Clubs, Societies and Circles: Select Chronology, 1855–c.1950

1855 Saturday Club, Boston

1869 Edinburgh Evening Club

1872 Metaphysical Club, Cambridge, MA

c.1887 Lamprecht group, Leipzig

1905 Eranos Circle, Heidelberg

1908 Galileo Circle, Budapest

c.1915 Sunday Circle, Budapest

c.1922 Vienna Circle

1923 History of Ideas Club, Baltimore

1928 Prague Circle

1932 Pareto Circle, Cambridge, MA

1949 Ratio Club, London

c.1949 Innominate Club, Chicago

c.1954 Glasgow group

Long before the term 'interdisciplinarity' was coined, the desire for general knowledge and wide-ranging discussion led to the foundation of societies such as 'The Club' (1764), established by Samuel Johnson and Joshua Reynolds and meeting in a London tavern. The historian of music Charles Burney remembered that 'It was Johnson's wish that our club should be composed of the heads of every liberal and literary profession, that we might not talk nonsense on any subject that might be started, but have somebody to refer to in our doubts and discussions, by whose science we might be enlightened'.[12]

In the nineteenth century, clubs of this kind proliferated. The Edinburgh Evening Club, which met twice a week from November to July, was described by a member, William Robertson Smith, as a 'talking club', including 'a whole circle of literary and scientific men in or near Edinburgh, the object being to have one man at least well up in every conceivable subject'.[13] It both presupposed specialization and offered a sociable response to it.

At the University of Leipzig, a group known as 'the Leipzig Circle' met for after-dinner coffee and conversation on Friday evenings at the Café Hannes in the years around 1900. It included Wilhelm Wundt, Wilhelm Ostwald, Karl Lamprecht and Friedrich Ratzel, all four of them polymaths in their different ways. Wundt was a psychologist best known for his experimental method, but he was also a physician, physiologist and philosopher, interested in 'the psychology of peoples' (*Völkerpsychologie*) and in a synthesis between the humanities and the social sciences.[14] Ostwald, a professor of chemistry, was also interested in philosophy and published a biography of Auguste Comte. Lamprecht, like Wundt, was interested in collective psychology and drew on it in his historical works, shocking his more conservative colleagues but inspiring French historians of 'mentalities' in the early twentieth century.[15] As for Ratzel, he is usually classified as a geographer, but his interests were much wider. It was his experience as a journalist, travelling widely, that awakened his interest in geography. As a professor of the subject, he took an active interest in neighbouring fields such as ethnology and politics.[16]

In his autobiography, Ostwald refers to meeting Wundt 'from time to time in a small informal circle that for a number of years met for an hour or so once a week after dinner in the theatre café'. It would be fascinating to know what the group talked about, to discover how much history Ratzel learned from Lamprecht, for instance, or how much psychology Lamprecht learned from Wundt. Ostwald's *Energetische Grundlagen der Kulturwissenschaft* (*Energy and the Foundations of the Science of Culture*, 1909) certainly bears the marks of his intellectual debt to Lamprecht.[17]

In Heidelberg, the Eranos Circle, composed in the main of Protestant scholars, discussed papers that focused on religion, viewing it from the perspective of various disciplines, from economics to law. Members of the Circle included the theologian Ernst Troeltsch, the art historian Henry Thode, the philosopher Wilhelm Windelband and the polymath Max Weber. It was to this Circle that Weber first presented his famous ideas on what he called 'the Protestant Ethic'.[18]

In Budapest, the 'Sunday Circle' did not last long (from 1915 to 1919), but it was vigorous while it lasted. Members included the critic Georg Lukács, who soon became the leader of the group; the art historian Frederick Antal; the sociologist Karl Mannheim; and the chemist Michael Polanyi (who was already interested in philosophy and economics). The Circle included 'a remarkably large number of talented women' (including the psychologist Júlia Lang, who later married Mannheim), who were able to participate 'without feeling the condescension of the male intellectual toward the woman'. According to one participant, 'it was always impossible to terminate the discussions', and one lasted until the next morning.[19]

Still better known are two groups that were formed in the 1920s. The Prague Circle, composed both of Czech and of exiled Russian scholars (including Roman Jakobson), meeting in the Café Derby, discussed problems of language, literature, folklore and semiotics. The Vienna Circle, meeting in the Café Central on Thursday evenings, was mainly composed of philosophers, inclding Rudolf Carnap and Moritz Schlick, but as one of its leading figures, Otto Neurath, explained, 'not one of the members is a so-called "pure" philosopher; all of them have done work in a special field of science' such as mathematics or physics.[20] The Vienna Circle was not the only group of its kind to be established in Vienna at this time. Viennese coffee-house culture may have encouraged this form of intellectual sociability.[21]

Interdisciplinary clubs emerged a little later in the English-speaking world and included the History of Ideas Club at Johns Hopkins University, the Pareto Circle at Harvard, the Ratio Club in London and a nameless but important group at the University of Glasgow.

The History of Ideas Club was founded in 1923, following a conversation at lunch between the philosophers Arthur Lovejoy and George Boas and Gilbert Chinard, who taught French literature but had many other interests. Six meetings a year were held on Thursdays in a seminar room at Johns Hopkins, with papers lasting from thirty-five to fifty minutes, followed by discussion. The constitution of the Club noted the choice of 'topics of common interest to representatives of diverse specialities' and the hope for 'a useful cross-fertilization'. Speakers came from a variety of disciplines but the Club's core membership was drawn from philosophy, history and literature.[22]

The Pareto Circle (founded in 1932) was the idea of the polymath Lawrence J. Henderson, who was interested in biological and social systems and attracted to Vilfredo Pareto as an alternative to Marx. He organized a seminar at Harvard that 'met for a couple of hours late in the afternoon', mainly to listen to Henderson interpreting Pareto's *General Treatise on Sociology* and to discuss it. The Circle included an anthropologist, an economist, a sociologist, a historian and a psychologist (another polymath, James G. Miller). Of all the interdisciplinary groups discussed here, it was the most sharply focused.[23]

The Ratio Club, founded in London in 1949, has been described as 'a hub of British cybernetics'. It met every couple of months in the National Hospital for Nervous Diseases to drink beer, listen to papers and discuss what was becoming known as 'cybernetics'. The group included psychologists, physiologists, mathematicians, physicists and engineers, among them the polymaths Alan Turing and W. Ross Ashby, a psychiatrist who moved into neuroscience, biophysics and general systems theory. In order to keep the proceedings informal, the club adopted a 'No Professors' rule, which inevitably led to its extinction in 1958 after its members had been promoted.[24]

As for the Glasgow group, 'about a dozen' academics met every few weeks in member's homes from about 1954 onwards to listen to and discuss a paper presented by one of them. The group's interests centred on theology, philosophy, literature and psychology. R. D. Laing is probably the best known of its members.[25] Another member, the Romanian sociologist Zevedei Barbu, migrated to the University of Sussex, where he joined a similar group, founded in the 1960s and calling itself the 'Humans' (in homage to David Hume).[26]

Groups of this semi-formal kind encourage the free expression of different points of view and educate their members by offering ideas that are new to some of them. Their success illustrates the argument that when problems need to be solved, even more important than ability is 'cognitive diversity'. In other words, two or three points of view are better than one. These interdisciplinary groups also illustrate the sociological theory of 'collaborative circles'.[27] They are small and mainly composed of young adults in their twenties and thirties who gradually formalize their meetings by fixing times and places. The groups tend to last about ten years from formation to dissolution. Their short life may not be a bad thing, since spontaneity and even semi-formality are difficult to maintain after a decade has passed.

UNIFYING KNOWLEDGE IN THEORY AND PRACTICE

Groups such as the ones discussed above might be described as a form of guerrilla warfare against the advance of specialization and the fragmentation of knowledge. They illustrate the modest approach to the problem, discussing specific themes and involving only a handful of people, even if there is a kind of 'multiplier effect' when each of these individuals talk to others. A more ambitious general approach is offered by the movement or movements for unified science.

The idea of unification goes back a long way for, as we have seen, the synthesis of fragmented knowledges was already part of the pansophic ideal of Comenius and his followers.[28] In the nineteenth century, Alexander von Humboldt viewed knowledge of the cosmos, like the cosmos itself, as an organic whole. Auguste Comte was concerned with the common principles of the sciences, while Herbert Spencer believed in a unified system of knowledge based on the laws of evolution.

An organized movement to unify the disciplines, on the other hand, emerged in the 1930s. As we have seen, the Austrian polymath Otto Neurath was a leader and an organizer of this movement, extending his concern with central planning and co-ordinated action from the economic to the intellectual sphere.[29] The philosopher Rudolf Carnap testified that 'In our discussion in the Vienna Circle, chiefly under the influence of Neurath, the principle of the unity of science became one of the main tenets of our general philosophical conceptions.'[30] All the same, 'it is curiously hard to say precisely what Neurath thought that the unity of science was'. He described one of the main aims of the movement as 'to further all kinds of scientific synthesis' but he was sceptical of systematization, preferring 'the stressed incompleteness of an encyclopaedia' with 'the anticipated completeness of *the* system'.[31] He was more interested in bridge-building than in a unifying 'theory of everything'.

Other attempts to unify knowledge depend on the concept of system. In biology, the polymaths Ludwig von Bertalanffy and Anatol Rapoport founded the Society for the Advancement of General Systems Theory (1954), now the International Society for the Systems Sciences. As we have seen, Bertalanffy developed the idea of an 'open system', while Rapoport was concerned with what he called 'the fundamental interconnectedness of everything with everything else'.[32] Another biologist concerned with the unity of knowledge is Edward O. Wilson, who was 'captured by the dream of unified learning' when he was eighteen. Wilson adopted the term 'consilience', in the sense of 'connection', from the Victorian polymath William Whewell. He argues that 'a united system of knowledge ... frames the most productive questions for future inquiry'.[33]

INTERDISCIPLINARY RESEARCH IN THE UNIVERSITIES

Less ambitious than attempts to unify science, a number of collective projects for research in fields that cut across disciplines were formally established in universities in the first half of the twentieth century. An early example, and one of the most famous, is the Institute for Social Research (*Institut für Sozialforschung*) established at Frankfurt in 1923 and the cradle of the so-called 'Frankfurt School' of Marxist scholars.[34] The Institute was directed from 1930 onwards by Max Horkheimer, whose programme was to replace what he called 'chaotic specialization' by the union of philosophy, economics, sociology, history and psychoanalysis in a common enterprise.[35] Horkheimer was joined by the polymaths Leo Löwenthal (later Lowenthal), best known for his studies of the sociology of literature, and Theodor Adorno, with whom he wrote *Dialektik der Aufklärung* (*Dialectic of the Enlightenment*, 1944), which included a famous account of popular culture as an 'industry'.[36] Two more polymaths, Walter Benjamin and Siegfried Kracauer (best known for his contribution to film studies, but a man of many talents), were active on the margins of the Frankfurt School.

After Hitler came to power the Institute was evacuated to Switzerland in 1933 and the United States in 1934, and it was there that Adorno and a number of collaborators began work on a major interdisciplinary study, *The Authoritarian Personality* (1949), examining the formation of that type of personality from different points of view: sociological, political and psychological. The Institute returned to Frankfurt after 1945. In its second generation it was directed by Jürgen Habermas, another polymath who may be equally well described as a philosopher or a sociologist, and it has also contributed to the disciplines of law and history.[37]

Collective projects were especially important in the United States, where philanthropic foundations, universities themselves and finally the government all encouraged interdisciplinary approaches to both the natural and the social sciences. Beardsley Ruml, for instance, a former psychologist who directed the Rockefeller Foundation programme for the social sciences from 1922 to 1929, described the current disciplinary divisions between 'history, economics, sociology, psychology and so forth' as 'sterile', so many obstacles to 'the development of social science as a whole'.[38] Warren Weaver, who was Director of the Division of Natural Sciences at the Rockefeller Foundation from 1932 to 1955, supported research on the frontiers of the disciplines of biology and chemistry. At the Ford Foundation in the 1950s, Bernard Berelson supported 'problem areas' that were common to different social sciences, 'Values and Beliefs', for example, or 'Social and Cultural Change'.

Some leading American universities attempted to unite the social sciences in super-departments. At Yale, for instance, James Angell, a psychologist who became president of the university in 1921 (and had formerly supervised Ruml's dissertation at the University of Chicago), founded an Institute for Social Relations in 1929. The Institute brought together in one building individuals working in the fields of psychology, medicine, neurology, economics, law, sociology and political science in order to launch a 'co-operative scientific attack' on 'the urgent problems of personal and social adjustment'. Seminars at the Institute on Monday nights were expected to produce integration.[39]

At the University of Chicago, it was the arrival of Robert Hutchins as a dynamic new president, aged only thirty at the time of his appointment, that led to the formation of an interdisciplinary research group in the social sciences. The group was housed in the Social Science Research Building, inaugurated in 1929 with an interdisciplinary conference that included representatives of medicine and neurology as well as law, economics, sociology and anthropology. In his 'Address of Dedication', prefaced to the volume, Hutchins emphasized what he called 'co-operative research' (the word 'interdisciplinary' had not yet come into general use).[40] Hutchins appointed Ruml dean of the social sciences in 1931 in order to assist the work of integration.[41]

A number of multidisciplinary committees were established for the same purpose. The Committee on Human Development (1940) was concerned to link the natural with the social sciences. The Committee on Social Thought (1942) encouraged the integration of the humanities as well. The Committee on the Behavioral Sciences (1949) was the brainchild of the physicist Enrico Fermi and the psychologist James G. Miller.

After helping to design the atomic bomb during the Second World War, Fermi was concerned to understand 'why men fight and kill'. He suggested to Miller that he work with colleagues in other disciplines to integrate the biological and the social sciences. Miller agreed, and became the chair of a group planning the institutionalization of what he claimed to have been the first to call 'behavioral science' (which, unlike 'social science', included psychology). The group was encouraged by President Hutchins and fitted into the Chicago tradition, but six years of discussion between 1949 and 1955 failed to establish an Institute of Behavioral Sciences at Chicago.

At Harvard, a Department of Social Relations was established in 1946, on the initiative of a group of psychologists and others who wished to reach out to other disciplines. The new department was dominated by the sociologist Talcott Parsons (a former member of the Pareto Circle), who established a division of labour between economists, psychologists, sociologists and anthropologists (who were awarded 'culture', leaving 'society' to their colleagues in sociology). The department, which included the polymaths Henry Murray and Barrington Moore, made an important contribution to the interdisciplinary theory of modernization, dominant in the 1950s and 1960s.[42]

Some of these attempts at co-operation between disciplines did not last. The Great Crash of 1929 reduced the funds for new developments.

There was also opposition to the new projects. In the case of Miller's 'behavioral science', opposition from colleagues who defended their territories or opposed the high-handed methods employed by President Hutchins made it impossible to 'walk the tightrope' between the biological and the social sciences.[43]

GENERAL EDUCATION

Some heads of American universities had been complaining about over-specialized curricula from the 1890s onwards. A response to this complaint was the movement for 'general education', the equivalent of *Bildung* in nineteenth-century Germany.[44] At Columbia University, for instance, President Nicholas Butler supported the idea of education for citizenship and so a course on 'Contemporary Civilization' was set up in 1919, the joint creation of professors from the departments of history, economics, philosophy and government.[45]

In Britain, a course in Philosophy, Politics and Economics (PPE) was established at Oxford in 1920. Besides attracting future polymaths such as Kenneth Boulding, PPE has played an important role in the formation of Britain's political elite.[46] In Scotland too there was a reaction against over-specialization at this time, taking the form of encouraging the study of philosophy by students in different disciplines. As late as the 1960s, 'a substantial number of students were annually exposed to philosophy'.[47]

The best-known attempt to address the need for general education took place at the University of Chicago when Robert Hutchins was president, from 1929 to 1945. Hutchins had been a professor of law but he was an individual of wider interests that led him later to become the chair of the board of editors of the *Encyclopedia Britannica*. Although he was the president of a major research university, and attempted, as we have seen, to establish a unified social science, Hutchins believed that too much attention was being paid to research and too little to teaching.

According to Hutchins, what was needed was a general education, emphasizing what he called 'a common stock of fundamental ideas', acquired from the study of the classics of literature and thought from the ancient Greeks onwards, a common course based on 'Great Books'. Hutchins was impressed if not inspired by the polymath Ortega y Gasset's denunciation of over-specialization. He reviewed Ortega's essay on the mission of the university, expressing his agreement with the author's critique of specialization.[48]

The Great Books course did not last for many years, but the idea of a general education survived. To this day, undergraduates at the University of Chicago follow a common 'Core Curriculum' that takes up about a third of their time and includes topics in the humanities, natural sciences and social sciences.[49] Two polymaths who studied at the University of Chicago, Herbert Simon and George Steiner, have testified to the importance for them of this broad learning experience. Other polymaths who studied there include Susan Sontag, Ralph Gerard, Anatol Rapoport and Thomas Sebeok.

An alternative attempt to promote integration, at least in the humanities, was the creation of a course in the history of Western Civilization, a historicization of an earlier course on Contemporary Civilization at Columbia. For a time courses in 'Western Civ' flourished in leading American universities, emphasizing the development of Western democracy and so contributing to what might be described as the Cold War of ideas.

THE ROLE OF GOVERNMENT

From the Second World War onwards, the US government supported interdisciplinary research, especially in the natural sciences. During the war, this was done via the Office of Scientific Research and Development (1941), headed by the polymath engineer Vannevar Bush. The most famous project was the construction of an atomic bomb at Los Alamos, involving collaboration between physicists, chemists and engineers. Its success illustrated the advantages of a problem-oriented approach as opposed to a discipline-oriented one.

After 1945, thanks to the Cold War, new institutions for research were established with money from the US government. They included the National Aeronautics and Space Administration (NASA), founded in

1958 as a response to the Soviet launch of Sputnik a year earlier, and the Advanced Research Project Agency (ARPA), which was dependent on the Department of Defense. Its private communication system, ARPANET, inspired the public Internet, a striking example of the importance of unintended consequences in the history of technology.[50]

In the social sciences, the Center for International Studies was established at MIT in 1952 with funds from the CIA. It housed economists, political scientists and sociologists who were committed to modernization theory and also intellectual warriors against Communism.[51]

AREA STUDIES

A joint enterprise of foundations and government was the interdisciplinary programme for 'Area Studies' launched in the United States soon after the Second World War.

Wars have often encouraged the participants to take an interest in other parts of the world. In London, the School of Slavonic Studies was founded in 1915, while the School of Oriental Studies (later the School of Oriental and African Studies, SOAS) followed a year later. In the United States, the rise of Japanese Studies was 'fuelled by confrontation with an enemy in war'. The anthropologist Ruth Benedict wrote her famous book *The Chrysanthemum and the Sword* (published in 1946) on commission from the Foreign Morale Analysis Division of the Office of War Information.[52]

During the Cold War, William Langer, assistant director of the CIA, argued that the government should support Area Studies, while McGeorge Bundy, a National Security Advisor to two presidents and himself president of the Ford Foundation, expressed the hope that there would be 'a high measure of interpenetration between universities with area programs and the information-gathering agencies of the government of the United States'.[53] On the principle of 'know your enemy', US foundations and the US government poured money into Russian studies. The best known of the fruits of this policy is probably the Russian Research Center (RRC) at Harvard, established in 1948, funded by the Carnegie Corporation and maintaining 'close but informal ties with the

CIA'.[54] Its first director, the anthropologist Clyde Kluckhohn, described the research as 'interdisciplinary in character', emphasizing 'anthropology, psychology and sociology', though scholars working on economics, economic history and politics were also active in the Center's projects.[55]

On the model of the RRC, Middle East Institutes were founded in Washington in 1946 and at Columbia and Harvard in 1954, while a Harvard professor received 100,000 dollars for secret research on Saudi Arabia.[56] Centres of South-East Asian studies were established at Yale, Cornell and elsewhere during the Vietnam War.[57] After Fidel Castro took power in Cuba, more money was forthcoming for the study of Latin America. As Eric Hobsbawm once remarked, 'We owe it to Castro.' The Institute for Latin American Studies at Columbia, for instance, was founded in 1962.

Some money from US foundations also went to academic institutions elsewhere, to St Antony's College, Oxford, for instance, to the Osteuropa Institut ('Institute for East European Studies') in Berlin, and to the École des Hautes Études in Paris, where Area Studies was grafted on to the local tradition of *aires culturelles*. The expectations of the funders may be illustrated from the relation between the officials of the Rockefeller Foundation and the historian Fernand Braudel, director of the Centre for Historical Research at the École. The Foundation was happy to give money to support the study of Chinese history but objected to Braudel's choice of two scholars, one because he was a member of the French Communist Party and the other because he worked on the twelfth century (research viewed as too remote to be useful). Braudel refused to back down, and the two scholars were appointed.[58]

In the case of the humanities and social sciences, unlike that of the natural sciences, the results of these initiatives were disappointing, at least insofar as interdisciplinarity was concerned. The centres for Area Studies provided information and published monographs but they were weaker in synthesis. The Russian Research Center at Harvard, for instance, soon 'dissolved into disciplines'. More generally, Herbert Simon criticized Area Studies programmes because they 'seemed to aim at training disciplinary specialization within area specialization: experts on the Russian economy, the Chinese government, the Indonesian family'.[59] It seems that a general concern with a particular region or 'area' does not displace disciplinary identities as effectively as a focus on a practical problem.

NEW UNIVERSITIES

The controversies surrounding both 'Great Books' and 'Western Civ', as well as opposition to attempts to unite the social sciences in Chicago, Harvard and Yale, suggest, among other things, that it is often easier to found a new institution than to reform an old one.[60] On the positive side, two new universities of the early twentieth century encouraged interdisciplinary co-operation, Strasbourg (discussed later in the chapter) and Hamburg.

In its early days, the University of Hamburg, founded in 1919, already harboured an interdisciplinary Institute for the Study of the Environment (Institut für Umweltsforschung) and the Institute for Foreign Policy (Institut für auswärtige Politik). The university also collaborated with the Library for Cultural Studies (Kulturwissenschaftlicher Bibliothek) founded by the polymath Aby Warburg. One polymath active in the university in the 1920s, the biologist Jakob von Uexküll, inspired the work of another, the philosopher Ernst Cassirer. Cassirer was also close to Warburg and his Library.[61]

In the second half of the twentieth century, the spread of interdisciplinary approaches owed a great deal to the foundation of new universities.

New Universities, 1950–75

1950 University of North Staffordshire (Keele)

1961 University of Sussex

1962 University of Bochum

1966 University of Konstanz

1967 La Trobe University

1969 University of Bielefeld

1970 University of Linköping

1971 Griffith University

1972 University of Roskilde

1974 Deakin University

1975 Murdoch University

As the table shows, the 1960s and early 1970s witnessed the foundation of a number of new universities in Britain, Germany, Scandinavia and Australia, offering some form of general education alongside training in particular disciplines. A pioneer in this respect was the University of North Staffordshire, now known as Keele University, founded in 1950, where the undergraduate course lasted for four years (instead of the three that are customary in England), beginning with a 'General Foundation Year' that attempted to bridge the gap between the 'two cultures', nine years before C. P. Snow formulated the concept. In the second year, Arts students were obliged to take a 'subsidiary' paper in the natural sciences, and vice versa.[62]

Again, the University of Sussex was founded in 1961 in order to 'redraw the map of learning', as the historian Asa Briggs, who helped plan the university, famously put it.[63] Originally there were no departments, only larger 'schools of studies'. 'English and American Studies' made a reference to the interdisciplinary courses in 'American Studies' in universities in the United States. 'European Studies' and 'African and Asian Studies' followed the model of 'Area Studies' – without either Cold War militancy or US money.

At Sussex, undergraduates chose a 'core' discipline on which to specialize but spent much of their time (half in arts, a third in the sciences) on other subjects, known as 'contextuals', which varied according to their School. In Social Studies, all the students took a contextual paper on 'Contemporary Britain', for instance, while in European Studies they took 'The Modern European Mind', approached via a reading list that included Marx, Dostoyevsky, Nietzsche and Freud. On the Arts side, introductory courses on philosophy and history were compulsory, while seminars led by two teachers (for instance one in history and one in literature) were common in the early years, focusing on interdisciplinary topics such as 'Science, Poetry and Religion in Seventeenth-Century England', or 'Literature and Society in the Age of Louis XIV'.[64] I can testify to the value of these seminars, not least as a way of educating the teachers.[65]

Interdisciplinary education became an international trend in the 1960s and 1970s and remains very much alive in some places. The University of Konstanz advertises interdisciplinary research projects. The University of Bielefeld has an interdisciplinary mission statement published on its website.[66] The University of Roskilde states that 'We employ an interdisciplinary approach because no major problems are ever resolved on the basis of any single academic discipline alone.'[67] Three Australian universities, Griffith, Deakin and Murdoch, still advertise interdisciplinary programmes. 'Integrative Studies' or 'Integrated Studies' is another name for a few centres, courses and degrees in the United States and elsewhere.

The story of these ventures includes failures as well as successes, and on occasion the disillusionment of former supporters of an interdisciplinary approach. At La Trobe University in Australia, founded in the 1960s, interdisciplinary schools were replaced by departments before the end of the decade. In 2003, after more than forty years of interdisciplinarity, the University of Sussex abandoned this form of organization and at least some of the aims associated with it. In Germany, the philosopher Hans Blumenberg and the historian Reinhart Koselleck began by supporting interdisciplinarity but Blumenberg came to regret that he had ever believed in it, while Koselleck became disillusioned with the practice as he had experienced it at the University of Bielefeld.[68]

On the other hand, an increasing number of interdisciplinary courses were established in more traditional universities. From the 1960s, courses on Western Civilization were increasingly criticized for their emphasis on white male Europeans, and they were gradually abandoned.[69] Their place was taken by programmes for the study of groups that had formerly been neglected by the academic world: Blacks, women and Latinos.

Programmes in African-American Studies or Black Studies were established at major US universities, sometimes, as at Cornell, as the result of direct action by students.[70] Women's Studies developed in the wake of the Feminist movement of the 1970s, followed by Gender Studies. The rise of Chicano Studies, later Latino or Latina/o Studies, was more gradual, sometimes building on or combining with Latin American Studies. As in the case of Area Studies, interdisciplinarity was encouraged by politics, but this time it was politics from below.

Other interdisciplinary programmes focused on a period, including Medieval, Renaissance, Eighteenth-Century and Victorian Studies (Classical Studies, formerly known in Germany as *Altertumswissenschaft*, goes back to the early nineteenth century). The menu has expanded to include Business Studies, Cognitive Studies, Cultural Studies, Development Studies, Media Studies, Memory Studies, Postcolonial Studies, Religious Studies, Science Studies, Urban Studies and Visual Studies.

Many of these programmes focus on topics that do not fit easily into a single discipline. Some illustrate a widening vision of a discipline, such as the shift from theology to religious studies or from the history of 'art' to the study of visual culture. Others represent combinations: Cognitive Studies joins psychology to linguistics and computer science, for instance, while Renaissance Studies brings together art, history and literature. Memory Studies bridges the two cultures, bringing together experimental psychologists, cognitive scientists and historians.

Cultural Studies, at least in Britain, has combined literature and socology with history (especially British history from the nineteenth century onwards), notably at the Centre for Contemporary Cultural Studies at the University of Birmingham (1964), directed from 1972 to 1979 by the cultural theorist Stuart Hall.[71] As in the case of American Studies in the United States, the movement for Cultural Studies emerged from a certain dissatisfaction with the way in which literature was taught, placing the emphasis on 'Great Books', often described as 'the canon', but failing to pay much attention to the social context of literature, to popular culture, to women writers or to authors from minorities.[72]

It is probably Urban Studies that holds the record for the number of disciplines involved in its programmes in different universities – anthropology, archaeology, architecture, economics, geography, history, literature, politics and sociology – held together by a concern with major urban problems such as poverty and violence. This is a field that has long attracted polymaths, from Georg Simmel and his former student Robert Park to Patrick Geddes, his former disciple Lewis Mumford and Richard Sennett, a polymath whose books might equally well be classified as contributions to the study of architecture, sociology, history and philosophy.

JOURNALS AND INSTITUTES

As we have seen, the emergence of particular academic disciplines in the nineteenth and twentieth centuries was encouraged by the foundation of specialist journals. In similar fashion, so is the movement for interdisciplinarity. Two well-known examples of such journals were founded in the middle of the twentieth century, *Diogenes* (founded in 1953 by the French polymath Roger Caillois) and *Daedalus* (1955). Other journals with a similar range include two that began publication in 1974, the *Internationales Jahrbuch für interdisziplinäre Forschung* and *Critical Inquiry*. A more recent example is *Common Knowledge* (1992).

The various forms of 'studies' have generated their own journals in parallel with disciplinary ones, among them *Urban Studies* (1964); *Signs: Journal of Women in Culture and Society* (1975); *Cultural Studies* (1984); and *Memory Studies* (2008). Unlike the nineteenth-century journals such as the *Edinburgh Review* which appealed, as we saw in chapter 5, to the general educated reader, the journals just mentioned target the academic community.

Conversation or collaboration between different disciplines was and still is a hallmark of research institutes, which often employ the phrase 'Advanced Studies' in their title, on the model of the Institute of

Advanced Studies at Princeton (1931). Early members of the Institute included Albert Einstein, the polymath John von Neumann and the art historian Erwin Panofsky. Another model for later institutes is the Center for Advanced Studies in the Behavioral Sciences at Palo Alto in California, founded in 1954 and funded by the Ford Foundation. On the advice of the polymath Herbert Simon, it was planned as a site remote from academic hierarchies and focused on research and writing. As we have seen, the Center brought together a diverse group of gifted individuals who discovered their common interest in the general theory of systems.

These research institutes proliferated, like the new universities, from the 1960s onwards.

Select Institutes for Advanced Studies, 1923–2008

1923 Institut für Sozialforschung, Frankfurt

1931 Institute for Advanced Studies, Princeton

1954 Centre for Advanced Studies in the Behavioral Sciences, Palo Alto

1962 Maison des Sciences de l'Homme, Paris

1963 Institut für Höhere Studien, Vienna

1968 Zentrum für interdisziplinäre Forschung, Bielefeld

1969 Institute for Advanced Studies in the Humanities, Edinburgh

1970 Netherlands Institute for Advanced Studies, Wassenaar

1970–81 Max Planck Institut, Starnberg

1972 Humanities Research Centre, Canberra

1980 Wissenschaftskolleg, Berlin

1985 Swedish Collegium for Advanced Studies, Uppsala

1986 Instituto de Estudos Avançados, São Paulo

1987 Rice University Humanities Research Centre, Houston

1992–2011 Collegium Budapest

1992 Centre for Advanced Studies, Oslo

1994 School of Advanced Study, London

1998 Max-Weber-Kolleg, Erfurt

2006 Institute for Advanced Studies, Durham

2007 Institute for Advanced Studies, Konstanz

2007 Institute for Advanced Studies, Paris

2008 Institute for Advanced Studies, Freiburg

Some of these institutes, such as the one in Vienna, founded as early as 1963, are confined to the social sciences, on the model of Palo Alto. Others are confined to the humanities, as at Edinburgh or Canberra, while still others are open to scholars working in any discipline. Some place particular emphasis on interdisciplinarity, for instance the Maison des Sciences de l'Homme in Paris or the Centre for Interdisciplinary Research at Bielefeld (the ZiF).[73]

Some of these institutes, such as Princeton, welcome individual scholars who come with their own projects. Others encourage collective projects, which are sometimes focused on a particular range of problems. The ZiF, for instance, focuses on a different theme every year. The Max Planck Institute at Starnberg in Bavaria, directed by the polymaths Carl von Weizsäcker and Jürgen Habermas, studies 'living conditions in the scientific and technical world', while another Max Planck Institute, at Göttingen, focuses on multicultural societies.

Whether or not these institutes were or are explicitly committed to interdisciplinarity, they have facilitated dialogues between scholars from different disciplines, sometimes formally, in seminars where papers are presented for general discussion, and more often informally, over cups of coffee in the intervals between bouts of reading or writing.

INTERDISCIPLINARY HISTORY

As a case study of attempts by scholars in one discipline to learn from their neighbours, this section focuses on history. An early example is that of Karl Lamprecht, mentioned earlier, whose cultural history was inspired by the collective psychology of his friend Wilhelm Wundt. Lamprecht's work was widely read by the general public, but rejected by most of his colleagues, with important exceptions such as the Dutch historian Johan Huizinga.

Huizinga surely qualifies as a polymath. He began his academic career as a philologist, writing a dissertation on the ways in which perceptions of light and sound were expressed in the Indo-Germanic languages. For his doctoral thesis, he turned to literature and studied the figure of the jester in ancient Sanskrit drama. When he did become a historian, Huizinga 'never specialized in a particular field, period, country or subject'.[74] His masterpiece, *The Autumn of the Middle Ages* (1919), owes not a little to his wide reading, from social anthropology to the study of Buddhism. Huizinga was also active as a literary critic, a cultural critic and a theorist, most famous for his analysis of the play element in culture, *Homo Ludens* (1938).

In the 1930s it was already possible for economic historians to draw on economic theory without losing professional respectability. They included Earl Hamilton, who studied the 'price revolution' in sixteenth-century Spain, and Eli Heckscher, who investigated the theory and practice of mercantilism. The new discipline of sociology also attracted some historians at this time, among them Marc Bloch, who learned from the work of Durkheim, Otto Hintze, who drew on the theories of Max Weber, and Lewis Namier, who made use of ideas from Vilfredo Pareto.

Namier also took an interest in Freud. It was not until the second half of the twentieth century, however, that leading professional historians began to make explicit use of ideas from psychoanalysis, as in the case of Peter Gay's *Freud for Historians* (1985). Gay's sustained engagement with Freud included professional training at the Western New England Institute of Psychoanalysis.

From the 1960s onwards, a number of cultural and social historians became fascinated by social and cultural anthropology, among them

Jacques Le Goff in France, Keith Thomas in Britain and Carlo Ginzburg in Italy. Like Huizinga, Ginzburg may be described as a polymath. He made his reputation in the 1970s for his studies of sixteenth-century religion and popular culture, but since then he has published books on art history and literature as well as collections of wide-ranging essays.

Engagement with other disciplines has sometimes been supported by institutions. The *Journal of Interdisciplinary History* was founded in 1970 by two American historians interested in what historians could learn from a whole range of other disciplines. In Britain, Asa Briggs, whose books drew on economics and sociology, was one of the founders of the University of Sussex.

In France, the so-called 'Annales School' was and remains a group of historians committed to learning from their neighbours. The school, or better, the movement, began when Lucien Febvre met Marc Bloch at the University of Strasbourg after the First World War. Strasbourg was effectively a new university, since the city had become part of France in 1919. In the early years, a Saturday seminar attracted a number of professors in the humanities and social sciences.

Febvre himself may be described as a polymath who edited an encyclopaedia, wrote on geography and linguistics, and was inspired by psychologists and anthropologists in his investigation of sixteenth-century mentalities. Febvre's editorial launching of the journal *Annales* (1929) amounted to a declaration of war on the division between history and the social sciences, declaring that 'The walls are so high that they often impede the view.' The editorial committee included a geographer, an economist, a sociologist and a political scientist.[75]

The second generation of the group was led by Fernand Braudel, who was at home in geography, economics and sociology and sometimes drew on other disciplines as well, in pursuit of what he called 'total history', including every type of human activity. As he once wrote, 'To try to marry history with geography or history with economics . . . is a waste of time. It is necessary to do everything at once. It is necessary to redefine problems in a total manner [*recréer des problématiques totalisantes*].'[76]

In the second decade of the twenty-first century, new partners for historians are emerging. Environmental history, for instance, a new sub-discipline attracting more and more interest in an age of environmental crisis, requires some knowledge of geology, botany, climatology and other disciplines in the natural sciences. Historians of the 'co-evolution' of humans with other animals study biology, while some historians of the emotions have discovered neuroscience.[77]

Few historians are able to emulate Braudel and 'do everything at once'. The main result of all the efforts described above has been the establishment of what are effectively hybrid disciplines such as historical anthropology, historical sociology or bio-history.

AMBITION VERSUS MODESTY

Earlier in this chapter I distinguished between modest and ambitious approaches to interdisciplinarity. The ambitious ones, from the movement for unified science to more recent discussions of post-disciplinarity, have not produced lasting results, while some experiments in education have been abandoned, at the University of La Trobe, for instance, and the University of Sussex. On the other hand, more modest approaches have had a certain degree of success, as in the case of the *Annales* group discussed in the previous section, or of teams focused on particular problems or topics such as fear and trust rather than on interdisciplinarity in general.[78]

Today, at both institutional and individual levels, the situation is so varied as to be confusing. We might be said to live in an age of coexistence between disciplines and interdisciplinarity, or more exactly in what Spaniards call *convivencia*, emphasizing interaction rather than simple existence. Academic departments, better described as compartments, have not withered away, but many interdisciplinary centres have been erected side by side with them on campuses in the United States and elsewhere.[79]

At an individual level, it no longer raises eyebrows when historians, for instance, make use of Weber, Freud or Foucault in writing about the ancient world or medieval or early modern Europe. There are current prospects for more exchanges between the notorious 'two cultures' in fields such as bio-history, bio-politics and bio-sociology. The interdisciplinary enterprise continues. Indeed, it is more necessary than ever before in our digital age, the moment of a third crisis, discussed in the coda that follows.

CODA
TOWARDS A THIRD CRISIS

We have arrived at last in the digital age, often defined as beginning in 1990 with the World Wide Web. Some writers refer to the 'digital revolution', others to the 'search engine society' (Internet Explorer was launched in 1995, Firefox and Yahoo in 2004, Google Chrome in 2008 and Bing in 2009).[1] The history of encyclopaedias tells us something about recent changes in the history of knowledge. The 1,507 individuals who contributed articles to the 1911 edition of the *Encyclopedia Britannica* or even the 4,000 who contributed to the fifteenth edition have become very few by comparison with the number of contributors to Wikipedia (nearly 34 million in 2018).[2] The tradition of 'citizen science', drawing on contributions by amateurs, has widened into what might be called 'citizen knowledge'.

Much knowledge has become more accessible, but recent changes are not all for the better. We may be experiencing a third crisis of knowledge. We are certainly living through a period of rapid change, turbulence and anxiety. For an older generation, at least, one reason for anxiety is the gradual decline and on occasion the rapid destruction of printed books, replaced by e-books. In the Netherlands, for instance, a number of university libraries have pulped most of their books or thrown them away. 'The idea is that one paper copy of each book is sufficient for the whole of the Netherlands.' The debate over this policy is of course part of a wider discussion about the future of the book.[3]

Underlying the competition between two kinds of book is the competition between two styles of reading, perceptively discussed in two relatively recent studies. Maryanne Wolf's *Proust and the Squid* (2007) draws on neuroscience to tell 'the story of the reading brain'. The author encourages us to marvel at the plasticity of the brain, the way it has recycled circuits of neurons in order to make use of the different writing systems invented in the last few thousand years. Wolf also expresses alarm at the rise of a new form of recycling neurons, encouraging the rapid scanning of information at the expense of slower reading. She alerts her readers – while there are still readers – to the danger of becoming 'a society of decoders of information' without the time for the thought necessary to transform information into knowledge.[4]

Nicolas Carr's *The Shallows* (2011) also draws on neuroscience, focusing on changes in 'the way we think, read and remember' in the age of the Internet. The book is all the more persuasive because the author is no enemy of the Internet but an enthusiast, or at least an ex-enthusiast who describes his 'uncomfortable sense that someone, or something, has been tinkering with my brain', impeding concentration on the narrative or the argument of a book or a long article.[5] The plasticity of the brain that made reading possible in the first place is now making it increasingly difficult.

In short, both these authors view the Internet as a problem. It is one of many examples in history of the way in which a solution to a problem sooner or later generates problems of its own. In this case the problem that the Internet seemed to solve is that of overload or 'overflow', a problem that has become a serious one for the third time, at both the individual level and that of society at large. For individuals, the new media of communication have produced an over-abundance of messages. For society, the amount of new information and the speed at which it arrives does not allow its 'cooking', in other words its transformation into knowledge.

No wonder then that the phrase 'information anxiety' is often heard.[6] There is even a glut of books on the glut of information, otherwise known as a 'flood', 'deluge' or 'tsunami'.[7]

As so often happens, revolution was preceded by more gradual change, a run up to the high jump. Once again, new words offer clues to perceptions of change. It was in 1964 that the phrase 'information explosion' was first used in English, according to the *Oxford English Dictionary*, while it was in 1970 that the American journalist Alvin Toffler coined the now ubiquitous phrase 'information overload'.[8]

Some statistics support this sense of change. There was a sharp rise in the number of books published in the second half of the twentieth century: from 332,000 titles published in 1960 to 842,000 in 1990.[9] The twenty-first century has witnessed a much more rapid rise in digital data. It has been estimated that 150 exabytes of digital data were produced in 2005 but around 1,200 exabytes were expected to be generated in 2010.[10] This amount has since come to seem small and calculations are now expressed in zettabytes (1,000 exabytes = 1 zettabyte). 'The total amount of data in the world was 4.4 zettabytes in 2013. That is set to rise steeply to 44 zettabytes by 2020.'[11]

There have of course been advances in the handling of 'Big Data'. At an everyday level, finding information on a variety of topics has become easier and faster than ever before, thanks to a variety of search engines. Companies, governments and scholars have all benefited from this digital revolution.[12] There is also a downside, however. For example, the reason that the attack on 9/11 was not detected in advance, despite warnings from the security services, was that the warnings were lost in the 'flood' of data. As Condoleeza Rice put it, there was 'a lot of chatter in the system'.[13]

The problem of bias in search engines, whether to increase the sale of certain products or to support political (including racist) agendas, has been the subject of much recent discussion. We have long been familiar with the 'surveillance state', but we now have to accustom ourselves to 'surveillance capitalism', the idea that when we search Google, for instance, Google is searching us.[14] The challenges presented by what are known as 'Big Data' include storage, analysis, verification and invasions of privacy.[15]

The turbulence we are experiencing makes it difficult to descry the long-term consequences of the shift from printed books and newspapers to online information. Wolf and Carr are not the only individuals to fear that the skill of 'slow reading' or 'close reading' in a continuous, linear, attentive manner will be lost, replaced by rapid scanning. There was a time when courses in rapid reading were offered to students who were used to going through a text from beginning to end. Today, courses on slow reading are becoming necessary. Optimists take comfort from the fact that skimming books is a skill that has co-existed for a long time with the ability to read with care.

Turbulence also obscures our vision of changes in the structure of knowledge. It has been suggested that we are entering a 'post-disciplinary' era.[16] What would such an era be like? Divisions between forms of knowledge would surely persist, because it is impossible to learn everything at once and because different methods are needed to attack different problems. In any case, specialization continues its relentless progress. The different branches of the tree of knowledge are constantly producing new twigs.

What is all too visible today is the threat to traditional niches for polymaths. There was a time, as we have seen, when wide-ranging scholars such as Leibniz were appointed librarians. Today, librarians are expected to be managers. Museums have moved in the same direction as libraries, from the age of the scholar–keeper to the age of the manager. Universities too are less welcoming to polymaths than they used to be. Heavier teaching loads and the proliferation of meetings are reducing the time available for both thinking and research. I wonder how a vice-chancellor would respond today to a professor of chemistry who announced (as Michael Polanyi did at the University of Manchester in 1948) that he wanted to teach philosophy.

Again, the cultural journals that have offered opportunities to members of the species from the later seventeenth century onwards are now facing diminishing sales. They may survive in online versions, but this solution is less satisfactory for these journals than for newspapers, because their articles are longer. It is no surprise to find that for some decades a number of distinguished freelance journalists have been coming in from the cold and joining universities. The polymath Perry Anderson, editor of the *New Left Review*, became a professor at the New School for Social Research in the 1980s. Timothy Garton Ash, a former foreign editor of *The Spectator*, joined St Antony's College, Oxford, in 1989. The former freelance writer Ian Buruma joined Bard College in 2003.

Despite these problems, a few many-sided scholars survive. Living polymaths include three controversial individuals who were mentioned earlier: George Steiner, Peter Sloterdijk and Slavoj Žižek. Somewhat less controversial, the Frenchman Bruno Latour has been described as 'a prolific writer on an amazing variety of topics', without respect for disciplinary boundaries. He might equally well be described as a philosopher, a sociologist, an anthropologist or a worker in the interdisciplinary field of the 'social studies of science'. In fact, his range is wider still. When Latour received the Holberg Prize in 2013, the committee described his work as making a contribution to 'the history of science, art history, history, philosophy, anthropology, geography, theology, literature and law'.[17] He has argued against the idea of modernity, emphasized the importance of 'centres of calculation' in the history of science, carried out 'fieldwork' in a laboratory and also in a court (the Conseil d'État in Paris), and developed what he calls 'actor-network theory', which resembles the figurational sociology of Norbert Elias but includes ideas and material objects in the network alongside people.

As I write, in January 2019, living examples of the species 'polymath' include Jürgen Habermas, who has been described as 'arguably our era's version' of Aristotle; the essayist Perry Anderson, whose interests span history, philosophy, politics, economics and sociology; the judge, economist and philosopher Richard Posner, whose publications have been described as 'almost absurdly wide ranging in subject matter'; the Italian Giorgio Agamben, who has written on philosophy, literature, law and history; and the Brazilian Roberto Mangabeira Unger, who helped to found the movement known as Critical Legal Studies as well as criticizing classical economics and writing about politics, religion and, most recently, on cosmology.[18] The number of living female polymaths, as we have seen, is higher than ever before, consisting mainly of clustered polymaths who concentrate on philosophy, literature, psychoanalysis, history and the interdisciplinary field of gender studies (Aleida Assmann, Mieke Bal, Margaret Boden, Judith Butler, Hélène Cixous, Luce Iragiray, Julia Kristeva, Juliet Mitchell, Griselda Pollock and Gayatri Chakravorty Spivak).

On the side of the natural sciences, the American scientist Edward O. Wilson offers an obvious example of a living polymath. Like Geddes and Herbert Fleure, Wilson suffers from eye problems, which in his case led to his turning his attention away from mammals and towards close studies of insects (especially ants and 'ant societies'). Again, Wilson's interest in what he calls 'socio-biology', studying humans and their societies as the products of evolution, is reminiscent of the 'bio-sociology' of Geddes. As we have seen, his theory of 'consilience' emphasizes the unity of knowledge.[19]

Another example is the Australian Robert May. May studied engineering, took his Ph.D in theoretical physics, taught mathematics, carried out research on biology and ecology, and has combined his interests by employing mathematical techniques to study animal populations.

A few polymaths bridge the famous 'two cultures'. In Britain, Nikolas Rose, who was trained in biology, has moved into sociology, psychology, philosophy and neuroscience. In the United States, Jared Diamond, who began his career as a physiologist, moved into ornithology and ecology and is perhaps most widely known today for his essays on world history, notably *Guns, Germs and Steel* (1997) and *Collapse* (2005), to say nothing of his lifelong interest in languages. His work has often been criticized by specialists but it has also been taken seriously. The American Anthropological Association responded to *Collapse* by holding a symposium in 2006, which led to a book with contributions not only by anthropologists but by historians and archaeologists as well.[20] One might say of Diamond – as one might say of other serial polymaths – that whether or not one agrees with his answers, the questions that this outsider has asked in the disciplines to which he has migrated have been original and fruitful ones.

Will polymaths survive, or is the species about to become extinct? The examples cited so far, and others that come to mind – to my mind, at least – are all limited to scholars who were already middle-aged before the digital revolution occurred. Noam Chomsky was born in 1928; Jürgen Habermas, George Steiner and Edward O. Wilson were all born in 1929; Luce Iragiray in 1930; Margaret Boden and Robert May in 1936; Hélène Cixous and Jared Diamond in 1937; Perry Anderson in 1938; Charles Jencks and Richard Posner in 1939; Juliet Mitchell in 1940; Julia Kristeva in 1941; Gayatri Chakravorty Spivak and Giorgio Agamben in 1942; Richard Sennett and Vaclav Smil in 1943; Raymond Tallis in 1946; Aleida Assmann, Bruno Latour, Nikolas Rose, Peter Sloterdijk and Roberto Mangabeira Unger in 1947; Jacqueline Rose and Slavoj Žižek in 1949; Judith Butler in 1956; Daniel Levitin and Robert Sapolsky in 1957. The drop around 1950 may be an alarm signal.

New challenges require new responses, so we should place our hopes – if we are optimists – in the digital generation.[21] In any case, an elegy for the species is still premature. This is just as well, since within the current division of intellectual labour we still need generalists in the sense of individuals who are able to perceive what Isaac Barrow back in the seventeenth century called the 'connection of things, and dependence of notions'. As Leibniz once declared, 'what we need are universal men. For one who can connect all things can do more than ten people.'[22] In an age of hyper-specialization, we need such individuals more than ever before.

APPENDIX
500 WESTERN POLYMATHS

This list of western polymaths active from the early fifteenth century onwards is not intended to form a canon: I am sure that I have missed some important figures, especially when they come from countries whose languages I cannot read. A round number has been chosen in order to make obvious the necessarily arbitrary nature of this kind of choice, dependent on the knowledge of a single individual. It is not assumed that the contributions of all these 500 individuals were equally important: Leibniz, for instance, contributed more to knowledge than Kircher. Living polymaths are absent from this list, though some have been mentioned from time to time in the text.

The 500 individuals selected for inclusion here have been chosen according to several different criteria. The majority have made original contributions to several (if not 'many') disciplines, but passive polymaths such as Aldous Huxley and Jorge Luis Borges have also been included, familiar with a range of disciplines without contributing to any; encyclopaedists such as Alsted, Diderot and Lucien Febvre; classifiers of knowledge such as Bacon, Comte and Melvil Dewey; managers of knowledge such as Warren Weaver; and polyglot scholars such as Lorenzo Hervás.

1. Filippo Brunelleschi, 1377–1446, Italian. Architect, engineer, mathematician, inventor, artist.
2. Mariano da Jacopo 'Taccola', 1382–c.1453, Italian. Notary, sculptor, engineer, inventor.

3. Paolo Toscanelli, 1397–1482, Italian. Mathematics, astronomy, geography.

4. Nicholas of Cusa, 1401–64, German. Bishop and cardinal. Philosophy, theology, law, astronomy, mathematics.

5. Leonbattista Alberti, 1404–72, Italian. Priest. Humanist, architect, mathematician.

6. Niccolò Leoniceno, 1428–1524, Italian. Philosophy, medicine, botany.

7. Francesco di Giorgio Martini, 1439–1501, Italian. Architect, engineer.

8. Rodolphus Agricola, 1443–85, Dutch. Humanist, philosopher, artist, musician.

9. Donato Bramante, 1444–1514, Italian. Architect, painter, poet, musician.

10. Leonardo da Vinci, 1452–1519, Italian. Artist, engineer, inventor, student of mathematics, natural history, etc.

11. Johannes Trithemius, 1462–1516, German, Benedictine abbot. History, philosophy, cryptography.

12. Giovanni Pico della Mirandola, 1463–94, Italian. Aristocrat. Attempted to master every discipline.

13. Cassandra Fedele, c.1465–1558, Italian. Philosophy, mathematics, astronomy, education.

14. Desiderius Erasmus, 1466–1536, Netherlander. Canon regular, then secular priest. Philology, philosophy, theology.

15. Laura Cereta, 1469–99, Italian. Rhetoric, philosophy, mathematics, astronomy.

16. Nicolaus Copernicus, 1473–1543, German/Polish. Canon, physician. Astronomy, medicine, law, humanities.

17. Celio Calcagnini, 1479–1541, Italian. Theology, law, medicine, rhetoric, astronomy.

18. Gasparo Contarini, 1483–1542, Italian. Cardinal, bishop. Theology, philosophy, astronomy.

19. Heinrich Cornelius Agrippa, 1486–1535, German. Philosophy, medicine, law, alchemy, occult sciences.

20. Sebastian Münster, 1488–1552, German. Franciscan turned Lutheran. Cartography, cosmography, biblical studies, oriental languages, mathematics.
21. Juan Luis Vives, 1493–1540, Spanish. Philosophy, medicine, education,.
22. Georg Agricola (Bauer), 1494–1555, German. Physician. Medicine, history, geology, mineralogy.
23. François Rabelais, c.1494–1553, French. Franciscan, then physician. Medicine, law, theology.
24. Philip Melanchthon, 1497–1560, German. Lutheran minister. Philosophy, theology, astronomy, astrology, anatomy, botany, mathematics.
25. Gerolamo Cardano, 1501–76, Italian. Physician. Medicine, mathematics, astrology, music, geology.
26. Cosimo Bartoli, 1503–72, Italian. Mathematics, art, architecture, literature, history.
27. Fernão de Oliveira, 1507–81, Portuguese, Dominican. Grammar, history, navigation.
28. Guillaume Postel, 1510–81, French. Languages, history, theology, geography, politics, astrology.
29. Miguel Servet, c.1511–53, Spanish. Physician. Protestant. Medicine, anatomy, astrology, astronomy, geography, theology.
30. Wolfgang Lazius, 1514–65, Austrian. Physician. Philosophy, medicine, history, geography.
31. Petrus Ramus, 1515–72, French. Calvinist. Philosophy, rhetoric, mathematics.
32. Conrad Gessner, 1516–65, Swiss. Physician. Medicine, natural history, languages, bibliography.
33. Ulisse Aldrovandi, 1522–1605, Italian. Medicine, natural history, antiquities.
34. Benito Arias Montano, 1527–98, Spanish. Rhetoric, theology, antiquities, oriental studies.
35. John Dee, 1527–1608, English. Mathematics, geography, astrology, alchemy, geography, antiquities, magic.

36. Jean Bodin, 1530–96, French. Carmelite, then layman. Natural philosophy, history, politics, political economy.
37. Hugo Blotius, 1533–1608, Netherlander. Librarian. Rhetoric, law, bibliography.
38. Theodor Zwinger the Elder, 1533–88, Swiss. Physician. Medicine, oriental languages, philosophy.
39. Giambattista Della Porta, 1535–1615, Italian. Gentleman, founder of the Otiosi. Cryptography, optics, mnemonics, meteorology, physics, astrology, physiognomy, mathematics, etc.
40. Joseph Scaliger, 1540–1609, French. Philology, chronology, oriental studies, astronomy.
41. Johann Thomas Freigius, 1543–83, Swiss. Calvinist. Philosophy, law, history, mathematics, political economy.
42. Tycho Brahe, 1546–1601, Danish. Aristocrat. Astronomy, astrology, alchemy, medicine.
43. Justus Lipsius, 1547–1606, Netherlander. Catholic and Protestant at different times. Philology, philosophy, chronology, etc.
44. Giordano Bruno, 1548–1600, Italian. Dominican. Philosophy, theology, cosmology, art of memory, mathematics.
45. Francisco Suárez, 1548–1617, Spanish. Jesuit. Philosophy, theology, law.
46. Paolo Sarpi, 1552–1623, Italian. Servite friar. History, law, philosophy, theology, mathematics, anatomy.
47. Walter Raleigh, 1554–1618, English. Courtier. History, chemistry.
48. Isaac Casaubon, 1559–1614, French. Calvinist. Philology, literature, history, theology, geography.
49. James Crichton, 1560–c.1585, Scottish. Gentleman. Attempted to master every discipline.
50. Francis Bacon, 1561–1626, English. Law, history, philosophy, natural philosophy.
51. Marie de Gournay, 1565–1645, French. Humanities, alchemy and a treatise on the equality of men and women.
52. Johannes Bureus, 1568–1652, Swedish. Antiquities, alchemy, occult studies.

53. Tommaso Campanella, 1568–1639, Italian. Dominican.
Philosophy, theology, astrology, astronomy, physiology, politics.

54. Bartholomäus Keckermann, c.1572–1608, German. Calvinist.
Philosophy, theology, politics, law, rhetoric, astronomy, geography,
physics.

55. Christoph Besold, 1577–1638, German. Jurist. Convert to
Catholicism. Law, history, theology, politics.

56. Robert Burton, 1577–1640, English. Anglican clergyman.
Librarian. Medicine, philosophy, theology, astrology.

57. Gerard Johannes Vossius, 1577–1649, Dutch. Theology, philology,
literature, history.

58. Nicolas-Claude Peiresc, 1580–1637, French. Nobleman.
Antiquities, natural history, anatomy, astronomy, etc.

59. Hugo Grotius, 1583–1645, Dutch. Calvinist. Law, history, theology.

60. John Selden, 1584–1654, English. Law, history, antiquities,
philology, oriental studies.

61. Peter Lauremberg, 1585–1639, German. Protestant. Anatomy,
mathematics, botany, philology.

62. Joseph Mede, 1586–1638, English. Anglican clergyman. Theology,
philosophy, chronology, mathematics, natural history, anatomy,
Egyptology.

63. Johann Heinrich Alsted, 1588–1638, German. Calvinist minister.
Encyclopaedist.

64. Ole Worm, 1588–1654, Danish. Physician. Medicine, antiquities,
natural history.

65. Claude Saumaise (Salmasius), 1588–1653, French. Protestant.
Classics, philology, antiquities, oriental studies.

66. Franciscus Junius (de Jon), 1591–1677, Netherlander. Philology,
antiquities, literature.

67. Jan Amos Comenius (Komenský), 1592–1670, Czech. Cleric.
Philosophy, languages, education.

68. Pierre Gassendi, 1592–1655, French. Priest. Philosophy,
astronomy, physics.

69. Emmanuele Tesauro, 1592–1675, Italian. Jesuit. Rhetoric, philosophy, history.
70. Johannes Marcus Marci, 1595–1667, Czech. Catholic. Medicine, optics, mechanics, mathematics, astronomy.
71. Juan Eusebio Nieremberg, 1595–1658, Spanish. Jesuit. Theology, philosophy, natural history, astronomy.
72. René Descartes, 1596–1650, French. Philosophy, geometry, optics, astronomy, music, medicine.
73. Lucas Holstenius, 1596–1661, German. Librarian. Convert to Catholicism. History, antiquities, theology.
74. Constantijn Huygens, 1596–1687, Dutch. Protestant. Natural philosophy, anatomy, medicine, languages.
75. Giambattista Riccioli, 1598–1671, Italian. Jesuit. Astronomy, geography, chronology, theology, mechanics, prosody.
76. Samuel Bochart, 1599–1667, French. Calvinist minister. Theology, geography, philology, oriental studies.
77. Samuel Hartlib, c.1600–62, Polish. Information go-between.
78. Bathsua Makin (née Reynolds), c.1600–c.1681, English. Education, medicine, languages.
79. Gabriel Naudé, 1600–53, French. Librarian. History, politics, bibliography.
80. Athanasius Kircher, 1602–80, German. Jesuit. Egyptology, sinology, magnetism, mathematics, mining, music. Inventor.
81. Kenelm Digby, 1603–65, English. Catholic gentleman. Attempted to master every discipline.
82. John Jonston, 1603–75, Scottish. Physician. Medicine, natural history, theology, antiquities.
83. Johann Heinrich Bisterfeld, 1605–55, German. Calvinist. Philosophy, theology, mathematics, physics.
84. Thomas Browne, 1605–82, English. Physician. Medicine, antiquities, philosophy, natural history.
85. Hermann Conring, 1606–81, German. Lutheran. Physician. Medicine, law, history, politics.

86. Juan Caramuel y Lobkowitz, 1606–82, Spanish. Cistercian. Theology, philosophy, mathematics, history, etc.

87. Anna Maria van Schurman, 1607–78, Dutch. Languages, philosophy, theology, education.

88. John Wilkins, 1614–72, English. Bishop. Philosophy, theology, astronomy, mathematics, languages, cryptography.

89. Thomas Bartholin the Elder, 1616–80, Danish. Physician. Medicine, mathematics, theology, antiquities.

90. Nicolás Antonio, 1617–84, Spanish. Law, bibliography.

91. Elias Ashmole, 1617–92, English. Law, astrology, alchemy, magic, heraldry, antiquities.

92. Elisabeth, Princess Palatine, 1618–80, English. Protestant abbess. Mathematics, philosophy, astronomy, history.

93. Isaac Vossius, 1618–89, Dutch. Philology, chronology, geography, physics, antiquities, mathematics.

94. Henry Oldenburg, c.1619–77, German. Theology, natural philosophy, information go-between.

95. François Bernier, 1620–88, French. Medicine, oriental studies, philosophy.

96. John Evelyn, 1620–1706, English. Gentleman. Anatomy, chemistry, natural history, mathematics, mechanics.

97. Johann Heinrich Hottinger, 1620–67, Swiss. Oriental studies, theology, history.

98. Marcus Meibom, 1621–1710, Danish. Antiquities, philology, mathematics.

99. Blaise Pascal, 1623–62, French. Mathematics, physics, philosophy, theology. Inventor.

100. William Petty, 1623–87, English. Inventor. Medicine, anatomy, natural philosophy, mathematics, political economy, demography.

101. Margaret Cavendish (née Lucas), c.1624–74, English. Natural philosophy, alchemy.

102. Hiob Ludolf, 1624–1704, German. Languages.

103. János Apáczai Csere, 1625–59, Hungarian. Calvinist. Mathematician and encyclopaedist.

104. Erhard Weigel, 1625–99, German. Mathematics, astronomy, theology. Also architect, inventor.

105. Queen Christina of Sweden, 1626–89. Philosophy, theology, mathematics, alchemy, astronomy, astrology.

106. Francesco Redi, 1626–97, Italian. Medicine, natural philosophy, literature.

107. Robert Boyle, 1627–91, English. Aristocrat. Philosophy, theology, physics, physiology, medicine, chemistry.

108. Peter Lambeck, 1628–80, German. Protestant, then Catholic. Librarian, historian of literature.

109. Christiaan Huygens, 1629–95, Dutch. Gentleman. Mathematics, astronomy, physics, mechanics.

110. Pierre-Daniel Huet, 1630–1721, French. Bishop. Mathematics, astronomy, anatomy, natural history, chemistry, oriental studies, history, theology, philosophy.

111. Isaac Barrow, 1630–77, English. Anglican clergyman. Mathematics, optics, theology, antiquities.

112. Olof Rudbeck the Elder, 1630–1702, Swedish. Anatomy, languages, music, botany, ornithology, antiquities.

113. Johann Georg Graevius, 1632–1703, German. Calvinist. Philology, rhetoric, history, classics, antiquities.

114. Samuel Pufendorf, 1632–94, German. Law, politics, history, philosophy, theology, political economy.

115. Christopher Wren, 1632–1723, English. Architecture, mathematics, astronomy, optics, mechanics, medicine, meteorology.

116. Antonio Magliabechi, 1633–1714, Italian. Librarian. Information go-between.

117. Johann Joachim Becher, 1635–82, German. Mineralogy, alchemy, natural history, education, philosophy, politics, political economy.

118. Robert Hooke, 1635–1703, English. Mathematics, physics, astronomy, chemistry, medicine, biology, geology. Inventor.

119. Lorenzo Magalotti, 1637–1712, Italian. Natural philosophy, geography.
120. Nicholas Steno, 1638–86, Danish. Convert to Catholicism. Bishop. Medicine, anatomy, natural history, philosophy.
121. Daniel Georg Morhof, 1639–91, German. Librarian. History, alchemy.
122. Olof Rudbeck the Younger, 1660–1740, Swedish. Anatomy, botany, ornithology, philology.
123. Nicolaes Witsen, 1641–1717, Dutch. Patrician. Geography, ethnography, antiquities, natural history.
124. Conrad Samuel Schurzfleisch, 1641–1708, German. Protestant. Librarian. Rhetoric, history, philosophy, law, geography.
125. Vincent Placcius, 1642–99, German. Law, philosophy, theology, medicine, bibliography, history.
126. Gilbert Burnet, 1643–1715, Scottish. Bishop. History, theology, philosophy.
127. Isaac Newton, 1643–1727, English. Mathematics, physics, alchemy, chronology, theology.
128. Otto Mencke, 1644–1707, German. Theology, philosophy, information go-between.
129. Eusebio Kino (Kühn), 1645–1711, Italian/Austrian. Jesuit. Languages, geography, astronomy, philosophy.
130. Carlos Sigüenza y Góngora, 1645–1700, Mexican. Mathematics, astronomy, astrology, geography, antiquities.
131. Elena Cornaro Piscopia, 1646–84, Italian. Languages, theology, philosophy, mathematics, music.
132. Gottfried Wilhelm Leibniz, 1646–1716, German. Philosophy, mathematics, history, languages, law, physics, chemistry, natural history, medicine.
133. Pierre Bayle, 1647–1706, French. Protestant minister. History, philosophy, natural philosophy, theology.
134. Sister Juana Inés de la Cruz, 1651–95, Mexican. Theology, philosophy, natural philosophy, law, theory of music.

135. Henri Basnage, 1656–1710, French. Protestant. History, lexicography, theology, mechanics.
136. Bernard de Fontenelle, 1657–1757 (*sic*), French. Philosophy, history, natural sciences.
137. Jean Leclerc, 1657–1736, Swiss. Protestant minister. Philosophy, philology, theology, history, literature.
138. Luigi Marsili, 1658–1730, Italian. Engineering, geography, hydrography, astronomy, natural history, history.
139. Jacob von Melle, 1659–1743, German. History, antiquities, palaeontology, lexicography.
140. Hans Sloane, 1660–1745, Irish. Medicine, anatomy, chemistry, botany, antiquities.
141. Giuseppe Averani, 1662–1739, Italian. Law, physics, theology, astronomy, mathematics.
142. Pedro de Peralta y Barnuevo, 1664–1743, Peruvian. Mathematics, astronomy, natural philosophy, metallurgy, law, history, etc.
143. John Woodward, c.1665–1728, English. Natural history, antiquities.
144. Herman Boerhaave, 1668–1738, Dutch. Philosophy, medicine, botany, chemistry.
145. Johann Albert Fabricius, 1668–1736, German. Rhetoric, philosophy, theology, bibliography, *historia literaria*.
146. Johann Peter von Ludewig, 1668–1743, German. History, law, antiquities.
147. Giambattista Vico, 1668–1744, Italian. Law, rhetoric, history, philosophy, philology.
148. Burkhard Gotthelf Struve, 1671–1738, German. Philosophy, politics, history, law, alchemy.
149. Johann Jacob Scheuchzer, 1672–1733, Swiss. Geology, palaeontology, meteorology, geography, antiquities.
150. Johannes Alexander Döderlein, 1675–1745, German. History, antiquities, philology, theology, oriental languages.
151. Scipione Maffei, 1675–1755, Italian. Politics, history, antiquities.

152. Benito Jerónimo Feijoó, 1676–1764, Spanish. Benedictine. Theology, philosophy, philology, history, medicine, natural history.

153. Ephraim Chambers, c.1680–1740, English. Encyclopaedist and lexicographer.

154. René de Réaumur, 1683–1757, French. Mathematics, metallurgy, meteorology, natural history.

155. Matthias Bél, 1684–1749, Hungarian/Slovak. History, geography, grammar, rhetoric, languages.

156. Daniel Gottlieb Messerschmidt, 1684–1735, German. Natural history, antiquities.

157. Nicholas Fréret, 1688–1749, French. History, chronology, geography, religion.

158. Emanuel Swedenborg, 1688–1772, Swedish. Theology, philosophy, metallurgy, chemistry, astronomy, anatomy, physiology.

159. Montesquieu (Charles de Secondat), 1689–1755, French. Law, history, geography, geology.

160. Carlo Lodoli, 1690–1761, Italian. Franciscan. Mathematics, architecture, physics, philosophy, theology.

161. Voltaire (François-Marie Arouet), 1694–1778, French. History, philosophy, natural history.

162. François Quesnay, 1694–1774, French. Political economy, medicine, politics, geometry.

163. Hermann Samuel Reimarus, 1694–1768, German. Theology, philosophy, oriental languages, mathematics, history, political economy, natural history.

164. Johann Andreas Fabricius, 1696–1769, German. Rhetoric, philosophy, philology, history.

165. Henry Home, Lord Kames, 1696–1782, Scottish. Law, philosophy, history, literary criticism, political economy.

166. Louis de Jaucourt, 1704–79, French. Anatomy, botany, chemistry, physiology, pathology, history.

167. Émilie du Châtelet, 1706–49, French. Physics, mathematics, philosophy.
168. Benjamin Franklin, 1706–90, English/American. Physics, meteorology, politics. Inventor.
169. Comte de Buffon (Georges-Louis Leclerc), 1707–88, French. Mathematics, geology, biology, palaeontology, physiology.
170. Leonhard Euler, 1707–83, Swiss. Mathematics, optics, ballistics, music.
171. Carl Linnaeus, 1707–78, Swedish. Natural history, medicine, political economy, ethnography.
172. Albrecht von Haller, 1708–77, Swiss. Anatomy, physiology, botany, bibliography, theology.
173. Johann Georg Gmelin, 1709–55, German. Natural history, chemistry, medicine.
174. Samuel Johnson, 1709–84, English. Lexicography, literary criticism, history.
175. Rudjer Bošković, 1711–87, Croat. Jesuit. Mathematics, astronomy, physics, cartography, philosophy, archaeology.
176. David Hume, 1711–76, Scottish. Philosophy, history, political economy.
177. Mikhail Lomonosov, 1711–65, Russian. Chemistry, mathematics, physics, metallurgy, history, philology.
178. Denis Diderot, 1713–84, French. Edited the *Encyclopédie*.
179. James Burnett, Lord Monboddo, 1714–99. Scottish. Law, language, philosophy.
180. Jean d'Alembert, 1717–83, French. Mathematics, physics, philosophy, music theory, history.
181. Johann David Michaelis, 1717–91, German. Theology, oriental studies, geography, law.
182. Maria Gaetana Agnesi, 1718–99, Italian. Mathematics, philosophy, theology.
183. Adam Ferguson, 1723–1816, Scottish. Protestant minister. Philosophy, history, politics.

184. Adam Smith, 1723–90, Scottish. Political economy, philosophy, rhetoric, theology, law.

185. Anne Robert Turgot, 1727–81, French. Political economy, philosophy, physics, philology.

186. Christian Gottlob Heyne, 1729–1812, German. Philology, rhetoric, antiquities.

187. Erasmus Darwin, 1731–1802, English. Medicine, physiology, natural history, philosophy.

188. Joseph Priestley, 1733–1804, English. Philology, education, rhetoric, history, theology, physics, chemistry.

189. Lorenzo Hervás y Panduro, 1735–1809, Spanish. Languages, palaeography, archives, education.

190. John Millar of Glasgow, 1735–1801, Scottish. Law, history, philosophy.

191. August von Schlözer, 1735–1809, German. History, languages, *Völkerkunde, Statistik.*

192. José Antonio de Alzate, 1737–99, Mexican. Natural history, astronomy.

193. Nicolas Masson de Morvilliers, 1740–89, French. Geography, encyclopaedist.

194. Peter Simon Pallas, 1741–1811, German. Natural history, geography, languages.

195. José Mariano da Conceição Veloso, 1742–1811, Brazilian. Natural history, chemistry, mathematics, linguistics, political economy.

196. Joseph Banks, 1743–1820, English. Natural history, languages, ethnography.

197. Thomas Jefferson, 1743–1826, American. Languages, natural history. Inventor.

198. Antoine Lavoisier, 1743–94, French. Chemistry, geology, physiology, agriculture.

199. Nicholas, Marquis de Condorcet, 1743–94, French. Philosophy, mathematics, political economy, politics, history.

200. Johann Gottfried Herder, 1744–1803, German. Protestant minister. Philosophy, theology, history, linguistics, literary and art criticism, music.

201. Gaspar Melchor de Jovellanos, 1746–1811, Spanish. Medicine, language, political economy, education, law, historical geography, theology, botany, mining.

202. William Jones, 1746–94, Welsh. Law, oriental studies, botany.

203. John Playfair, 1748–1819, Scottish. Protestant minister. Mathematics, geology, astronomy.

204. Johann Wolfgang von Goethe, 1749–1832, German. Anatomy, physics, chemistry, botany, geology.

205. Johann Gottfried Eichhorn, 1752–1827, German. Theology, oriental studies, history, numismatics.

206. Stanisław Staszic, 1755–1826, Polish. Priest. History, education, geology.

207. William Playfair, 1759–1823, Scottish. Engineering, political economy, statistics. Inventor.

208. Jan Potocki, 1761–1815, Polish. Engineering, Egyptology, languages, history.

209. Daniel Encontre, 1762–1818, French. Protestant minister. Literature, mathematics, theology, philosophy.

210. Germaine de Staël, 1766–1817, Swiss. Politics, literature, geography.

211. William Wollaston, 1766–1828, English. Physiology, optics, chemistry, geology.

212. Wilhelm von Humboldt, 1767–1835, German. Philosophy, languages, history, politics, literature, medicine.

213. Georges Cuvier, 1769–1832, French. Protestant. Palaeontology, natural history, comparative anatomy, history of science.

214. Alexander von Humboldt, 1769–1859, German. Geography, natural history, anatomy, politics, archaeology, demography.

215. Dorothea Schlözer, 1770–1825, German. Studied mathematics, botany, zoology, optics, religion, mineralogy, art history.

216. Samuel Taylor Coleridge, 1772–1834, English. Literary critic, philosopher. Interest in astronomy, botany, chemistry, geology, medicine, history, languages.

217. Francis Jeffrey, 1773–1850, Scottish. Literary criticism, history, philosophy, law, political science, religion, geography.

218. Thomas Young, 1773–1829, English. Medicine, physiology, physics, languages, Egyptology.

219. Henry Peter Brougham, 1778–1868, Scottish. Journalist. Law, physics, education.

220. Mary Somerville, 1780–1872, Scottish. Mathematics, astronomy, geography.

221. Andrés Bello, 1781–1865, Venezuelan. Law, philosophy, philology.

222. Thomas De Quincey, 1785–1859, English. Philosophy, political economy, history, physiology.

223. Carl Gustav Carus, 1789–1869, German. Medicine, physiology, zoology, psychology, philosophy, literature.

224. Jules Dumont d'Urville, 1790–1842, French. Cartography, languages, botany, entomology.

225. Charles Babbage, 1791–1871, English. Mathematics, physics, theology. Inventor.

226. John Herschel, 1792–1871, English. Astronomy, mathematics, physics, chemistry, botany, geology.

227. William Whewell, 1794–1866, English. Anglican clergyman. Mathematics, mechanics, mineralogy, astronomy, philosophy and history of science, theology.

228. Thomas Carlyle, 1795–1881, Scottish. Philosophy, literature, history, mathematics.

229. Auguste Comte, 1798–1857, French. Philosophy, sociology, history of science.

230. Thomas B. Macaulay, 1800–59, Scottish. History, essays.

231. William Henry Fox Talbot, 1800–77, English. Mathematics, physics, botany, astronomy, chemistry, photography, Assyriology. Inventor.

232. Carlo Cattaneo, 1801–69, Italian. Political economy, history, mathematics.

233. Antoine Cournot, 1801–77, French. Mechanics, mathematics, political economy.

234. Gustav Fechner, 1801–87, German. Philosophy, physics, experimental psychology.

235. George P. Marsh, 1801–82, American. Philology, archaeology, geography, ecology.

236. Gustav Klemm, 1802–67, German. Archaeology, ethnology, history.

237. Harriet Martineau, 1802–76, English. Theology, political economy, education, history.

238. Charles Sainte-Beuve, 1804–69, French. Literary criticism, philosophy, history.

239. Alexis de Tocqueville, 1805–59, French. Political science, history, sociology, ethnography.

240. Frédéric Le Play, 1806–82, French. Engineering, metallurgy, economics, sociology.

241. John Stuart Mill, 1806–73, English. Philosophy, economics, politics, history.

242. Louis Agassiz, 1807–73, Swiss. Botany, geology, zoology, anatomy.

243. Harriet Taylor (née Hardy), 1807–58, English. Co-author with John Stuart Mill.

244. Charles Darwin, 1809–82, English. Zoology, botany, geology, palaeontology, philosophy.

245. Domingo Sarmiento, 1811–88, Argentinian. Education, philosophy, society, law, politics.

246. Mark Pattison, 1813–84, English. Anglican clergyman. History, theology, philosophy, literature.

247. George Boole, 1815–64, English. Mathematics, logic, education, history, psychology, ethnography.

248. Benjamin Jowett, 1817–93, English. Anglican clergyman. Classics, philosophy, theology.

249. George Henry Lewes, 1817–78, English. Literary criticism, history, philosophy, biology, physiology, psychology.
250. Alfred Maury, 1817–92, French. Medicine, psychology, folklore, archaeology, geography, geology.
251. Jacob Burckhardt, 1818–97, Swiss. History, philosophy of history, art history, art criticism.
252. Karl Marx, 1818–83, German. Philosophy, history, economics, sociology, politics.
253. Marian Evans ('George Eliot'), 1819–80, English. History, philosophy, geology, biology, physics, astronomy, anatomy.
254. John Ruskin, 1819–1900, English. Art criticism, geology, history, economics, philosophy.
255. Herbert Spencer, 1820–1903, English. Engineering, philosophy, sociology, phrenology, biology, psychology.
256. Hermann von Helmholtz, 1821–94, German. Medicine, anatomy, physics, the perception of art, theory of music.
257. Rudolf Virchow, 1821–1902, German. Medicine, anatomy, physical anthropology, ethnology, prehistory, biology.
258. Matthew Arnold, 1822–88, English. Education, cultural criticism.
259. Francis Galton, 1822–1911, English. Biology, psychology, mathematics, statistics, physical anthropology, meteorology.
260. Joseph Leidy, 1823–91, American. Anatomy, natural history, forensic medicine, palaeontology.
261. Ernest Renan, 1823–92, French. Priest, then layman. Philosophy, philology, oriental languages, history of religion, archaeology.
262. Paul Broca, 1824–80, French. Medicine, anatomy, physical anthropology.
263. Thomas Henry Huxley, 1825–95, English. Medicine, physiology, anatomy, zoology, geology, palaeontology.
264. Ferdinand Lassalle, 1825–64, German. Philosophy, law, economics.
265. Adolf Bastian, 1826–1905, German. Psychology, ethnography, geography, history.
266. Hippolyte Taine, 1828–93, French. Philosophy, literature, history, psychology.

267. Lothar Meyer, 1830–95, German. Medicine, physiology, chemistry, physics.
268. Paolo Mantegazza, 1831–1910, Italian. Medicine, natural history, ethnography.
269. Wilhelm Wundt, 1832–1920, German. Physiology, psychology, philosophy.
270. Ernst Haeckel, 1834–1919, German. Anatomy, zoology, physical anthropology, ecology, philosophy of science.
271. John Lubbock, 1834–1913, English. Private means. Archaeology, anthropology, natural history, prehistory.
272. Léon Walras, 1834–1910, French. Mathematics, mechanics, economics.
273. Cesare Lombroso, 1835–1909, Italian. Forensic medicine, psychiatry, parapsychology, criminology, physical anthropology.
274. James Bryce, 1838–1922, Irish. Law, history, politics, botany, 'mental and moral science'.
275. Ernst Mach, 1838–1916, Austrian. Physics, psychology, philosophy, history of science.
276. Friedrich Althoff, 1839–1908, German. Administrator of education and science.
277. Charles Sanders Peirce, 1839–1914, American. Philosophy, mathematics, chemistry, linguistics, semiotics, psychology, economics.
278. John Theodore Merz, 1840–1922, English/German. Astronomy, engineering, philosophy, history.
279. Gustave Le Bon, 1841–1931, French. Medicine, anthropology, psychology, geography, sociology.
280. Giuseppe Pitrè, 1841–1916, Italian. Medicine, psychology, folklore.
281. Rudolf Sohm, 1841–1917, German. Law, theology, history, religion.
282. Lester Frank Ward, 1841–1913, American. Botany, geology, palaeontology, sociology.
283. William James, 1842–1910, American. Philosophy, psychology, religion, education.

284. Manuel Sales y Ferré, 1843–1910, Spanish. Philosophy, law, sociology, history, geography, archaeology.

285. Gabriel Tarde, 1843–1904, French. Law, anthropology, psychology, philosophy, sociology.

286. Alfred Espinas, 1844–1922, French. Philosophy, education, zoology, psychology, sociology.

287. Andrew Lang, 1844–1912, Scottish. History, literary criticism, folklore, anthropology.

288. Friedrich Ratzel, 1844–1904, German. Geography, anthropology, politics.

289. William Robertson Smith, 1846–94, Scottish. Protestant minister, but expelled. Mathematics, physics, theology, oriental studies, anthropology, comparative religion.

290. Karl Bücher, 1847–1930, German. Economics, history, geography, journalism studies.

291. Vilfredo Pareto, 1848–1923, Italian. Engineering, economics, sociology, political science.

292. Frederic William Maitland, 1850–1906, Scottish. Law, history, philosophy.

293. Thomas Masaryk, 1850–1937, Czech. Sociology, philosophy, philology, international relations.

294. Melvil Dewey, 1851–1931, American. Bibliography, classification of knowledge.

295. Wilhelm Ostwald, 1853–1932, German. Chemistry, philosophy, history, 'energetics'.

296. Patrick Geddes, 1854–1932, Scottish. Botany, biology, sociology, urban studies.

297. James Frazer, 1854–1941, Scottish. Classics, comparative religion, anthropology.

298. Henri Poincaré, 1854–1912, French. Mathematics, physics, astronomy, philosophy of science.

299. Franklin H. Giddings, 1855–1931, American. Sociology, economics, politics, cultural history.

300. Alfred Haddon, 1855–1940, English. Zoology, anthropology, sociology.
301. Rafael Salillas, 1855–1923, Spanish. Medicine, law, psychology, anthropology, philology, history.
302. Karl Lamprecht, 1856–1915, German. History, psychology.
303. Benedetto Croce, 1856–1952, Italian. Philosophy, history, literary and art criticism.
304. Marcelino Menéndez Pelayo, 1856–1912, Spanish. Philology, literary criticism, history.
305. Sigmund Freud, 1856–1939, Austrian. Medicine, physiology, psychology.
306. Karl Pearson, 1857–1936, English. Mathematics, history, philosophy, statistics, eugenics.
307. Thorstein Veblen, 1857–1929, American. Economics, philosophy, sociology.
308. Franz Boas, 1858–1942, German-American. Physics, geography, anthropology.
309. Émile Durkheim, 1858–1917, French. Philosophy, psychology, political economy, sociology, anthropology.
310. Salomon Reinach, 1858–1932, French. Classics, art history, archaeology, anthropology, religious studies.
311. Georg Simmel, 1858–1918, German. Philosophy, psychology, sociology.
312. John Dewey, 1859–1952, American. Philosophy, psychology, education, religious studies.
313. Ludwik Krzywicki, 1859–1941, Polish. Economics, sociology, politics, history, ethnography.
314. Théodore Reinach, 1860–1928, French. Law, classics, mathematics, musicology, history.
315. Henri Berr, 1863–1954, French. Philosophy, history, psychology.
316. Henri-Alexandre Junod, 1863–1934, Swiss. Protestant minister. Medicine, ethnography, botany, entomology.

317. Robert E. Park, 1864–1944, American. Philosophy, sociology, urban studies.

318. William H. Rivers, 1864–1922, English. Medicine, neurology, psychology, anthropology.

319. Max Weber, 1864–1920, German. History, philosophy, law, economics, sociology.

320. Jacob von Uexküll, 1864–1944, Estonian. Physiology, biology, ecology, biosemiotics.

321. Themistocles Zammit, 1864–1935, Maltese. History, archaeology, chemistry, medicine.

322. Ernst Troeltsch, 1865–1923, German. Protestant minister. Theology, philosophy, history, sociology, religious studies.

323. Aby Warburg, 1866–1929, German. History of images, cultural studies.

324. Herbert George Wells, 1866–1946, English. Biology, history, futurology.

325. Karl Camillo Schneider, 1867–1943, Austrian. Zoology, anatomy, animal psychology, parapsychology, futurology.

326. Vladimir Vernadsky, 1867–1945, Russian. Mineralogy, geochemistry, radiogeology, biochemistry, philosophy.

327. Paul Otlet, 1868–1944, Belgian. Classified the world.

328. James R. Angell, 1869–1949, American. Philosophy, psychology, education.

329. Nicolae Iorga, 1871–1940, Romanian. History, philosophy, criticism. Also politician, poet and playwright.

330. Johan Huizinga, 1872–1945, Dutch. Oriental studies, history, cultural criticism.

331. Marcel Mauss, 1872–1950, French. Sociology, anthropology, philology, religious studies.

332. Alexander Bogdanov, 1873–1928, Russian. Medicine, psychology, philosophy, economics. Also science fiction.

333. Arthur Lovejoy, 1873–1962, American. Philosophy, philology, history of ideas.

334. Abel Rey, 1873–1940, French. Philosophy, history of science, sociology.

335. Carl Gustav Jung, 1875–1961, Swiss. Medicine, psychiatry, psychoanalysis, religious studies.

336. Herbert John Fleure, 1877–1969, from Guernsey. Zoology, geology, anthropology, prehistory, folklore, geography.

337. Lawrence J. Henderson, 1878–1942, American. Physiology, chemistry, biology, philosophy, sociology.

338. Lucien Febvre, 1878–1956, French. History, geography. Encyclopaedist.

339. Othmar Spann, 1878–1950, Austrian. Philosophy, sociology, economics.

340. Alfred Zimmern, 1879–1957, English. Classics, history, international relations.

341. George Elton Mayo, 1880–1949, Australian. Psychology, sociology, management theory.

342. Alfred Wegener, 1880–1930, German. Astronomy, meteorology, geophysics.

343. Gilbert Chinard, 1881–1972, French. Literature, history.

344. Fernando Ortiz, 1881–1969, Cuban. Law, ethnography, folklore, history, philology, geography, economics, musicology.

345. Pierre Teilhard de Chardin, 1881–1955, French. Jesuit. Geology, palaeontology, philosophy, theology.

346. Eugenio d'Ors, 1881–1954, Spanish. Essayist on art, literature, etc.

347. Pavel Florensky, 1882–1937, Russian. Priest. Mathematics, philosophy, theology, art history, electrical engineering.

348. Otto Neurath, 1882–1945, Austrian. Economics, politics, sociology, history, literature. Encyclopaedist.

349. John Maynard Keynes, 1883–1946, English. Economics, history.

350. José Ortega y Gasset, 1883–1955, Spanish. Philosopher, sociologist, historian.

351. Philipp Frank, 1884–1966, Austrian. Physics, mathematics, philosophy.

352. Edward Sapir, 1884–1939, American. Linguistics, anthropology, psychology, philosophy.

353. György Lukács, 1885–1971, Hungarian. Philosophy, literary criticism, history, sociology.

354. Karl Polanyi, 1886–1964, Hungarian. Economics, history, anthropology, sociology, philosophy.

355. Julien Cain, 1887–1974, French. History, art history. Encyclopaedist.

356. Julian Huxley, 1887–1975, English. Zoology, physiology.

357. Gregorio Marañón, 1887–1960, Spanish. Medicine, psychology, history, philosophy.

358. Erwin Schrödinger, 1887–1961, Austrian. Physics, experimental psychology, biology, philosophy.

359. Erich Rothacker, 1888–1965, German. Philosophy, sociology, psychology, history.

360. Robin George Collingwood, 1889–1943, English. Philosophy, archaeology, history.

361. Gerald Heard, 1889–1971, English. Science, religion, para-psychology.

362. Siegfried Kracauer, 1889–1966, German. Art history, philosophy, sociology, film studies.

363. Charles Ogden, 1889–1957, English. Psychology, language, education.

364. Alfonso Reyes, 1889–1959, Mexican. Philosophy, literature.

365. Arnold Toynbee, 1889–1975, English. Classics, history, international relations.

366. Vannevar Bush, 1890–1974, American. Engineering, computer science. Inventor.

367. Victoria Ocampo, 1890–1979, Argentinian. Criticism, biography.

368. Michael Polanyi, 1891–1976, Hungarian. Chemistry, economics, philosophy.

369. Walter Benjamin, 1892–1940, German. Philosophy, literature, history.

370. John B. S. Haldane, 1892–1964, English. Genetics, physiology, biochemistry, biometry.

371. Karl Mannheim, 1893–1947, Hungarian. Sociology, history, philosophy.

372. Henry A. Murray, 1893–1988, American. Physiology, biochemistry, psychology, literature.

373. Ivor Richards, 1893–1979, English. Philosophy, literature, language, psychology, education.

374. Aldous Huxley, 1894–1963, English. Essayist and passive polymath.

375. Harold Innis, 1894–1952, Canadian. History, economics, communications.

376. Friedrich Pollock, 1894–1970, German. Economics, sociology.

377. Beardsley Ruml, 1894–1960, American. Statistics, economics, social sciences.

378. Warren Weaver, 1894–1978, American. Engineering, mathematics, agriculture, computer science.

379. Norbert Wiener, 1894–1964, American. Mathematics, philosophy engineering, cybernetics.

380. Joseph Henry Woodger, 1894–1981, English. Zoology, philosophy, mathematics.

381. Mikhail Bakhtin, 1895–1975, Russian. Philosophy, literary criticism, language, theology.

382. Richard Buckminster ('Bucky') Fuller, 1895–1983, American. Engineer, inventor, futurologist.

383. Max Horkheimer, 1895–1973, German. Philosophy, sociology, history, psychology.

384. Ernst Jünger, 1895–1998, German. Entomology, philosophy.

385. Lewis Mumford, 1895–1990, American. Criticism, sociology, history, interest in geography, geology, economics, biology, ecology.

386. Edmund Wilson, 1895–1972, American. Criticism, history, sociology.

387. Roman Jakobson, 1896–1982, Russian. Philology, literature, psychology, folklore.

388. Georges Bataille, 1897–1962, French. Librarian. Philosophy, economics, sociology, anthropology.
389. Kenneth Burke, 1897–1993, American. Criticism, rhetoric, philosophy, sociology.
390. Norbert Elias, 1897–1990, German. Philosophy, sociology, psychology, history.
391. Károly Kérenyi, 1897–1973, Hungarian. Classics, philosophy, psychology.
392. Benjamin Lee Whorf, 1897–1941, American. Engineering, linguistics, anthropology.
393. Roger Bastide, 1898–1974, French. Philosophy, sociology, anthropology, psychoanalysis.
394. Georges Dumézil, 1898–1986, French. Philology, comparative religion.
395. Warren McCulloch, 1898–1969, American. Mathematics, philosophy, psychology, neuroscience, cybernetics.
396. Jean Piaget, 1896–1980, Swiss. Psychology, philosophy, botany, biology.
397. Leo Szilard, 1898–1964, Hungarian. Engineering, physics, biology. Inventor.
398. Jorge Luis Borges, 1899–1986, Argentinian. Philosophy, languages, mathematics, history.
399. Friedrich (von) Hayek, 1899–1992, Austrian. Economics, political science, psychology, philosophy of science.
400. Robert M. Hutchins, 1899–1977, American. Law, education.
401. Vladimir Nabokov, 1899–1977, Russian. Comparative literature, entomology.
402. Nicolas Rashevsky, 1899–1972, Russian. Physics, mathematical biology.
403. Alfred Schütz, 1899–1959, Austrian. Philosophy, sociology.
404. Gilberto Freyre, 1900–87, Brazilian. History, sociology, anthropology.
405. Erich Fromm, 1900–80, German. Psychology, history, philosophy, sociology.

406. Ralph W. Gerard, 1900–74, American. Medicine, biophysics, biochemistry, neuroscience and GST.
407. Leo Lowenthal, 1900–93, German. Sociology, literature, philosophy, history.
408. Joseph Needham, 1900–95, English. Biology (embryology), sinology, history of science.
409. Franz Leopold Neumann, 1900–54, German. Law, political science.
410. John D. Bernal, 1901–71, Irish. Crystallography, biology, physics, history and sociology of science.
411. Ludwig von Bertalanffy, 1901–72, Austrian. Philosophy, biology, psychology, GST.
412. Paul Lazarsfeld, 1901–76, Austrian. Mathematics, psychology, sociology.
413. Charles W. Morris, 1901–79, American. Engineering, psychology, philosophy, semiotics.
414. Linus Pauling, 1901–94, American. Physical chemistry, mathematical physics, biology, medicine.
415. Mortimer J. Adler, 1902–2001, American. Philosophy, law, education, psychology, economics.
416. Fernand Braudel, 1902–85, French. History, geography, economics, sociology.
417. Harold Lasswell, 1902–78, American. Political science, psychology, law, sociology.
418. Oskar Morgenstern, 1902–77, German. Economics, mathematics.
419. Theodor W. Adorno, 1903–69, German. Philosophy, sociology, psychology, musicology.
420. William Ross Ashby, 1903–72, English. Medicine, psychiatry, neurology, cybernetics.
421. Peter A. Boodberg (Piotr Alekseevich Budberg), 1903–72, Russian. Linguist, sinologist.
422. Henry Corbin, 1903–78, French. Philosophy, theology, history, Islamic studies.

423. George Evelyn Hutchinson, 1903–91, English. Zoology, ecology, art history, archaeology, psychoanalysis.

424. Konrad Lorenz, 1903–89, Austrian. Zoology, psychology, ethology, ecology.

425. John von Neumann, 1903–57, Hungarian-American. Mathematics, computer science, biology, history.

426. Gregory Bateson, 1904–80, English. Anthropology, psychology, biology.

427. Raymond Aron, 1905–83, French. Philosophy, politics, sociology, history.

428. Jean-Paul Sartre, 1905–80, French. Philosophy, criticism, politics.

429. Charles P. Snow, 1905–80, English. Physical chemistry, education.

430. Edward Haskell, 1906–86, American. Sociology, anthropology, philosophy, unified science.

431. Samuel Hayakawa, 1906–92, American. Linguistics, psychology, philosophy, musicology.

432. Marie Jahoda, 1907–2001, Austrian. Psychology, sociology, science studies.

433. Jacob Bronowski, 1908–74, English. Mathematics, biology, history of science, ideas.

434. Ernesto de Martino, 1908–65, Italian. Ethnology, philosophy, history, interest in archaeology, psychoanalysis.

435. Pedro Laín Entralgo, 1908–2001, Spanish. Medicine, history, philosophy.

436. Isaiah Berlin, 1909–97, English. Philosophy, history, Russian studies.

437. Norberto Bobbio, 1909–2004, Italian. Philosophy, law, political science.

438. Peter Drucker, 1909–2005, Austrian-American. Economics, sociology, psychology, management theory.

439. Ernst Hans Gombrich, 1909–2001, Austrian-English. History, art history, drew on experimental psychology, biology.

440. David Riesman, 1909–2002, American. Sociology, psychology, education, law, politics.

441. Joseph Jackson Schwab, 1909–88, American. Biology, education.
442. Kenneth Boulding, 1910–93, English. Economics, but also wrote on society, knowledge, conflict, peace, ecology and history.
443. Marjorie Grene (née Glickman), 1910–2009, American. Philosophy, biology, history and philosophy of science.
444. George C. Homans, 1910–89, American. Sociology, history, anthropology.
445. Paul Goodman, 1911–72, American. Literary critic, psychotherapist, philosopher, sociologist.
446. Louis Henry, 1911–91, French. Demography, history.
447. Marshall McLuhan, 1911–80, Canadian. Literature, media studies.
448. Anatol Rapoport, 1911–2007, Russian. Mathematics, biology, psychology, GST.
449. Bernard Berelson, 1912–79, American. Literature, sociology, knowledge management.
450. Karl Deutsch, 1912–92, Czech. Law, international relations, political science, cybernetics.
451. Alan Turing, 1912–54, English. Mathematician, philosopher, cryptanalyst, engineer, biologist.
452. Carl Friedrich von Weizsäcker, 1912–2007, German. Astronomy, physics, philosophy, sociology.
453. Roger Caillois, 1913–78, French. Literature, sociology.
454. Barrington Moore, 1913–2005, American. Sociology, politics, history.
455. Paul Ricoeur, 1913–2005, French. Philosophy, psychoanalysis, history, literature.
456. Zevedei Barbu, 1914–93, Romanian. Philosophy, psychology, sociology, history.
457. Daniel Boorstin, 1914–2004, American. History, law, sociology.
458. Julio Caro Baroja, 1914–95, Spanish. History, anthropology, linguistics.
459. Constantinos Doxiadis, 1914–75, Greek. History, geography, anthropology, 'ekistics'.

460. Roland Barthes, 1915–80, French. Criticism, linguistics, sociology, semiotics.

461. Albert Hirschman, 1915–2012, German-American. Economics, politics, history, anthropology.

462. Donald T. Campbell, 1916–96, American. Psychology, sociology, anthropology, biology and philosophy.

463. James G. Miller, 1916–2002, American. Psychology, pharmacology, biology, GST.

464. Claude Shannon, 1916–2001, American. Mathematics, engineering, genetics, computer science. Inventor.

465. Herbert Simon, 1916–2001, American. Political science, economics, psychology, artificial intelligence.

466. Edward N. Lorenz, 1917–2008, American. Mathematics, meteorology.

467. Ray Birdwhistell, 1918–94, American. Anthropology, linguistics, comunication, 'kinesics'.

468. Richard Feynman, 1918–88, American. Physics, biology, astronomy.

469. Jack Goody, 1919–2015, English. Anthropology, history, sociology.

470. Hans Blumenberg, 1920–96, German. Philosophy, intellectual history, theology, literature ('metaphorology').

471. John Maynard Smith, 1920–2004, English. Engineering, biology, mathematics.

472. George A. Miller, 1920–2012, American. Linguistics, psychology, cognitive science.

473. Thomas Sebeok, 1920–2001, Hungarian-American. Linguistics, anthropology, folklore, semiotics, 'zoosemiotics'.

474. Edmund S. Carpenter, 1922–2011, American. Anthropology, archaeology, communication studies.

475. Yuri Lotman, 1922–93, Russian. Philology, literature, history, semiotics.

476. Darcy Ribeiro, 1922–97, Brazilian. Anthropology, sociology, history, education.

477. René Girard, 1923–2015, French. History, philosophy, literature, theory of violence.

478. David Lowenthal, 1923–2018, American. Geography, history, heritage studies.

479. Walter Pitts, 1923–69, American. Mathematics, philosophy, biology, neuroscience.

480. Jacob Taubes, 1923–87, Austrian. Theology, philosophy, sociology.

481. Benoit Mandelbrot, 1924–2010, French. Mathematician. Geometry, physics, geology, economics.

482. Michel de Certeau, 1925–86, French. Jesuit. Philosophy, theology, psychoanalysis, history, sociology, anthropology.

483. Gilles Deleuze, 1925–95, French. Philosopher, critic of literature, art, film.

484. Ernest Gellner, 1925–95, Czech/English. Philosophy, anthropology, history, sociology.

485. Michel Foucault, 1926–84, French. Philosophy, history, geography, sociology, politics.

486. Niklas Luhmann, 1927–98, German. Sociology, law, economics, politics, art, religion, ecology, psychology.

487. Marvin Minsky, 1927–2016, American. Mathematics, psychology, engineering, computer science.

488. Allen Newell, 1927–92, American. Maths, psychology, computer science.

489. Giorgio Prodi, 1928–87, Italian. Medicine, biology, philosophy, biosemiotics.

490. André Gunder Frank, 1929–2005, German-American. Economics, sociology, history, anthropology.

491. Pierre Bourdieu, 1930–2002, French. Philosophy, anthropology, sociology.

492. Jacques Derrida, 1930–2004, Algerian-French. Philosophy, linguistics, literary criticism.

493. Pierre-Félix Guattari, 1930–92, French. Psychoanalysis, philosophy, semiology, 'ecosophy'.

494. Ronald Dworkin, 1931–2013, American. Law, philosophy, politics.
495. Umberto Eco, 1932–2016, Italian. Philosophy, literature, semiotics.
496. Oliver Sacks, 1933–2015, English. Neurology, psychiatry, botany, biology, history of science.
497. Susan Sontag (née Rosenblatt), 1933–2004, American. Philosophy, criticism, photography, etc.
498. Edward Said, 1935–2003, American. Criticism, philosophy, history, postcolonial theory, music.
499. Tristan Todorov, 1939–2017, Bulgarian. Philosophy, literary criticism, history, sociology, politics.
500. Stephen J. Gould, 1941–2002, American. Geology, palaeontology, biology.

NOTES

LIST OF ABBREVIATIONS

ANB   *American National Biography*, 24 vols. (New York, 1999)

DBI   *Dizionario Biografico degli Italiani* (Rome, 1960–)

DSB   Charles C. Gillespie (ed.), *Dictionary of Scientific Biography*, 16 vols. (New York, 1970)

GDLI   *Grande Dizionario della Lingua Italiano*, 21 vols. (Turin, 1961–2002)

IESBS   *International Encyclopedia of Social and Behavioral Sciences*, 2nd edn, ed. James Wright, 26 vols. (Amsterdam, 2015)

JHI   *Journal of the History of Ideas* (University of Pennsylvania Press, 1940–)

ODNB   *Oxford Dictionary of National Biography*, eds. Henry Matthew and Brian Harrison, 60 vols. (Oxford, 2004)

PREFACE

1. See in particular Peter Burke, 'The Polymath: A Cultural and Social History of an Intellectual Species', in D. F. Smith and H. Philsooph (eds.), *Explorations in Cultural History: Essays for Peter McCaffery* (Aberdeen, 2010), 67–79.

INTRODUCTION

1. Alexander Murray (ed.), *Sir William Jones, 1746–1794* (Oxford, 1998), v.
2. Edward Dyker, *Dumont Durville: Explorer and Polymath* (Dunedin, 2014); D. Ben Rees, *The Polymath: Reverend William Rees* (Liverpool, 2002).
3. Edward Carr, 'The Last Days of the Polymath', *Intelligent Life*, Autumn 2009; Burke, 'The Polymath', in Smith and Philsooph (eds.), *Explorations in Cultural History*, 67–79; Eric Monkman and Bobby Seagull, 'Polymathic Adventure', BBC Radio 4, 21 August 2017. For a recent general view, working with a wider definition of 'polymath' than mine, see Waqas Akbar Ahmed, *The Polymath: Unlocking the Power of Human Versatility* (Chichester, 2019).
4. Quoted by Woodruff D. Smith, *Politics and the Sciences of Culture in Germany, 1840–1920* (New York, 1991), 138.
5. www.dubage.com/API/ThePolymath.html, accessed 15 July 2016.
6. The friend was Leonard Woolf, quoted in Richard Davenport-Hines, *Universal Man: The Seven Lives of John Maynard Keynes* (London, 2015), 7; Keynes quoted in ibid., 137.
7. For a comparative analysis of the early stages of 'disciplining', see Geoffrey Lloyd, *Disciplines in the Making* (Oxford, 2009).
8. Carr, 'The Last Days of the Polymath', on Judge Richard Posner. A similar example is that of Amartya Sen in the fields of economics and philosophy.

9. 'la prosopographie des savants . . . a toujours été une de mes passions' (Pierre Bayle to his brother Jacob, 1675, quoted in Hubert Bost, *Pierre Bayle* [Paris, 2006], 387). Such a prosopography was provided by Christian Gottlieb Jöcher in his *Allgemeines Gelehrten-Lexicon* (Leipzig, 1750).

10. Augustine, *De vera religione*, section 49.

11. Peter Burke, *Exiles and Expatriates in the History of Knowledge, 1500–2000* (Waltham, MA, 2017).

12. Leo Rosten, 'Harold Lasswell: A Memoir', in Arnold A. Rogow (ed.), *Politics, Personality and Social Science in the 20th Century* (Chicago, 1969), 1–13, at 5.

13. 'Henry Holorenshaw', 'The Making of an Honorary Taoist', in Mikuláš Teich and Robert Young (eds.), *Changing Perspectives in the History of Science* (London, 1973), 1–20, at 1.

14. Johann Heinrich Alsted, *Encyclopaedia* (1630), preface.

15. Isaiah Berlin, *The Hedgehog and the Fox: An Essay on Tolstoy's View of History* (London, 1953). Cf. Stephen J. Gould, *The Hedgehog, the Fox and the Magister's Pox* (London, 2003), a plea for 'a fruitful union of these seemingly polar opposites' (5).

16. Pamela H. Smith, *The Business of Alchemy: Science and Culture in the Holy Roman Empire* (Princeton, NJ, 1994), 14; Mikuláš Teich, 'Interdisciplinarity in J. J. Becher's Thought', in Gotthardt Frühsorge and Gerhard F. Strasser (eds.), *Johann Joachim Becher* (Wiesbaden, 1993), 23–40.

17. Paula Findlen (ed.), *The Last Man Who Knew Everything* (London, 2004).

18. Andrew Robinson, *Thomas Young: The Last Man Who Knew Everything* (London, 2006); Leonard Warren, *Joseph Leidy: The Last Man Who Knew Everything* (New Haven, 1998); David Schwartz, *The Last Man Who Knew Everything: The Life and Times of Enrico Fermi* (New York, 2017), 365. No fewer than eighteen individuals are listed in Hmolpedia, 'Last person to know everything', http://www.eoht.info/page/Last+person+to+know+everything.

19. Sandro Montalto (ed.), *Umberto Eco: l'uomo che sapeva troppo* (Pisa, 2007). Cf. Stephen Inwood, *The Man Who Knew Too Much: The Strange and Inventive Life of Robert Hooke* (London, 2002), and David Leavitt, *The Man Who Knew Too Much: Alan Turing and the Invention of the Computer* (London, 2006).

20. Croce was so described by Antonio Gramsci, Simon by Ha-Joon Chang, *23 Things They Don't Tell You about Capitalism* (London, 2011), 173; Maurice Goldsmith, *Joseph Needham: Twentieth-Century Renaissance Man* (Paris, 1995); Steiner, described by Antonia Byatt; Florensky, by Avril Pyman, *Pavel Florensky, a Quiet Genius: The Tragic and Extraordinary Life of Russia's Unknown Da Vinci* (New York, 2010); Lasswell, by Steven A. Peterson, 'Lasswell, Harold Dwight', in Glenn H. Utter and Charles Lockhart (eds.), *American Political Scientists: A Dictionary* (2nd edn, Westport, CT, 2002), 228–30, at 229, and by Bruce L. Smith, 'The Mystifying Intellectual History of Harold D. Lasswell', in Arnold A. Rogow (ed.), *Politics, Personality and Social Science in the 20th Century* (Chicago, 1969), 41.

21. N. J. Pearce, 'Janet Beat: A Renaissance Woman', *Contemporary Music Review* 11 (1994), 27; Melanie Davis, 'Sandra Risa Leiblum, Ph.D: Sexology's Renaissance Woman', *American Journal of Sexuality Education* 5 (2010), 97–101.

22. Cf. Robert K. Merton, 'The Matthew Effect in Science', *Science* 159 (1968), Issue 3810, 56–63, which discusses the later attribution to major scientists of the discoveries made by minor ones, illustrating the idea expressed in the Gospel of St Matthew that 'To him who hath shall be given'.

23. Burnet to Leibniz, 27 February 1699, quoted in Maria Rosa Antognazza, *Leibniz: An Intellectual Biography* (Cambridge, 2009), 559.

CHAPTER 1

1. However, this fragment has survived only because it was recorded by a later philosopher, Diogenes Laertius, who had his own agenda. In any case, it may be better to translate *noos* not as 'understanding' but as the faculty of sense. My thanks to Geoffrey Lloyd for pointing this out.

2. Isaiah Berlin, *The Hedgehog and the Fox* (London, 1953).

3. W. K. C. Guthrie, *The Sophists* (Cambridge, 1971), 280–5; Patricia O'Grady, 'Hippias' in O'Grady (ed.), *The Sophists* (London, 2008), 56–70.

4. There is a huge secondary literature on Aristotle, including Maurice Manquat, *Aristote naturaliste* (Paris, 1932), and Geoffrey Lloyd, *Aristotle: The Growth and Structure of his Thought* (Cambridge, 1968). See also G. E. L. Owens, D. M. Balme and Leonard G. Wilson, 'Aristotle', *DSB* 1, 250–81 (taking three specialists to assess his contributions to the natural sciences).

5. Christian Jacob, 'Un athlète du savoir', in C. Jacob and F. de Polignac (eds.), *Alexandrie* (Paris, 1992), 113–27; Klaus Geus, *Eratosthenes von Kyrene* (Oberhaid, 2011, 32–4).

6. This argument repeats much from Plato's *Gorgias*. Thanks again to Geoffrey Lloyd for pointing this out.

7. Quintilian, *Institutio Oratoria*, 12.xi.21–4.

8. Vitruvius, *De Architectura*, 1.i.1, 1.i.3.

9. Cicero, *De Oratore*, 3.xxxiii.135.

10. Quintilian, *Institutio*, 12.xi.24. Cf. D. J. Butterfield (ed.), *Varro Varius: The Polymath of the Roman World* (Cambridge, 2015).

11. Trevor Murphy, *Pliny the Elder's Natural History: The Empire in the Encyclopaedia* (Oxford, 2004), 13.

12. Howard L. Goodman, 'Chinese Polymaths 100–300 AD', *Asia Major* 18 (2005), 101–74, at 110.

13. John Chaffee, *The Thorny Gates of Learning in Sung China: A Social History of Examinations* (Cambridge, 1985); Benjamin A. Elman, *A Cultural History of Civil Examinations in Late Imperial China* (Berkeley, CA, 2000).

14. Quoted in John Meskill (ed.), *Wang An-shih: Practical Reformer?* (Boston, MA, 1963), 8.

15. Wang Yangming, *Instructions for Practical Living* (English translation, New York, 1963), 13, 62. Cf. Benjamin A. Elman, *On Their Own Terms* (Cambridge, MA, 2005), 4–7.

16. Hellmut Wilhelm, 'The Po-Hsüeh Hung-ju Examination of 1679', *Journal of the American Oriental Society* 71 (1951), 60–6.

17. Geoffrey Lloyd, *Disciplines in the Making* (Oxford, 2009), 10, 45.

18. *Zhuangxi*, chapter 33, in *Complete Works of Chuang Tzu* (New York, 1968), 374, 377. Cf. Angus G. Graham, *Disputers of the Tao* (Chicago, 1989), 76–81, 174–83.

19. Joseph Needham and Wang Ling, *Science and Civilization in China* (Cambridge, 1965), vol. 4, part 1, 446–65.

20. Needham and Wang Ling, *Science and Civilization* (Cambridge, 1954), vol. 1, 135. Thanks yet again to Geoffrey Lloyd for making me aware of Shen's importance.

21. Joël Brenier et al., 'Shen Gua (1031–1095) et les sciences', *Revue d'histoire des sciences* 42, 333–50. On his 'vast' knowledge, 335. Nathan Sivin, 'Shen Gua', *Science in Ancient China: Researches and Reflections* (Aldershot, 1995, vol. III, 1–53), notes his 'unlimited curiosity' and the comparisons to Leibniz and Lomonosov, the latter made 'in an era of happy relations between China and the Soviet Union' (11).

22. Daiwie Fu, 'A Contextual and Taxonomic Study of the "Divine Marvels" and "Strange Occurrences" in the *Mengxi bitan*', *Chinese Science* 11 (1993–4), 3–35.

23. Geoffrey Lloyd, *The Ambitions of Curiosity: Understanding the World in Ancient Greece and China* (Cambridge, 2002).

24. Sivin, 'Shen Gua', 53.

25. Tertullian, *De praescriptione haereticorum*, Book 7, ch. 14; Augustine, *Confessiones*, Book 12, ch. 14.

26. Richard Southern, *The Making of the Middle Ages* (London, 1953), 210.

27. Other major figures include Cassiodorus, Bede and Alcuin of York.

28. Cassiodorus, *Variarum Libri XII*, ed. Å. J. Fridh (Turnhout, 1973), Book I, no. 44.

29. Henry Chadwick, *Boethius* (Oxford, 1981); Lorenzo Minio-Paluello, 'Boethius', *DSB* 2 (New York, 1981), 228–36.

30. Isidore of Seville, *Etymologies* (English translation, Cambridge, 2006). On him, John Henderson, *The Medieval World of Isidore of Seville* (Cambridge, 2007).

31. Pierre Riché, *Gerbert d'Aurillac, le pape de l'an mil* (Paris, 1987).
32. William of Malmesbury, *Gesta Regum Anglorum*, ed. and trans. R. A. B. Mynors (Oxford, 1998), Book II, sections 167–9, 172.
33. Tarif Khalidi, *Images of Muhammad* (New York, 2009), 104–5. My thanks to Professor Khalidi for help with this section.
34. Quoted in Robert Irwin, *Ibn Khaldun: An Intellectual Biography* (Princeton, NJ, 2018), 24.
35. Geert Jan Van Gelder, 'Compleat Men, Women and Books', in Peter Binkley (ed.), *Pre-Modern Encyclopaedic Texts* (Leiden, 1997), 241–59, at 247; George Makdisi, *The Rise of Humanism in Classical Islam and the Christian West* (Edinburgh, 1990), 110.
36. Michael Chamberlain, *Knowledge and Social Practice in Medieval Damascus* (Cambridge, 1994), 86.
37. Other leading scholars were Jabir ibn Hayyan (c.721–c.815), known in the West as 'Geber'; Ibn Bajja (c.1085–1138: 'Avempace'); Al-Farabi (872–950: 'Alpharabius'); Al-Biruni (973–c.1050); and Ibn Hazm (994–1064).
38. Quoted in George N. Atiyeh, *Al-Kindi: Philosopher of the Arabs* (Rawalpindi, 1966), 9.
39. Peter Adamson, *Al-Kindi* (Oxford, 2007), 7. Cf. Fritz W. Zimmerman, 'Al-Kindi', in M. J. L. Young, J. D. Latham and R. B. Serjeant (eds.), *Religion, Learning and Science in the Abbasid Period* (Cambridge, 2014), 364–9.
40. G. C. Anawati and Albert Z. Iskander, 'Ibn Sina', *DSB Supplement* 1, 495–501; Lenn E. Goodman, *Avicenna* (revised edn, Ithaca, NY, 2006); Robert Wisnovsky, 'Avicenna and the Avicennian Tradition', in Peter Adamson and Richard C. Taylor (eds.), *The Cambridge Companion to Arabic Philosophy* (Cambridge, 2006), 92–136.
41. Dominque Urvoy, *Ibn Rushd (Averroes)* (London, 1991).
42. Warren E. Gates, 'The Spread of Ibn Khaldun's Ideas on Climate and Culture', *Journal of the History of Ideas* 28 (1967), 415–22; Aziz al-Azmeh, *Ibn Khaldun in Modern Scholarship: A Study in Orientalism* (London, 1981); Robert Irwin, *Ibn Khaldun: An Intellectual Biography* (Princeton, NJ, 2018).
43. Thomas Aquinas is omitted because this great scholar concentrated on theology and philosophy.
44. Studies of Hugh focus on either his theology, his history or his 'psychology', so many signs of the fragmentation of knowledge in our own time.
45. Serge Lusignan and Monique Paulmier-Foucart (eds.), *Lector et compilator: Vincent de Beauvais* (Grâne, 1997).
46. Tom McLeish, 'In Conversation with a Medieval Natural Philosopher', *Emmanuel College Magazine* 100 (Cambridge, 2018), 147–62, at 147.
47. Alistair C. Crombie, *Robert Grosseteste and the Origins of Experimental Science* (Oxford, 1953); Richard W. Southern, *Robert Grosseteste* (Oxford, 1986); idem., 'Grosseteste, Robert', *ODNB* 24, 79–86.
48. Alistair C. Crombie and John North, 'Bacon, Roger', *DSB* 1 (New York, 1981), 377–85; G. Mollant, 'Bacon, Roger', *ODNB* 3, 176–81.
49. Giovanni da Pian del Carpine, Benedict of Poland and William of Rubruck. See Bert Roest, *Reading the Book of History: Intellectual Contexts and Educational Functions of Franciscan Historiography, 1226–c.1350* (Groningen, 1996), 114, 120.
50. Ulrich of Strasbourg, quoted in Irven M. Resnick (ed.), *A Companion to Albert the Great* (Leiden, 2013), 1. Cf. James A. Weisheipl (ed.), *Albertus Magnus and the Sciences* (Toronto, 1980); Gerbert Meyer and Albert Zimmermann (eds.), *Albertus Magnus, Doctor Universalis 1280/1980* (Mainz, 1980), which includes chapters on his contribution to medicine, zoology and botany.
51. Paolo Rossi, *Clavis Universalis: arti mnemoniche e logica combinatoria da Lullo a Leibniz* (Milan and Naples, 1960), esp. 61–74; Dominique Urvoy, *Penser l'Islam. Les présupposés Islamiques de l'"art" de Lull* (Paris, 1980); Umberto Eco, *The Search for the Perfect Language* (Oxford, 1995), 53–72, at 53; John N. Crossley, *Raymond Llull's Contributions to Computer Science* (Melbourne, 2005); Anthony Bonner, *The Art and Logic of Ramon Llull: A User's Guide* (Leiden, 2007).

CHAPTER 2

1. Agnes Heller, *Renaissance Man* (1982: English translation, London 1984); Dorothy Koenigsberger, *Renaissance Man and Creative Thinking* (Atlantic Highlands, NJ, 1979).

2. Jacob Burckhardt, *The Civilisation of the Renaissance in Italy* (1860: English translation, London 1878), ch. 2, section 2.

3. Edgar Quinet, *Révolutions d'Italie* (Paris, 1849), quoted and translated in J. B. Bullen, *The Myth of the Renaissance in Nineteenth-Century Writing* (Oxford, 1994), 175.

4. George Eliot, *Romola* (1863), quoted in Bullen, *Myth*, 218.

5. William H. Woodward, *Vittorino da Feltre and Other Humanist Educators* (Cambridge, 1897), 1–92, drawing on Bartolomeo Platina's life of Vittorino.

6. Matteo Palmieri, *Vita Civile*, ed. Gino Belloni (Florence, 1982), 43.

7. Eliza M. Butler, *The Fortunes of Faust* (Cambridge, 1952), ch. 1.

8. James J. Supple, *Arms versus Letters: The Military and Literary Ideals in the Essais of Montaigne* (Oxford, 1984).

9. Baldassare Castiglione, *Il Cortegiano* (1528: ed. Bruno Maier, Turin 1964), Book 1, sections 44–9.

10. Maximilian, *Weisskunig*, ed. H. T. Musper (Stuttgart, 1956), part 2. However, Jan-Dirk Müller, *Gedachtnus: Literatur und Hofgesellschaft um Maximilian I* (Munich, 1982), 242, rejects the interpretation of this text in terms of the Renaissance man.

11. François Rabelais, *Pantagruel* (c.1532), ch. 8; *Gargantua* (1534), chs. 23–4. The phrase 'abysme de science' was later used to describe the learning of the French polymath Guillaume Postel.

12. William Caxton, *Chronicle* (1520), quoted in *Oxford English Dictionary* under 'universal'.

13. Thomas Elyot, *The Book Named the Governor* (1531: facsimile edn, Menston, 1980), ch. 8.

14. Castiglione, *Il Cortegiano*, Book 2, section 39.

15. Werner Kaegi, *Jacob Burckhardt: eine Biographie* (6 vols., Basel, 1947–77); Hugh R. Trevor-Roper, 'Jacob Burckhardt', *Proceedings of the British Academy* 70 (1984), 359–78. Cf. J. B. Bullen, *The Myth of the Renaissance in Nineteenth-Century Writing* (Oxford, 1994).

16. Riccardo Fubini and Anna Nenci Gallorini, 'L'autobiografia di Leon Battista Alberti', *Rinascimento* 12 (1972), 21–78, at 68; English translation in James B. Ross and Mary M. McLaughlin (eds.), *The Portable Renaissance Reader* (revised edn, Harmondsworth 1978), 480. Cf. Anthony Grafton, *Leon Battista Alberti: Master Builder of the Italian Renaissance* (London, 2001), 17–29.

17. Cristoforo Landino, *Apologia di Dante*, quoted in Joan Gadol, *Leon Battista Alberti: Universal Man of the Early Renaissance* (Chicago, 1969), 3.

18. Werner Straube, 'Die Agricola-Biographie des Johannes von Plieningen', in Wilhelm Kühlmann, *Rudolf Agricola 1444–1485* (Bern, 1994), 11–48.

19. Stephen Greenblatt, *Sir Walter Ralegh: The Renaissance Man and his Roles* (New Haven, 1973); Mark Nicholls and Penry Williams, 'Raleigh, Walter', *ODNB* 45, 842–59; Nicholls and Williams, *Sir Walter Raleigh in Life and Legend* (London, 2011).

20. Aldo Manutio, *Relatione de Iacomo di Crettone* (Venice, 1581); James H. Burns, 'Crichton, James', *ODNB* 14, 183–6, at 184.

21. Paolo Rossi, *Francis Bacon, from Magic to Science* (1957: English translation, London 1968); J. Martin, *Francis Bacon, the State, and the Reform of Natural Philosophy* (Cambridge, 1992).

22. André Godin, 'Erasme: Pia/Impia curiositas', in Jean Céard (ed.), *La curiosité à la Renaissance* (Paris, 1986), 25–36; Brian Cummings, 'Encyclopaedic Erasmus', *Renaissance Studies* 28 (2014), 183–204, at 183.

23. Dino Bellucci, 'Mélanchthon et la défense de l'astrologie', *Bibliothèque d'Humanisme et Renaissance* 50 (1988), 587–622; Sachiko Kusukawa, *The Transformation of Natural Philosophy: The Case of Philip Melanchthon* (Cambridge, 1995).

24. Chaim Wirszubski, *Pico della Mirandola's Encounter with Jewish Mysticism* (Cambridge, MA, 1989), 121, 259.

25. Eugenio Garin, *Giovanni Pico della Mirandola: vita e dottrina* (Florence, 1937); Frances Yates, 'Pico della Mirandola and Cabalist Magic', in *Giordano Bruno and the Hermetic*

Tradition (London, 1964), 84–116; William G. Craven, *Giovanni Pico della Mirandola, Symbol of his Age* (Geneva, 1981); Steve A. Farmer, *Syncretism in the West: Pico's 900 Theses* (Tempe, AZ, 1998).

26. W. Craven, *Giovanni Pico della Mirandola* (Geneva, 1981), stresses Pico's medieval heritage and denies that Pico's theses dealt with all subjects.

27. Yates, 'Cornelius Agrippa's Survey of Renaissance Magic', in *Giordano Bruno*,130–43; Charles G. Nauert Jr., *Agrippa and the Crisis of Renaissance Thought* (Urbana, IL, 1965); Rudolf Schmitz, 'Agrippa, Heinrich Cornelius', *DSB* 1, 79–81; Christoph I. Lehrich, *The Language of Demons and Angels: Cornelius Agrippa's Occult Philosophy* (Leiden, 2003).

28. Hugh R. Trevor-Roper, *The European Witch-Craze of the 16th and 17th centuries* (1969: Harmondsworth, 1978 edn), 47.

29. Beatrice Reynolds (ed. and trans.), *Method for the Easy Comprehension of History* (New York, 1945), 2 (the dedication), 79, 81. On Bodin's studies of law, history and politics, Julian H. Franklin, *Jean Bodin and the Sixteenth-Century Revolution in the Methodology of Law and History* (New York, 1963); Donald R. Kelley, 'The Development and Context of Bodin's Method' (1973: rpr. Julian H. Franklin [ed.], *Jean Bodin* [Aldershot, 2006], 123–50).

30. Denis P. O'Brien, 'Bodin's Analysis of Inflation' (2000: rpr. in Franklin [ed.], *Jean Bodin*, 209–92).

31. Marion Kuntz, 'Harmony and the *Heptaplomeres* of Jean Bodin', *Journal of the History of Philosophy* 12 (1974), 31–41; Noel Malcolm, 'Jean Bodin and the Authorship of the "Colloquium Heptaplomeres", *Journal of the Warburg and Courtauld Institutes* 69 (2006), 95–150.

32. On Scaliger as one of the 'Wündermännern des Gedächtnisses', Immanuel Kant, *Gesammelte Schriften* 7 (Berlin, 1907), 184; as a 'titan', Anthony Grafton, *Joseph Scaliger: A Study in the History of Classical Scholarship*, 2 vols. (Oxford, 1983–93), vol. 2, 22.

33. Jakob Bernays, *Joseph Justus Scaliger* (Berlin, 1855); Grafton, *Joseph Scaliger*, vol. 2.

34. Peter J. French, *John Dee: The World of an Elizabethan Magus* (London, 1972), 209; Nicholas H. Clulee, *John Dee's Natural Philosophy* (London, 1988); J. Roberts and A. Watson, *John Dee's Library Catalogue* (London, 1990); William H. Sherman, *John Dee: The Politics of Reading and Writing in the English Renaissance* (Amherst, MA: University of Massachusetts Press, 1995); R. Julian Roberts, 'Dee, John', *ODNB* 15, 667–75; Stephen Clucas (ed.), *John Dee: Interdisciplinary Studies in English Renaissance Thought* (Dordrecht, 2006).

35. Helmut Zedelmaier, *Bibliotheca universalis und Bibliotheca selecta: das Problem der Ordnung des gelehrten Wissens in der frühen Neuzeit* (Cologne, 1992), 101, 297n.

36. Ann Blair, 'Humanism and Printing in the Work of Conrad Gessner', *Renaissance Quarterly* 70 (2017), 1–43, at 9.

37. Ibid., 14; cf. Alfredo Serrai, *Conrad Gesner* (Rome, 1990); Massimo Danzi, 'Conrad Gessner (1516–1565: Universalgelehrter und Naturforscher der Renaissance', *Bibliothèque d'Humanisme et Renaissance* 78 (2016), 696–701; Urs B. Leu and Mylène Ruoss (eds.), *Facetten eines Universums: Conrad Gessner, 1516–2016* (Zurich, 2016).

38. Christopher, Bellitto, Thomas M. Izbicki and Gerald Christianson (eds.), *Introducing Nicholas of Cusa: A Guide to a Renaissance Man* (New York, 2004).

39. Garin, *Pico*, 120n.

40. William J. Bouwsma, *The Career and Thought of Guillaume Postel* (Cambridge, MA, 1957); Marion Kuntz, *Guillaume Postel: Prophet of the Restitution of all Things* (The Hague, 1981).

41. Franklin, *Sixteenth-Century Revolution*, 59; Kelley, 'Development', 145; Marion D. Kuntz, 'Harmony and the Heptaplomeres of Jean Bodin', *Journal of the History of Philosophy* 12 (1974), 31–41; Ann Blair, *The Theater of Nature: Jean Bodin and Renaissance Science* (Princeton, NJ, 1997), 7.

42. The word calculation comes from Ann Blair, 'Revisiting Renaissance Encyclopaedism', in Jason König and Greg Woolf (eds.), *Encyclopaedism from Antiquity to the Renaissance* (Cambridge, 2013), 379–97, at 385.

43. Erwin Panofsky, 'Artist, Scientist, Genius', in Wallace K. Ferguson (ed.), *The Renaissance: Six Essays* (New York, 1962), 121–82.

44. Helmut M. Wilsdorf, 'Agricola, Georgius', *DSB* 1, 77–9.
45. Eugenio Battisti, *Filippo Brunelleschi* (Florence, 1976); Bertrand Gille, 'Brunelleschi, Filippo', *DSB* 2, 534–5.
46. Bertrand Gille, *The Renaissance Engineers* (1964: English translation, Cambridge, MA, 1966), 81–7; Paul L. Rose, 'Taccola', *DSB* 13, 233–4.
47. Gille, *The Renaissance Engineers*, 101–15; Ladislao Reti, 'Martini, Francesco di Giorgio', *DSB* 9, 146–7.
48. Quoted in Martin Warnke, *The Court Artist* (1985: English translation, Cambridge 1993), 177.
49. General studies of Leonardo include Vasilii Zubov, *Leonardo da Vinci* (1961: English translation, Cambridge, MA 1968); Martin Kemp, *Leonardo da Vinci: The Marvellous Works of Nature and Man* (London, 1981); Walter Isaacson, *Leonardo: The Life* (New York, 2017).
50. Emmanuel Winternitz, *Leonardo da Vinci as a Musician* (New Haven, 1982).
51. Raffaele Giacomelli, 'Leonardo da Vinci aerodinamico' and Luigi Tursini, 'La navigazione subacquea in Leonardo', in *Atti del Convegno di Studi Vinciani* (Florence, 1953), 353–73 and 344–52; Mario Taddei and Edoardo Zanon, *Le macchine di Leonardo* (Milan, 2005).
52. Quoted in Martin Kemp, *Leonardo* (Oxford, 2011), 45.
53. Leonardo, 'Codice Atlantico', 119, a passage discussed in Kemp, *Marvellous Works*, 102–3.
54. Giorgio di Santillana, 'Léonard et ceux qu'il n'a pas lus', in *Léonard de Vinci et l'expérience scientifique* (Paris, 1953), 43–9.
55. Martin Clayton and Ron Philo, *Leonardo Anatomist* (London, 2012), 7.
56. Francesca Fiorani and Alessandro Nova (eds.), *Leonardo da Vinci and Optics* (Venice, 2013).
57. Zubov, *Leonardo*, 188–9, 109; Mario Taddei and Edoardo Zanon (eds.), *Leonardo, l'acqua e il Rinascimento* (Milan, 2004).
58. F. Sherwood Taylor, 'Léonard de Vinci et la chimie de son temps', in *Léonard de Vinci et l'expérience scientifique* (Paris, 1953), 151–62.
59. Ann Pizzorusso, 'Leonardo's Geology', *Leonardo* 29 (1996), 197–200.
60. Annalisa Perissa Torrini, 'Leonardo e la botanica', in Perissa Torrini (ed.), *Leonardo da Vinci uomo universale* (Florence, 2013), 99–107.
61. F. S. Bodenheimer, 'Léonard de Vinci, biologiste', in *Léonard de Vinci et l'expérience,* 171–88.
62. Roberto Almagià, 'Leonardo da Vinci geografo e cartografo', in *Atti del Convegno di Studi Vinciani* (Florence, 1953), 451–66.
63. Fra Pietro da Novellara, quoted in Kenneth Clark, *Leonardo da Vinci* (1936: new edn, Harmondsworth, 1958), 63.
64. Kemp, *Leonardo*, 4.
65. Zubov, *Leonardo*, 65.
66. Edna E. Kramer, 'Hypatia', *DSB* 6, 615–6; Charlotte Booth, *Hypatia: Mathematician, Philosopher, Myth* (London, 2017).
67. Sabina Flanagan, *Hildegard of Bingen, 1098–1179, a Visionary Life* (London, 1989); Charles Burnett and Peter Dronke (eds.) *Hildegard of Bingen: The Context of her Thought and Art* (London, 1998), especially the essays by Burnett, Jacquart and Moulinier; Heinrich Schipperges, *The World of Hildegard of Bingen* (Collegeville, MN, 1999).
68. Margaret Brabant (ed.), *Politics, Gender, and Genre: The Political Thought of Christine de Pizan* (Boulder, CO, 1992); Kate Forhan, *The Political Theory of Christine de Pizan* (Aldershot, 2002).
69. Castiglione, *Il Cortegiano*, Book 3, section 9.
70. Margaret L. King, 'Book-Lined Cells: Women and Humanism in the Early Italian Renaissance', in Patricia H. Labalme (ed.), *Beyond Their Sex: Learned Women of the European Past* (New York, 1980), 66–90, at 81n. Cf. Paul O. Kristeller, 'Learned Women of Early Modern Italy', in Labalme, *Beyond Their Sex*, 91–116; Lisa Jardine, 'The Myth of the Learned Lady', *Historical Journal* 28 (1985), 799–819.
71. Lisa Jardine, 'Isotta Nogarola', *History of Education* 12 (1983), 231–44; Margaret King, 'Isotta Nogarola', in Ottavia Niccoli (ed.), *Rinascimento al femminile* (Rome and Bari, 1991), 3–34.

72. Albert Rabil Jr, *Laura Cereta: Quattrocento Humanist* (Binghamton, NY, 1981); M. Palma, 'Cereta, Laura', *DBI* 23, 729–30.

73. C. Cavazzana, 'Cassandra Fedele erudita veneziana del Rinascimento', *Ateneo veneto*, XXIX (1906), 74–91, 249–75, 361–97; Franco Pignatti, 'Fedele, Cassandra', *DBI* 45, 566–8.

74. Rabil, *Laura Cereta*, 25.

75. King, 'Book-Lined Cells', 69.

76. Georg Deichstetter (ed.), *Caritas Pirckheimer, Ordensfrau und Humanistin* (Cologne, 1982).

77. Almudena de Arteaga, *Beatriz Galindo, La Latina, maestra de reinas* (Madrid, 2007).

78. Retha M. Warnicke, 'Women and Humanism in the English Renaissance', in Albert Rabil Jr (ed.), *Renaissance Humanism* (Philadelphia, 1988), vol. 2, 39–54.

79. Marjorie H. Ilsley, *A Daughter of the Renaissance: Marie Le Jars de Gournay* (The Hague, 1963); Eva Sartori, 'Marie de Gournay', *Allegorica* 9 (1987), 135–42; Michèle Fogel, *Marie de Gournay: itinéraires d'une femme savante* (Paris, 2004).

CHAPTER 3

1. Hermann Boerhaave, *Methodus studii medici* (Amsterdam, 1751), 73. In *Middlemarch*, George Eliot preferred 'hero of erudition', but Richard Feynman's autobiography mentions 'monster minds' such as John von Neumann's.

2. Hans Blumenberg, *Die Legitimität der Neuzeit* (1966: English translation, The Legitimacy of the Modern Age, Cambridge, MA, 1983), 191–200. Neil Kenny warns against viewing Bacon as 'baldly' in favour of curiosity in his *Uses of Curiosity*, 167.

3. Nicholas Jardine, *The Birth of History and Philosophy of Science: Kepler's A Defence of Tycho against Ursus* (Cambridge, 1984).

4. Erwin Panofsky, *Galileo as a Critic of the Arts* (The Hague, 1954).

5. Stephen Gaukroger, *Descartes: An Intellectual Biography* (Oxford, 1995).

6. Meric Casaubon, *Generall Learning: A Seventeenth-Century Treatise on the Formation of the General Scholar*, ed. Richard Serjeantson (Cambridge, 1999), 149.

7. *Parentalia, or memoirs of the family of the Wrens* (London, 1750), 343: https://books.google.co.uk/books?id=Tm1MAAAAcAAJ

8. Adrian Tinniswood, *His Invention So Fertile: A life of Christopher Wren* (London, 2001); Lisa Jardine, *On a Grander Scale: The Outstanding Career of Sir Christopher Wren* (London, 2002); Kerry Downes, 'Wren, Christopher', *ODNB* 60, 406–19.

9. Betty J. T. Dobbs, *The Foundations of Newton's Alchemy* (Cambridge, 1975); Karin Figala, 'Newton's Alchemy', in I. Bernard Cohen and George E. Smith (eds.), *Cambridge Companion to Newton* (Cambridge, 2002), 370–86. Frank E. Manuel, *Isaac Newton, Historian* (Cambridge, 1963); idem., *The Religion of Isaac Newton* (Oxford, 1974); Rob Iliffe, *Priest of Nature: The Religious Worlds of Isaac Newton* (Oxford, 2017).

10. Yaël Nazé, 'Astronomie et chronologie chez Newton', *Archives Internationales d'Histoire des Sciences* 62 (2012), 717–65; Jed. Z. Buchwald and Mordechai Feingold, *Newton and the Origin of Civilization* (Princeton, NJ, 2013), 244.

11. Jean R. Brink, 'Bathsua Makin: Educator and Linguist', in Brink (ed.), *Female Scholars* (Montreal, 1980), 86–100; Frances Teague, *Bathsua Makin, Woman of Learning* (Lewisburg, PA, 1998); Carol Pal, 'Bathsua Makin', in *Republic of Women* (Cambridge, 2012), 177–205.

12. Una Birch, *Anna van Schurman* (London, 1909); Mirjam de Baar et al. (eds.), *Choosing the Better Part: Anna Maria van Schurman* (Dordrecht, 1996); Joyce L. Irwin, 'Anna Maria van Schurman and her Intellectual Circle', in Anna Maria van Schurman, *Whether a Christian Woman should be Educated* (Chicago, 1998), 1–21; Pieta van Beek, *The First Female University Student: A. M. van Schurman* (Utrecht, 2010).

13. Pal, *Republic of Women*, 22–51.

14. Eileen O'Neill, *Margaret Cavendish, Duchess of Newcastle, Observations upon Experimental Philosophy* (Cambridge, 2001); Lisa Walters, *Margaret Cavendish: Gender, Science and Politics* (Cambridge, 2014); Richard Holmes, 'Margaret Cavendish', *This Long Pursuit* (London, 2016), 111–32.

15. Evelyn is quoted in Holmes, *Long Pursuit*, 126.
16. Sten Stolpe, *Queen Christina* (2 vols., 1960–1: abbreviated English translation, London, 1966); Sten G. Lindberg, 'Christina and the Scholars', in *Christina, Queen of Sweden* (Stockholm, 1966), 44–53; Susanna Åkerman, *Queen Christina of Sweden and her Circle* (Leiden, 1991).
17. Åkerman, *Queen Christina*, 49.
18. R. Derosas, 'Corner, Elena Lucrezia', *DBI* 29, 174–9.
19. Ludwig Pfandl, *Die Zehnte Muse von Mexico* (1946); Octavio Paz, *Sor Juana: Her Life and her World* (1982: English translation, London 1988); Gerard Flynn, 'Sor Juana Inés de la Cruz', in Brink, *Female Scholars*, 119–36.
20. Helmut Zedelmaier, ' "Polyhistor" und "Polyhistorie" ' (2002: rpr. in *Werkstätten des Wissens zwischen Renaissance und Aufklärung* [Tübingen, 2015], 112).
21. By Michael Neander, *Orbis terra*, 1583, quoted in Zedelmaier, *Bibliotheca Universalis und Bibliotheca Selecta* (Cologne, 1992), 297n. Cf. Anthony Grafton, 'The World of the Polyhistors', *Central European History* 18 (1985), 31–47, rpr. in his *Bring Out Your Dead* (Cambridge, MA, 2001), 166–80.
22. For English, here and subsequently, I follow the *Oxford English Dictionary* (1888: revised edn, online, 2000); for French, Emile Littré, *Dictionnaire de la langue française* (1863: revised edn, 7 vols., Paris 1956–8).
23. Claudia Bareggi, *Il mestiere di scrivere* (Rome, 1988).
24. Oliver Impey and Arthur MacGregor (eds.), *The Origins of Museums: The Cabinet of Curiosities in 16th- and 17th-Century Europe* (Oxford, 1985); Krysztof Pomian, *Collectors and Curiosities* (1987: English translation, Cambridge 1990); Jaś Elsner and Roger Cardinal (eds.), *The Cultures of Collecting* (London, 1994); Arthur MacGregor, *Curiosity and Enlightenment: Collectors and Collections from the Sixteenth to the Nineteenth Century* (New Haven, CT, 2007).
25. Neil Kenny, *The Uses of Curiosity in Early Modern France and Germany* (Oxford, 2004), 52, 64, 69–70; Jean-Marc Chatelain, 'Philologie, pansophie, polymathie, encyclopédie', in Waquet, *Morhof*, 15–30.
26. Serjeantson (ed.), *Generall Learning*.
27. Johannes Wower, *De polymathia* (1603: Leipzig 1665 edn), 19. Cf. Luc Deitz, 'Johannes Wower of Hamburg, Philologist and Polymath', *Journal of the Warburg and Courtauld Institutes* 58 (1995), 132–51.
28. Marcus Boxhorn, *De polymathia* (Leiden, 1632); Jack Fellman, 'The First Historical Linguist', *Linguistics* 41 (1974), 31–4.
29. Pietro Rossi, *Clavis Universalis: arti mnemoniche e logica combinatorial da Lullo a Leibniz* (Milan-Naples, 1960), ix–xv, 178–200; Frances Yates, *The Rosicrucian Enlightenment* (London, 1972), a speculative reconstruction; Frank E. Manuel and Fritzie P. Manuel, 'Pansophia: A Dream of Science' in their *Utopian Thought in the Western World* (Oxford, 1979), 205–21; Chatelain, 'Philologie, pansophie'; Howard Hotson, 'Outsiders, Dissenters, and Competing Visions of Reform', in Ulinka Rublack (ed.), *Oxford Handbook of the Protestant Reformations* (Oxford, 2017), 301–28.
30. Howard Hotson, *Johann Henrich Alsted, 1588–1638: Between Renaissance, Reformation and Universal Reform* (Oxford, 2000); idem., 'The Ramist Roots of Comenian Pansophia', in *Ramus, Pedagogy and the Liberal Arts: Ramism in Britain and the Wider World*, eds. Steven John Reid and Emma Annette Wilson (Farnham, 2011), 227–52; idem., 'Outsiders', 306–9.
31. Imre Bán, *Apáczai Csere János* (Budapest, 1958), 563–85.
32. Johann Heinrich Alsted, *Encyclopaedia septem tomis distincta* (Herborn, 1630); Hotson, *Alsted*, 144–81, 163–72; idem., 'Ramist Roots', 233n.
33. Jan Amos Comenius, *Via Lucis* (1668). Cf. Umberto Eco, *The Search for the Perfect Language* (Oxford, 1995), 214–16, at 215.
34. Jan Amos Comenius, *Pansophiae Praeludium* (1637), rpr. in *Works* 15/2 (Prague, 1989), 13–53, at 32, 41. On his career, Milada Blekastad, *Comenius. Versuch eines Umrisses von Leben, Werk und Schicksal des Jan Amos Komenský* (Oslo, 1969).

35. Robert F. Young, *Comenius in England* (Oxford, 1932), 32–3.
36. Jan Amos Comenius, *Prodromus*, ed. and trans. Herbert Hornstein (Dusseldorf, 1963), 12; Samuel Hartlib (trans.), *A Reformation of Schools* (London, 1642); Comenius, *Pansophiae Diatyposis* (1643; English translation, London, 1651).
37. Jan Amos Comenius, *Conatum Pansophicorum Dilucidatio* (1638), rpr. in *Works* 15/2, 59–79, at 63.
38. Jan Amos Comenius, *De rerum humanarum emendatio*, rpr. in *Works* 19/1 (Prague, 2014), 58–9; cf. Blekastad, *Comenius*, 688–700.
39. H. D. Schepelern, *Museum Wormianum* (Aarhus, 1971); idem., 'Worm, Ole', *Dansk Biografisk Leksikon* 16 (1984), 45–51; Glyn Daniel, 'Worm, Ole', *DSB* 14, 505.
40. James Delbourgo, *Collecting the World: The Life and Curiosity of Hans Sloane* (London, 2017).
41. Rubens to Pierre Dupuy, 1628, quoted and translated in Peter N. Miller, *Peiresc's Mediterranean World* (Cambridge, MA, 2015), 1, 449. Peiresc, long neglected, has been put back on the intellectual map by Miller.
42. Many of Peiresc's letters have been published: see *emloportal.bodleian.ox.ac.uk/collections/?catalogue=nicolas...peiresc*. On him, Peter N. Miller, *Peiresc's Europe: Learning and Virtue in the Seventeenth Century* (New Haven, CT, 2000); idem., *Peiresc's History of Provence: Antiquarianism and the Discovery of a Medieval Mediterranean* (Philadelphia, 2011); idem., *Peiresc's Orient* (Farnham, 2012). On his Egyptian studies, Sydney Aufrère, *La momie et la tempête* (Avignon, 1990).
43. Arnaldo Momigliano, *The Classical Foundations of Modern Historiography* (Berkeley, 1990), 54.
44. Miller, *Peiresc's Mediterranean World*, 334–7; idem., 'Peiresc in Africa', in Marc Fumaroli (ed.), *Les premiers siècles de la république européenne des lettres* (Paris, 2005), 493–525.
45. Miller, *Peiresc's Mediterranean World*, 108–11.
46. On his concern with the natural sciences, Harcourt Brown, 'Peiresc', *DSB* X, 488–92. On astronomy, Miller, *Peiresc's Mediterranean World*, 241–6.
47. Miller, *Peiresc's Mediterranean World*, 18, 65, 266–8, 347.
48. Jacopo Antonio Tadisi, *Memorie della Vita di Monsignore Giovanni Caramuel di Lobkowitz* (Venice, 1760), v; Alfredo Serra, *Phoenix Europae: Juan Caramuel y Lobkowicz in prospettiva bibliografica* (Milan, 2005).
49. The term was also applied to the philologist Joseph Scaliger, the Mexican nun Sor Juana and the Jesuit Athanasius Kircher.
50. Bianca Garavelli (ed.), *Caramuel: vescovo eclettico* (Bergamo, 2016), 38–9, 105–7.
51. Dino Pastine, *Juan Caramuel: probabilismo ed enciclopedia* (Florence, 1975); Augusto De Ferrari and Werner Oechslin, 'Caramuel Lobkowicz, Juan', *DBI* 19, 621–6; Paolo Pissavino (ed.), *Le meraviglie del probabile: Juan Caramuel* (Vigevano, 1990); Julia Fleming, *Defending Probabilism: The Moral Theology of Juan Caramuel* (Washington DC, 2006); Petr Dvořák and Jacob Schmutz (eds.), *Juan Caramuel Lobkowitz, the Last Scholastic Polymath* (Prague, 2008); Bianca Garavelli, *Caramuel, Vescovo Eclettico* (Bergamo, 2016).
52. Cesare Vasoli, 'Introduzione' to Pissavino, *Le meraviglie del probabile*, 13–17; María Elisa Navarro, 'The Narrative of the Architectural Orders', in Dvořák and Schmutz, *Caramuel*, 257–72, at 257.
53. *Rudbecksstudier* (Uppsala, 1930); Sten Lindroth, *Svensk Lärdomshistoria*, vol. 4, *Stormaktstiden* (Stockholm, 1975), 414–32, translated in Lindroth, *Les chemins du savoir en Suède* (Dordrecht, 1888), 57–70; idem., 'Rudbeck, Olaus', *DSB* XI, 586–8.
54. Lindroth, *Stormaktstiden*, 284–96, translated in *Les Chemins*, 71–82; Gunnar Eriksson, *The Atlantic Vision: Olaus Rudbeck and Baroque Science* (Canton, MA, 1994), 45, 50, 54–5, 100–12.
55. Kurt Johannesson, *The Renaissance of the Goths in Sixteenth-Century Sweden* (Berkeley, CA, 1991).
56. Håkan Håkansson, 'Alchemy of the Ancient Goths: Johannes Bureus's Search for the Lost Wisdom of Scandinavia', *Early Science and Medicine* 17 (2012), 500–22.

57. Ole Klindt-Jensen, *A History of Scandinavian Archaeology* (English translation, London, 1975), 30.
58. Paula Findlen (ed.), *Athanasius Kircher: The Last Man Who Knew Everything* (London, 2003); Joscelyn Godwin, *Athanasius Kircher: A Renaissance Man and the Quest for Lost Knowledge* (London, 1979), 5.
59. Daniel Stolzenberg, *Egyptian Oedipus: Athanasius Kircher and the Secrets of Antiquity* (Chicago, 2013).
60. Malcolm, 'Private and Public Knowledge', 297.
61. John T. Waterman (ed. and trans.), *Leibniz and Ludolf on Things Linguistic* (Berkeley, CA, 1977), 51, 53.
62. On the tradition, Erik Iversen, *The Myth of Egypt and its Hieroglyphs in European Tradition* (1961: 2nd edn, Princeton, NJ, 1993).
63. Peiresc described Kircher as 'a little too credulous', while an Englishman who visited Rome at this time (Robert Southwell, later President of the Royal Society) reported that Kircher 'is reputed very credulous': Findlen, *Last Man*, 141, 384.
64. Thomas Leinkauf, *Mundus Combinatus: Studien zur Struktur der barocken Universalwissenschaft am Beispiel Athanasius Kirchers SJ (1602–1680)* (Berlin, 1993), 75 and passim.
65. Pierre Bayle, *Oeuvres Diverses* (The Hague, 1737), vol. 1, 75.
66. Elisabeth Labrousse, *Pierre Bayle* (The Hague, 1963–4); *eadem, Bayle* (Oxford, 1983); Helena H. M. van Lieshout, *The Making of Pierre Bayle's Dictionnaire historique et critique* (Amsterdam, 2001); Wiep van Bunge, 'Pierre Bayle et l'animal-machine', in Hans Bots (ed.), *Critique, savoir et erudition au siècle des lumières* (Amsterdam-Maarssen, 1998), 375–88, at 386.
67. bayle-correspondance.univ-st-etienne.fr/. Cf Miranda Lewis, 'At the centre of the networked early modern world: Pierre Bayle', *www.culturesofknowledge.org/?p=7326*.
68. Marc Fumaroli, 'Nicolas Claude Fabri de Peiresc, prince de la république des lettres' (1996: rpr. Fumaroli, *La République des Lettres* [Paris, 2015], 56–90).
69. Nicholas Jolley (ed.), *The Cambridge Companion to Leibniz* (Cambridge, 1995), which is the work of twelve professors of philosophy. For a corrective to this emphasis, see Maria Rosa Antognazza, *Leibniz: An Intellectual Biography* (Cambridge, 2007).
70. Sigrid von der Schulenberg, *Leibniz als Sprachforscher* (Frankfurt, 1973), 68–114; Daniel Droixhe, 'Leibniz et le finno-ougrien', in Tullio De Mauro and Lia Formigari (eds.), *Leibniz, Humboldt and the Origins of Comparativism* (Amsterdam and Philadelphia, 1990), 3–29; Shane Hawkins, ' "Selig wer auch Zeichen gibt": Leibniz as historical linguist', *The European Legacy* 23 (2018), 510–21.
71. Louis Davillé, *Leibniz historien* (Paris, 1909); Carl J. Friedrich, 'Philosophical Reflections of Leibniz on Law, Politics and the State', *Natural Law Forum* 11 (1966), 79–91; Patrick Riley (ed.), *The Political Writings of Leibniz* (Cambridge, 1972); Franklin Perkins, *Leibniz and China* (Cambridge, 2004).
72. Miller, *Peiresc's Mediterranean World*, 394.
73. Maria Rosa Antognazza, *Leibniz: An Intellectual Biography* (Cambridge, 2009), 2, 206.
74. Delia K. Bowden, *Leibniz as Librarian* (1969); Hans G. Schulte-Albert, 'Gottfried Wilhelm Leibniz and Library Classification', *Journal of Library History* 6 (1971), 133–52; Margherita Palumbo, *Leibniz e la res bibliothecaria* (Rome, 1993); Antognazza, *Leibniz: An Intellectual Biography*, 195–280.
75. Anna Rosa Antognazza, *Leibniz: A Very Short Introduction* (Oxford, 2016), 6.
76. Antognazza, *Leibniz: An Intellectual Biography*, 559.
77. Ibid, 1.
78. Christian Gottlieb Jöcher, 1733, quoted in Wellmon, *Organizing Enlightenment*, 49; Emil Du Bois-Reymond, *Reden*, quoted in Lorraine Daston, 'The Academies and the Unity of Knowledge: The Disciplining of the Disciplines', *Differences* 10 (1998), 67–86, at 76.
79. Schulte-Albert, 'Gottfried Wilhelm Leibniz'; Palumbo, *Leibniz*.
80. Antognazza, *Leibniz: An Intellectual Biography*, 236, 244.

81. István Hont, 'Samuel Pufendorf and the Theoretical Foundations of the Four-Stage Theory' (1986: rpr. in his *Jealousy of Trade*, Cambridge, MA, 2005, 159–84); Detlef Döring, 'Biographisches zu Samuel von Pufendorf', in Bodo Geyer and Helmut Goerlich (eds.), *Samuel Pufendorf und seine Wirkungen bis auf die heutige Zeit*, Baden-Baden 1996, 23–38; Mordechai Feingold (ed.), *Before Newton: The Life and Times of Isaac Barrow* (Cambridge, 1990); idem., 'Barrow, Isaac', *ODNB* 4, 98–102, at 102; Françoise Waquet (ed.), *Mapping the World of Learning: The* Polyhistor *of Daniel Georg Morhof* (Wiesbaden, 2000).

82. Pierre-Daniel Huet, *Commentarius* (The Hague, 1718); Charles Sainte-Beuve, *Causeries de Lundi*, 15 vols. (Paris, 1851–62).

83. Christopher Ligota, 'Der apologetischen Rahmen der Mythendeutung im Frankreich des 17. Jahrhunderts (P. D. Huet)', in Walter Killy (ed.), *Mythographie der frühen Neuzeit* (Wiesbaden, 1984), 149–62, at 151.

84. Alphonse Dupront, *Pierre-Daniel Huet et l'exégèse comparatiste au XVII siècle* (Paris, 1930); Alain Niderst, 'Comparatisme et syncrétisme religieux de Huet', in Suzanne Guellouz (ed.), *Pierre-Daniel Huet* (Tübingen, 1994), 75–82; Elena Rapetti, *Pierre-Daniel Huet: erudizione, filosofia, apologetica* (Milan, 1999); April G. Shelford, *Transforming the Republic of Letters: Pierre-Daniel Huet and European Intellectual Life, 1650–1720* (Rochester, NY, 2007).

85. Fabienne Gégou (ed.), *Traité sur l'origine des romans* (Paris, 1971), introduction.

86. Léon Tolmer, *Pierre-Daniel Huet: humaniste, physicien* (Bayeux, 1949), 189–90, 215–18; M. de Pontville, 'Pierre-Daniel Huet, homme des sciences', in Guellouz, *Huet*, 29–42.

87. Quoted in David S. Berkowitz, *John Selden's Formative Years* (Washington DC, 1988), 296.

88. Harold D. Hazeltine, 'Selden as Legal Historian', *Festschrift H. Brunner* (Weimar, 1910), 579–630; Paul Christianson, 'Selden, John', *ODNB* 49, 694–705; Gerald J. Toomer, *John Selden: A Life in Scholarship*, 2 vols. (Oxford 2009); Timothy Brook, *Mr Selden's Map of China* (London, 2015).

89. John Stoye, *Marsigli's Europe* (New Haven, CT, 1994); Giuseppe Gullino and Cesare Preti, 'Marsili, Luigi Fernando', *DBI* 70, 771–81.

90. Igor Wladimiroff, *De kaart van een verzwegen vriendschap. Nicolaes Witsen en Andrej Winius en de Nederlandse cartografie van Rusland* (Groningen, 2008), 148–9.

91. Brun Naarden, 'Witsen's Studies of Inner Eurasia', in Siegfried Huigen, Jan L. de Jong and Elmer Kotfin (eds.), *The Dutch Trading Companies as Knowledge Networks* (Leiden 2010), 211–39.

92. Marion Peters, *De wijze koopman. Het wereldwijde onderzoek van Nicolaes Witsen (1641–1717), burgemeester en VOC-bewindhebber van Amsterdam* (Amsterdam, 2010).

93. Prager and Scaglia, *Brunelleschi*, 111, 129, 144.

94. Richard S. Westfall, *Never at Rest: A Biography of Isaac Newton* (Cambridge, 1980), 714–15, 727; Thomas Sonar, *Die Geschichte des Prioritätsstreits zwischen Leibniz und Newton* (Heidelberg, 2016).

95. 'Altissimum planetam tergeminum observavi'.

96. 'anulo cingitur, tenui, plano, nusquam cohaerente, ad eclipticam inclinato'.

97. 'ut tensio, sic vis'.

98. Jacob Thomasius, *De plagio literario* (1673); Theodor Jansson van Almeloveen, 'Plagiorum syllabus', in his *Opuscula* (1686); Johannes Fabri, *Decas decadum, sive plagiariorum centuria* (1689); Jacques Salier, *Cacocephalus, sive de plagiis* (1693).

99. Wolfgang Behringer, 'Communications Revolutions', *German History* 24 (2006), 333–74.

100. Philippe Tamizey de Larroque (ed.), *Lettres de Peiresc*, 7 vols. (Paris 1888–98).

101. Elisabeth Labrousse et al. (eds.), *Correspondance de Pierre Bayle*, 14 vols. (Oxford, 1999–2017). Cf. *emlo-portal.bodleian.ox.ac.uk/collections/?catalogue=pierre-bayle*

102. Kircher's correspondence is available online at http://web.stanford.edu/group/kircher/cgi-bin/site/?page_id=303. On magnetic variation, Michael John Gorman, 'The Angel and the Compass: Athanasius Kircher's Magnetic Geography', in Paula Findlen (ed.), *The Last Man Who Knew Everything* (New York, 2003), 229–51, at 245.

103. Marie Boas Hall, *Henry Oldenburg* (Oxford, 2002).

104. M. Albanese, 'Magliabechi, Antonio', *DBI* 67, 422–7.

105. Mordechai Feingold, 'The Humanities', in Nicholas Tyacke (ed.), *History of the University of Oxford*, vol. 4 (Oxford, 1997), 211–357, at 218.
106. Paul Hazard, *The Crisis of the European Mind, 1680–1715* (1934: English translation, New York 2013), Hugh R. Trevor-Roper, 'The General Crisis of the Seventeenth Century', *Past & Present* 16 (1959), 31–64.
107. Malcolm Gladwell, *The Tipping Point: How Little Things Can Make a Big Difference* (London, 2000).
108. Eduard J. Dijksterhuis, *The Mechanization of the World Picture* (English translation, Oxford, 1961).
109. Richard H. Popkin, *The History of Scepticism from Erasmus to Spinoza* (1960: revised edn, Berkeley, CA, 1979).
110. Elisabeth Labrousse, *Bayle* (Oxford, 1983), 12, 22, 51.
111. Ann M. Blair, *Too Much to Know: Managing Scholarly Information before the Modern Age* (New Haven, CT, 2010).
112. Andrew Pettegree, 'The Renaissance Library and the Challenge of Print', in Alice Crawford (ed.), *The Meaning of the Library: A Cultural History* (Princeton, NJ, 2015), 72–90, at 75, 84.
113. Peter Burke, 'Gutenberg Bewältigen. Die Informationsexplosion im frühneuzeitlichen Europa', *Jahrbuch für Europäische Geschichte* 2 (2001), 237–48. Cf. the special issue of the *Journal of the History of Ideas* 64 (2003), no. 1; Blair, *Too Much to Know*.
114. Robert Burton, *Anatomy of Melancholy* (1621), Book 1, section 10; Adrien Baillet, *Jugemens des sçavans* (Paris, 1685), translated and quoted in Blair, *Too Much to Know*, 59.
115. Adrien Baillet, *Jugements des Savants sur les principaux ouvrages des anciens*, 4 vols (Paris, 1685–6), preface; Gottfried Wilhelm Leibniz, *Philosophische Schriften*, 7 vols. (Berlin 1875–90), vol. 7, 160.
116. Blair, *Too Much to Know*, 93–6.
117. David Gledhill, *The Names of Plants* (4th edn, Cambridge 2008), 7.
118. Richard S. Wurman, *Information Anxiety* (New York, 1989).
119. Johannes Wower, *De polymathia* (1603); Daniel Georg Morhof, *Polyhistor* (Lübeck, 1688). Cf. Luc Deitz, 'Joannes Wower', *Journal of the Warburg and Courtauld Institutes* 58 (1995), 132–51; Françoise Waquet (ed.), *Mapping the World of Learning: The Polyhistor of Daniel Georg Morhof* (Wiesbaden, 2000).
120. Morhof, *Polyhistor*, 2.
121. Jan Amos Comenius, *Pansophia Praeludium* (1637), rpr. in *Works* 15/2 (Prague, 1989), 22.
122. Quoted and translated in Daniel Murphy, *Comenius: A Critical Introduction to his Life and Work* (Dublin, 1995), 20.
123. John Donne, *An Anatomy of the World* (written in 1611). The poem argues in conventional fashion for 'the decay of the world', but this particular argument is a fresh one.
124. John Selden, *Titles of Honour* (London, 1614), dedication.
125. Richard Baxter, *Holy Commonwealth* (London, 1659), 493; he seems to be quoting Comenius, 'uno intuitu OMNIA . . . exhibens' (*Consultatio Catholica*, Prague 1966, 28).
126. Thomas Fuller, *The Holy State* (London, 1642), Book 2, ch. 7.
127. Isaac Barrow, *Sermons and Expository Treatises* (Edinburgh, 1839), 492.
128. Morhof, *Polyhistor* (1688: expanded edn, Lübeck, 1747), 4.
129. Casaubon, *Generall Learning*, 88, 146.
130. Burnet is quoted in Antognazza, *Leibniz: An Intellectual Biography*, 559; John Cockburn, *A Specimen of Some Free and Impartial Remarks occasion'd by Dr Burnet's History of His Own Times* (London, 1724), 27–8, quoted in Helen C. Foxcroft (ed.), *Supplement to Burnet's History of His Own Time* (Oxford, 1902), 456n.
131. Quoted in Lisa Jardine, *The Curious Life of Robert Hooke* (London, 2003), 6.
132. Walter E. Houghton, 'The English Virtuoso in the Seventeenth Century', *Journal of the History of Ideas* 3 (1942), 51–73; on fashions, Krzysztof Pomian, 'Médailles/coquilles=érudition/philosophie', *Transactions of the IVth International Congress on the Enlightenment* 4 (1976), 1677–1705; Delbourgo, *Collecting the World*, 164. The phrase 'master of only scraps' was used by a contemporary critic of Sloane, the lawyer William King.

133. Pamela H. Smith, *The Business of Alchemy: Science and Culture in the Holy Roman Empire* (Princeton, NJ, 1994), 14.
134. John Fletcher (ed.), *Athanasius Kircher und seine Beziehungen zum gelehrten Europa seiner Zeit* (Wiesbaden, 1988), 111.
135. Antognazza, *Leibniz: An Intellectual Biography*, 232 (cf. 325).
136. Ibid., 171, 321.
137. Jardine, *Curious Life*, 3, 22.
138. Tinniswood, *His Invention So Fertile*, 246; Derek T. Whiteside, 'Wren the Mathematician', *Notes and Records of the Royal Society of London* 15 (1960), 107–11, at 107.
139. David Brading, *The First America* (Cambridge, 1991), 393; John Stoye, *Marsigli's Europe* (New Haven, CT, 1994), viii, 25.

CHAPTER 4

1. Pierre-Daniel Huet, *Huetiana* (Paris, 1722), 1–2.
2. Giambattista Vico, letter to the French Jesuit Édouard de Vitry, in *Opere*, ed. Roberto Parenti, 2 vols. (Naples, 1972), vol. 1, 452, 454.
3. Louis Davillé, *Leibniz historien* (Paris, 1909), 407, 522–3.
4. Contemporary critics include Johan Hadorph, Claudius Örnhielm and Johann Scheffer.
5. Peter Miller, 'Copts and Scholars', in Findlen, *Last Man*, 135, 141.
6. Findlen, *Last Man*, 5–6.
7. Quoted in Eric Jorink and Dirk van Miert (eds.), *Isaac Vossius* (Leiden, 2012), 211.
8. Dijksterhuis, *De Mechanisering*; Marjorie H. Nicolson, *The Breaking of the Circle: Studies in the Effect of the 'New Science' upon Seventeenth-Century Poetry* (Evanston, IL, 1950), 108.
9. Conrad Wiedemann, 'Polyhistors Glück und Ende: Von D. G. Morhof zum jungen Lessing', *Festschrift Gottfried Weber* (Bad Homburg, 1967), 215–35; Helmut Zedelmaier, '"Polyhistor" und "Polyhistorie"' (2002: rpr. in *Werkstätten des Wissens zwischen Renaissance und Aufklärung* [Tübingen, 2015], 109, 115).
10. Quoted and translated in Jan. C. Westerhoff, 'A World of Signs: Baroque Pansemioticism, the Polyhistor and the Early Modern *Wunderkammer*', *Journal of the History of Ideas* 62 (2001), 633–50, at 641.
11. Gunter E. Grimm, *Literatur und Gelehrtentum in Deutschland* (Tübingen, 1983), 346. Cf. Wilhelm Kühlmann, *Gelehrtenrepublik und Fürstenstaat* (Tübingen, 1982), 286–454, though he laments the lack of a history of pedantry (287, note 2).
12. Paul Raabe, 'Lessing und die Gelehrsamkeit', in Edward P. Harris and Richard E. Schade (eds.), *Lessing in heutiger Sicht* (Bremen, 1977), 65–88; Wilfred Barner, 'Lessing zwischen Bürgerlichkeit und Gelehrtheit', in Rudolf Vierhaus (ed.), *Bürger und Bürgerlichkeit* (Heidelberg, 1981), 165–204.
13. Ussher's remark was recorded by John Evelyn, *Diary*, ed. E. S. de Beer, 6 vols. (Oxford 1955), vol. 3, 156. Wren is quoted in Steven Shapin and Simon Schaffer, *Leviathan and the Air-Pump: Hobbes, Boyle and the Experimental Life* (Princeton, NJ, 1985), 31. Like Descartes, the English gentleman Robert Payne compared Kircher to fellow Jesuits: 'enough of these Mountebankes' (quoted by Noel Malcolm, 'Private and Public Knowledge: Kircher, Esotericism and the Republic of Letters', in Findlen, *Last Man*, 300).
14. 'Le Jesuite a quantité de farfanteries: il est plus charlatan que sçavant': René Descartes to Constantijn Huygens, 14 January 1643, in Marin Mersenne, *Correspondence* (Paris, 1972), vol. 12, no. 1160. Johann Burckhardt Mencke, *De Charlataneria Eruditorum* (1715), English translation *The Charlatanry of the Learned* (New York, 1937), 85–6, also discusses Kircher, not as an impostor but as an easily deceived worshipper of antiquity.
15. Marian Füssel, '"The Charlatanry of the Learned": On the Moral Economy of the Republic of Letters in Eighteenth-Century Germany', *Cultural and Social History* 3 (2006), 287–300.
16. Jacques Roger, *Buffon: A Life in Natural History* (1989: English translation, Ithaca, NY 1997), 434.

17. Samuel Johnson, *The Rambler* (1750–2: ed. W. J. Bate and Albrecht B. Strauss, New Haven, CT, 1969), nos. 180, 121.
18. Quoted in Richard Yeo, *Encyclopaedic Visions: Scientific Dictionaries and Enlightenment Culture* (Cambridge, 2001), xi.
19. Preface to vol. 6 of the *Bibliothèque Françoise*, quoted in Jean Sgard (ed.), *Dictionnaire des Journaux, 1600–1789*, 2 vols. (Paris 1991), vol. 1, 162. My translation.
20. Maria Luisa Altieri Biagi, *Lingua e cultura di Francesco Redi, medico* (Florence, 1968); Gabriele Bucchi and Lorella Mangani, 'Redi, Francesco', *DBI* 86, 708–12; Georges Güntert, *Un poeta scienziato del Seicento* (Florence, 1966); L. Matt, 'Magalotti, Lorenzo', *DBI* 67, 300–5.
21. Steven Shapin, 'The Man of Science', in Lorraine Daston and Katharine Park (eds.), *Early Modern Science* (Cambridge History of Science, vol. 3, Cambridge, 2006), 179–91; Londa Schiebinger, 'Women of Natural Knowledge', ibid., 192–205.
22. Dena Goodman, 'Enlightenment Salons: The Convergence of Female and Philosophic Ambitions', *Eighteenth-Century Studies* 22 (1989), 329–50. Cf. Antoine Lilti, *Le monde des salons: sociabilité et mondanité à Paris au XVIIIe siècle* (Paris, 2005).
23. Sylvia H. Myers, *The Bluestocking Circle* (Oxford, 1990).
24. Isobel Grundy, 'Montagu, Lady Mary Wortley', *ODNB* 38, 754–9.
25. Robert Shackleton, *Montesquieu, an Intellectual and Critical Biography* (Oxford, 1961), vii.
26. Judith N. Shklar, *Montesquieu* (Oxford, 1987), 10; Muriel Dodds, *Les récits de voyages: sources de L'Esprit des lois de Montesquieu* (Paris, 1929).
27. Theodore Besterman, *Voltaire* (London, 1969).
28. John Henry Brumfitt, *Voltaire historian* (Oxford, 1958).
29. Besterman, *Voltaire*, 124, 525.
30. Esther Ehman, *Madame du Châtelet* (Leamington, 1986); Judith P. Zinsser and Julie C. Hayes (eds.), *Émilie du Châtelet: Rewriting Enlightenment Philosophy and Science* (Oxford, 2006); Judith P. Zinsser, *Émilie du Châtelet: Daring Genius of the Enlightenment* (New York, 2007).
31. Thomas Hankins, *Jean d'Alembert, Scientist and Philosopher* (Ithaca, NY, 1964); J. Morton Briggs, 'Alembert, Jean Le Rond d', *DSB* 1, 110–17.
32. René Pomeau, *Diderot* (Paris, 1967); Charles C. Gillespie, 'Diderot, Denis', *DSB* 4, 84–90.
33. Jacques Roger, *Buffon: A Life in Natural History* (1989: English translation, Ithaca, NY, 1997).
34. Keith M. Baker, *Condorcet: From Natural Philosophy to Social Mathematics* (Chicago, IL, 1975), ix. Cf. Gilles Granger, 'Condorcet, Marie-Jean-Antoine-Nicolas Caritat, Marquis de', *DSB* 3, 383–8.
35. J. B. Gough, 'Réaumur, René-Antoine Ferchault de', *DSB* 11, 327–35; Jean Torlais, *Un esprit encyclopédique en dehors de l'Encyclopédie: Réaumur* (Paris, 1961); Henry Guerlac, 'Lavoisier, Antoine-Laurent', *DSB* 8, 66–91; Arthur Donovan, *Antoine Lavoisier* (Cambridge, 1993); Rhoda Rappoport, 'Turgot, Anne-Robert-Jacques', *DSB* 13, 494–7; Anthony Brewer, 'Turgot: Founder of Classical Economics', *Economica* 54 (1987), 417–28.
36. Peter Loewenberg, 'The Creation of a Scientific Community', in *Fantasy and Reality in History* (New York, 1995), 46–89; Martin Mulsow and Marcelo Stamm (eds.), *Konstellationsforschung* (Frankfurt, 2005).
37. Ernest C. Mossner, *The Life of David Hume*, 2nd edn (Oxford, 1980), 3. Cf. James A. Harris, *Hume: An Intellectual Biography* (Cambridge, 2015), 14–24.
38. Quoted in Nicholas Philippson, *Adam Smith: An Enlightened Life* (London, 2010), 214.
39. Ian S. Ross, *The Life of Adam Smith*, 2nd edn (Oxford, 2010), 241.
40. Alastair J. Durie and Stuart Handley, 'Home, Henry, Lord Kames', *ODNB* 27, 879–81; Iain Maxwell Hammett, 'Burnett, James, Lord Monboddo', *ODNB* 8, 941–3.
41. Fania Oz-Salzberger, 'Ferguson, Adam', *ODNB* 19, 341–7.
42. Robert DeMaria, Jr., *The Life of Samuel Johnson* (Oxford, 1993), 45, 97.
43. Quoted in J. P. Hardy, *Samuel Johnson: A Critical Study* (London, 1979), 28.
44. James Boswell, *Life of Samuel Johnson* (1791: ed. A. Napier, 2 vols., London 1884), vol. 2, 365. The cousin's name was Cornelius Ford.

45. Richard Cumberland, *Memoirs* (London, 1807), 77.
46. DeMaria, *Johnson's Dictionary and the Language of Learning* (Oxford, 1986).
47. Vincenzo Ferrone, 'The Man of Science', in Michel Vovelle (ed.), *Enlightenment Portraits* (1995: English translation, Chicago, IL, 1997), 190–225, at 211.
48. Robert E. Schofield, *The Enlightenment of Joseph Priestley* (University Park, PA, 1997), ix.
49. Robert E. Schofield, *The Enlightened Joseph Priestley* (University Park PA, 2004); idem., 'Priestley, Joseph', *ODNB* 45, 351–9.
50. Jenny Uglow, *The Lunar Men* (London, 2003).
51. Richard Gombrich in Alexander Murray (ed.), *Sir William Jones, 1746–94: A Commemoration* (Oxford, 1998), 3. Cf. Michael J. Franklin, *Oriental Jones: Sir William Jones, Poet, Lawyer and Linguist, 1746–1794* (Oxford, 2011).
52. Marisa González Montero de Espinosa, *Lorenzo Hervás y Panduro, el gran olvidado de la ilustración española* (Madrid, 1994); Antonio Astorgano Abajo, *Lorenzo Hervás y Panduro (1735–1809)* (Toledo, 2010).
53. Javier Varela, *Jovellanos* (Madrid, 1988); AA.VV., *Jovellanos: el hombre que soñó España* (Madrid, 2012).
54. Quoted from the ecclesiastical approbation of the seventh volume of Feijoo's *Teatro Crítico* by Gregorio Marañón, *Las ideas biológicas del Padre Feijoo* (1933: 2nd edn, Madrid, 1941), 15.
55. Ivy L. McClelland, *Benito Jerónimo Feijoo* (New York, 1969); Inmaculada Urzainqui and Rodrigo Olay Valdés (eds.), *Con la razón y la experiencia: Feijoo 250 años después* (Oviedo, 2016).
56. Edna E. Kramer, 'Agnesi, Maria Gaetana', *DSB* 1, 75–7; M. Gliozzi and G. F. Orlandelli, 'Agnesi, Maria Gaetana', *DBI* 1, 441–3.
57. Peter Burke, *Vico* (Oxford, 1985); Joseph Mali, *The Rehabilitation of Myth: Vico's New Science* (Cambridge, 1992); Mark Lilla, *G. B. Vico: The Making of an Anti-Modern* (Cambridge, MA, 1993); H. S. Stone, *Vico's Cultural History* (Leiden, 1997).
58. Lisbet Koerner, *Linnaeus: Nature and Nation* (Cambridge, MA, 1999).
59. Ernst Benz, *Emanuel Swedenborg: Visionary Savant in the Age of Reason* (1948: English translation, West Chester, PA, 2002).
60. B. M. Kedrov, 'Lomonosov, Mikhail Vasilievich', *DSB* 8, 467–72; Galina Pavlova and Alexander Fyodorov, *Mikhail Lomonosov, Life and Work* (Moscow, 1984); Ludmilla Schulze, 'The Russification of the St Petersburg Academy of Sciences', *British Journal for the History of Science* 18 (1985), 305–35.
61. Elizabeth Hill, 'Roger Boscovich', in Lancelot L. Whyte (ed.), *Roger Joseph Boscovich* (London, 1961), 17–201; Piers Bursill-Hall (ed.), *R. J. Boscovich* (Rome, 1993).
62. Irving A. Leonard, 'Pedro de Peralta: Peruvian Polygraph', *Revista Hispánica Moderna* 34 (1968), 690–9, at 698. Cf. David Brading, *The First America* (Cambridge, 1991), 391–9; Mark Thurner, *History's Peru: The Poetics of Colonial and Post-Colonial Historiography* (Gainesville, FL, 2011), 58–81.
63. P. Ford, *The Many-Sided Franklin* (1899); Carl Van Doren, *Benjamin Franklin* (New York, 1938); Alfred O. Aldridge, *Benjamin Franklin, Philosopher and Man* (Philadelphia, PA, 1965); I. Bernard Cohen, 'Franklin, Benjamin', *DSB* 5, 129–39.
64. Karl Lehmann, *Thomas Jefferson, American Humanist* (1947: Charlottesville, VA, 1985).
65. Catherine E. Ross, '"Trying all things": Romantic Polymaths, Social Factors and the Legacies of a Rhetorical Education', *Texas Studies in Literature and Language* 53 (2011), 401–30, at 406.
66. Richard Holmes, *Coleridge: Early Visions* (1989: new edn, London 1998), 130. Cf. Trevor H. Levere, 'Coleridge and the Sciences', in Andrew Cunningham and Nicholas Jardine (eds.), *Romanticism and the Sciences* (Cambridge, 1990), 295–306.
67. Josephine McDonagh, *De Quincey's Disciplines* (Oxford, 1994). Cf. Grevel Lindof, 'Quincey, Thomas Penson de', *ODNB* 45, 700–6.
68. Alexander Wood, *Thomas Young, Natural Philosopher* (Cambridge, 1954), 256–71, 286.
69. Wood, *Thomas Young*, 227–55; Edgar W. Morse, 'Young, Thomas', *DSB* 14, 562–72; Andrew Robinson, *The Last Man Who Knew Everything: Thomas Young, the anonymous polymath who*

proved Newton wrong, explained how we see, cured the sick and deciphered the Rosetta Stone, among other feats of genius (New York, 2005).

70. David S. Evans, 'Herschel, John', *DSB* 6, 323–8, at 327. Cf. Günter Buttmann, *The Shadow of the Telescope: A Biography of John Herschel* (1965: English translation, New York, 1970); Michael J. Crowe, 'Herschel, John Frederick William', *ODNB* 26, 825–31; Richard Holmes, *The Age of Wonder: How the Romantic Generation Discovered the Beauty and Terror of Science* (2008: new edn, London, 2009), 387–411; James A. Secord, 'The Conduct of Everyday Life: John Herschel's *Preliminary Discourse on the Study of Natural Philosophy*', in his *Visions of Science* (Oxford, 2014), 80–106.

71. Laura J. Snyder, *The Philosophical Breakfast Club: Four Remarkable Friends who Transformed Knowledge and Changed the World* (New York, 2011).

72. Robert E. Butts, 'Whewell, William', *DSB* 14, 292–5; Richard Yeo, *Defining Science: William Whewell, Natural Knowledge, and Public Debate in Early Victorian Britain* (Cambridge, 1993); idem., 'Whewell, William', *ODNB* 58, 463–70.

73. John Herschel, *Proceedings of the Royal Society* 16 (1867–8), liii.

74. Yeo, *Defining Science*, 57; J. M. F. Wright, *Alma Mater* (London, 1827).

75. R. A. Hyman, *Charles Babbage* (London, 1982); Doron Swade, *The Cogwheel Brain: Charles Babbage and the Quest to Build the First Computer* (London, 2000); idem., 'Babbage, Charles', *ODNB* 3, 68–74; James A. Secord, 'The Economy of Intelligence: Charles Babbage's Reflections on the Decline of Science in England', in his *Visions of Science* (Oxford, 2014), 52–79.

76. Isaiah Berlin, 'Herder and the Enlightenment', in *Vico and Herder* (London, 1976), 145–216; Jürgen Trabant, 'Herder and Language', in Hans Adler and Wolf Koepke (eds.), *Companion to the Works of Johann Gottfried Herder* (Rochester, NY, 2009), 117–39.

77. Walter H. Bruford, *Culture and Society in Classical Weimar, 1775–1806* (Cambridge, 1962), 174–235; Peter H. Reill, 'Herder's Historical Practice and the Discourse of Late Enlightenment Science', in Wulf Koepke (ed.), *Johann Gottfried Herder, Academic Disciplines and the Pursuit of Knowledge* (Columbia, SC, 1996), 13–21; Elías Palti, 'The "Metaphor of Life": Herder's Philosophy of History and Uneven Developments in Late Eighteenth-Century Natural Sciences', *History and Theory* 38 (1999), 322–47; Dalia Nassar, 'Understanding as Explanation: The Significance of Herder's and Goethe's Science of Describing', in Anik Waldow and Nigel DeSouza (eds.), *Herder: Philosophy and Anthropology* (Oxford, 2017), 106–25.

78. Nicholas Boyle, *Goethe: The Poet and the Age*, 2 vols. (Oxford 1991–2000).

79. Katharina Mommsen, *Goethe and the Poets of Arabia* (1988: English translation, Rochester, NY, 2014).

80. Hugh A. Nisbet, *Goethe and the Scientific Tradition* (1972); George A. Wells, *Goethe and the Development of Science* (Alphen, 1978); F. Amrine et al., *Goethe and the Sciences* (Dordrecht, 1987).

81. Paul R. Sweet, *Wilhelm von Humboldt: A Biography*, 2 vols. (Columbus, OH, 1978–80); Tilman Borsche, *Wilhelm von Humboldt* (Munich, 1990); Peter H. Reill, 'Science and the Construction of the Cultural Sciences in Late Enlightenment Germany: The Case of Wilhelm von Humboldt', *History and Theory* 33 (1994), 345–66; K. Muller-Vollmer, 'Wilhelm von Humboldt', *Stanford Encyclopaedia of Philosophy*, https://plato.stanford.edu/entries/wilhelm-humboldt.

82. Ole Hansen-Love, *La révolution copernicienne du langage dans l'oevre de Wilhelm von Humboldt* (Paris, 1972).

83. Ralph W. Emerson, *Works*, 17 vols. (London 1904–5), vol. XI, 458.

84. Kurt-R. Biermann and Ingo Schwarz (1997) 'Der polyglotte Alexander von Humboldt', *Mitteilungen der Alexander von Humboldt-Stiftung* H69, 39–44.

85. Bettina Hey'l, *Das Ganze der Natur und die Differenzierung des Wissens: Alexander von Humboldt als Schriftsteller* (Berlin, 2007), 7–10, 386–94 and passim.

86. *Die letzte Universalgelehrte*: Claudia Schülke, https://www.welt.de › Wissenschaft, 4 May 2009.

87. Auguste Comte, 'Préface personnelle', *Cours de Philosophie Positive*, 6 vols. (1830–42, rpr. Brussels, 1969), vol. 6, v–xxxviii. Cf. Mary Pickering, *Auguste Comte: An Intellectual Biography*, 3 vols. (Cambridge, 1993–2009).

88. Comte, *Cours*, vol. 1, 1–115. Cf. Johan Heilbron, 'Auguste Comte and Modern Epistemology', *Sociological Theory* 8 (1990), 153–62; Pickering, *Auguste Comte*, vol. 1, 445, 561–604.

89. Sydney Elsen, 'Herbert Spencer and the Spectre of Comte', *Journal of British Studies* 7 (1967), 48–67.

90. John D. Y. Peel, *Herbert Spencer: The Evolution of a Sociologist* (London, 1971); Greta Jones and Robert Peel, *Herbert Spencer: The Intellectual Legacy* (London, 2004); José Harris, 'Spencer, Herbert', *ODNB* 51, 851–61.

91. General studies of the man and his work range from Isaiah Berlin, *Karl Marx* (London, 1939), to Gareth Stedman Jones, *Karl Marx: Greatness and Illusion* (London, 2016).

92. Lawrence Krader (ed.), *The Ethnological Notebooks of Karl Marx* (Assen, 1972).

93. Quoted in Eric Hobsbawm, 'Marx, Karl', *ODNB* 37, 57–66, at 60.

94. Jones, *Karl Marx*, 434, 593.

95. René Wellek, *A History of Modern Criticism* 1750–1950, 4 vols. (Cambridge 1955–65), vol. 3, 34–72; Wolf Lepenies, *Sainte-Beuve: Auf der Schwelle zur Moderne* (Munich, 1997).

96. François Furet and Françoise Mélonio, 'introduction' to Tocqueville, *Oeuvres*, vol. 1 (Paris, 2004); Raymond Aron, *Main Currents in Sociological Thought*, 2 vols. (Harmondsworth, 1968–70), vol. 1, 183–232; Melvin Richter, 'Tocqueville on Algeria', *The Review of Politics* 25 (1963), 362–98.

97. Jean-Louis Benoît, *Tocqueville* (Paris, 2005), xii.

98. Richard Swedberg, *Tocqueville's Political Economy* (Princeton, NJ, 2009), 73.

99. H. W. Wardman, *Ernest Renan: A Critical Biography* (London, 1964), 211. Cf. Jean-Pierre Van Deth, *Renan* (Paris, 2012); Henry Laurens (ed.), *Ernest Renan* (Paris, 2013).

100. The historian Gabriel Monod, quoted in Laurens, *Renan*, 10.

101. Leo Weinstein, *Hippolyte Taine* (New York, 1972); Regina Pozzi, *Hippolyte Taine: scienze umane e politica nel 'Ottocento* (Venice, 1993); Nathalie Richard, *Hippolyte Taine: histoire, psychologie, littérature* (Paris, 2013).

102. Pozzi, *Hippolyte Taine*, 24.

103. Richard, *Hippolyte Taine*, 81.

104. Quoted in Weinstein, *Hippolyte Taine*, 26.

105. Ann P. Robson, 'Mill, Harriet', *ODNB* 38, 143–6; Dale E. Miller, 'Harriet Taylor Mill', in Edward N. Zalta (ed.), *The Stanford Encyclopaedia of Philosophy* (Stanford, CA, 2015): https://plato.stanford.edu/archives/win2015/entries/harriet-mill

106. Nicholas Capaldi, *John Stuart Mill: A Biography* (Cambridge, 2004); Jose Harris, 'Mill, John Stuart', *ODNB* 38, 155–75.

107. Timothy Hilton, *John Ruskin*, 2 vols. (New Haven CT, 1985–2000); Robert Hewison, 'Ruskin, John', *ODNB* 48, 173–92.

108. Quoted in Peter Stansky, *William Morris* (Oxford, 1983), 1.

109. E. P. Thompson, *William Morris, Romantic to Revolutionary* (London, 1955); Fiona McCarthy, *William Morris* (London, 1994).

110. Stefan Collini, *Matthew Arnold: A Critical Portrait* (Oxford, 1994), 54; idem., 'Arnold, Matthew', *ODNB* 2, 487–94. Cf. Wellek, *Modern Criticism*, vol. 4, 155–80.

111. William E. Buckler, '"On the Study of Celtic Literature": A Critical Reconsideration', *Victorian Poetry* 27 (1989), 61–76, at 62; S. Nagarajan, 'Arnold and the *Bhagavad Gita*', *Comparative Literature* 12 (1960), 335–47.

112. Maria Fairweather, *Madame de Staël* (London, 2004); Michel Winock, *Madame de Staël* (Paris, 2010); Richard Holmes, *This Long Pursuit* (London, 2016), 153–68.

113. Bärbel Kern and Horst Kern, *Madame Doctorin Schlözer: ein Frauenleben in den Widersprüchen der Aufklärung* (Munich, 1988), 52ff.

114. Robert K. Webb, 'Martineau, Harriet', *ODNB* 37, 13–19.

115. Gordon S. Haight, *George Eliot: A Biography* (1968); Sally Shuttleworth, *George Eliot and 19th-Century Science* (Cambridge, 1984); Beryl Gray, 'George Eliot and the "Westminster Review"', *Victorian Periodicals Review* 33 (2000) 212–24; Diana Postlethwaite, 'George Eliot and Science', in George Levine (ed.), *The Cambridge Companion to George Eliot* (Cambridge, 2001), 98–118; Rosemary Ashton, 'Evans, Marian', *ODNB* 18, 730–43.

116. Valerie A. Dodd, *George Eliot: An Intellectual Life* (1990), 284.

117. Rosemary Ashton, *George Henry Lewes* (London, 1991); eadem., 'Lewes, George Henry', *ODNB* 33, 563–8.

118. Gillian Beer, *Darwin's Plots* (London, 1983), 149, 154.

119. Haight, *George Eliot*, 344–50.

120. Kathryn A. Neeley, *Mary Somerville: Science, Illumination and the Female Mind* (Cambridge, 2001), 2.

121. Mary Somerville, *Personal Recollections* (London, 1873), 140.

122. Elizabeth C. Patterson, 'Somerville, Mary', *DSB* 12, 521–5; idem., *Mary Patterson and the Cultivation of Science, 1815–1840* (The Hague, 1984); Mary R. S. Creese, 'Somerville, Mary', *ODNB* 51, 617–9; James A. Secord, 'General Introduction' to Mary Somerville, *Scientific Papers and Reviews* (London, 2004), xv–xxxix; idem., 'Mathematics for the Million? Mary Somerville's *On the Connexion of the Physical Sciences*, in *Visions of Science* (Oxford, 2014), 107–37; Richard Holmes, *This Long Pursuit: Reflections of a Romantic Biographer* (London, 2016), 197–216.

123. Sydney Ross, ' "Scientist": The Story of a Word', *Annals of Science* 18 (1962), 65–85.

124. G. Granger, 'Cournot, Antoine-Augustin', *DSB* 3, 450–4; Franck Bourdier, 'Cuvier, Georges', *DSB* 3, 521–8; idem., 'Geoffroy Saint-Hilaire, Étienne', *DSB* 5, 355–8.

125. Quoted in Ian F. McNeely, *'Medicine on a Grand Scale': Rudolf Virchow, Liberalism and the Public Health* (London, 2002), 5.

126. McNeely, *'Medicine on a Grand Scale'*, 7.

127. Guenther B. Risse, 'Virchow, Rudolf', *DSB* 14, 39–45; T. James, 'Rudolf Virchow and Heinrich Schliemann', *South African Medical Journal* 56 (1979), 111–14.

128. Lorenz Krüger (ed.), *Universalgenie Helmholtz* (Berlin, 1994).

129. R. Steven Turner, 'Helmholtz, Hermann von', *DSB* 6, 241–53, at 253.

130. Michel Meulden, *Helmholtz: From Enlightenment to Neuroscience* (2001: English translation, Cambridge, MA, 2010).

131. Wilhelm Bölsche, *Haeckel: His Life and Work* (English translation, London, 1906, 173); Georg Uschmann, 'Haeckel, E. H. P.', *DSB* 6, 6–11; Andrea Wulf, *The Invention of Nature: The Adventures of Alexander von Humboldt, the Lost Hero of Science* (London, 2016), 298–314; David Lowenthal, *G. P. Marsh: Prophet of Conservation* (Seattle, WA, 2000).

132. Letter to his friend the botanist Joseph Hooker, quoted in Peter Brent, *Charles Darwin: A 'man of enlarged curiosity'* (London, 1981), 98.

133. Ibid., 174.

134. Gillian Beer, *Darwin's Plots* (London, 1983).

135. Gavin de Beer, 'Darwin, Charles Robert', *DSB* 3, 565–77; Janet Browne, *Charles Darwin*, 2 vols. (London, 1995–2002); Adrian Desmond, Janet Browne and James Moore, 'Darwin, Charles Robert', *ODNB* 15, 177–202; Oliver Sacks, 'Darwin and the Meaning of Flowers', in *The River of Consciousness* (2017), 3–26.

136. Wesley C. Williams, 'Huxley, Thomas Henry', *DSB* 6, 589–97; Adrian Desmond, *T. H. Huxley*, 2 vols. (1994–7); idem., 'Huxley, Thomas Henry' *ODNB* 29, 99–111.

137. Norman T. Gridgeman, 'Galton, Francis', *DSB* 5, 265–7; Ruth S. Cowan, 'Galton, Francis', *ODNB* 21, 346–9; Nicholas W. Gillham, *A Life of Sir Francis Galton* (Oxford, 2001); Michael Bulmer, *Francis Galton* (Baltimore, MD, 2003).

138. H. J. P. Arnold, *William Henry Fox Talbot: Pioneer of Photography and Man of Science* (London, 1977); Larry J. Schaff, 'Talbot, William Henry Fox', *ODNB* 53, 730–3. An exhibition in Cambridge in 2012, 'Talbot Beyond Photography', celebrated his many achievements.

139. Diderot, letter, 16 December 1748.
140. Adam Smith, *Lectures on Jurisprudence* (1763); idem., *Wealth of Nations* (1776), 18. Cf. Jerry A. Jacobs, *In Defense of Disciplines: Interdisciplinarity and Specialization in the Research University* (Chicago, IL, 2013), 55–60.
141. Immanuel Kant, *Groundwork for the Metaphysics of Morals* (1785: English translation, ed. Alan Wood, New Haven, CT, 2002), preface.
142. Charles Babbage, *On the Economy of Machinery and Manufactures* (2nd edn, London 1832), 131–63.
143. Herbert Spencer, 'Progress: Its Law and Cause' (1857), in *Essays*, media.bloomsbury. com/.../primary-source-131-herbert-spencer-progress-its-law-and-cause.pdf, 2.
144. Quoted in Ross, 'Scientist', 71.
145. Quoted in Crosbie Smith and William Agar (eds.), *Making Space for Science* (Basingstoke 1998), 184.
146. Jean-Pierre Chaline, *Sociabilité et erudition: les sociétés savantes en France, XIXe–XXe siècles* (Paris, 1995). Chaline quotes one exception, the 'Société polymathique de Morbihan' (1826).
147. Holmes, *The Age of Wonder*, 393.

CHAPTER 5

1. Schiller quoted in Andrea Wulf, *The Invention of Nature* (London, 2016), 33.
2. Smith is quoted in Richard Yeo, *Encyclopaedic Visions* (Cambridge, 2001), 249; William Hazlitt, 'Samuel Taylor Coleridge', *The Spirit of the Age* (London, 1825), 61–79, at 61.
3. Alexander Wood, *Thomas Young* (Cambridge, 1954), 230, 237.
4. Dubois-Reymond quoted in Paul Bishop (ed.), *Companion to Goethe's Faust* (Woodbridge, 2006), 195. Cf. Richard Hibbitt, *Dilettantism and its Values* (London, 2006), especially the introduction.
5. Frédéric Barbier (ed.), *Les trois révolutions du livre* (Geneva, 2001); Simon Eliot, 'From Few and Expensive to Many and Cheap: The British Book Market, 1800–1890', in Eliot and Jonathan Rose (eds.), *A Companion to the History of the Book* (Oxford, 2007), 291–302; Aileen Fyfe, *Steam-Powered Knowledge: William Chambers and the Business of Publishing, 1820–1860* (Chicago, IL, 2012), 1–11.
6. Bernard Lightman, *Victorian Popularizers of Science: Designing Nature for New Audiences* (Chicago, IL, 2007), 66. On Germany, see Andreas W. Daum, *Wissenschaftspopularisierung in 19 Jht: bürgerliche Kultur, naturwissenschaftliche Bildung und die deutsche Öffentlichkeit, 1848–1914* (Munich, 1998).
7. Thomas De Quincey, *Suspiria de profundis* (London, 1845), ch. 1.
8. Emma C. Spary, 'L'invention de "l'expédition scientifique"', in Marie-Noëlle Bourguet et al. (eds.), *L'invention scientifique de la Méditerranée* (Paris, 1998), 119–38.
9. Oliver MacDonagh, 'The Nineteenth-Century Revolution in Government: A Reappraisal', *Historical Journal* 1 (1958), 52–67; Martin Bulmer (ed.), *The Social Survey in Historical Perspective* (Cambridge, 1991); Edward Higgs, *The Information State in England* (Basingstoke, 2004).
10. Ian Hacking, *The Taming of Chance* (Cambridge, 1990), 3. Cf. Alain Desrosières, *The Politics of Large Numbers* (1993: English translation, Cambridge, MA, 1998).
11. Studies of this topic abound. Important examples include Chris A. Bayly, *Empire and Information: Intelligence Gathering and Social Communication in India, 1780–1870* (Cambridge, 1996); Bernard S. Cohn, *Colonialism and its Forms of Knowledge* (Princeton, NJ, 1996); Emmanuelle Sibeud, *Une science impériale pour l'Afrique? La construction des savoirs africanistes en France, 1878–1930* (Paris, 2002).
12. Haia Shpayer-Makov, *The Ascent of the Detective* (Oxford, 2011), 125.
13. JoAnne Yates, 'Business Use of Information and Technology during the Industrial Age', in Alfred D. Chandler Jr. and James W. Cortada (eds.), *A Nation Transformed by Information* (New York, 2003), 107–36.

14. Jacques-Bernard Durey de Noinville, *Table alphabétique des dictionnaires* (Paris, 1758). Cf. Peter Burke with Joseph McDermott, 'The Proliferation of Reference Books, 1450–1850', in McDermott and Burke (eds.), *The Book Worlds of East Asia and Europe, 1450–1850: Connections and Comparisons* (Hong Kong, 2015), 283–320.
15. Quoted in Mark S. Phillips, *Society and Sentiment: Genres of Historical Writing in Britain, 1740–1820* (Princeton, NJ, 2000), 294.
16. Quoted by Nick Jardine in Marina Frasca-Spada and Nick Jardine (eds.), *Books and the Sciences in History* (Cambridge, 2000), 402.
17. The journal *Modern Business* in 1908, quoted in the *OED*.
18. John Higham, 'The Matrix of Specialization', in Alexandra Oleson and John Voss, *The Organization of Knowledge in Modern America, 1860–1920* (Baltimore, MD, 1979), 3–18, at 9.
19. Comte also wrote of 'l'esprit de spécialité, l'âge de spécialité, le régime de spécialité': *Cours de Philosophie Positive* (6 vols., 1830–42: rpr. Brussels, 1969), vol. 1, 31: vol. 6, 15, 293, 304, 341.
20. Fritz Ringer, *Fields of Knowledge: French Academic Culture in Comparative Perspective, 1890–1920* (Cambridge, 1992), 303.
21. Émile Durkheim, *La division du travail social* (1893); cf. Marcel Fournier, *Émile Durkheim* (2007: English translation, Cambridge 2013), 427–9, 432.
22. Quoted in Ruth Kinna, 'William Morris: Art, Work and Leisure', *JHI* 61 (2000), 493–512, at 499, 503–4.
23. Max Weber, 'Science as a Vocation', in Hans H. Gerth and C. Wright Mills (eds.), *From Max Weber* (New York, 1946), 129–56.
24. George Rosen, *The Specialization of Medicine with Particular Reference to Ophthalmology* (New York, 1944).
25. George E. Davie, *The Democratic Intellect: Scotland and her Universities in the Nineteenth Century* (1961: 3rd edn, Edinburgh, 2013).
26. Chad Wellmon, *Organizing Enlightenment: Information Overload and the Invention of the Modern Research University* (Baltimore, MD, 2015) 4–5, 10–11, 40, 122 and passim.
27. James Hart, *German Universities* (1874), 264.
28. Basil Gildersleeve, quoted in James Axtell, *Wisdom's Workshop: The Rise of the Modern University* (Princeton, NJ, 2016), 248.
29. Durkheim quoted in Fournier, *Émile Durkheim*, 67.
30. Sheldon Pollock, 'Introduction' to *World Philology*, ed. Pollock et al. (Cambridge, MA, 2015), 1–24.
31. Michael G. Brock and M. C. Curthoys (eds.), *History of the University of Oxford* (Oxford, 2000), vol. 7, part 2, 361–84, 397–428.
32. Davie, *The Democratic Intellect*, 6–7, 65–6, 79; idem., *The Crisis of the Democratic Intellect: The Problem of Generalism and Specialization in Twentieth-Century Scotland* (New York, 1987).
33. Tony Becher and Paul R. Trowler, *Academic Tribes and Territories: Intellectual Inquiry and the Cultures of Disciplines* (1989: second edn, Buckingham, 2001): an investigation of the late twentieth century. Robert Ardrey's *The Territorial Imperative: A Personal Enquiry into the Animal Origins of Property and Nations* (London, 1972) was followed by many extensions of the idea from zoology to sociology. For a geographer's view, see Robert David Sack, *Human Territoriality: Its Theory and History* (Cambridge, 1986).
34. Quoted in Mary O. Furner and Barry Supple (eds.), *The State and Economic Knowledge* (Cambridge, 1990), 303.
35. Alfred N. Whitehead, *Science and the Modern World* (Cambridge, 1926).
36. Charles E. McClelland, *State, Society and University in Germany, 1700–1914* (Cambridge, 1980), 281, 285.
37. Marie B. Hall, *All Scientists Now: The Royal Society in the Nineteenth Century* (Cambridge, 1984), 216–17.
38. My thanks to Michael Hunter for help on this question.

39. Eckhardt Fuchs, 'The Politics of the Republic of Learning: International Scientific Congresses in Europe, the Pacific Rim and Latin America', in Fuchs and Benedikt Stuchtey (eds.), *Across Cultural Borders* (Lanham, MD, 2002), 205–44; Wolf Feuerhahn (ed.), *La fabrique internationale de la science: les congrès internationales de 1865 à 1945* (Paris, 2010).

40. Denis Pernot, 'Brunetière', in Dominique Kalifa et al. (eds.), *La civilisation du journal: histoire culturelle et littéraire de la presse française au XIXe siècle* (Paris, 2011), 1,261–5.

41. Lorraine Daston, 'The Academies and the Unity of Knowledge', *Differences* 10 (1998), 67–86, at 73.

42. C. P. Snow, *The Two Cultures* (1959: ed. Stefan Collini, Cambridge, 2001), 2, 14–15.

43. Helmut Kreuzer (ed.), *Die zwei Kulturen* (Munich, 1987); W. W. Mijnhardt and B. Theunissen (eds.) *De Twee Culturen* (Amsterdam, 1988); Giorgio Olcese (ed.), *Cultura scientifica e cultura umanistica: contrasto o integrazione?* (Genoa, 2004); Emma Eldelin, *"De två kulturerna" flyttar hemifrån: C. P. Snows begrepp i svensk idédebatt, 1959–2005* (Stockholm, 2006); Jost Halfmann and Johannes Rohbeck (eds.), *Zwei Kulturen Der Wissenschaft, Revisited* (Göttingen, 2007).

44. Benedict Anderson, *Imagined Communities: Reflections on the Origin and Spread of Nationalism* (1983: revised edn, London, 1991).

45. Frank Horner, *The French Reconnaissance: Baudin in Australia, 1801–1803* (Melbourne, 1987), 72.

46. Peter E. Carels and Dan Flory, 'J. H. Zedler's Universal Lexicon', in Frank A. Kafker (ed.), *Notable Encyclopaedias of the Seventeenth and Eighteenth Centuries* (Oxford, 1981), 165–95; Frank A. Kafker, *The Encyclopaedists as Individuals* (Oxford, 2006).

47. Herman Kogan, *The Great EB: The Story of the* Encyclopaedia Britannica (Chicago, IL, 1958), 168; Gabriele Turi, *Il mecenate, il filosofo e il gesuita: l'*Enciclopedia Italiana, *specchio della nazione* (Bologna, 2002), 50, 57.

48. Steven Shapin, *The Scientific Life: A Moral History of a Late Modern Vocation* (Chicago, IL, 2008), 169–78; Jeffrey A. Johnson, *The Kaiser's Chemists: Science and Modernization in Imperial Germany* (Chapel Hill, NC, 1990), 34; Daniel P. Todes, *Pavlov's Physiological Factory* (Baltimore, MD, 2002), 88.

49. Laurent Mucchielli, *La découverte du social: naissance de la sociologie en France, 1870–1914* (Paris, 1998), 213; Marcel Fournier, *Émile Durkheim* (2007: English translation, Cambridge 2013), 66.

50. John Ruscio, quoted in Becher and Trowler, *Academic Tribes and Territories*, 66.

51. Rudolf Stichweh, 'Differenzierung der Wissenschaft', in *Wissenschaft, Universität, Professionen* (Frankfurt, 1994).

52. Ian McNeely with Lisa Wolverton, *Reinventing Knowledge from Alexandria to the Internet* (New York, 2008), xix, 163. Cf. Immanuel Wallerstein et al., *Open the Social Sciences* (Stanford, CA, 1996).

53. George Weisz, *The Emergence of Modern Universities in France, 1863–1914* (Princeton, NJ, 1983), 225–69).

54. Bernhard vom Brocke, 'Friedrich Althoff: A Great Figure in Higher Education Policy in Germany', *Minerva* 29 (1991), 269–93, at 272.

55. Axtell, *Wisdom's Workshop*, 263.

56. Fournier, *Émile Durkheim*, 91, 411.

57. Wallerstein, *Open the Social Sciences*, 34.

58. Pierre Bourdieu, *Distinction* (1979: English translation, London 1984); idem., *Homo Academicus* (1984: English translation, Cambridge 1988).

59. P. Boardman, *The Worlds of Patrick Geddes: Biologist, Town Planner, Re-Educator, Peace-Warrior* (London, 1978), 1; Israel Zangwill, 'Introduction' to Amelia Defries, *The Interpreter: Geddes, the Man and his Gospel* (London, 1927), 10.

60. The acquaintance was the planner Patrick Abercrombie. Paddy Kitchen, *A Most Unsettling Person: An Introduction to the Ideas and Life of Patrick Geddes* (London, 1975), 237.

61. Lewis Mumford, *Sketches from Life: The Autobiography of Lewis Mumford* (New York, 1982), 153.

62. Quoted in Davie, *The Democratic Intellect*, ix.
63. Helen Meller, *Patrick Geddes: Social Evolutionist and City Planner* (London, 1990); idem., 'Geddes, Patrick', *ODNB* 21, 701–6.
64. Françoise Levie, *L'homme qui veut classer le monde* (Brussels, 2006); Alex Wright, *Cataloguing the World: Paul Otlet and the Birth of the Information Age* (Oxford, 2014).
65. Marie Neurath and Robert S. Cohen (eds.), *Otto Neurath: Empiricism and Sociology* (Dordrecht, 1973), 14, 46.
66. Otto quoted in Neurath and Cohen, *Otto Neurath*, 4. His estimate was 13,000 books. His wife Marie is quoted ibid., 59.
67. Jordi Cat, Nancy Cartwright and Hasok Chang, 'Otto Neurath: Politics and the Unity of Science', in Peter Galison and David J. Stump (eds.), *The Disunity of Science* (Stanford, CA, 1996), 347–69. It seems paradoxical that it takes three authors to discuss one man's view of the unity of knowledge, but the article does illustrate the international co-operation dear to its protagonist.
68. Nader Vossoughian, 'The Language of the World Museum: Otto Neurath, Paul Otlet, Le Corbusier', *Associations Transnationales* (2003), 82–93.
69. Otto Neurath, 'Unified Science as Encyclopaedic Integration', in Otto Neurath, Rudolf Carnap and Charles Morris (eds.), *International Encyclopaedia of Unified Science*, vol. 1 (Chicago, IL, 1955), 1–27.
70. Guy V. Beckwith, 'The Generalist and the Disciplines: The Case of Lewis Mumford', *Issues in Integrative Studies* 14 (1996), 7–28. Mumford became increasingly critical of Geddes, as is clear from his article 'The Disciple's Rebellion', *Encounter* (September, 1966), 11–20.
71. Quoted in Donald L. Miller, *Lewis Mumford: A Life* (New York, 1989), 163.
72. Ibid., 427, quoting from the Mumford papers; Lewis Mumford, *The Myth of the Machine* (1966), 16–17.
73. Ibid., 16.
74. Allen Davis, 'Lewis Mumford: Man of Letters and Urban Historian', *Journal of Urban History* 19 (1993), 123–31, at 123. Cf. Thomas P. Hughes and Agatha Hughes (eds.), *Lewis Mumford: Public Intellectual* (New York, 1990).
75. Norman and Jean Mackenzie, *The Time Traveller: The Life of H. G. Wells* (London, 1973), 41, 402–3.
76. Nicholas Murray, *Aldous Huxley: A Biography* (London, 2003), 171.
77. Ibid., 127, 161.
78. Stefan Collini, *Absent Minds: Intellectuals in Britain* (Oxford, 2008), 458.
79. Interview with Borges, cited in Jaime Alazraki, *Borges and the Kabbalah* (Cambridge, 1988), 5.
80. My thanks to my friend Steven Boldy for comments on the draft of this section. Cf. his *Companion to Jorge Luis Borges* (Woodbridge, 2009).
81. Borges, 'An Autobiographical Essay', in *The Aleph and Other Stories* (London, 1971), 203–60, at 245.
82. Iván Almeida, 'Borges and Peirce, on Abduction and Maps', *Semiotica* 140 (2002), 113–31, 22, and, more generally, Alfonso de Toro (ed.), *Jorge Luis Borges: Ciencia y Filosofía* (Hildesheim, 2007), and Guillermo Martínez, *Borges and Mathematics* (West Lafayette, IN, 2012).
83. Mark Krupnick, 'George Steiner's Literary Journalism', *New England Review* 15 (1993), 157–67, at 157.
84. It was the novelist and critic Antonia Byatt who called Steiner a 'Renaissance man'. On Steiner as a 'monster' of learning, see Guido Almansi, 'The Triumph of the Hedgehog', in Nathan A. Scott Jr. and Ronald A. Sharp (eds.), *Reading George Steiner* (Baltimore, MD, 1994), 58–73, at 60.
85. Robert Boyers, 'Steiner as Cultural Critic', in Scott and Sharp, *Reading George Steiner*, 14–42.
86. George Steiner, *Errata: An Examined Life* (New Haven, CT, 1997), 278.
87. Quoted in Daniel Schreiber, *Susan Sontag: A Biography* (2007: English translation, Evanston, IL, 2014), 196, 153.

88. Ibid., 15.
89. Susan Sontag, *Against Interpretation* (New York, 1966), 11, 88, 93ff, 299.
90. All the same, Sontag often approached photography through literature. Her essay 'America, Seen Through Photographs, Darkly', begins with Walt Whitman and later refers to Stéphane Mallarmé, Paul Valéry, Hart Crane, Herman Melville, Marcel Proust, Thomas Mann, J. G. Ballard, Thomas Hardy, William Carlos Williams and D. H. Lawrence.
91. Schreiber, *Susan Sontag*, 111–12.
92. Donald T. Campbell, 'Ethnocentrism of Disciplines and the Fish-Scale Model of Omniscience', in Muzafa Sherif and Carolyn W. Sherif (eds.), *Interdisciplinary Relationships in the Social Sciences* (Boston, MA, 1969), 328–48.
93. Max Weber to Robert Liefmann (1920), quoted in Guenther Roth and Wolfgang Schluchter, *Max Weber's Vision of History* (Berkeley, CA, 1984), 120.
94. Peter Ghosh, *Max Weber and the Protestant Ethic: Twin Histories* (Oxford, 2014), 35.
95. Cynthia Kerman, *Creative Tension: The Life and Thought of Kenneth Boulding* (Ann Arbor, MI, 1974), quotations at 6, 8, 43; Deborah Hammond, *The Science of Synthesis* (Boulder, CO, 2003), 197–241.
96. Leo Rosten, 'Harold Lasswell: A Memoir', in Arnold A. Rogow (ed.), *Politics, Personality and Social Science in the 20th Century* (Chicago, IL, 1969), 1–13.
97. Quoted in Steven A. Peterson, 'Lasswell, Harold Dwight', in Glenn H. Utter and Charles Lockhart (eds.), *American Political Scientists: A Dictionary* (2nd edn, Westport, CT, 2002), 228–30.
98. From the huge secondary literature on Foucault, see Didier Eribon, *Michel Foucault* (1989: English translation, Cambridge, MA, 1991); Alan Megill, 'The Reception of Foucault by Historians', *Journal of the History of Ideas* 48 (1987), 117–41; Moya Lloyd and Andrew Tucker (eds.), *The Impact of Michel Foucault on the Social Sciences and Humanities* (Basingstoke, 1997); Jeremy W. Crampton and Stuart Elden (eds.), *Space, Knowledge and Power: Foucault and Geography* (Basingstoke, 2007); Ben Golder and Peter Fitzpatrick (eds.), *Foucault and Law* (Farnham, 2010).
99. Egon S. Pearson, *Karl Pearson: An Appreciation of Some Aspects of his Life and Work* (Cambridge, 1938); Churchill Eisenhart, 'Pearson, Karl', *DSB* 10, 447–73; Joanne Woiak, 'Pearson, Karl', *ODNB* 43, 331–5.
100. Nathan Reingold, 'Weaver, Warren', *ANB* 22, 838–41; Robert E. Kohler, *Partners in Science: Foundations and Natural Scientists, 1900–1945* (Chicago, IL, 1991), 265–302.
101. Giuseppe Armocida and Gaetana S. Rigo, 'Mantegazza, Paolo', *DBI* 69, 172–5.
102. Fabio Dei, 'Pitré, Giuseppe', *DBI* 84, 293–7.
103. Giuseppe Armocida, 'Lombroso, Cesare', *DBI* 65, 548–53; Mary Gibson, *Born to Crime* (Westport, CT, 2002).
104. Fiorenzo Monati, 'Pareto, Vilfredo', *DBI* 81, 341–7. G. Eisermann, *Vilfredo Pareto* (Tübingen, 1987); Bernard Valade, *Pareto: la naissance d'une autre sociologie* (Paris, 1990).
105. Paul Lazarsfeld, 'Notes on the History of Quantification in Sociology', *Isis* 52 (1961), 277–333; Kevin Donnelly, *Adolphe Quételet, Social Physics and the Average Men of Science* (Pittsburgh, PA, 2015).
106. Tarde's reputation, long eclipsed by Durkheim's, is currently undergoing a revival. See Elihu Katz, 'Rediscovering Gabriel Tarde', *Political Communication* 23 (2006), 263–70.
107. A comment made when Simmel was considered for a chair in philosophy in Heidelberg. He was not appointed. David Frisby, *Georg Simmel* (1984: revised edn, London, 2002), 31.
108. Clifford H. Scott, *Lester Frank Ward* (Boston, MA, 1976); Laurel N. Tanner, 'Ward, Lester Frank', *ANB* 22, 641–3.
109. Alfred Glucksmann, 'Norbert Elias on his Eightieth Birthday', prefaced to Peter Gleichmann, Johan Goudsblom and Hermann Korte (eds.), *Human Figurations: Essays for/Aufsätze für Norbert Elias* (Amsterdam, 1977). My thanks to Stephen Mennell for this reference.
110. Norbert Elias, 'Scientific Establishments' (1982, rpr. in his *Collected Works*, vol. 14, Dublin, 2009), 107–60). Cf. Stephen Mennell, *Norbert Elias* (Oxford, 1989); Dennis Smith,

Norbert Elias and Modern Social Theory (Cambridge, 2001); Florence Delmotte, *Norbert Elias, la civilisation et l'Etat: enjeux épistémologiques et politiques d'une sociologie historique* (Brussels, 2007); Marc Joly, *Devenir Norbert Elias* (Paris, 2012).

111. Woodruff Smith, 'Wilhelm Wundt: *Völkerpsychologie* and Experimental Pyschology', in *Politics and the Sciences of Culture* (New York, 1991), 120–8.

112. James quoted in Horst Gundlach, 'William James and the Heidelberg Fiasco', *Journal of Psychology and Cognition* (2017), 58. Cf. Gerald E. Myers, *William James* (New Haven, CT, 1986).

113. Robert A. Nye, *The Origins of Crowd Psychology: Gustave Le Bon and the Crisis of Mass Democracy in the Third Republic* (Beverly Hills, CA, 1975); Benoît Marpeau, *Gustave Le Bon: parcours d'un intellectuel, 1841–1931* (Paris, 2000).

114. Peter Amacher, 'Freud, Sigmund', *DSB* 5, 171–83, at 173; Oliver Sachs, 'The Other Road: Freud as Neurologist', *The River of Consciousness* (London, 2017), 79–100, at 79.

115. Frank J. Sulloway, *Freud, Biologist of the Mind* (1979, 2nd edn, Cambridge, MA 1992); Joel Whitebook, *Freud: An Intellectual Biography* (Cambridge, 2017).

116. Marcel Fournier, *Marcel Mauss* (1994: English translation, Princeton, NJ, 2006), 92.

117. Douglas Cole, *Franz Boas: The Early Years, 1858–1906* (Seattle, WA, 1999); Ned Blackhawk and Isaiah L. Wilner (eds.), *Indigenous Visions: Rediscovering the World of Franz Boas* (New Haven, CT, 2018).

118. Herbert J. Fleure, 'Haddon, Alfred', *ODNB* 24, 411–12.

119. Michael Bevan and Jeremy MacClancy, 'Rivers, William Halse Rivers', *ODNB* 47, 48–9.

120. Robert Ackerman, *J. G. Frazer: His Life and Work* (Cambridge, 1987); idem., 'Frazer, Sir James George', *ODNB* 20, 892–3.

121. George Gordon, *Andrew Lang* (Oxford, 1928), 11.

122. George Gordon, 'Lang, Andrew', *DNB 1912–21*, 319–23; A. De Cocq, *Andrew Lang* (Tilburg, 1968); William Donaldson, 'Lang, Andrew', *ODNB* 32, 453–6.

123. Bernhard Maier, *William Robertson Smith* (Tübingen, 2009), 5, 243.

124. Thomas O. Beidelman, *W. Robertson Smith and the Sociological Study of Religion* (Chicago, IL, 1974); Henry R. Sefton, 'Smith, William Robertson', *ODNB* 51, 385–6.

125. Norbert Wiener, *Ex-Prodigy* (1953: new edn, Cambridge, MA 1964), and *I Am a Mathematician* (1956: new edn, Cambridge, MA, 1964); Leone Montagnini, *Le armonie del disordine: Norbert Wiener matematico-filosofo del '900* (Venice, 2005).

126. Leon Harmon, quoted in Pamela McCorduck, *Machines Who Think: A Personal Enquiry into the History and Prospects of Artificial Intelligence* (Natick, MA, 2004), 67.

127. William Aspray, *John von Neumann and the Origins of Modern Computing* (Cambridge, MA, 1990), 1.

128. Norman Macrae, *John von Neumann: The Scientific Genius who Pioneered the Modern Computer, Game Theory, Nuclear Deterrence and Much More* (New York, 1992); Giorgio Israel and Ana Millán Gasca, *The World as a Mathematical Game: John von Neumann and 20th-Century Science* (Basel, 2000).

129. Jimmy Soni and Rob Goodman, *A Mind at Play: How Claude Shannon Invented the Information Age* (New York, 2017).

130. Andrew Hodges, *Alan Turing: The Enigma* (London, 1983); David Leavitt, *The Man Who Knew Too Much: Alan Turing and the Invention of the Computer* (London, 2006); George Dyson, *Turing's Cathedral: The Origins of the Digital Universe* (London, 2012).

131. This remarkable man does not appear to have been the subject of a full biography. For a short account, see John Parascandola, 'Henderson, Lawrence Joseph', *DSB* 6, 260–2.

132. Mark Davidson, *Uncommon Sense: The Life and Thought of Ludwig Von Bertalanffy* (Los Angeles, CA, 1983); cf. Hammond, *The Science of Synthesis*.

133. Quoted in Hammond, *The Science of Synthesis*, 157.

134. Quoted in Davidson, *Uncommon Sense*, 18.

135. Beverley Kent, *Charles S. Peirce: Logic and the Classification of the Sciences* (Montreal, 1987); Paul J. Croce, 'Peirce, Charles Sanders', *ANB* 17, 252–4; Christopher Hookway, 'Peirce, Charles Sanders', in Edward Craig (ed.), *Routledge Encyclopedia of Philosophy*, 7, 269–84.

136. Daniel Armstrong and C. H. van Schooneveld (eds.), *Roman Jakobson: Echoes of his Scholarship* (Lisse, 1977), v, 1.
137. Roman Jakobson, 'Preface' to *Selected Writings*, vol. 4 (The Hague, 1966).
138. Roman Jakobson and Petr Bogatyrev, 'Folklore as a Special Form of Creation' (1929: repr. in *Selected Writings*, vol. 4, 1–15).
139. Elmar Holenstein, 'Jakobson's Philosophical Background', in Krystina Pomorska et al. (eds.), *Language, Poetry and Politics* (Amsterdam, 1987), 15–31.
140. José Marcos-Ortega, 'Roman Jakobson precursor de la neuropsicología cognitiva', in Mónica Mansour and Julieta Haidar (eds.), *La imaginación y la inteligencia en el lenguaje: Homenaje a Roman Jakobson* (Mexico City, 1996), 161–76.
141. Roman Jakobson, 'Two Aspects of Language and Two Aspects of Aphasic Disturbances' (1956: repr. in Roman Jakobson, *Selected Writings*, vol. 2 (The Hague, 1971), 239–59.
142. Richard Bradford, *Roman Jakobson: Life, Language, Art* (London, 1994), 129–42.
143. Edmund Leach, 'Roman Jakobson and Social Anthropology', in the collective volume *A Tribute to Roman Jakobson* (Berlin, 1983), 10–16; Holenstein, 'Philosophical Background', 17.
144. Roland Barthes, *Système de la Mode* (Paris, 1967); idem., *L'empire des signes* (Paris, 1970). On him, Louis-Jean Calvet, *Roland Barthes: A Biography* (1990: English translation, Bloomington, IN, 1994).
145. Quoted in Sandro Montalto (ed.), *Umberto Eco: l'uomo che sapeva troppo* (Pisa, 2005), 215. In fact, Eco did not approve of acquiring information for its own sake, although he doubtless relished the allusion in the title of this collection to Alfred Hitchcock's *The Man Who Knew Too Much*.
146. Peter Bondanella, *Umberto Eco and the Open Text* (Cambridge, 1997); Michael Caesar, *Umberto Eco: Philosophy, Semiotics and the Work of Fiction* (Cambridge, 1999).
147. Avril Pyman, *Pavel Florensky, a Quiet Genius: The Tragic and Extraordinary Life of Russia's Leonardo da Vinci* (New York, 2010). I should like to thank Robin Milner-Gulland for telling me, years ago, about Florensky's work.
148. William T. Scott and Martin X. Moleski, *Michael Polanyi: Scientist and Philosopher* (Oxford, 2005); Mary Jo Nye, *Michael Polanyi and his Generation* (Chicago, IL, 2011).
149. Maurice Goldsmith, *Joseph Needham: 20th-Century Renaissance Man* (Paris, 1995).
150. Needham's collaborator Wang Ling, quoted in Goldsmith, *Joseph Needham*, 136. Cf. Simon Winchester, *Bomb, Book and Compass: Joseph Needham and the Great Secrets of China* (London, 2008).
151. Goldsmith's interviews with Needham, quoted in *Joseph Needham*, 55, 45. On the 'Needham Question', Nathan Sivin, 'Why the Scientific Revolution Did Not Take Place in China – or Didn't It?', *Chinese Science* 5 (1982), 45–66.
152. David Lipset, *Gregory Bateson: Legacy of a Scientist* (Boston, MA, 1980), 115. Cf. Peter Harries-Jones, *A Recursive Vision: Ecological Understanding and Gregory Bateson* (Toronto, 1995).
153. Robert W. Rieber (ed.), *The Individual, Communication and Society: Essays in Memory of Gregory Bateson* (Cambridge, 1989), 2.
154. Lipset, *Gregory Bateson*, 184–238.
155. Ibid., 180. On the Macy conferences, see chapter 8 below.
156. Harries-Jones, *Recursive Vision*, 9.
157. Letter to Sigmund Koch, quoted in Hunter Crowther-Heyck, *Herbert A. Simon: The Bounds of Reason in Modern America* (Baltimore, MD, 2006), 312.
158. Ha-Joon Chang, *23 Things They Don't Tell You about Capitalism* (London, 2011), 173.
159. Herbert Simon, *Models of My Life* (New York, 1991), 189.
160. Michel de Certeau: *La prise de parole: pour une nouvelle culture* (Paris, 1968); idem., with Jacques Revel and Dominique Julia, *Une politique de la langue: la Révolution Française et les patois* (Paris, 1975).
161. Richard Creath, 'The Unity of Science: Carnap, Neurath and Beyond', in Peter Galison and David J. Stump, *The Disunity of Science* (Stanford, CA, 1996), 158–69, at 161.

162. Fournier, *Émile Durkheim*, 188, 206, 208.
163. Cynthia Kernan, *Creative Tension: The Life and Thought of Kenneth Boulding* (Ann Arbor, MI, 1974), 22.
164. Berlin quoted in Mary Jo Nye, *Michael Polanyi and His Generation* (Chicago, IL, 2011), 304.
165. Andrew Hodges, *Alan Turing, the Enigma* (1983: new edn, London, 2012), 411.
166. Miller, *Lewis Mumford*, 532.
167. Reported by Carlo Ginzburg in Maria Lúcia G. Pallares-Burke, *The New History: Confessions and Comparisons* (Cambridge, 2002), 209.
168. www.critical-theory.com/noam-chomsky-calls-jacques-lacan-a-charlatan, accessed 3 August 2017.
169. Quoted in Michael Moran, *The Metaphyiscal Imagination* (Peterborough, 2018), 660–1.
170. Blake Morrison, 'Too Clever by Half: George Steiner', *Independent*, 15 October 1994; Jeet Heer, 'George Steiner's Phony Learning', *sans everything*, 16 May 2009; https://www.wsws.org/en/articles/2010/11/zize-n12.html, accessed 3 August 2017.
171. Stuart Elden, *Sloterdijk Now* (Cambridge, 2012), 3.
172. Stuart Elden (ed.), *Sloterdijk Now* (Cambridge, 2011); Jamil Khader and Molly Anne Rothenberg (eds.), *Žižek Now* (Cambridge, 2013).
173. Rebecca Mead, 'The Marx Brother: How a Philosopher from Slovenia Became an International Star', *New Yorker*, 5 May 2005.
174. George S. Gordon, 'Lang, Andrew', *DNB 1912–21*, 319–23, at 322; idem., *Andrew Lang* (Oxford, 1928), 10. Robert R. Marett, who worked in this field himself, called Lang 'a great anthropologist' (*The Raw Material of Religion*, Oxford, 1929, 3).
175. Max Weber, *The Protestant Ethic and the Spirit of Capitalism* (1904: English translation, London, 1930), 32.

CHAPTER 6

1. Josh Clark, 'How Curiosity Works', https://science.howstuffworks.com › Science › Life Science › Evolution
2. Peter Miller, 'Peiresc in Africa', in Marc Fumaroli (ed.), *Les premiers siècles de la république européenne des lettres* (Paris, 2005), 493–525, at 501.
3. Pierre-Daniel Huet, *Commentarius* (The Hague, 1718), 15; *Huetiana* (Paris, 1722), quoted in Elena Rapetti, *Pierre-Daniel Huet: erudizione, filosofia, apologetica* (Milan, 1999), 5n.
4. Richard S. Westfall, *Never at Rest: A Biography of Isaac Newton* (Cambridge, 1980), 103.
5. Benjamin Franklin, *Autobiography*, ed. J. A. Leo Lemay and P. M. Zall (New York, 1986), 9.
6. Alexander von Humboldt, *Cosmos* (English translation, New York, 1858), preface; Jean-Louis Benoît, *Tocqueville* (Paris, 2005), vol. 1, p. 818.
7. Hippolyte Taine, *Correspondance*, 4 vols. (Paris, 1902–6), vol. 1, 56.
8. Peter Gay, *Freud: A Life for Our Time* (London, 1988), 13–14, 25.
9. Bertrand Russell, *Autobiography*, 3 vols. (London, 1967–9), vol. 1, 13.
10. Fernando Ortiz, *La africanía de la música folklorica de Cuba* (Havana, 1950), xiii.
11. Anna Rosa Antognazza, *Leibniz: A Very Short Introduction* (Oxford, 2016), 6.
12. Edmund Hector, quoted in Robert DeMaria Jr., *The Life of Samuel Johnson* (Oxford, 1993), 8.
13. Lewis Mumford, *The Condition of Man* (1944), 383.
14. George Dyson, *Turing's Cathedral* (London, 2012), 44.
15. Quoted in Gareth Dale, *Karl Polanyi: A Life on the Left* (New York, 2016), 8.
16. Lewis M. Dabney, *Edmund Wilson: A Life* (New York, 2005), xii.
17. Quoted in Didier Eribon, *Michel Foucault* (1989: English translation, Cambridge, MA 1991), 9.
18. 'l'intérêt passioné . . . qu'il porte à toutes choses': quoted in François Dosse, *Michel de Certeau: Le marcheur blessé* (Paris, 2002), 176.
19. Daniel Horowitz, 'David Riesman: From Law to Social Criticism', *Buffalo Law Review* 58 (2010), 1,005–29, at 1,012.

20. 'ragionando con amici e tra lo strepito de'suoi figliuoli, come ha uso di sempre o leggere o scrivere o meditare': Giambattista Vico, *Opere*, ed. Roberto Parenti (Naples, 1972), 384.

21. Klári von Neumann, quoted in Dyson, *Turing's Cathedral*, 54.

22. Mary Somerville, *Personal Recollections* (London, 1873), 164.

23. Andrew Clark, *The Life and Times of Anthony Wood*, 3 vols. (Oxford, 1891–4), vol. 1, 282.

24. John Aubrey, *Brief Lives*, ed. Oliver L. Dick (London, 1960), 20.

25. Westfall, *Never at Rest*, 103, 191.

26. Robert Shackleton, *Montesquieu: A Critical Biography* (Oxford, 1961), 77–8.

27. Pierre Boutroux and Etienne Toulouse, quoted in Jeremy Gray, *Henri Poincaré: A Scientific Biography* (Princeton, NJ, 2013), 25.

28. Dale, *Karl Polanyi*, 216–17.

29. Hector, quoted in DeMaria, *The Life of Samuel Johnson*, 8.

30. Julie de Lespinasse, quoted in Keith M. Baker, *Condorcet: From Natural Philosophy to Social Mathematics* (Chicago, IL, 1975), 25.

31. Sarah Lee, *Memoirs of Baron Cuvier* (London, 1833), 9, 11.

32. George O. Trevelyan, *Life and Letters of Lord Macaulay* (1876: rpr. Oxford, 1978), vol. 1, 48, and vol. 2, 142–3, citing Macaulay's friend and editor, the polymath Francis Jeffrey.

33. Ferdinand Denis, quoted in A. G. Lehmann, *Sainte-Beuve* (Oxford, 1962), 233.

34. Quotations from Dyson, *Turing's Cathedral*, 41, and Pamela McCorduck (the interviewer), in *Machines Who Think* (San Francisco, CA 1979), 67.

35. Maurice Goldsmith, *Joseph Needham: Twentieth-Century Renaissance Man* (Paris, 1995), 3, 137.

36. Foxcroft, *Supplement*, 456.

37. The French geologist Jules Marcou, quoted in Edward Lurie, *Louis Agassiz: A Life in Science* (Chicago, IL, 1960), 18.

38. Trevelyan, *Life and Letters*, vol. 1, 48, 50.

39. James Bryce, quoted in Bernhard Maier, *William Robertson Smith* (Tübingen, 2009), 202; Boulding quoted in Deborah Hammond, *The Science of Synthesis* (Boulder, CO, 2003), 154.

40. Steve J. Heims, *The Cybernetic Group* (Cambridge, MA, 1991), 44.

41. Wang Ling in Goldsmith, *Joseph Needham*, 141.

42. Quoted in Thomas Hager, *Force of Nature: A Life of Linus Pauling* (New York, 1995), 53.

43. Nancy G. Slack, *G. Evelyn Hutchinson and the Invention of Modern Ecology* (New Haven, CT, 2010), 320–33.

44. McCorduck, *Machines Who Think*, 86.

45. Quoted in Peter Brent, *Charles Darwin* (1981: new edn, London, 1983), 300; McCorduck, *Machines Who Think*, 154.

46. Nathan Sivin, 'Shen Gua', *Science in Ancient China: Researches and Reflections* (Aldershot, 1995), vol. III, 53.

47. Johann Gottfried Herder, 'Vom Erkennen und Empfinden der menschlichen Seele', in *Werke*, eds. Jürgen Brummack and Martin Bollacher (Frankfurt, 1985–2000), vol. 4, 330; Max Black, *Models and Metaphors* (Ithaca, NY, 1962); Mary B. Hesse, *Models and Analogies in Science* (London, 1963).

48. C. Scott Littleton, *The Comparative Indo-European Mythology of Georges Dumézil* (Bloomington, IN, 1964).

49. Donald A. Schön, *Displacement of Concepts* (London, 1963).

50. Cosimo Bartoli, Giordano Bruno, Celio Calcagnini, Erasmus Darwin, Kenelm Digby, Tommaso Campanella, Hugo Grotius, Albert von Haller, Constantijn Huygens, Samuel Johnson, William Jones, Gaspar Melchor de Jovellanos, Mikhail Lomonosov, Lorenzo Magalotti, Pedro Peralta, Francesco Redi, Carlos de Sigüenza y Góngora, Rudjer Bošković.

51. Andrés Bello, Jorge Luis Borges, Aldous and Julian Huxley, Kenneth Boulding, Jacob Bronowski, Kenneth Burke, Roman Jakobson, Andrew Lang and Georges Bataille.

52. Novels were also published by Albrecht von Haller, Germaine de Staël, George Henry Lewes, Karl Pearson, Siegfried Kracauer, Kenneth Burke, Ludwig von Bertalanffy, Gilberto Freyre, Roger Caillois, Darcy Ribeiro and Susan Sontag.

53. William Lloyd, sermon at the funeral of John Wilkins, quoted in Barbara J. Shapiro, *John Wilkins* (Berkeley, CA, 1969), 214, 312.

54. Basnage quoted in Hubert Bost, Pierre Bayle (Paris, 2006), 518.

55. Foxcroft, *Supplement*, 455.

56. Jacques Roger, *Buffon: A Life in Natural History* (1989: English translation, Ithaca, NY, 1997), 24, 28.

57. Paul R. Sweet, *Wilhelm von Humboldt: A Biography*, 2 vols. (Columbus, OH, 1978–80), vol. 1, 160.

58. Karl Lehmann, *Thomas Jefferson, American Humanist* (Chicago, IL, 1947), 13; Lurie, *Louis Agassiz*, 24.

59. Quoted in Fiona MacCarthy, *William Morris* (London, 1994), 499, 523.

60. McCorduck, *Machines Who Think*, 131.

61. Bruce L. Smith, 'The Mystifying Intellectual History of Harold D. Lasswell', in Arnold A. Rogow (ed.), *Politics, Personality and Social Science in the 20th Century* (Chicago, IL, 1969), 41–105, at 44.

62. Berr's friend Lucien Febvre, quoted in Agnès Biard, Dominique Bourel and Eric Brian (eds.), *Henri Berr et la culture du XXe siècle* (Paris, 1997), 11.

63. Mumford, *Condition of Man*, 383.

64. Mark Elvin, 'Introduction' to a symposium on the work of Joseph Needham, *Past and Present* 87 (1980), 17–20, at 18; Christopher Cullen, in Needham, *Science and Civilization in China*, vol. 7, part 2, xvi.

65. David Rieff, quoted in Daniel Schreiber, *Susan Sontag* (2007: English translation, Evanston, IL, 2014), 55.

66. Roger, *Buffon*, 28.

67. MacCarthy, *William Morris*, 262, 562.

68. Wang Ling in Goldsmith, *Joseph Needham*, 135; Marie Neurath and Robert S. Cohen (eds.), *Otto Neurath, Empiricism and Sociology* (Dordrecht, 1973), 13, 28, 52, 59, 64.

69. Hager, *Force of Nature*, 139.

70. Pamela H. Smith, *The Business of Alchemy: Science and Culture in the Holy Roman Empire* (Princeton, NJ, 1994), 14.

71. Quoted in MacCarthy, *William Morris*, 230.

72. Umberto Eco, 'In Memory of Giorgio Prodi', in Leda G. Jaworksi (ed.), *Lo studio Bolognese* (Stony Brook, NY, 1994), 77. As for Eco himself, I can offer personal testimony about the speed with which he moved. I was once on the same panel as Eco at a conference in Italy. He arrived just in time for his paper, shook hands with each member of the panel, delivered his paper, shook hands again and left – presumably for another conference!

73. To Hugh O'Neill, quoted in Scott and Moleski, *Polanyi*, 193.

74. Quoted in Robert Olby, 'Huxley, Julian S.', *ODNB* 29, 92–5, at 93.

75. Robert W. Rieber, 'In Search of the Impertinent Question: An Overview of Bateson's Theory of Communication', in Rieber (ed.), *The Individual, Communication and Society: Essays in Memory of Gregory Bateson* (Cambridge, 1989), 1–28, at 2.

76. George Steiner, *Errata: An Examined Life* (New Haven, CT, 1997), 276.

77. Edward Said, *Out of Place: A Memoir* (London, 1999).

78. Herbert Simon, *Models of My Life* (1991: 2nd edn, Cambridge, MA, 1996), ix.

79. George C. Homans, *Coming to My Senses: The Autobiography of a Sociologist* (New Brunswick, 1984), 164.

80. Johann Georg Graevius, preface to Junius, *De pictura* (Rotterdam, 1694).

81. Neumann's daughter Marina, quoted in Dyson, *Turing's Cathedral*, 55.

82. Linda Gardiner, 'Women in Science', in Samia I. Spencer (ed.), *French Women and the Age of Enlightenment* (Bloomington, IN, 184), 181–93, at 189; Judith P. Zinsser, *Émilie du Châtelet: Daring Genius of the Enlightenment* (New York, 2007).

83. Laurel N. Tanner, 'Ward, Lester Frank', *ANB* 22, 641–3.

84. Leonard Warren, *Joseph Leidy: The Last Man Who Knew Everything* (New Haven, CT, 1998), 5.

85. Karl Pearson's autobiography, quoted in E. S. Pearson, *Karl Pearson* (London, 1938), 2.

86. Russell, *Autobiography*, vol. 1, 71.

87. Simon, *Models*, 112, 200, 238.

88. Quoted in Hager, *Force of Nature*, 55.

89. Klára von Neumann, preface to John von Neumann, *The Computer and the Brain* (New Haven, CT, 1958).

90. Wang Ling in Goldsmith, *Joseph Needham*, 134, 137, 143.

91. Eribon, *Foucault*, 13, 325; Stuart Elden, *Foucault's Last Decade* (Cambridge, 2016), 1.

92. Thomas O. Beidelman, *W. Robertson Smith and the Sociological Study of Religion* (Chicago, IL, 1974), 11.

93. Wilhelm Ostwald, *The Autobiography* (1926: English translation, n.p., 2017), 202.

94. Frederick W. Maitland, *Life and Letters of Leslie Stephen* (London, 1906), 374, quoted in Alan Bell, 'Stephen, Leslie', *ODNB* 52, 447–57, at 454.

95. H. S. Jones, *Intellect and Character in Victorian England: Mark Pattison and the Invention of the Don* (Cambridge, 2007), 150.

96. Anthony D. Nuttall, *Dead from the Waist Down: Scholars and Scholarship in Literature and the Popular Imagination* (New Haven, CT, 2003), 142.

97. R. H. Robbins, 'Browne, Thomas', *ODNB* 8, 215.

98. Westfall, *Never at Rest*, 192.

99. Quoted in Sweet, *Wilhelm von Humboldt*, vol. 2, 372.

100. Quoted in Günter Buttmann, *The Shadow of the Telescope: A Biography of John Herschel* (1965: English translation, New York, 1970), 14.

101. Charles Darwin, letter to his sister Susan, 1836, in *Life and Letters of Charles Darwin*, 2 vols. (London, 1887), 266.

102. Quoted in Brent, *Charles Darwin*, 209.

103. Annette Vowinckel, ' "Ich fürchte mich vor den Organisationslustigen": Ein Dialog zwischen Hans Blumenberg und Reinhart Koselleck', *Merkur* 68 no.6, 546–50, at 548.

104. Joachim Radkau, *Max Weber* (2005: English translation, Cambridge 2009), 122–4, 145.

105. Mackenzie, *Time Traveller*, 46, 329, 338.

106. Montesquieu quoted in Shackleton, *Montesquieu*, 234; Young quoted in Gurney, 42; Dewey quoted in Wayne Wiegand, *Irrepressible Reformer*, 192.

107. Gerald Toomer, *John Selden* (2 vols., Oxford 2009), 490.

108. Edmund Hector, quoted in John Hawkins, *Life of Samuel Johnson*, 7.

109. Simon, *Models*, 110; Homans, *Coming to My Senses*, 57.

110. Norbert Elias, *Über Sich Selbst* (Frankfurt, 1990), 138.

111. Young, letter to Gurney, quoted in Robinson, 183.

112. 'Henry Holorenshaw', 'The Making of an Honorary Taoist', in Mikuláš Teich and Robert Young (eds.) *Changing Perspectives in the History of Science* (London, 1973), 1–20, at 12.

113. Maria Lúcia G. Pallares-Burke, *The New History: Confessions and Comparisons* (Cambridge, 2002), 186.

114. Heims, *The Cybernetic*, 37, 45.

115. McCorduck, *Machines Who Think*, 121.

116. Isaiah Berlin, *The Hedgehog and the Fox: An Essay on Tolstoy's View of History* (London, 1953). Cf. Stephen J. Gould, *The Hedgehog, the Fox and the Magister's Pox* (London, 2003).

117. Rieber, 'In Search of the Impertinent Question', 3.

118. Constantin Fasolt, 'Hermann Conring and the Republic of Letters', in Herbert Jaumann (ed.), *Die Europäische Gelehrtenrepublik im Zeitalter des Konfessionalismus* (Wiesbaden, 2001), 141–53, at 150; cf. Michael Stolleis, *Die Einheit der Wissenschaften – zum 300. Todestag von Hermann Conring* (Helmstedt, 1982).

119. Pyman, *Pavel Florensky*, 40, 27; Steven Cassedy, 'P. A. Florensky and the Celebration of Matter', in Judith D. Kornblatt and Richard F. Gustafson (eds.), *Russian Religious Thought* (Madison, WI, 1996), 95–111, at 97.

120. Teich and Young, 'Holorenshaw', 'Honorary Taoist', 2, 19–20.

121. Simon quoted in Hunter Crowther-Heyck, *Herbert A. Simon: The Bounds of Reason in Modern America* (Baltimore, MD, 2005), 316.

122. Bronowski's unpublished autobiographical sketch, quoted by Sheets-Pyenson, 'Bronowski', 834.
123. Marie Jahoda, 'PFL: Hedgehog or Fox?', in Robert Merton, James Coleman and Peter Rossi (eds.), *Qualitative and Quantitative Social Research* (Glencoe, IL, 1979), 3–9, at 3.
124. Guido Almansi, 'The Triumph of the Hedgehog', in Nathan A. Scott Jr. and Ronald A. Sharp (eds.), *Reading George Steiner* (Baltimore, MD, 1994), 58–73.
125. Ginzburg quoted in Pallares-Burke, *The New History*, 194.
126. Vasilii Zubov, *Leonardo da Vinci* (1961: English translation, Cambridge, MA, 1968), 65; Martin Kemp, *Leonardo* (Oxford, 2011), 4.
127. Kurt-R. Biermann, 'Humboldt, F. W. H. A. von', *DSB* 6, 551.
128. François Dosse, *Michel de Certeau: le marcheur blessé* (Paris, 2002).
129. Michelle Perrot, 'Mille manières de braconner', *Le Débat* 49 (1988), 117–21.
130. Peter Burke, 'The Art of Re-Interpretation: Michel de Certeau', *Theoria* 100 (2002), 27–37.
131. Michael Hunter, 'Hooke the Natural Philosopher', in Jim Bennet et al., *London's Leonardo* (Oxford, 2003), 105–62, at 151.
132. George Peacock, *Life of Thomas Young* (London, 1855), 397.
133. Quoted in Eric Hobsbawm, 'Marx, Karl', *ODNB* 37, 57–66, at 60.
134. Quoted by Gay, *Freud*, from Ernest Jones, *Sigmund Freud: Life and Work*, vol. 1 (London 1954), 50.
135. Helen Meller, 'Geddes, Patrick', *ODNB* 21, 706.
136. Richard Creath, 'The Unity of Science: Carnap, Neurath and Beyond', in Peter Galison and David J. Stump (eds.), *The Disunity of Science: Boundaries, Contexts and Power* (Stanford, CA, 1996), 158–69, at 161.
137. Scott and Moleski, *Polanyi*, 208.
138. Dosse, *Michel de Certeau*, 176.

CHAPTER 7

1. For speculation about Vico's knowledge of the ideas of Ibn Khaldun, see Warren E. Gates, 'The Spread of Ibn Khaldun's Ideas on Climate and Culture', *Journal of the History of Ideas* 28 (1967), 415–22.
2. Sue Prideaux, *Strindberg: A Life* (New Haven, CT, 2012).
3. Egil Johansson, 'Literacy Studies in Sweden', in Johansson (ed.), *Literacy and Society in a Historical Perspective* (Umeå, 1973), 41–65.
4. Bruno Latour, 'Centres of Calculation', *Science in Action* (Cambridge, MA, 1987) 215–57; Christian Jacob (ed.), *Lieux de Savoir*, 2 vols. (Paris 2007–11); on the Dutch, see Graham Gibbs, 'The Role of the Dutch Republic as the Intellectual Entrepôt of Europe in the 17th and 18th Centuries', *Bijdragen en Mededelingen betreffende de geschiedenis der Nederlanden* 86 (1971), 323–49; Karel Davids, 'Amsterdam as a Centre of Learning in the Dutch Golden Age', in Patrick O'Brien et al. (eds.), *Urban Achievement in Early Modern Europe* (Cambridge, 2001), 305–25.
5. The six are Wower, Holstenius, Lambeck, Placcius, Fabricius and Reimarus. Cf. Johann Otto Thiess, *Versuch einer Gelehrtengeschichte von Hamburg* (Hamburg, 1783).
6. In chronological order: Sigüenza y Góngora, Sor Juana, Peralta, Alzate, Conceição Veloso, Bello, Sarmiento, Ortiz, Reyes, Borges, Freyre, Ribeiro.
7. Enrico Mario Santí, *Fernando Ortiz: contrapunteo y transculturación* (Madrid, 2012); Peter Burke and Maria Lúcia G. Pallares-Burke, *Gilberto Freyre: Social Theory in the Tropics* (Oxford, 2008).
8. Robert K. Merton, 'Science, Technology and Society in Seventeenth-Century England', *Osiris* 4 (1938), 360–620; Reijer Hooykaas, 'Science and Reformation', *Cahiers d'Histoire Moderne* 3 (1956), 109–38.
9. The nine Jesuit polymaths in the appendix are Suárez, Tesauro, Nieremberg, Riccioli, Kircher, Kino, Bošković, Teilhard and Certeau. On Eco, Claudio Paolucci, *Umberto Eco* (Milan, 2016), 40–1.

10. The others are Isaac Casaubon, Johann Heinrich Bisterfeld, Herman Conring, Gerard Voss, Samuel Pufendorf, Conrad Schurzfleisch, Johann Joachim Becher, John Millar of Glasgow, John and William Playfair, Daniel Encontre, Gustav Fechner, Mark Pattison, William Robertson Smith, Frank Giddings, Wilhelm Wundt, James G. Miller and Edward Haskell.

11. Friedrich Nietzsche, *Der Antichrist* (1895), chapter 10.

12. Stefan Müller-Doohm, *Habermas: A Biography* (2014: English translation, Cambridge, 2016), 13.

13. Bertrand Russell, *Autobiography*, 3 vols. (London, 1967–9), vol. 1, 71.

14. Thorstein Veblen, 'The Intellectual Pre-Eminence of Jews in Modern Europe', *Political Science Quarterly* 34 (1919), 33–42.

15. Norbert Wiener, *Ex-Prodigy* (New York, 1953), 120.

16. Peter Burke, *Exiles and Expatriates in the History of Knowledge* (Waltham, MA, 2017).

17. Wiener, *Ex-Prodigy*, 63; idem., *I am a Mathematician* (London, 1956), 20; Gerard quoted in Deborah Hammond, *The Science of Synthesis* (Boulder, CO, 2003), 147.

18. Cynthia E. Kerman, *Creative Tension: The Life and Thought of Kenneth Boulding* (Ann Arbor, MI, 1974).

19. Andrew Hodges, *Andrew Turing: The Enigma* (1983: 2nd edn, London, 2014), 43; Herbert Simon, *Models of My Life* (New York, 1991), 9, 40.

20. Hans Rudoolf Velten, 'Die Autodidakten', in Jutta Held (ed.), *Intellektuelle in der Frühe Neuzeit* (Munich, 2002), 55–81, at 66.

21. Alexander Wood, *Thomas Young, Natural Philosopher* (Cambridge, 1954), 11.

22. Ibid., 5.

23. Norman and Jeanne Mackenzie, *The Life of H. G. Wells: The Time Traveller* (London, 1987), 47.

24. George C. Homans, *Coming to My Senses: The Autobiography of a Sociologist* (New Brunswick, NJ, 1984), 46.

25. Jorge Luis Borges, 'Autobiographical Essay', in *The Aleph* (London, 1971), 203–60, at 209.

26. Wiener, *Ex-Prodigy*, 62–3; Otto Neurath, *Empiricism and Sociology*, eds. Marie Neurath and Robert S. Cohen (Dordrecht, 1973), 4, 14, 46.

27. Cassandra Fedele, Laura Cereta, Marie de Gournay, Bathsua Makin, Anna Maria van Schurman, Elisabeth Princess Palatine, Margaret Cavendish, Queen Christina, Elena Cornaro, Sor Juana, Émilie du Châtelet, Maria Agnesi.

28. Most of this group are happily still alive and so excluded from the list in the appendix.

29. Michael John Gorman, 'The Angel and the Compass: Athanasius Kircher's Magnetic Geography', in Paula Findlen (ed.), *The Last Man Who Knew Everything* (New York, 2003), 229–51, at 245.

30. Charles Darwin, notebook, July 1838, ms in Cambridge University Library, https://www.darwinproject.ac.uk/tags/about-darwin/family-life/darwin-marriage.

31. Ernst Gombrich, *Aby Warburg: An Intellectual Biography* (Oxford, 1986), 22.

32. Homans, *Coming to My Senses*, 295.

33. John Aubrey, *Brief Lives*, ed. Oliver L. Dick (London, 1960), 254.

34. Quoted in Peter Brent, *Charles Darwin: A Man of Enlarged Curiosity* (London, 1981), 137.

35. Gerald Toomer, *John Selden: A Life in Scholarship*, 2 vols. (Oxford, 2009), 332, 447.

36. Detlef Döring, 'Biographisches zu Samuel von Pufendorf', in Bodo Geyer and Helmut Goerlich (eds.), *Samuel Pufendorf und seine Wirkungen bis auf die heutige Zeit* (Baden-Baden, 1996), 23–38, at 27.

37. Russell, *Autobiography*, vol. 2, 34.

38. Peter F. Drucker, *Adventures of a Bystander* (London, 1978), 126; on Cécile, see Gareth Dale, *Karl Polanyi: The Limits of the Market* (Cambridge, 2010), 15.

39. J. W. Scott, 'Ogden, Charles Kay', *ODNB* 41, 558–9; Richard Storer, 'Richards, Ivor Armstrong', *ODNB* 46, 778–81.

40. Michel Surya, *Georges Bataille: An Intellectual Biography* (1992: English translation, London, 2002); Alain Bosquet, *Roger Caillois* (Paris, 1971).

41. On masters and disciples, George Steiner, *Lessons of the Masters* (Cambridge, 2003), and Françoise Waquet, *Les enfants de Socrate: filiation intellectuelle et transmission du savoir, XVIIe–XXie siècle* (Paris, 2008).

42. Interview with Lewis Mumford, www.patrickgeddestrust.co.uk/LM%20on%20PG%20 BBC%201969.htm, accessed 6 February 2017. Cf. Mumford, 'The Disciple's Rebellion', cited in Frank G. Novak Jr. (ed.), *Lewis Mumford and Patrick Geddes: The Correspondence* (London, 1995).

43. Harriet Wanklyn, *Friedrich Ratzel: A Biographical Memoir and Bibliography* (Cambridge, 1961), 7.

44. Mark Davidson, *Uncommon Sense: The Life and Work of Ludwig von Bertalanffy* (Los Angeles, CA, 1983), 191.

45. Sten Lindroth, *Svensk lärdomshistoria*, vol. 1 (Stockholm, 1975), 152–61, 237–49; Håkan Håkansson, 'Alchemy of the Ancient Goths: Johannes Bureus's Search for the Lost Wisdom of Scandinavia', *Early Science and Medicine* 17 (2012), 500–22.

46. John Fletcher (ed.), *Athanasius Kircher und seine Beziehungen zum gelehrten Europa seiner Zeit* (Wiesbaden, 1988), 3, 111.

47. Maria Rosa Antognazza, *Leibniz: An Intellectual Biography* (Cambridge, 2009), 324; Andrea Wulf, *The Invention of Nature: The Adventures of Alexander von Humboldt, the Lost Hero of Science* (London, 2015), 240.

48. Wilhelm Adolf Scribonius moved from the University of Marburg to the gymnasium at Korbach. Conrad Samuel Schurzfleisch also taught at Korbach. Teachers at the gymnasium at Hamburg, the Johanneum, included Peter Lambeck, Vincent Placcius, Johann Albert Fabricius and Hermann Samuel Reimarus.

49. Daniel J. Wilson, *Arthur O. Lovejoy and the Quest for Intelligibility* (Chapel Hill, NC, 1980), 186–7.

50. Wanklyn, *Friedrich Ratzel*, 3.

51. Michael Stolleis, 'Die Einheit der Wissenschaften: Hermann Conring', in Stolleis, ed., *Conring* (Berlin, 1983), 11–34. Cf. Alberto Jori, *Hermann Conring (1606–1681): Der Begründer der deutschen Rechtsgeschichte* (Tübingen, 2006).

52. Benoît Marpeau, *Gustave Le Bon: parcours d'un intellectuel, 1841–1931* (Paris, 2000); G. Armocida and G. S. Rigo, 'Mantegazza, Paolo', *DBI* 69, 172–5.

53. On one kind of renegade, see Peter Burke, 'Turn or Return? The Cultural History of Cultural Studies, 1500–2000', in Mihaela Irimia and Dragoş Ivana (eds.), *Literary into Cultural History* (Bucharest, 2009), 11–29.

54. Bayle, writing in 1681, quoted in Helena H. M. van Lieshout, 'The Library of Pierre Bayle', in Eugenio Canone (ed.), *Bibliothecae Selectae da Cusano a Leopardi* (Florence, 1993), 281–97, at 281.

55. Other listed polymaths who were active as librarians were Johannes Bureus and Isaac Voss in Stockholm, Marcus Meibom in Stockholm and Copenhagen, Robert Burton at Christ Church, Oxford, Daniel Morhof in Kiel, Lucas Holste in France and Rome, Peter Lambeck in Vienna, Vincentius Placcius in Padua, Conrad Schurzfleisch in Weimar, Georges Bataille in Paris and Daniel Boorstin in Washington.

56. Gordon Stevenson and Judith Kramer-Greene (eds.), *Melvil Dewey: The Man and the Classification* (Albany, NY, 1983); Françoise Levie, *L'Homme qui voulait classer le monde: Paul Otlet et le mundaneum* (Brussels, 2006); Alex Wright, *Cataloging the World: Paul Otlet and the Birth of the Information Age* (New York, 2014).

57. Franck Bourdier, 'Cuvier, Georges', *DSB* 3, 521–8, at 524.

58. Samuel Johnson, *Dictionary of the English Language* (London, 1755), preface.

59. John Clive, *Macaulay: The Shaping of the Historian* (London, 1973), 100.

60. L. Kellner, Alexander von Humboldt and the Organization of International Collaboration in Geophysical Research', *Contemporary Physics* 1 (1959), 35–48; Kurt-R. Biermann, 'Alexander

von Humboldt als Initiator und Organisator internationaler Zusammenarbeit auf geophysikalischen Gebiet', in E. G. Forbes (ed.), *Human Implications of Scientific Advance* (Edinburgh, 1978), 126–38; Frank Holl (ed.), *Alexander von Humboldt: Netzwerke des Wissens* (Ostfildern, 2009); Otmar Ette, *Alexander von Humboldt und die Globalisierung* (Frankfurt, 2009), 20.

61. Lazarsfeld's collaborators included Marie Jahoda (his first wife), Elihu Katz and Robert Merton. Needham's assistants, some of whom pursued academic careers of their own, included Lu Gwei-Jen (his second wife), Wang Ling, Gregory Blue, Francesca Bray and Toshio Kusamitsu.

62. Simon, *Models*, 64.

63. Stuart Elden, *Foucault's Last Decade* (Cambridge, 2016), 8.

CHAPTER 8

1. For a general guide, see Robert Frodeman (ed.), *The Oxford Handbook of Interdisciplinarity* (Oxford, 2010); for a history, see Harvey J. Graff, *Undisciplining Knowledge: Interdisciplinarity in the Twentieth Century* (Baltimore, MD, 2015).

2. Roberta Frank, 'Interdisciplinary: The First Half-Century', in E. G. Stanley and T. F. Hoad (eds.), *Words* (Cambridge, 1988), 91–101.

3. Leonard S. Reich, *The Making of American Industrial Research* (Cambridge, 1985).

4. Herbert Simon, *Models of My Life* (Cambridge, MA, 1991), 170.

5. *Manchester Guardian*, 1 January 1901.

6. Beardley Ruml, 'Recent Trends in Social Science', in Leonard D. White (ed.), *The New Social Science* (Chicago, IL, 1930); Martin Bulmer and Joan Bulmer, 'Philanthropy and Social Science in the 1920s', *Minerva* 19 (1981), 347–407, at 358.

7. James R. Angell, 'Yale's Institute of Human Relations', *Religious Education* 24 (1929), 583–8, at 585; cf. J. G. Morawski, 'Organizing Knowledge and Behavior at Yale's Institute of Human Relations', *Isis* 77 (1986), 219–42, at 219.

8. Guy V. Beckwith, 'The Generalist and the Disciplines: The Case of Lewis Mumford', *Issues in Integrative Studies* 14 (1996), 7–28, at 15; Norbert Elias, 'Scientific Establishments', in Elias, Herminio Martins and Richard Whitely (eds.), *Scientific Establishments and Hierarchies* (Dordrecht, 1982), 3–69; Simon, *Models of My Life*, 173.

9. José Ortega y Gasset, *Misión de la universidad* (1930, rpr. in his *Obras*, vol. 4, 4th edn, Madrid, 1957), 313–53); Antón Donoso, 'The University Graduate as Learned Ignoramus according to Ortega', in *Ortega y Gasset Centennial* (Madrid, 1985), 7–18.

10. Donald T. Campbell, 'Ethnocentrism of Disciplines and the Fish-Scale Model of Omniscience', in Muztafa Sherif and Carolyn W. Sherif (eds.), *Interdisciplinary Relationships in the Social Sciences* (Boston, MA, 1969), 328–48.

11. Andreas Gelz, *Tertulia: Literatur und Soziabilität im Spanien des 18. Und 19. Jahrhunderts* (Frankfurt, 2006); William Clark, 'The Research Seminar', in *Academic Charisma and the Origins of the Research University* (Chicago, IL, 2006), 141–82.

12. Marshall Waingrow (ed.), *The Correspondence and other Papers of James Boswell* (2nd edn, New Haven, CT, 2000), 331.

13. Bernhard Maier, *William Robertson Smith* (Tübingen, 2009).

14. Solomon Diamond, 'Wundt, Wilhelm', *DSB* 14, 526–9, considers him only as an experimental psychologist; contrast Woodruff Smith, 'Wilhelm Wundt: *Völkerpsychologie* and Experimental Psychology', in *Politics and the Sciences of Culture* (New York, 1991), 120–8.

15. Roger Chickering, *Karl Lamprecht: A German Academic Life (1856–1915)* (Atlantic Highlands, NJ, 1993).

16. Johannes Steinmetzler, *Die Anthropogeographie Friedrich Ratzels und lhre Ideengeschichtlich Würzeln* (Bonn, 1956); Wanklyn, *Friedrich Ratzel*.

17. Wilhelm Ostwald, *The Autobiography* (1926: English translation, n.p., 2017, 191–206; Woodruff D. Smith, 'The Leipzig Circle', in *Politics and the Sciences of Culture in Germany, 1840–1920* (New York, 1991), 204–9.

18. Hubert Treiber, 'Der Eranos: Das Glanzstück im Heidelberger Mythenkranz', in W. Schluchter and F. W. Graf (eds.), *Asketischer Protestantismus und der „Geist" des modernen Kapitalismus* (Tübingen, 2005), 75–153.

19. Mary Gluck, 'The Sunday Circle', in *Georg Lukács and his Generation, 1900–1918* (Cambridge, MA, 1985), 13–42; Eva Káradi and Erzsebet Vezér (eds.), *Georg Lukács, Karl Mannheim und der Sonntagskreis* (Frankfurt, 1985); Lee Congdon, *Exile and Social Thought: Hungarian Intellectuals in Germany and Austria, 1919–33* (Princeton, NJ, 1991), 10–11, 52ff.

20. Otto Neurath, *Empiricism and Sociology*, eds. Marie Neurath and Robert S. Cohen (Dordrecht, 1973), 304.

21. Charlotte Ashby, Tag Gronberg and Simon Shaw-Miller (eds.), *The Viennese Café and Fin-de-Siècle Culture* (New York, 2013).

22. Dorothy Stimson, 'The History of Ideas Club', in George Boas et al., *Studies in Intellectual History* (Baltimore, MD, 1953), 174–96; Irmeline Veit-Brause, 'The Interdisciplinarity of History of Concepts: A Bridge Between Disciplines', *History of Concepts Newsletter* 6 (2003), 8–13.

23. Barbara Heyl, 'The Harvard "Pareto Circle"', *Journal of the History of the Behavioral Sciences* 4 (1968), 316–34; George Homans, *Coming to My Senses: The Autobiography of a Sociologist* (New Brunswick, NJ, 1984), 105.

24. Philip Husbands and Owen Holland, 'The Ratio Club' in Husbands, Holland and Michael Wheeler (eds.), *The Mechanical Mind in History* (Cambridge, MA, 2008), 91–148.

25. Kenneth Collins, 'Joseph Schorstein: R. D. Laing's "rabbi"', *History of Psychiatry* 19 (2008), 185–201, at 195–7.

26. Besides Barbu, the Sussex group included literary scholars (John Cruickshank, Cecil Jenkins, Gabriel Josipovici, Tony Nuttall), philosophers (Bernard Harrison, István Mészaros) and historians (Peter Hennock, John Rosselli and myself). Among the texts discussed were Hume's *Dialogues on the Natural History of Religion*, Martin Buber's *I and Thou*, some short stories by Kafka, Claude Lévi-Strauss's *Anthropologie structurale*, and the *Mahabharata*. My thanks to Gabriel Josipovici for sharing his memories of the meetings.

27. Scott Page, *The Difference* (Princeton, NJ, 2007); Michael P. Farrell, *Collaborative Circles* (Chicago, IL, 2001).

28. Jordi Cat, 'The Unity of Science', in Edward N. Zalta (ed.), *The Stanford Encyclopedia of Philosophy* (Spring 2017 Edition), URL = https://plato.stanford.edu/archives/spr2017/entries/scientific-unity; David Lowenthal, *Quest for the Unity of Knowledge* (London, 2019).

29. Georg A. Reisch, 'Planning Science: Otto Neurath and the "International Encyclopedia of Unified Science"', *British Journal for the History of Science* 27 (1994), 153–75; Jordi Cat, Nancy Cartwright and Hasok Chang, 'Otto Neurath: Politics and the Unity of Science', in Peter Galison and David J. Stump (eds.), *The Disunity of Science* (Stanford, CA, 1996), 347–69.

30. Carnap quoted in Neurath, *Empiricism and Sociology*, 43; Otto Neurath, 'Zur Theorie der Sozialwissenschaften', rpr. in his *Schriften* (1981). Cf. John Symons, Olga Pombo and Juan Manuel Torres (eds.), *Otto Neurath and the Unity of Science* (Dordrecht, 2004).

31. Neurath, 'Politics and the Unity of Science'; Richard Creath, 'The Unity of Science: Carnap, Neurath and Beyond', in Galison and Stump, *The Disunity of Science*, 158–69, at 161.

32. Quoted in Deborah Hammond, *The Science of Synthesis* (Boulder, CO, 2003), 157.

33. Edward O. Wilson, *Consilience: The Unity of Knowledge* (New York, 1999), 3, 8, 298.

34. Martin Jay, *The Dialectical Imagination: A History of the Frankfurt School and the Institute for Social Research 1923–1950* (Boston, MA, 1973); Stuart Jeffries, *Grand Hotel Abyss: The Lives of the Frankfurt School* (London, 2016).

35. Max Horkheimer, 'The Present State of Social Philosophy and the Tasks of an Institute for Social Research' (1931: English translation in Horkheimer, *Between Philosophy and Social Science*, Cambridge, MA, 1993, 1–14), at 9.

36. Stefan Müller-Doohm, *Adorno: A Biography* (Cambridge, 2005).

37. Stefan Müller-Doohm, *Habermas: A Biography* (Cambridge, 2016).

38. Ruml, 'Recent Trends in Social Science', 99–111, at 104.

39. Howard Spiro and Priscilla W. Norton, 'Dean Milton C. Winternitz at Yale', *Perspectives in Biology and Medicine* 46 (2003), 403–12; Mary Ann Dzuback, *Robert M. Hutchins: Portrait of an Educator* (Chicago, IL, 1991), 43–66.

40. The proceedings of the conference were published in Leonard D. White (ed.), *The New Social Science* (Chicago, IL, 1930).

41. Dzuback, *Hutchins*, 111.

42. Nils Gilman, *Mandarins of the Future: Modernization Theory in Cold War America* (Baltimore, MD, 2003), 72–112; Joel Isaac, *Working Knowledge: Making the Human Sciences from Parsons to Kuhn* (Cambridge, MA, 2012), 174–9.

43. Dzuback, *Hutchins*, 214–5; Hammond, *The Science of Synthesis*, 143–96; Philippe Fontaine, 'Walking the Tightrope: The Committee on the Behavioral Sciences and Academic Cultures at the University of Chicago, 1949–1955', *Journal of the History of the Behavioral Sciences* 52 (2016), 349–70.

44. Roy Pascal, '*Bildung* and the Division of Labour', *German Studies presented to W. H. Bruford* (Cambridge, 1962), 14–28

45. Gilbert Allardyce, 'The Rise and Fall of the Western Civilization Course', *American Historical Review* 87 (1982), 695–725, at 703, 707.

46. Andy Beckett, 'PPE: The Oxford Degree that Runs Britain', *Guardian*, 23 February 2017, https://www.theguardian.com/.../2017/.../ppe-oxford-university-degree-that-rules-brita, accessed 4 April 2018.

47. George E. Davie, *The Crisis of the Democratic Intellect: The Problem of Generalism and Specialisation in Twentieth-century Scotland* (Edinburgh, 1986), 11–26, 46–7, 158.

48. Robert M. Hutchins, *The Higher Learning in America* (New Haven, CT, 1936), 60, 78, 81; idem., review of Ortega, *Annals of the American Academy of Political and Social Science* 239 (1945), 217–20. Cf. Dzuback, *Hutchins*, 88–108, 101–24; Donoso, 'The University Graduate', 12.

49. https://college.uchicago.edu/academics/college-core-curriculum

50. Stuart W. Leslie, *The Cold War and American Science* (New York, 1993); Erin C. Moore, 'Transdisciplinary Efforts at Public Science Agencies', in Frodeman, *Oxford Handbook*, 337–8.

51. Gilman, *Mandarins*, 155–202.

52. Richard D. Lambert, 'Blurring the Disciplinary Boundaries: Area Studies in the United States', in David Easton and Corinne S. Schelling (eds.), *Divided Knowledge* (Thousand Oaks, CA, 1991), 171–94; Alan Tansman, 'Japanese Studies: The Intangible Act of Translation', in David L. Szanton (ed.), *The Politics of Knowledge: Area Studies and the Disciplines* (Berkeley, CA, 2002), 184–216, at 186.

53. Robin W. Winks, *Cloak and Gown: Scholars in America's Secret War* (London, 1987), 81; Bundy quoted in Sigmund Diamond, *Compromised Campus: The Collaboration of Universities with the Intelligence Community, 1945–55* (New York, 1992), 10.

54. David C. Engerman, *Know Your Enemy: The Rise and Fall of America's Soviet Experts* (Oxford, 2009), 48.

55. Clyde Kluckhohn, 'Russian Research at Harvard', *World Politics* 1 (1949), 266–71.

56. Timothy Mitchell (2004) 'The Middle East in the Past and Future of Social Science', in Szanton, *Politics of Knowledge*, 74–118.

57. Benedict Anderson, *The Spectre of Comparisons: Nationalism, Southeast Asia and the World* (London, 1998), 8–12.

58. Brigitte Mazon, *Aux origines de l'EHESS. Le role du mécenat américain (1920–60)* (Paris, 1988).

59. Engerman, *Know Your Enemy*, 70, 75, 255, 259; Simon, *Models*, 173.

60. Peter Burke, *A Social History of Knowledge*, vol. 2, *From the Encyclopédie to Wikipedia* (Cambridge, 2012), 239–43.

61. Barend van Heusden, 'Jakob von Uexküll and Ernst Cassirer', *Semiotica* 134 (2001), 275–92; Frederik Stjernfelt, 'Simple Animals and Complex Biology: The Double von Uexküll Inspiration in Cassirer's Philosophy', *Synthese* 179 (2009), 169–86.

62. W. B. Gallie, *A New University: A. D. Lindsay and the Keele Experiment* (London, 1960).
63. David Daiches (ed.), *The Idea of a New University: An Experiment at Sussex* (London, 1964), 67.
64. For a vivid account of these joint seminars by a leading participant, see Laurence Lerner, *Wandering Professor* (London, 1999), 146–57.
65. Daiches, *The Idea of a New University*; personal knowledge (I taught in the School of European Studies, 1962–78).
66. https://www.uni-bielefeld.de/(en)/Universitaet/Serviceangebot/.../leitbild.html
67. https://ruc.dk/en
68. Annette Vowinckel, ' "Ich fürchte mich vor den Organisationslustigen": Ein Dialog zwischen Hans Blumenberg und Reinhart Koselleck', *Merkur* 68, no. 6 (2014), 546–50.
69. Frederic Cheyette, 'Beyond Western Civilization', *The History Teacher* 10 (1977), 533–8; Allardyce, 'Rise and Fall', 720–4.
70. Lewis R. Gordon and Jane A. Gordon (eds.), *A Companion to African-American Studies* (Oxford, 2006).
71. The Centre became the nucleus of a Department of Cultural Studies, abruptly closed in 2002.
72. Toby Miller (ed.), *A Companion to Cultural Studies* (Oxford, 2006). Rather different approaches are employed in German *Kulturwissenschaft*. See Heide Appelsmeyer and Elfriede Billmann-Mahecha (eds.), *Kulturwissenschaft* (Göttingen, 2001).
73. Jürgen Kocka, 'Realität und Ideologie der Interdisziplinarität: Erfahrung am ZiF Bielefeld', in *Einheit der Wissenschaften* (Berlin, 1991), 127–44; Wolf Lepenies, 'Interdisziplinarität und Institutes for Advanced Study', in ibid., 145–61.
74. Johan Huizinga, 'My Path to History' (1943: English translation in Huizinga, *Dutch Civilization in the 17th Century and Other Essays*, London, 1968, 244–75), at 273–4.
75. Peter Schöttler, 'Die frühen *Annales* als interdisziplinäre Projekt', in Matthias Middell (ed.), *Frankreich und Deutschland im Vergleich* (Leipzig, 1992), 112–86; Peter Burke, *The French Historical Revolution: The Annales School, 1929–2014* (2nd edn, Cambridge, 2015).
76. Quoted in Pierre Daix, *Braudel* (Paris, 1995). My translation.
77. Edmund Russell, 'Coevolutionary History', *American Historical Review* 119 (2014) 1,514–28.
78. Jan Plamper and Benjamin Lazier (eds.), *Fear Across the Disciplines* (Pittsburgh, PA, 2012); Diego Gambetta (ed.), *Trust: Making and Breaking Cooperative Relations* (Oxford, 1988).
79. For a guide to the situation today, see Frodeman, *Oxford Handbook*, and Graff, *Undisciplining Knowledge*.

CODA

1. Alexander Halavais, *Search Engine Society* (Cambridge, 2009).
2. https://en.wikipedia.org/wiki/Wikipedia:Wikipedians.
3. Rudolf Dekker, *The Road to Ruin: Dutch Universities, Past, Present and Future* (Amsterdam, 2015), 144; Angus Phillips, 'Does the Book Have a Future?', in Simon Eliot and Jonathan Rose (eds.), *A Companion to the History of the Book* (Oxford, 2007), 547–59.
4. Maryanne Wolf, *Proust and the Squid: The Story and Science of the Reading Brain* (London, 2008), 226.
5. Nicholas Carr, *The Shallows: How the Internet is Changing the Way we Think, Read and Remember* (New York, 2011).
6. Richard S. Wurman, *Information Anxiety* (2nd edn, New York, 2000).
7. Alex Wright, *Glut: Mastering Information through the Ages* (Washington DC, 2007). Cf. David W. Shenk, *Data Smog: Surviving the Information Glut* (London, 1997).
8. Alvin Toffler, *Future Shock* (1970, rpr. London, 1971), 11–12, 317–23. Cf. William van Winkle, 'Information Overload', www.gdrc.org/icts/i-overload/infoload.html, accessed 19 July 2012.
9. UNESCO statistical yearbook, quoted in Michael Gibbons et al., *The New Production of Knowledge* (London, 1994), 94.

10. 'Data Deluge', *The Economist*, 25 February 2010. An exabyte is equivalent to a billion giga-bytes or a quintillion bytes.

11. Mikal Khoso, 'How Much Data is Produced Every Day?', 13 May 2016, www.northeastern. edu › Home › Authors › Posts by Mikal Khoso.

12. Jo Guldi and David Armitage, *The History Manifesto* (Cambridge, 2014).

13. Quoted in Jeffreys Jones, *The FBI: A History* (New Haven, CT, 2007), 232.

14. 'How Google's Search Algorithm Spreads False Information with a Rightwing Bias', *Guardian*, 12 December 2016, https://www.theguardian.com, accessed 18 July 2017. On bias on the web in general, see Halavais, *Search Engine Society*, 55–60, 64–5. Cf. Shoshana Zubov, *The Age of Surveillance Capitalism* (London, 2019).

15. Wikipedia, 'Big Data', accessed 18 July 2017.

16. 'Tourism in a Post-Disciplinary Era' was the subject of a conference at the University of Neuchâtel in 2013.

17. Gerard De Vries, *Bruno Latour* (Cambridge, 2016), 3 and *passim*.

18. Stefan Müller-Doohm, *Habermas: A Biography* (Cambridge, 2016): the comparison with Aristotle, by Martin Jay, appears on the back cover. On Anderson, see Stefan Collini, *Absent Minds* (Oxford, 2006), 469; on Posner, see James Ryerson, 'The Outrageous Pragmatism of Judge Richard Posner', *Lingua Franca* 10 (2000), 26–34; Roberto M. Unger and Lee Smolin, *The Singular Universe and the Reality of Time* (Cambridge, 2014).

19. Edward O. Wilson, *Sociobiology: The New Synthesis* (1975); idem., *Consilience: The Unity of Knowledge* (New York, 1998).

20. Patricia A. McAnany and Norman Yoffee (eds.), *Questioning Collapse* (Cambridge, 2010).

21. John Palfrey and Urs Gasser, *Born Digital: Understanding the First Generation of Digital Natives* (New York, 2008).

22. Quoted in Maria Rosa Antognazza, *Leibniz: An Intellectual Biography* (Cambridge, 2009), 210. I have modified the translation.

FURTHER READING

General studies of polymaths are rare. A recent one is Waqas Ahmed's *The Polymath* (Chichester, 2018), based mainly on interviews with living members of the species. On the trend towards increasing specialization that polymaths resist, see Peter Burke, 'Dividing Knowledges', in *A Social History of Knowledge*, vol. 2 (Cambridge, 2012), 160–83. On interdisciplinarity, Robert Frodeman, Julie T. Klein and Carl Mitcham (eds.), *The Oxford Handbook of Interdisciplinarity* (Oxford, 2010).

Some polymaths have written their autobiographies, including the following:

Charles Darwin, *Autobiography* (c.1876–82: reprinted London, 1958)
Benjamin Franklin, *Autobiography* (1793: reprinted, London 1936)
Wilhelm Ostwald, *Autobiography* (1926: English translation, Cham, 2017)
Bertrand Russell *Autobiography* (1931: 3 vols., London, 1967–9)
Giambattista Vico, *Autobiography* (1728: English translation, Ithaca, NY, 1975)
Norbert Wiener, *Ex-Prodigy* (New York, 1953)

Biographies of individual polymaths are listed below, in order of the subject, not the author:

David Lipset, *Gregory Bateson* (Boston, MA, 1982)
Howard Eiland and Michael W. Jennings, *Walter Benjamin: A Critical Life* (Cambridge, MA, 2014)
Jacques Roger, *Buffon: A Life in Natural History* (1989: English translation, Ithaca, NY, 1997)
Lisa Walters, *Margaret Cavendish: Gender, Science and Politics* (Cambridge, 2014)
François Dosse, *Le marcheur blessé: Michel de Certeau* (Paris, 2002)
Judith P. Zinsser, *Emilie du Châtelet, Daring Genius of the Enlightenment* (New York, 2007)
Susanna Åkerman, *Queen Christina of Sweden* (Leiden, 1991)
Richard Holmes, *Coleridge* (2 vols., London, 1989–99)
Adrian Desmond and James Moore, *Darwin* (New York, 1991)
Claudio Paolucci, *Umberto Eco tra Ordine e Avventura* (Milan, 2016)
Rosemary Ashton, *George Eliot* (Oxford, 1983)
Avril Pyman, *Pavel Florensky, a Quiet Genius* (London, 2010)
Didier Eribon, *Michel Foucault* (1989: English translation, Cambridge, MA, 1991)
Paddy Kitchen, *A Most Unsettling Person: An Introduction to the Ideas and Life of Patrick Geddes* (London, 1975)
Nicholas Boyle, *Goethe* (2 vols., Oxford, 1991–9)
Andrea Wulf, *The Invention of Nature: The Adventures of Alexander von Humboldt* (London, 2015)
James A. Harris, *Hume: An Intellectual Biography* (Cambridge, 2015)

Nicholas Murray, *Aldous Huxley* (London, 2003)

Octavio Paz, *Sor Juana Inés de la Cruz* (1983: English translation, Cambridge, MA, 1988)

Michael J. Franklin, *Orientalist Jones: Sir William Jones, Poet, Lawyer and Linguist, 1746–1794* (Oxford, 2011)

Paula Findlen (ed.), *Athanasius Kircher: The Last Man Who Knew Everything* (London, 2004)

Maria Rosa Antognazza, *Leibniz* (Cambridge, 2008)

Leonard Warren, *Joseph Leidy: The Last Man Who Knew Everything* (New Haven, CT, 1998)

Martin Kemp, *Leonardo* (1981: revised edition, Oxford, 2006)

Robert Shackleton, *Montesquieu: A Critical Biography* (Oxford, 1961)

Fiona McCarthy, *William Morris* (London, 1994)

Donald L. Miller, *Lewis Mumford* (New York, 1989)

Maurice Goldsmith, *Joseph Needham: A 20th-Century Renaissance Man* (London, 1995)

Norman Macrae, *John von Neumann* (New York, 1992)

Alex Wright, *Cataloging the World: Paul Otlet and the Birth of the Information Age* (New York, 2014)

Peter N. Miller, *Peiresc's Mediterranean World* (Cambridge, MA, 2015)

Gareth Dale, *Karl Polanyi: A Life on the Left* (New York, 2016)

Mary Jo Nye, *Michael Polanyi and his Generation* (Chicago, IL, 2010)

Gunnar Eriksson, *The Atlantic Vision: Olof Rudbeck and Baroque Science* (Canton, MA, 1994)

Hunter Crowther-Heyck, *Herbert A. Simon: The Bounds of Reason in Modern America* (Baltimore, MD, 2005)

Ian S. Ross, *The Life of Adam Smith* (2nd edn, Oxford, 2010)

Kathryn A. Neeley, *Mary Somerville* (Cambridge, 2001)

Daniel Schreiber, *Susan Sontag: A Biography* (2007: English translation, Evanston, IL, 2014)

Michel Winock, *Madame de Staël* (Paris, 2010)

Andrew Robinson, *The Last Man Who Knew Everything: Thomas Young* (London, 2006)

INDEX

abduction, 146, 160, 163
absent-mindedness, 173
academies, 66, 89, 91, 92, 101, 106, 125, 164
Adab, 20
Addison, Joseph, 87
Adorno, Theodor, 203, 222–3
Agamben, Giorgio, 244, 246
Agassiz, Louis, 175, 178, 192, 194
Agnesi, Maria Gaetana, 89, 99, 118, 197
Agricola, Georg, 38
Agricola, Rudolf, 30, 121
Agrippa, Heinrich Cornelius, 33–5, 204
Albert of Saxony, 24
Albert the Great, 24, 31, 35
Alberti, Leonbattista, 27, 29–30, 38, 121, 182
Alexander VII, Pope, 206
Alexander of Miletus, 13
Al-Farabi, 31
Al-Kindi, 21, 41
Alsted, Johann Heinrich, 6, 54–5, 56, 79, 194
amateur, 11, 28, 50, 53, 59, 74, 120, 168, 240
analogies, 38–9, 43, 62, 64, 97, 106, 122, 176–7, 187, *see also* metaphors
Anderson, Benedict, 137
Anderson, Perry, 243–4, 246
Angell, James R., 215, 223
Antal, Frederick, 218
Apáczai Csere, János, 55
Aquinas, Thomas, 60, 162
Archilochus, 6
Area Studies, 227–9
Arias Montano, Benito, 4, 209
Aristotle, 12, 18, 21–4, 45, 56, 108, 176, 185

Arnold, Matthew, 115–16, 123, 177
ARPA, 227
asceticism, 3, 182
Ash, Timothy Garton, 244
Ashby, W. Ross, 220
assistants, 16, 59, 98, 105, 108, 183, 211, *see also* collaboration; informants
Assmann, Aleida, 199, 245–6
Athenaeum (Amsterdam), 193
athletics, 12, 30, 121
Aubrey, John, 173, 201
Augustine, 4–5, 17, 188
Averroes (Ibn Rushd) 21–2, 113
Avicenna (Ibn Sina), 21

Babbage, Charles, 104, 119, 125, 200, 203
Bacon, Francis, 6, 31, 47, 99–100, 171, 204
Bacon, Roger, 23–4, 35, 41
Bagehot, Walter, 198
Baillet, Adrien, 77
Bal, Mieke, 199, 245
Balzac, Honoré de, 177
Banks, Joseph, 126
Barbu, Zevedei, 220
Barrow, Isaac, 67, 79–80, 173, 246
Barthes, Roland, 160, 162
Bartholin, Thomas, the Elder, 61, 72
Bartoli, Daniele, 87
Basnage, Henri, 64
Basnage, Jacques, 178
Bastian, Adolf, 180, 209
Bataille, Georges, 203–4
Bateson, Gregory, 163, 165, 179–80, 185, 204
Baudin, Nicolas, 138
Bauhin, Caspar, 74, 78

ERNEST RENAN   PAUL BROCA   HERBERT SPENCER   THOMAS HENRY HUXLE

PAOLO MANTEGAZZA   WILHELM WUNDT   KARL MARX   ERNST HAECK

ERNST MACH   FRIEDRICH ALTHOFF   CHARLES SANDERS PEIRCE   J

LESTER FRANK WARD   WILLIAM JAMES   MANUEL SALES Y FERRÉ

WILLIAM ROBERTSON SMITH   KARL BÜCHER   VILFREDO PARETO   FREDE

PATRICK GEDDES   JAMES FRAZER   HENRI POINCARÉ   FRANKLIN H. GIDDING

MARCELINO MENÉNDEZ PELAYO   SIGMUND FREUD   KARL PEARSON   T

SALOMON REINACH   GEORG SIMMEL   JOHN DEWEY   LUDWIK KRZYWICKI

WILLIAM H. RIVERS   MAX WEBER   JACOB VON UEXKÜLL   THEMISTO

KARL CAMILLO SCHNEIDER   VLADIMIR VERNADSKY   PAUL OTLET

ALEXANDER BOGDANOV   ARTHUR LOVEJOY   ABEL REY   CARL GUSTA

OTHMAR SPANN   ALFRED ZIMMERN   GEORGE ELTON MAYO   ALFRED W

EUGENIO D'ORS   PAVEL FLORENSKY   OTTO NEURATH   JOHN MAY

GYÖRGY LUKÁCS   KARL POLANYI   JULIEN CAIN   JULIAN HUX

ROBIN GEORGE COLLINGWOOD   GERALD HEARD   GEORGE HENRY LEWES

VANNEVAR BUSH   VICTORIA OCAMPO   MICHAEL POLANYI   WALTE

IVOR RICHARDS   ALDOUS HUXLEY   HAROLD INNIS   FRIEDRIC

JOSEPH HENRY WOODGER   MIKHAIL BAKHTIN   RICHARD BUCKMINSTER FULL

ROMAN JAKOBSON   GEORGES BATAILLE   KENNETH BURKE   NC

GEORGES DUMÉZIL   WARREN MCCULLOCH   JEAN PIAGET   LEO S

VLADIMIR NABOKOV   NICOLAS RASHEVSKY   ALFRED SCHÜTZ

JOSEPH NEEDHAM   FRANZ LEOPOLD NEUMANN   JOHN D. BERNAL

LINUS PAULING   MORTIMER J. ADLER   FERNAND BRAUDEL   HAROLD L

PETER A. BOODBERG   HENRY CORBIN   GEORGE EVELYN HUTCHINSON

JEAN-PAUL SARTRE   CHARLES P. SNOW   EDWARD HASKELL   SAMUE

ERNESTO DE MARTINO   ISAIAH BERLIN   NORBERTO BOBBIO   PETER D

KENNETH BOULDING   MARJORIE GRENE   GEORGE C. HOMANS   P

BERNARD BERELSON   KARL DEUTSCH   ALAN TURING   CARL FRIEDRIC

ZEVEDEI BARBU   DANIEL BOORSTIN   JULIO CARO BAROJA   ROLAN

CLAUDE SHANNON   HERBERT SIMON   EDWARD N. LORENZ   RAY E

GEORGE A. MILLER   THOMAS SEBEOK   EDMUND S. CARPENTER

WALTER PITTS   JAC   BENOIT MANDELBROT   MICHEL

JACQUES DERRIDA   PIE   DWORKIN   UMBERT

TRISTAN TODOROV   STEPHEN J. GOULD   CHARLES DARWIN   JAC